MY GOD TODAY

Dr. Lori Alyse Croom

Copyright © 2020 Lori Croom Enterprises LLC
All rights reserved.

2020 – First Edition

Cover Design by Justin Foster; Photography by Danny Austin Photography

No copyright is claimed in reference to any quoted song lyric or title contained in this book, and to the extent that material may appear to be infringed, I assert that such is permissible under fair use principles in U.S. copyright laws.

www.loricroom.com

I would like to dedicate this book to the Holy Spirit.

IN MEMORY OF

Mr. Ronald E. Croom (my dad)

Mr. Jessie M. Simon, Jr. (my godfather/mentor/person)

Mrs. Ellease Croom (my grandmother/best friend)

Mr. Sam Jones & Mrs. Ruth M. Jones (my grandparents)

ACKNOWLEDGMENTS

I am grateful for the following people/places/things:

Gloria Croom (my mom)

Charity & Christen Jasper (my daughters)

Rev. Dr. J.W. Croom, Jr. (my grandfather and first pastor)

Adrienne M. Nixon (my God-ordained friend)

Dr. Randall M. Croom (my big brother and writing mentor)

Randall, Brandon, Elliot, Alexandria, Renita, & Rollin (my siblings)

Dr. Kelvin M. Bryant (my pastor) & Faith Walkers Church

First Baptist Church Graymont

Dr. Christian Dotson-Pierson (for suggesting I write a book)

Erroll Hickenbottom (for buying the first copy)

Tacos (because they are good, act like you know)

Chalak Richards, JD, Shelton Marshall, JD, Melanie Gardner, Michael V. Williams, Dr. Aundrea Vereen Eady, LaTosha Williams

Dr. Ayesha Kidd, Dr. Kre Johnson, Jimele Hill, Jessica West, Gina Presley Peterson, Geaneé Quinney, Kaye Jones

The Croom, Jones, McHenry, and Simon Families

Spelman College & Hillman College

All Sorors of Delta Sigma Theta Sorority, Inc. & P.R.E.S.T.I.G.E.

Jasmine Young and Every Patient of NowVision Eye Care

Bishop L. Spenser Smith, Dr. Jeronn C. Williams

Mr. Fred Hammond & Mr. John-Mark McGaha

INTRODUCTION

Let me tell you who this book is for. This book is for all of God's children who don't live in a bubble. Who are we kidding? We love the Lord, but we know more than just gospel music. If you love the Lord but still run to the dance floor when you receive notification that Cash Money Records plans to take over not only for the 99, but also for the 2000, then this book is for you. If you have a playlist on your phone specifically for trap music, then this book is for you. If you can rap all of Biggie's lyrics right along with him, then this book is for you. If you've been to some ratchet places and seen some ratchet things in your lifetime, then this book is for you. If you've ever been guilty of doing hoodrat stuff with your friends, then this book is for you. Most importantly, if you want to grow up in God, this book is for you.

You may be wondering where this book comes from. All I can tell you is that different people have different talents and abilities. Some people can sing, dance, act, or play an instrument. I have the uncanny ability to hear God talking to me through song lyrics, no matter how ratchet they may otherwise be. I can literally be listening to THE most ratchet song and in the middle of it, you will see me quicken and exclaim "My God Today! That was a whole WORD!" Think of me as your ratchet whisperer/interpreter. Over the next 365 days, I will teach you some of life's greatest lessons by transforming and translating many of your favorite lyrics into spiritual commentary. I understand that the original meaning of the lyrics may be different than my transformative spiritual review of them, but I consider this book to be a lighthearted and "respectful" parody of sorts. Afterall, preachers have been taking Bible verses and using them to mean whatever they want them to mean for years, right? I think the Bible scholars call it an eisegesis. This book is nothing more than my spiritual eisegesis of some of the greatest Hip Hop and R&B lyrics of all time. I pray that you have as much fun reading it as I have had writing it. This one's #ForTheCulture. We needed this. Let's go!

JANUARY 1

"SITUATIONS WILL ARISE IN OUR LIVES, BUT YOU GOTTA BE SMART ABOUT IT."
-USHER

Have you ever been in a situation where you found yourself...in a situation? Perhaps a loved one passed away with no insurance and stuck you with the bill. Maybe you caught a flat tire out of nowhere. Perhaps the person you've been dating for six months turned out to be somebody's husband or wife. Perhaps you lost your job unexpectedly and now find yourself unemployed. Maybe a global pandemic came along and wreaked havoc on your way of life.

The crazy thing about situations is that they tend to simply arise. We are always optimistic and hopeful that a new year will be better than the last. If we are honest, however, we know that unexpected situations will continue to arise in our lives. The difference between this year and last year has to be **you.** You have to be smart about how you will approach everything from money to relationships to health. So, what is the smartest thing you can do this year? You can pray **more**. The Bible tells us that if we need more wisdom, we can simply ask God for it, and He will give it to us liberally. When we find ourselves in situations, Satan will try to trick us into thinking that we don't have to call (on the Lord)...That we're okay...and that we will be alright tonight. Don't fall for that. Be smart about all of your situations this year and pray about **everything**. This book will take you on a journey of 365 different "situations" and will provide Godly wisdom on how to approach each one. Happy New Year! Let's go!

READ TODAY: JAMES 1:5-6

JANUARY 2

"I PULL UP TO THE CLUB V.I.P. GAS TANK ON E, BUT ALL DRANKS ON ME."
-FOXX A MILLIYONE

Have you ever been in a situation where you didn't know where your "next" was coming from? Perhaps no one around you even knew that you were struggling because you always managed to look like the VIP that you are. Yes, you may have pulled up to the club. Yes, you may have been dressed as if you were VIP, but only you and God knew that your gas tank was really on "E." You decided to trust Him though, and you kept going anyway. By the end of the day, not only did He provide for you, but He also allowed you to be a blessing to those around you. "All drinks on me!" Look at you being a cheerful giver and whatnot!

You never know how and when God is going to move on your behalf. I challenge you to put your trust in God today. Boldly and confidently put your trust in the One who has the power to change your situation from needing help one moment, to being in a position to help others the next. Do not allow your uncertainty of the future to paralyze you with fear. When you trust and obey God, He **will** come through. Continue to move forward in faith, and continue to pull up to the places where God is sending you. He will not let you be put to shame.

READ TODAY: PSALMS 31:1-4

JANUARY 3

"I PULL UP TO THE CLUB V.I.P. GAS TANK ON E, BUT ALL DRANKS ON ME." (2)
-FOXX A MILLIYONE

Have you ever been in a situation where you found yourself to be empty? Perhaps it seems as if you have nothing left, but somehow you continue to pour out and give to others. You haven't even been able to fill up your own gas tank, yet you are busy making sure that friends, family, and children are taken care of at your expense. There are so many people looking for you to pick up the tab on their "drinks," and yet you are thirsty.

This kind of lifestyle eventually leads to burnout. The burnout may actually come from your job, church work, volunteer activities, or domestic responsibilities. These are all tasks that seem pretty noble. It is dangerous, however, to ride around with your gas tank on "E," because you will be tempted to seek fulfillment in **unhealthy** places. This can include excessive drinking, drugs, sex, inappropriate relationships, or other habits that are hard to break. Take time for self-care. The ultimate self-care will come when you spend intentional alone time with God and allow Him to fill you back up. Allow Him to re-energize you for your purpose and show you which things on your plate aren't even meant to be there. Not everyone will be happy that you are tending to yourself, but that's their problem.

READ TODAY: ISAIAH 55:1-2

JANUARY 4

"I.N.D.E.P.E.N.D.E.N.T. DO YOU KNOW WHAT THAT MEANS?" -WEBBIE

Have you ever been in a situation where you weren't really in a situation? Ladies, perhaps your bills are paid. Maybe you have a job that you enjoy. Perhaps you've been drinking water, your skin is clear, your edges are still present/luxurious, and your curls are at their optimal poppage point. You are what this psalmist would call "a bad broad." Fellas, perhaps your beard has finally connected, the promotion/raise just came through at work, and you are now able to see the beginnings of a six-pack in your abdominal region. You don't need anybody to take care of you. You are…**INDEPENDENT.**

Aht! Aht! Not so fast. It's easy to get to a place of "winning" and feel like you got there independently. This is especially true when you've had to grind on your own and didn't seem to have help from family or friends along the way. The truth of the matter is that we can neither survive nor thrive for very long without a connection to God. We cannot do life **well** without being dependent on Him. This is why we must continue to do things every day to strengthen that connection. God is like the vine and we are like the branches connected to it. If you ain't on (the vine)…sit down and spend some one-on-one time re-connecting to your source.

READ TODAY: JOHN 15:5-7

JANUARY 5

"I'VE BEEN BLASTIN' AND LAUGHIN' SO LONG THAT EVEN MY MAMA THINKS THAT MY MIND IS GONE."
-COOLIO

Have you ever been in a situation where you had been messing up for so long, that messing up started to seem normal to you? Perhaps it became so normal that even your friends and family got used to it. Maybe even your own mother has lost hope in your ability to be anything more than what you have been. In today's society, people have assigned a word for this: toxic.

Hopefully you are not a toxic person, but do you have any toxic ways? Are there areas in your life where you have taken the wrong things and made them feel normal after so long? Toxic ways can affect you and those around you more than you realize. Consider your ways. Consider your thought processes. Consider how you react and respond when angry. Consider the things that you know are wrong but don't care enough to fix anymore. Consider everything. I want you to know that no matter how long it's been, and no matter who thinks your mind is gone, change is still possible with God.

READ TODAY: HAGGAI 1:5-7

JANUARY 6

"YOU USED TO CALL ME ON MY CELL PHONE... LATE NIGHT WHEN YOU NEED MY LOVE." -DRAKE

Have you ever been in a situation where you found yourself unable to sleep late at night? Perhaps you were tired, yet you tossed and turned all night long with something on your mind. Perhaps it was a problem on your job, a financial worry, or a problem in your relationship. In these difficult times you should remember that God has granted you direct access to Him 24 hours a day, 7 days a week, and 365 days a year. The old saints would tell you that Jesus was on the "Main Line" and to call Him up. Well in this day and age, we barely have landlines anymore, but we do have cell phones. God does too. Because our connection to Him is "cellular" this means that no matter His location, He can always be reached through prayer.

So why haven't you been calling Him on His "cell phone" like you used to? I know that life can get hectic. Between adulting, paying bills, taking care of children, trying to drink enough water, and keeping up with your Netflix shows, you have a lot on your plate. There is so much on your plate that sometimes you can't get your thoughts to quiet themselves late at night. The truth is, you need His love to help calm your spirit and overcome anxiety. Talk to Him like you used to, even if it's a late-night call. He is **always** there when you need His love. Let's set aside some extra time to pray tonight.

READ TODAY: ISAISH 55:6-12

JANUARY 7

"SHOOT, SHOOT, SHOOT, SHOOT, SHOOT, SHOOT, SHOOT."
-BLOCKBOY JB

Have you ever been in a situation where you wanted to do something, but you weren't sure if it was possible? Perhaps you wanted to start your business or go back to school. Maybe you wanted to write a book or a television show. Perhaps you were unsure if it was doable, so you ended up doing nothing instead. Sometimes God will give us dreams, visions, and goals that seem impossible. With God, however, all things are possible. The problem is that you will never know exactly what you can accomplish or what goals can be attained if you never shoot.

The phrase "shoot your shot" has become popular in recent years because it's actually pretty solid advice. You will miss 100% of the shots that you don't take. Maybe things won't turn out perfectly the first time you try, but the idea is to shoot, shoot, shoot, shoot again, and keep on shooting. I want you to think about that vision and that dream again. Pray and ask God to give you the right strategy. Ask God to coach you on the proper shooting technique, and then get your butt in the game!

READ TODAY: PHILIPPIANS 4:13

JANUARY 8

"TO THE LEFT, TO THE LEFT...EVERYTHING ABOUT YOU IN A BOX TO THE LEFT."
-BEYONCÉ

Have you ever been in a situation where you felt rejected? Maybe you feel as though you and everything about you was placed neatly inside of a box. Not only were you placed in a box, but said box was then taken and moved all the way over to the left. Rejection is difficult, but it is a part of life. Maybe you have experienced rejection from a job or a promotion that you applied for. Others have experienced rejection in romantic or even platonic relationships. Rejection hurts, and it can cut deeper than a knife. But consider this: rejection is a necessary part of life.

It's okay to feel hurt by an unexpected rejection. Let's be honest, you will probably be in your feelings at first. However, the quicker you can shift your feelings over from rejection to gratitude, the better. Why gratitude? Oftentimes God uses our rejection as a means of protection. God knows the things that will make us happy down the line, but we don't give Him enough credit for also knowing the things that will make us completely miserable. Sometimes the thing you **thought** you wanted would have been a hot mess had you gotten it. That job would have stressed you out. That man or woman would have sucked the very life out of you. Everything is not always as it appears y'all. Take time today and thank God for the times you were rejected.

READ TODAY: PSALMS 118:22-25

JANUARY 9

"TURN DOWN FOR WHAT?"
-LIL JON

    Have you ever been in a situation where you felt depressed? Perhaps you are facing discouragement because of a disappointment. Maybe you are experiencing grief from the loss of a loved one. Maybe you need to pay a bill but don't have the money. Don't feel bad. We all feel down from time to time. No matter the reason for feeling down, you have to be strategic about how you handle it.

    When you begin to turn down, it can be a very sensitive and even dangerous time. We have seen time and time again where people have taken what should have been a down moment and turned it into a down season. In some cases, a down season became a down lifetime. For what? It is because that person has lost their hope. No matter how difficult the situation is before you, you must savagely hold on to the hope that is in God. He has promised never to leave us nor forsake us. For those of us who love Him, He has promised to work **all things** together for our good. Life has a way of knocking us down from time to time, but the worst thing we can do is stay there. Stay down for what?

READ TODAY: PSALMS 42:11

JANUARY 10

"YEAH, OK."
-LIL JON

    Have you ever been in a situation where something kept nagging at you? Maybe it was just a thought that something was not right. Maybe it was something that you knew you should be doing that you hadn't done. Maybe it was a relationship that you were supposed to cut off. Maybe it was a dream or a goal that you were supposed to be pursuing. Do not ignore those recurring thoughts and feelings.

    Sometimes God will speak to us this way through the Holy Spirit. Don't be so quick to sweep these thoughts and feelings under the rug, especially if they are **recurring**. Yes, it may be something that seems hard or scary to do, but remember that God will always have your best interest in mind. All He needs from you is a "yeah" and an "okay." The sooner you stop bucking against it and realize that His will and His plans for your life are your best possible path, the better. I pray that God strengthen you for your assignment, whatever it may be.

READ TODAY: LUKE 22:41-43

JANUARY 11

"SHAKE IT LIKE A SALT-SHAKER."
-YING-YANG TWINS

Have you ever been in a situation where you felt like the outsider? Maybe you have always felt like you were a little different than those around you. Perhaps your differences have caused you to feel like a loner from time to time. It's important to understand why you could never and will never truly fit in. It's because you are salty.

The Bible refers to believers as "the salt of the earth." When applied correctly, salt has the ability to improve a dish by bringing out its flavor. Salt, or lack thereof, has been known to make or break the quality of an entire dish. May I submit you that perhaps the reason you have never been able to fit in is because you aren't supposed to? You are supposed to be the difference-maker amongst your family, your friends, and even on your job. These days, so much focus is placed on "getting yours." Just for a moment, let us suppose that you are also here to help other people get theirs. How can your life be used to improve someone else's? You are the salt, so get to shakin'?

READ TODAY: MATTHEW 1:13-16

JANUARY 12

"YOU'RE HERE, I'M PLEASED. I REALLY DIG YOUR COMPANY."
-JILL SCOTT

    Have you ever been in a situation where you felt lonely? Perhaps you recently suffered the loss of a loved one or endured a difficult break up. Maybe you are single and growing tired of coming home to an empty bed each night. Maybe you have a house full of people, but still no one seems to get you. Loneliness is a slippery slope that can give way to desperation.

    Before you send that "Hey Big Head," text to your toxic past, consider the Holy Spirit. God has given us His Holy Spirit inside of us so that no matter where we find ourselves in life, we are never truly alone. The old saints used to call Him a "Company Keeper." There is a huge difference between being alone and feeling lonely. Being alone may be a result of your situation. Feeling lonely has everything to do with your response to that situation. Respond by seeking God on the **purpose** for your alone time. Ok. I can see you're not convinced. Take me for example. I am currently alone. I could fall into feelings of despair and loneliness **or** I could sit down and let the Holy Spirit write a book through me. I'll let you guess which one I did as you read my book. *sips tea* I needed to be alone with the Holy Spirit in order to do this. Dear Holy Spirit, You're here and I'm pleased. I really dig your company. He's good company y'all, I promise.

    READ TODAY: JOHN 14:16-18

JANUARY 13

"QUEENS SHOULDN'T SWING, IF YOU KNOW WHAT I MEAN."
-JILL SCOTT

Have you ever been in a situation where you found yourself in a battle? Life is **full** of battles. Maybe it was a mental battle. Perhaps the battle was for your health or for your finances. Maybe the battle was for your children. Perhaps hands had to be physically thrown on sight and on site. Let's examine that.

As believers, we have a **known** enemy who wishes to steal, kill, and destroy us. The good news, however, is that we have a huge advantage in any battle. The advantage is that we don't have to do all that fighting for ourselves. Why not? Royalty doesn't sit on the front lines. The Bible tells us that we are a chosen generation and a royal priesthood. Why are you on the front lines fighting all the petty day-to-day battles that you encounter? Kings and Queens shouldn't swing. God sends His angel army to fight those battles for us. Our job is to wrestle not against flesh and blood, but to win on the spiritual battleground. Guard the castle of your heart through faith, prayer, praise, fasting, meditation, and daily communion with God.

READ TODAY: 2 CHRONICLES 20:15

JANUARY 14

"SLOWLY, SURELY...I WALK AWAY."
-JILL SCOTT

Have you ever been in a situation where the best thing you could do for the situation was to leave it? Maybe the situation was so toxic that staying would have killed you. Perhaps the toxic situation was a job. Maybe it was a bad relationship. It could have also been a bad habit that you held on to for years. Maybe you tried to fix it at first, but as time went on it became obvious that the best thing for you to do was to walk away.

Walking away can be difficult especially when it's something you have been attached to for a very long time. Sometimes we become comfortable with the dysfunction and become nervous about the unknowns of what life will be like without it. Change is good, but it's not always easy. Sometimes God will snatch you out of a situation suddenly, but sometimes your walking away happens as a process... slowly and surely...so that you can learn every lesson that He wants you to learn while you are there. Don't freak out if your changes don't happen overnight. The Bible says that He who has begun a good work in you shall complete it. That's a process. It may be slow, but it is sure.

READ TODAY: PHILIPPIANS 1:6

JANUARY 15

"YOU BROKE ME, BUT I'M HEALING."
-JILL SCOTT

Have you ever been in a situation that broke you? It's like you went into the situation one way and came out of the situation a completely different way. Maybe you went into the situation happy and came out of the situation sad. Maybe you went into the situation with money and came out of the situation in debt. Maybe you went into the situation healthy and in good shape and came out of the situation unhealthy and overweight. Maybe you went into the situation with your peace and came out of the situation battling depression. Maybe you went into the situation sweet and came out of the situation bitter. You came out of the situation feeling like you had been broken. The good news, however, is that you came out of the situation.

Now that you are **out** of the situation, it's important to focus on your healing. When you've been broken, you must heal properly. Proper healing of a broken bone requires temporary immobilization. Casts and other contraptions ensure that the broken areas are able to sit still long enough to go through the biological restoration process. It's the same thing with us. Be very careful about hopping up and moving so quickly after experiencing brokenness. We've all seen that person who jumps from one bad situation to the next trying to busy themselves and to avoid going through the healing process legitimately. Wisdom tells us to seek God for the lessons we are meant to learn while we sit still long enough for Him to restore us completely.

READ TODAY: JOEL 2:25-26

JANUARY 16

"MENDING MYSELF, NOT CONCEALING."
-JILL SCOTT

Have you ever been in a situation where you pretended to be doing better, but you weren't? Perhaps you were on the basketball team, and after your injury you told your coach that you were better so you could get back in the game. You were honestly still in pain. Maybe you were out sick from work on a job that pays by the hour. If you didn't work, you wouldn't make money. You pretended to be better, but you really needed to see a doctor. Perhaps you just got out of a bad relationship that did a number on your self-image. You probably should have spent more time focusing on yourself, healing, and figuring out why you were so willing to accept some of the things that you did. Instead, you hopped right back in the saddle with a new man or woman while pretending to be healed and whole from the relationship that hurt you.

Concealing is the act of covering up something that you don't want people to know is there. In makeup, concealer is used to hide bags under our eyes. These bags can be caused by stress, lack of sleep, water retention from a diet too high in salt, and excessive fat deposits. They are much easier to conceal than to address. Unfortunately, there will be times in life where we will experience trauma. Do you know how to seek help when you need it? Are we taking the proper steps to mend ourselves or are we just concealing? Do we seek God for true restoration or are we just too eager to get back in the game? Restoration is one of God's many specialties.

READ TODAY: JEREMIAH 30:17

JANUARY 17

"OR MAYBE WE COULD JUST BE SILENT."
-JILL SCOTT

Have you ever been in a situation where your mouth got you in trouble? Perhaps you were minding your own business when somebody tested your gangster, so you went ahead and scored the A+. Maybe they did not know where you were **really** from. You had to let them know that you may be educated now, but the streets raised you. Maybe your clap-back game was strong. We're not talking about simply throwing shade here. Before you knew it, you Mortal Kombatingly finished them and cut them down to the white meat as if your first name was Black, and your last name was Twitter. You said some things that were truly hurtful and may have even done permanent damage to that person's psyche. You didn't think before you spoke, and now that the words are out there, you can never get them back.

Our words are extremely powerful, and this is why the Bible teaches us to use self-discipline when it comes to our tongue. If you truly understood the weight that your own words carry, you would be a little more careful about how and when you weaponize them, even when provoked or angry. Nobody wants to be seen as the punk or the loser in an argument or confrontation, but oftentimes the silent one has the most inner peace. When you are secure and at peace with who and what you are, you don't have to work so hard to prove it to others. It's not always easy, but the next time someone tries us, we have a couple of options. We can engage in the foolishness, or maybe...we could just be silent.

READ TODAY: JAMES 1:26

JANUARY 18

"YOU LOVE ME ESPECIALLY DIFFERENT. YOU KEEP ME ON MY FEET."
-JILL SCOTT

Have you ever been in a situation where you slipped up and fell? Perhaps you were doing too much and lost balance. Maybe you were trying to walk in some shoes that you knew you couldn't walk in. Maybe you were simply not focused on what you were doing and missed some sort of hazard in your path. Falling while other people watch is one of the most embarrassing things that can happen. More than likely, people will laugh at you for falling. Read this paragraph again, but instead of a physical fall, think about an existential fall.

How dope is God? Think of Him like an elderly person's walker (I know, but just go with it okay?). When we make moves in life, we find safety when we hold tightly to Him **as we walk**. If we continue leaning and depending on Him, He is able to keep us from falling. He is able to keep us on our feet. God's love is so amazing and so especially different from anything we've known because even if we do fall, He can pick us up, dust us off, and get us right back on our feet once again. That's love. If you've experienced some sort of fall from grace, don't beat yourself up. We have a Father whose mercies are new every morning. God has the ability to keep you on your feet with His love.

READ TODAY: JUDE 1:24-25

JANUARY 19

"OUR THING IS SWEET. OUR THING IS STRONGER THAN ANY LIE YOU CAN TELL ON ME."
-JILL SCOTT

Have you ever been in a situation where somebody lied on you? Perhaps somebody lied on you at work just to cover up their own mistakes. Maybe a relationship or marriage ended, and someone lied on you to protect their own reputation. Maybe you know a habitual liar who lied on you just for the fun of it. Actually, you do know a habitual liar who lies on you just for the fun of it. This is what Satan does all day every day. He lies **to you** and **on you** because he is the father of lies. This means that all lies originate from him.

Satan is so low-down that he even attempts to lie to God Himself about you. He tells God that you are good for nothing and that you are no better than your last mistake. He tells God that you are not worthy of forgiveness and not worthy of living to see another day. But thanks be unto God for loving us the way that He does. His love for us is strong, and it is sweet. Our thing is stronger than any lie that Satan or any other person can tell on me or you. If you have been lied upon, take courage and be patient. It may take some time, but truth and love will win out. Believe that.

READ TODAY: JAMES 1:5-6

JANUARY 20

"I'M FEELING KINDA HUNGRY, CUZ MY HIGH IS COMING DOWN."
-ERYKAH BADU

Have you ever been in a situation where you found yourself enjoying something that you **knew** was bad for you? Perhaps the instant gratification of the moment was filled with adrenaline, and you had big fun. You had big, Vanessa Huxtable fun. But what happened once the moment was over? What happened once your high came down? Did you realize that the void you **thought** you were filling remained empty? Perhaps your high came down, and you realized that you were still hungry.

God offers us the amazing opportunity to eat the Bread of Life. Until we begin to eat His Daily Bread (aka His Word), we will always remain hungry. Our highs will continue to be followed by lows until we begin to consistently seek God as the source for everything we need. Do not underestimate just how completely satisfying and **healthy** it is to walk with the Lord and to live by His Word every day. Before the day is over, can you find and meditate on at least one promise that God has made to you in His Word?

READ TODAY: JOHN 6:32-25

JANUARY 21

"WHY CAN'T WE BE BY OURSELVES SOMETIMES?"
-ERYKAH BADU

     Have you ever been in a situation where you were an extrovert? Perhaps you don't like spending time alone. There's absolutely nothing wrong with being an extrovert. As an introvert, I admire how you all can do so much in social settings without getting tired. A major difference between extroverts and introverts would be that extroverts are energized by crowds, company, and social interactions, while introverts are drained by them. Many introverts can move just as well in these spaces but have to deplete their energy to partake. Introverts love returning to solitude to recharge their social batteries. In contrast, alone time for extroverts can be draining. They will long for social interaction to help recharge their batteries. If you are an extrovert, you must be careful not to fill up your social calendar so much that you don't have enough one-on-one time with the One who created you.

     I see God asking, "Why can't we be by ourselves sometimes?" If you live in a household full of people, it can be difficult to carve out alone time with God. I grew up in a household of seven, and my mom would wake up at 4am every morning JUST so that she could spend time with God before everyone woke up. She knew that as a working woman with a husband and 5 kids, her day would be trash if she didn't first center her mind on the things above. As you read this book, make sure you are also reading and **meditating** on the daily scriptures and praying. That's a good start, and I'm proud of you for intentionally setting aside daily time to commune with God. This is your secret weapon.

READ TODAY: MATTHEW 6:6

JANUARY 22

"I THINK I MADE A WRONG TURN BACK THERE SOMEWHERE."
-ERYKAH BADU

Have you ever been in a situation where you began to question your own decision-making abilities? Perhaps you look back at some of the choices you've made in absolute wonderment. How on earth could I have been **that** wrong while thinking that I was right? Why did I date him? Why did I marry her? Why did I have a baby by him? Why did I let such a good woman go? Why did I choose this career? Why did I move to this city? Why did I drop out of college? Why did I even go to college? Why did I purchase a car that I can't really afford? Why did I get so drunk that night? Why did I eat the entire pizza? Why did I send those nudes? The list goes on!

The first thing you need to know is that Jesus already took the death penalty for our sin. This means that even though you may have to live with certain consequences to your poor decisions, your whole life doesn't have to be over. Don't fret. You may have made a wrong turn back there somewhere, but it's not too late to re-route and get on the right path with God. You just have to be more intentional about seeking God's guidance on **everything** in your life moving forward. He has promised that if we acknowledge Him during our decision-making processes, He will help us make the right turns.

READ TODAY: PROVERBS 3:5-8

JANUARY 23

"ONE DAY, ALL THEM BAGS GONE GET IN YOUR WAY."
-ERYKAH BADU

Have you ever been in a situation where you let your past affect your present and future? Maybe you had been let down in the past, so you decided not to get your hopes up in the future. Maybe a black woman hurt you in the past, so you decided not to date black women in the future. Maybe a pastor betrayed your trust in the past, so you decided not to trust any pastor in the future. Perhaps someone took advantage of your kind heart in the past, so you decided never to be vulnerable again in the future. Maybe somebody made a joke about your legs in the past, so you decided never to wear shorts in the future. These are all examples of the heavy baggage that we tend to carry from one season into the next.

The truth of the matter is that at some point, all of the extra weight and the bags we carry will get in our way. Excess baggage can…my God today, this just came to me…too much baggage will cause you to miss your **flight**. We've all seen that one person in the airport rushing to catch a flight, but they can't move quickly because they are burdened with too much luggage. We've seen the person who gets denied entry at the gate because they are trying to board with a bag that is too big to be stowed as a carry-on. Listen, we have a destination in God…somewhere we need to go. Leave all of that extra baggage so that you can take off on time!

READ TODAY: HEBREWS 12:1-2

JANUARY 24

"KEEP YOUR HEAD UP. WHAT? KEEP YOUR HEAD UP. THAT'S RIGHT." -QUEEN LATIFAH

Have you ever been in a situation where you felt ashamed? Maybe you did something that you are not so proud to say that you did. Maybe you said something that you wish you could take back. Maybe you are embarrassed about how you handled a situation. Maybe you are the one who did somebody wrong. Guess what? Nobody is perfect.

One of Satan's most famous tricks is to use guilt and shame to control you. If he can get you to lower your head in shame, that means your eyes are no longer focused on God. You begin looking down and focusing on yourself and your own shortcomings. Shame is not God's will for our lives. Although our actions do have consequences attached, God's love for us remains unconditional. No matter what you have done, God is willing to forgive you and allow you to repent (change your mind) and move forward. Keep your head **up** and keep your eyes forever focused on God. That's right.

READ TODAY: PSALMS 3:3

JANUARY 25

"I BEEZ IN THE TRAP, BE-BEEZ IN THE TRAP."
-NICKI MINAJ

Have you ever been in a situation and realized that you needed to get out of said situation and fast? Perhaps you tested some limits and thought you wouldn't get yourself caught up. Maybe curiosity and temptation got the best of you. You knew that continuing to move forward in the situation would bring nothing but trouble, but you also felt that you had already gone too far to turn around. My mom used to tell me that sin takes you farther than you want to go, keeps you longer than you want to stay, and makes you pay more than you planned to pay. Ladies and gentleman, I present to you **the trap.**

Perhaps you be-beez in a trap right now. Getting caught up in a trap can be embarrassing. It's even more embarrassing when God warned us not to go there in the first place. We blew right past every red flag, and now we are ashamed to reach out to God for help. The good news is that He loves us so much that He will still hear our cry even **from** the trap. No matter how far we've gone, God is able to provide a way of escape. Ask God to get you out of the trap, and don't walk, but run to the nearest exit.

READ TODAY: 1 CORINTHIANS 10:12-13

JANUARY 26

"STARTED FROM THE BOTTOM, NOW THE WHOLE TEAM HERE."
-DRAKE

Have you ever been in a situation where you actually made something out of yourself? Perhaps you weren't supposed to succeed based on where you came from. Based on the statistics, you were supposed to end up dead, in jail, or living in poverty. Perhaps there are cycles that have repeated themselves within your family, and you were the one to break the curse. I want to say congratulations to you! You did that! That is a major flex, and I'm so proud of you. People don't tell you that enough.

That's a good place to stop and take a quick praise break! Don't worry, I'll wait. Did you do it? Listen, if God's grace and mercy had not **sustained** you, there's no telling where you would be now or what you would be doing. Gratitude has to be your posture, because we've all seen the person who makes advances and then forgets that God blesses us so that we will be able to be a blessing to others. Many assume that I'm talking about money, but sometimes it's just taking a moment to share some wisdom on how you started from the bottom but ended up "here." Sometimes it's taking time to help pray somebody through a situation. Sometimes it's sharing your story or taking an interest in someone else's journey. It's one thing to be able to say, "I'm here," but the next level of flexing is when you can say that "I'm here, and I brought a whole team here too."

READ TODAY: PHILIPPIANS 2:4-5

JANUARY 27

"IT AIN'T NUTHIN' BUT A 'G' THANG BABY."
-SNOOP DOGG

Have you ever been in a situation where people didn't understand your relationship with God? Perhaps you tried to explain it to them, but they just couldn't seem to understand. Maybe they didn't really want to understand. All they know is that they see you forgiving folks and praying for the people who did you wrong. They see you walking around with inner peace even in the midst of the turmoil going on around you. They see how you never stop giving to others when you could use a little help yourself. They see you with a sound mind even though others who experienced what you experienced are now locked in a padded room. They see how you may not have the money for the big and unexpected bill that's due, but you somehow remain as cool as a fan.

To be honest, there are some things that people won't understand until they try it for themselves. As hard as you try to explain that it's nuthin' but a "G" thang...a G-O-D thang, people will need to have their own personal relationship with the Lord in order to fully understand why you choose to live and believe the way that you do. Never waste time arguing with a person who is determined to misunderstand anyway. The best thing you can do is continue to live a life before them that makes them want to try this "G" thang out for themselves.

READ TODAY: PSALMS 23:1-6

JANUARY 28

"NEVER LET ME SLIP, 'CAUSE IF I SLIP, THEN I'M SLIPPIN."
-DR. DRE

    Have you ever been in a situation where you didn't feel as close to the Lord as you once were? Perhaps there was a time when you were more **excited** about your relationship with the Lord. You prayed more then. You were reading your Word all the time. You even had a little journal you would write stuff in as God would speak to you. You looked forward to Sunday service AND midweek Bible Study. Those were some of the most fulfilling times of your life. What happened? Did you start slipping? Slowly, surely, and bit by bit, you started slipping away from the thing that was giving you the most life.

    Life is full of distractions that can cause us to start slipping away from our walk with God. Sometimes they are unexpected situations that arise. It could be school, work, a new boo, a new baby, a new house, or new friends. Slipping is a gradual process that never happens all at once. This is one of Satan's slickest tricks. He wants us to fall back so gradually that we are miles away before we even know it. You start feeling an emptiness and don't even realize it's because you have slipped away from your First Love. Life changes are inevitable, so we must endeavor to hold on to God's unchanging hand. Hold **tightly** to His hand and don't let your grip slip. In what areas have you been slipping lately and why?

                                  READ TODAY: REVELATIONS 2:4

JANUARY 29

"IT'S LIKE THIS AND LIKE THAT AND LIKE THIS, AND UH."
-DR. DRE/SNOOP DOGG

Have you ever been in a situation where you didn't take your own advice? Perhaps you had all the answers and the explanations for everybody else's life, but you didn't apply them to yourself. Do you tell others the importance of self-care but do a bad job taking care of yourself? Have you told your homegirl to stop messing around with her toxic ex, but you keep entertaining yours? Have you encouraged a friend to follow their dream, but are too scared to do the same thing for yourself? I know you don't want to hear this, but perhaps no one takes your advice seriously because you are a hypocrite. We've all been hypocrites before, so don't freak out.

The thing about your advice is that it's actually pretty sound. The only reason why people don't take it is because they are not just looking at what you say. They are also looking at what you do, and they see the inconsistency in your **example**. Would you accept fitness advice from someone who is overweight and unhealthy? If you want your advice to be heard, you have to tighten up on your example. That way, when you try to explain to someone how it is, you can say, "it's like this and like that and like this, and uh…" and they will actually believe you because they've also seen you.

READ TODAY: 1 CORINTHIANS 11:1

JANUARY 30

"I WON'T NEVER SELL MY SOUL, AND I CAN BACK THAT."
-RODDY RICH

Have you ever been in a situation where you wanted things to be easier? How exhausting is it to actually study for a test when you could just cheat like everybody else? Why, oh why do you have to get up every day to go to work when you could be making a few drug runs instead? Why am I paying all my own bills when I have all these sugar daddy offers on the table? Why am I being faithful to my wife when all of my friends get away with cheating? Why am I actually paying for all my items at Wal-Mart when I could just *cough* go through the self-checkout? It can be exhausting, but as men and women of God, we've got to have a **code**.

Having a code means that no matter what Satan tries to tempt us with, we will never sell our souls. We stand on the Word of God to back that. Satan will always be trying to wave some quick and easy way in our face. Don't go for the instant gratification, because it's only a trick. You may seem to be getting the jump temporarily, but I can guarantee you that selling your soul is only going to end in destruction. We have to be smart enough to remember that the enemy comes to steal, kill, and destroy…that's it. But Jesus came that we might have life, and life more abundantly. Wait, I say, on the Lord.

READ TODAY: JOHN 10:10

JANUARY 31

"BIRTHDAYS WAS THE WORST DAYS. NOW WE SIP CHAMPAGNE WHEN WE THIRSTY" -THE NOTORIOUS B.I.G.

Have you ever been in a situation where you were expecting something big but got something small? Perhaps it was indeed your birthday that was the worst day. Maybe you left Thanksgiving dinner in tears. Maybe you got some of the worst news of your life on Christmas Day. You were all set for a glorious time but ended up having a day that was worse than the other 364. The disappointment was real. The first thing you need to know is that Satan takes no days off, and he doesn't care what day it is. If he can get you to feel down, discouraged, or depressed, he has done his job.

The second thing you need to know is that time is filled with swift transitions. This means that things in your life can change at any moment. God is the Master of the turnaround. Do not let one bad day, month, or even year, cause you to second-guess God's ability. He can literally take you from being so broke that you cannot afford to celebrate your birthday, to a place of so much **abundance** that you can literally sip champagne simply on the grounds that you are thirsty. My God Today! Savagely hold on to your faith, continue to be patient, and continue to sow good seeds so that you can reap an amazing harvest.

READ TODAY: 1 PETER 5:10-11

FEBRUARY 1

"YOU'VE GOT YOUR PROBLEMS BABY, AND I'VE GOT MINE."
-BLACKSTREET

Have you ever been in a situation where you felt like you were being judged incorrectly? Maybe it was by your own mother. Maybe it was by people who didn't even know you or what you were about. Maybe you felt like you were being judged in church, at work, or some other place where you didn't fit in. If you've ever been incorrectly judged, you know that it's a terrible feeling.

The Bible tells us that men look at your outward appearance, but God looks at your heart. The crazy thing is that not only do we **not** know for sure what's in somebody else's heart, but we can't even claim to **truly** know what's in our own heart! The Bible says that the heart is deceitful and wicked and asks us who can truly understand it? The truth of the matter is that you've got your problems baby, and I've also got mine. Nobody is perfect, but God. Wise people know that you don't have to spend so much energy trying to judge someone, because their fruit will eventually speak for itself. If you're honest, you'll admit that you've also judged people incorrectly while **knowing** you weren't all the way right yourself. Don't waste your energy trying to judge others, and don't waste it being frustrated about how others have judged you. Use your time wisely by making sure that your own fruit speaks well on your behalf.

READ TODAY: ROMANS 3:23

FEBRUARY 2

"BUT IF YOU WALK AWAY, YOU'LL MAKE THIS GROWN MAN CRY." -BLACKSTREET

Have you ever been in a situation where somebody tried to manipulate you? Perhaps it was your own baby. They did not like for you to put them down, so they would scream and cry until you picked them back up. Maybe it was someone who needed you to do them a favor. Instead of coming out and just asking for what they wanted, they'd call you with this terrible sob story knowing that you would feel guilty if you didn't help. Perhaps you were in a romantic relationship with a woman who knew that even if she was dead wrong, as long as she shed a couple of tears, she'd get her way. Perhaps you were in a relationship with a grown man who told you that his life would be ruined if you left and that your leaving would make him cry.

Manipulation is the language of the immature. As you can see, it starts as early as infancy. I definitely understand the need to make one's requests more marketable, but some people are just downright puppet masters. They learn your weaknesses and leverage them to their advantage. For even the strongest woman, seeing a grown man cry is difficult. We have to do a better job of recognizing manipulation and not giving in to it. The Bible tells us that we shouldn't give grudgingly or under compulsion. We should give cheerfully based on what is truly in our hearts to do. If you find yourself feeling forced by guilt to do something or to give something, that's not the Holy Spirit. Pray and ask God to reveal to you any manipulative schemes that may be happening in your life.

READ TODAY: ROMANS 3:23

FEBRUARY 3

"AIN'T NOBODY DOPE AS ME, I'M DRESSED SO FRESH, SO CLEAN."
-OUTKAST

Have you ever been in a situation where you got yourself dirty? Perhaps you got something on your clothes. I barely wear white anymore because there is a 99% chance that I will brush up against something dirty or spill something red on myself. Getting yourself dirty is frustrating and sometimes embarrassing. We can't wait to get home, take off our dirty clothes, hop in the shower, and put on fresh, clean clothes to relax our minds and calm our anxiety.

We should keep that same energy when it comes to our hearts. Sometimes we allow things into our hearts that will contaminate them. Our hearts can become dirty with anger, bitterness, jealousy, pride, fear, lust, and greed to name a few. We must be very intentional about searching our hearts to see if there are any unclean ways **within** us. Thankfully, God is able to cleanse and dress our hearts so that we may be dope, fresh, and clean once again. Do you have anything in your heart that needs to be cleaned up today?

READ TODAY: PSALMS 51:10-12

"HEY! WHO I'M IS? RUBBERBAND MAN..."
-T.I.

    Have you ever been in a situation where you got knocked down? Maybe you experienced the loss of a job and got knocked down financially. Perhaps you were emotionally knocked down when you discovered that the person you loved wasn't who you thought they were. Maybe you were knocked down by grief when you lost someone near and dear to your heart. Maybe you made a bad mistake and now everyone knows about it. If you live this life long enough, you **will** be knocked down from time to time.

    But just like a man composed completely of rubber bands, you have the God-given ability to bounce back. Getting knocked down can sometimes feel like the end, but as long as you have breath in your body, it is not. Thousands of people take their own lives every year because they felt that they could never bounce back from whatever knocked them down. If you are reading this, God is able to restore your money, your health, your peace, healthy relationships, and most importantly, He is able to restore your soul. If you've ever bounced a rubber ball, you know that when it hits the ground hard, not only does it bounce back...it bounces **higher**. Don't give up.

    READ TODAY: PSALMS 23:3

FEBRUARY 5

"TROUBLEMAN, ALWAYS IN TROUBLE MAN..."
-T.I.

    Have you ever been in a situation where you got into trouble? Perhaps it seems as if you are always in trouble man. Maybe you said to yourself, "Ugh. If it's not one thing, it's another." Perhaps you were simply minding your own business and found yourself in a minefield of trouble exploding all around you. How do you respond? Unfortunately, trouble causes many of us to freak out and do things that make matters worse. There is a better way.

    God never told us that we wouldn't have trouble, but He did say that He would be present with us **in** the trouble. When trouble comes, it seems like we call or text everybody about our business but God. Why is it that we have talked to our homegirl or co-worker about our problems, but we haven't talked to the One who actually has the answers? We take all kinds of questionable advice from people who don't even know how to get out of their own situations. Not only does God have the answers to get us out of the trouble, but He also knows how to comfort us and give us peace in the midst of it.

READ TODAY: PSALMS 46:1-2

FEBRUARY 6

"YOU COULD HAVE WHATEVER YOU LIKE..."
-T.I.

Have you ever been in a situation where you just really wanted something? I mean you **really** liked and wanted that thing. Maybe you interviewed for a job that you felt would be perfect for you. Maybe you found a new house that you felt would be just right for you and your family. Maybe you really wanted to marry that one man or woman. Maybe you wanted to get pregnant and have yourself a baby.

There's nothing wrong with having desires or things that you like. What's important is how you go about obtaining them. Sometimes we want a thing so badly that we will try to force it into existence. The Bible tells us that with God all things are possible, which is awesome and powerful news. The Word also tells us that if we spend our time delighting in the Lord, He will give us the desires of our hearts. Let me explain the part that nobody tells us though. When you begin to take delight in the Lord, the desires of your heart and the things that you like will begin to **change**. Your heart's desires will begin to align more with God's will for your life. You will then have a better picture of the things for which you will need to apply your work and your faith to obtain. I like to call it clarity. Always remember that you may think you like something, but God knows whether that thing will make you happy or miserable in the long run. Don't force anything. Just delight yourself in the Lord first, and let Him give you whatever it is that you would **really** like.

READ TODAY: PSALMS 37:4-5

FEBRUARY 7

"WHAT YOU KNOW ABOUT THAT?"
-T.I.

Have you ever been in a situation where you had to study hard to pass a big test? Perhaps you were taking an exam in school or needed to gain some sort of professional license. Either way, you knew that failing the test was **not** what you wanted to do. Tests these days can have big stakes and oftentimes determine if you will move forward in some area of your life. That's a lot of pressure, so you study your butt off to make sure you get the score needed to pass. On my journey to becoming a doctor, there were many times where I had to drink caffeine to stay up around the clock, neglect sleep, miss social functions, and stay away from social media in order to study. I had to be **sure** that I knew my stuff, and I was ready to do whatever it took to get the knowledge in my head.

Why is it then, that we will do all of that studying in an attempt to advance our lives in the natural realm, but we often neglect to study the things that will help us advance our lives in the spiritual realm? Just as our scholastic tests have big stakes, so do the tests and trials that we go through in life. It's important to be prepared spiritually. Life will tempt and try us in all kinds of ways and then rudely look back at us and ask, "What you know about *that*?" But if you study your Word, get good teaching, and continue to seek God for wisdom, you can answer life by saying, "I know all about that."

READ TODAY: 2 TIMOTHY 2:15

FEBRUARY 8

"BRING EM OUT, BRING EM OUT."
-T.I.

Have you ever been in a situation where you knew you were supposed to be doing something that you were not doing? Perhaps you are supposed to be writing a book that you haven't written. Maybe you have a great singing voice, and you are supposed to be using it. Maybe you have a great entrepreneurial mind, but all you do is go to work for "the man" every day. Are you always counseling your friends and family but won't go to school to become a licensed counselor? Do you know how to cook better than the restaurants? Do you have God-given gifts that seem to be going to waste?

Bring em out! Bring em out! If **God** has placed gifts or ideas inside of you, why won't you bring em out? What excuse have you been holding on to in order to convince yourself that you can't do it right now? Did God say it's not time yet, or did you say it's not time yet? Do you have a fear of rejection? Are you just too lazy to put in the work? Are you worried about how it's going to be possible? Pray and ask God to give you the proper **strategy** to get started, and don't put it off, even if you don't know exactly how it's going to work. Listen, I'm over here writing a book right now. Do you think I know exactly how it's going to get published and who gon' pay for it? Haaa! Almost cussed. I'm writing though. These words were inside of me and I finally decided to bring em out. I know God will make the rest happen.

READ TODAY: 2 TIMOTHY 1:6-7

FEBRUARY 9

"YOU MIGHT SEE ME IN THE STREET, BUT SHAWTY YOU DON'T KNOW ME."
-T.I.

Have you ever been in a situation where you thought you knew somebody, but you really didn't? Maybe you thought the person was one way, only to discover later that they were a completely different way. Perhaps it was a co-worker. You can't stand them at work, but you went out with them once and realized that they were actually as cool as a fan. Maybe it was your own grandmother you didn't know. All your life she's been this angelic woman of God on the battlefield for the Lord and sitting in Jesus' lap. When you actually did the calculations though, you realized that Nanna is only 16 years older than your mama, and the man you've been calling granddaddy was still living in Chicago around the time your mama was conceived. The point is, you assumed you knew somebody that you did not truly know simply because you had been **around** them a lot.

Sadly, there are so many of us who do this with God. You can go to church every time it opens, sing in the choir, listen to gospel music exclusively, do kind things for people, and still not know God. You've just been around Him a lot. You could get up to Heaven's gates, see the Lord standing in the street (paved with gold), only to have Him say…"You did all that **stuff**, but shawty you don't know **Me**, and I don't know you either." Whew chile! That would be a mess. Make sure you're not just in the habit of going to church or being a nice person. Make sure you are in a personal relationship with the Lord. Prayer is a great place to start.

READ TODAY: MATTHEW 7:21-23

FEBRUARY 10

"IF YA HATIN', GET ON YOUR JOB. IT'S MOTIVATION."
-T.I.

Have you ever been in a situation where you had a hater? Perhaps there is someone at work who doesn't like you for no apparent reason. Maybe there are people who talk badly about you behind your back even though you've never had beef with them personally. As much as I can't stand the word, I've come to realize that haters are real. For a long time, I just thought that people who were always talking about their "haters" needed these imaginary beings to fuel their inflated egos. Okay, I still think that to a degree...but haters do exist.

Not only are haters real, but they are necessary. ESPN broadcasted a documentary on the career of Michael Jordan wherein we learned that some of his most amazing performances were, in essence, his way of responding to a hater. There is something about the human nature that causes us to be motivated by people who underestimate us. Haters can be annoying, but the truth of the matter is that we need them to get on their jobs and motivate us. Having a hater is a great indicator that you are doing something dope. As you are reading this, does a certain person come to mind? (Spoiler Alert!) That person is not your **actual** hater, because we wrestle not against flesh and blood. Yes, some people may be allowing Satan to use them, but they are not your real enemies. They are only pawns. Stand up to your one **true** hater with God's Word, and use it as motivation.

READ TODAY: EPHESIANS 6:12-13

FEBRUARY 11

"SO I'M OUTSIDE OF THE CLUB, AND YOU THINK I'M A PUNK."
-BONE CRUSHER

Have you ever been in a situation where you felt like you had been left out? Maybe you logged on to social media to see that some of your friends had a get together that they so conveniently neglected to tell you about. Perhaps there was a whole entire trip that your friends took, but you had no clue until the pictures were posted. Perhaps you are aware of a group text that does not include you. We may see these kinds of things and wonder why we've been left out of the figurative club. Do they think I'm a punk?

Let's not beat around the bush here. You've changed. It's not that they think you're a punk. They just know that you no longer tolerate foolishness the way that you once did. Once you got serious about your walk with the Lord, you were transformed by the renewing of your mind. This means that you think about things differently now, and this new thinking has changed you. There was a time when you just wanted to do hoodrat stuff with your friends, but you're on to other things now. You're not invited on the trip because they know you're not into getting sloppy drunk anymore. They don't include you on the group text because your tolerance for gossip isn't what it used to be. It's called spiritual maturity, and that's nothing to be ashamed of. You have to understand that there will now be some clubs that you are left out of, and it's time to be okay with that. You're not a punk, friend. You're blessed.

READ TODAY: PSALMS 1:1-3

FEBRUARY 12

"IT'S A TAD BIT LATE…NATE DOGG AND WARREN G HAD TO REGULATE."
-NATE DOGG

     Have you ever been in a situation where it was just time to quit playing? Maybe you were in school and you knew if you didn't quit playing, you wouldn't graduate. Perhaps you got diagnosed with pre-diabetes and knew that if you didn't quit playing, you'd end up with an amputated leg. Maybe your favorite pair of pants wouldn't zip anymore, and you knew if you didn't quit playing, you'd end up getting featured on *My 600lb Life*. Maybe your period was three weeks late, and you knew if you didn't quit heauxing, you'd end up on stage with Maury pointing at a split screen to convince the audience that your baby has his nose. You knew it was well past time to get your "ish" together, and although it was a tad bit late, you knew you had to regulate.

     To regulate, by definition, means to control or maintain a thing so that it can operate properly. It often takes extreme circumstances or the threat of a negative consequence for us to realize that we need to quit playing and pull it together. What does this tell you? It tells me that it was all mental the whole time! So often we feel like we **can't** do better because it's too hard, but this isn't true at all. If you change your mind, you can regulate your life. It may be a tad bit late, but it's not **too** late. In what area of your life is it time to quite playing? What is it that you need to regulate?

                                        READ TODAY: ROMANS 12:2

FEBRUARY 13

"TO THE WINDOW...TO THE WALL."
-LIL JON

Have you ever been in a situation where someone took advantage of you? Maybe you allowed that person to stay at your place for a few nights that turned into a few months. Did you let someone borrow your car only for them to start acting like it was theirs? Perhaps you dated someone who only seemed to show interest in you around tax refund time. After you had been taken advantage of, you probably had some questions to ask yourself. What was wrong with me? Why did I allow that person into my life? Why did I give them a **window**? I should have given them a **wall**.

It happens to the best of us. We often allow people to come into our lives who should have never been given access. Once we emerge from whatever daze we were in, we begin to question our own judgement or discernment. Discernment is a gift that God gives us through the Holy Spirit that allows us to know certain things without knowing exactly how we know them. Too often, our discernment picks up on something, but we find ways to explain it away or ignore it because we want everything to work out a certain way. Listen to your discernment and allow yourself to be led by the Holy Spirit. We wait around for some sort of concrete proof to make it make sense, but by then all the damage has been done. If your spirit is troubled, listen to it, and stop giving windows to the people who should be given walls.

READ TODAY: MATTHEW 10:16

FEBRUARY 14

"KEEP YA HEART THREE STACKS. KEEP YA HEART."
-ANDRÉ 3000

Have you ever been in a situation where your heart was broken? Maybe you thought to yourself "Hey, it's already broken and dysfunctional. I may as well throw it away." Maybe you gave it your all and were committed, but it blew up in your face. Maybe you put your heart out there and it was taken for granted, used, abused, and then broken. It's very tempting to use that disappointment and broken heart as a reason to stop being the kind, good-hearted person that you have always been. It's just easier to go into a hard and protective turtle shell where we won't ever have to experience heartbreak again.

Sounds like a great plan, doesn't it? Oh yeah, it's the perfect plan until you realize that you have actually allowed something called **bitterness** to creep into your heart. When you see someone who is bitter, you are looking at someone who has allowed past experiences to harden their heart towards future ones. Bitter people are limited people because they have chosen what they feel will protect them but have sacrificed their true desires in order to do so. You will never experience success if you are shell-shocked and paralyzed from the failures. It's not easy, but you must fight like an absolute savage to keep your heart my friend, keep your heart **pure**.

READ TODAY: MATTHEW 5:8

FEBRUARY 15

"I APOLOGIZE A TRILLION TIMES."
-OUTKAST

Have you ever been in a situation where you were wrong? Maybe you accused someone of something that they didn't do. Maybe you talked badly about somebody behind their backs. Maybe you cheated on someone who really cared about you. Maybe you slapped your mama...just kidding. You wouldn't be alive to read this. Maybe you stole the leftovers that somebody was looking forward to eating. Maybe you stole your best friend's man. Maybe you lost your temper and threw hands on somebody. Maybe you weren't around to help raise your son or daughter. Whatever it was, you were dead wrong, and you knew it.

What did you do? How did you respond? Did you apologize? Many times, when we are wrong, a little thing called pride likes to creep in. Pride keeps us from humbly admitting our mistakes and hinders us from apologizing to the people we have wronged. For some situations, an apology **and** changed behavior can go a long way in mending fences. There are other situations, however, where the damage is done. In those cases, you could apologize a trillion times, and that person's heart isn't going to change towards you, which is fine. The important thing is that you don't let pride get in the way of doing what you know is right. They can choose to forgive or not forgive, but your heart will be lighter because you stood tall and refused to let pride get the best of you. Is there anyone you need to say "I'm sorry" to? Is her name Ms. Jackson? Oooh, I am for real... that would be so cool! You know what? Never mind. Just read this scripture.

READ TODAY: PROVERBS 29:23

FEBRUARY 16

"YOU CAN PLAN A PRETTY PICNIC, BUT YOU CAN'T PREDICT THE WEATHER." -OUTKAST

Have you ever been in a situation where your life didn't go as planned? Maybe you planned to be a college graduate by 21, married by 25, a parent by 27, a business owner by 30, out of debt and independently wealthy by 35, and retired to travel the world by 45. Maybe you wrote out a 10-year plan, but your life looks nothing like it. Aww that was cute. You tried it. You planned a really pretty picnic for your life but didn't account for the F5 tornado that blew through.

There is absolutely nothing wrong with creating a plan. First and foremost, we have to understand that any plans that we make need to be done so with the guidance of the Holy Spirit. The Holy Spirit is able to give you a vision, and the Bible actually tells us to write that vision down. We must understand, however, that the vision may not become a reality exactly in the **way** that we planned or **when** we planned. We have to be open and flexible to flow with God in the way that He sees fit for our lives. If you get impatient and try to rush the process, it's like inviting ants to your own picnic. You will end up way more miserable going rogue and forcing things. This is where trust comes in. Do you really trust that God has your best interest in mind and that He hasn't forgotten about you? We may not understand exactly why God does things the way that He does, but for all you know there was somebody waiting in that park to rob you. Maybe the postponed picnic saved your life.

READ TODAY: PROVERBS 3:5-6

FEBRUARY 17

"SHAKE IT LIKE A POLAROID PICTURE."
-OUTKAST

Have you ever been in a situation where you were shooketh? Shooketh, you know, it's the third person singular present tense adjective of the word "shake" in Old English. Okay. I made that part up. It's not even a real word, but you know what I mean. Maybe something came along and unexpectedly mixed some things up in your life. Maybe you found out you were pregnant. Maybe someone very close to you passed away unexpectedly. Maybe your husband or wife walked out on you. Maybe you found out that you were adopted. Whatever happened, it was at that moment where you felt as if your life had been shaken like one might shake a Polaroid picture

Why do we shake our Polaroid pictures? When a Polaroid picture first exits the camera, it is not completely developed. By shaking it, we (at least in our heads) are aiding in the developing process. Such is life. Sometimes our lives get shaken in ways we never would have imagined, but **perspective** is everything. Do you see your shaking as a reason to give up, or do you see it as an experience that you can use to help you grow and **develop** into a better picture of what God is calling you to be?

READ TODAY: JAMES 1:2-4

FEBRUARY 18

"I LIKE THE WAY YOU MOVE."
-OUTKAST

Have you ever been in a situation where you didn't know how things were going to work out? Maybe you were in a real crisis there for a minute. Things were reeeeallllly touch and go. Perhaps the house was on the verge of getting foreclosed on. Maybe you were on the verge of going out of business. Maybe your car quit on you, and you didn't have the money or the credit to purchase a new one. Maybe you lost your job a month after closing on your new home. You had absolutely no idea how things would work out. Your anxiety was through the roof, and you could barely sleep at night worrying about the problem. Your life was in complete turmoil then, but now it is a vague and fuzzy memory that you have mostly forgotten about.

What happened? God moved on your behalf. In the words of the church cliché, "He may not come when you want Him, but He's always on time!" We may not particularly enjoy the timing of His moves, but if we see it to completion, we will most certainly like the **way** He moves. If you really sit and think about all the times and ways that God moved for you, you will realize that He's never actually failed you. Even if you had to sleep in your car a few nights or miss a few meals, you made it. When you look at it that way, you begin to realize that the worry, the fear, the freak outs, and the anxiety attacks aren't so necessary. Next time you are on the verge of a meltdown, remember the places He's brought you from and the ways in which He has moved.

READ TODAY: PSALMS 42:6

FEBRUARY 19

"NOW WALK IT OUT."
-DJ UNK

Have you ever been in a situation where you decided to allow Jesus into your heart? Congratulations to you! That is the most excellent news ever and the absolute best decision you could have ever made for yourself and your family. That's awesome, but maybe you woke up the next day and still felt like hitting the blunt. Maybe you woke up the next day and were still tempted to respond to the "Hey Big Head..." text message and get you a lil' some. Maybe you woke up the next day and your tongue still felt like cussing somebody out.

What many people don't understand is that accepting Jesus doesn't instantly make you some perfect saint. Some things, yes, God will remove from your desires right away. Other times there will be a process, and you will have to work it out and walk it out with God's help. Shout out to my church (Faith Walkers Church in Birmingham, AL) where our church motto is literally "Walk It Out By Faith." Step by step and day by day you are on this **journey** to wholeness. We live in a suit made of flesh, so don't get too down on yourself if you don't get everything right immediately. Thankfully, God has given us all the tools we need. The most important things are a changed heart, a made-up mind, and the resolve never to quit working it out and walking it out by faith.

READ TODAY: PHILIPPIANS 2:12

FEBRUARY 20

"YOU MIGHT WIN SOME, BUT YOU JUST LOST ONE."
-LAURYN HILL

Have you ever been in a situation where somebody baited you into a stupid argument? Maybe you could tell when they started talking that they were desperate to pick a fight. Perhaps they lied, called you out of your name, or took a really low blow and insulted your character. It's like you knew exactly what they were trying to do, but you just couldn't resist the urge to clap right back and set the record straight. The next thing you knew, your blood pressure was up, and you were embroiled in a heated argument with some dummy. Well guess what? They won. They won (and you lost), the moment you decided to engage in the foolery.

To the other party's satisfaction, you allowed your time, energy, spirit, and possibly blood pressure to be disturbed. However, there exists a beautifully golden state of mind known as being "unbothered." When a person is truly unbothered it's because they have a very clear picture of who they are and of who God is. Don't go for the bait. Let the insults roll off as you remember that you have **nothing to prove** (least of all, to them). It will be at this moment that they will realize that although they might win some, they just lost one. Hold your peace. Hold it in your dominant hand and wave it like some unbothered flag of victory.

READ TODAY: PSALMS 34:14

FEBRUARY 21

"...FORCES YOU TO SCREAM MY NAME, THEN PRETEND THAT YOU CAN'T STAY."
-LAURYN HILL

Have you ever been in a situation where you felt used? Maybe you have a "friend" who only calls you when they need a favor. Perhaps you have a child who only calls home when they need money. Have you ever seen your phone ringing and you already knew they were about to ask you to watch their kids? Why do certain people always seem to have some kind of emergency? They are never calling just to check in with you, and once they get what they need, they are gone again until the next time. You probably know by now where we are going with this.

If we don't like it when someone does it to us, then why do we do it to God? When life forces us to scream His name and cry out to Him, we fast, we pray, and we are steady in our Word. We are **there**! What's crazy is that He doesn't mind us being there either. He actually prefers us to be near to Him. The only problem is that when He finally grants our requests, we pretend that we can't stay. We go back to business as usual. I don't know who this is for, but you **can** stay. Even when your life is not in a crisis, you can stay.

READ TODAY: PSALMS 27:4

FEBRUARY 22

"TELL ME WHO I HAVE TO BE TO GAIN SOME RECIPROCITY."
-LAURYN HILL

Have you ever been in a situation where you treated somebody better than they treated you? Maybe you went all out for their Christmas gift, but they got you a gift card to the wire hanger store. Maybe they had a tough day at work. You went the extra mile to provide a stress-free evening for them, but when you had a bad day, it was you, Jesus, that bottle of wine, and a frozen pizza. Maybe when they have a problem, they can come vent to you, but when you have a problem, they literally fall asleep while you're talking. Even though you don't do what you do to gain anything in return, it does make you feel undervalued when there is no reciprocity. You already know where we're about to go again.

We have a God who literally hung the stars with His words. We have a God who literally gave us His Son. We have a God who will never leave us nor forsake us. We have a God who forgives us when we mess up and heals us when we are sick. We have a God who loves us so much that He can take our mistakes and turn them into blessings. I can guarantee you that there is nobody doper and nobody who loves us more than He does. So tell me who exactly does He have to be to gain some reciprocity? We can never truly reciprocate what He does for us, but He tells us that if we love Him, we can reciprocate by keeping His commandments. Your obedience is your most effective demonstration of love towards Him.

READ TODAY: JOHN 14:15

FEBRUARY 23

"IT'S FUNNY HOW MONEY CHANGES SITUATIONS."
-LAURYN HILL

Have you ever been in a situation where you let money change you? Aww look at you already being judgey and stuff before we even get started. Maybe you were just getting ready to apply this word to somebody you know who got a "come up" and then wanted to act all bougie. Well having money isn't the only thing that changes people. Not having money does it too. Have you ever seen someone who changes into a completely different person when they have money troubles? They aren't themselves at all. They change into this person who is depressed, distant, detached, and distracted because of money. They have allowed money to change their **internal** situation.

If a storm comes along blowing a little wind, and you crumble, then there was already a problem with your foundation. True peace from God trumps what you see with your eyes. Don't get too down on yourself though. Your faith has the ability to grow and to be strengthened, but you do have to exercise it. I've got an exercise for you. The next time your money is funny, I challenge you not to allow it to change your internal situation. Hold on to your peace while you wait to see How God will provide this time.

READ TODAY: EXODUS 14:14

FEBRUARY 24

"MAMA SAID KNOCK YOU OUT."
-LL COOL J

    Have you ever been in a situation where the devil kept bothering you? Perhaps you were minding your own business, and he tried to remind you of that time you were living that heaux life and slept with two different guys from Tinder only 16 hours apart. Maybe he reminded you of the time you were addicted to watching porn. Perhaps he brought up how much you hurt your significant other by cheating. Maybe he reminded you of how much you miss your toxic ex. You didn't want these negative thoughts in your head, but Satan sure did. He wanted you to feel guilt, condemnation, shame, and eventually depression.

    When Satan tries to attack your mind, it's usually because He knows that you are close to some sort of breakthrough in life. He knows that he can't block the door that you're getting ready to walk into, but if he can get into your head, he can make you change your own mind about wanting to walk through it. If you were fortunate enough to grow up with a praying mother, she probably taught you how to pray. But don't forget about that other thing she taught you to do. She taught you how to **rebuke** the devil when he tries to show up in your life. The Bible teaches us that if you resist the devil, he will have to flee. It also tells us that the name of Jesus itself is powerful. The next time the enemy tries it with your mind, resist him, call on the name of Jesus for help, and tell the devil "Mama said knock you out..."

READ TODAY: LUKE 10:17

FEBRUARY 25

"WHEN I'M ALONE IN MY ROOM, SOMEITMES I STARE AT THE WALL."
-LL COOL J

Have you ever been in a situation where folks didn't want to let you be great? Perhaps you're overweight, and your mom won't quit frying chicken and telling you to come get a plate. You want to look like a snack, but you can't stop eating them. Maybe you wanted to stop being a jerk, but the girl at work won't stop asking you stupid questions. Maybe you want a better relationship with your spouse, but it seems like all they do is bring up what happened five years ago. It seems that, in your attempt to be great, you have hit a wall.

When we're alone in our rooms lying in bed at night, sometimes we stare at the wall. The wall is the thing that seems to be standing between us and our happiness or our greatness. Sometimes we can't even get to sleep because we are too busy thinking about our wall and about how impossible it seems to get to the other side of it. You know what's better than staring at your wall? Instead of being so focused on the obstacle, we should fix our eyes on the One who is able to move it, break through it, demolish it, or dissolve it with a dadgum Star Wars blaster if He felt like it. With God **all** things are possible. Take your focus off of the wall today and put it back on God.

READ TODAY: LUKE 1:37

FEBRUARY 26

"WHO'S THAT PEEKING IN MY WINDOW? POW! NOBODY NOW."
-GOODIE MOB

Have you ever been in a situation where you were depressed? Perhaps you didn't feel like doing anything anymore. Is all of your motivation gone? Are you tired all the time, even if you sleep all day? Did something happen to make you sad? Did you experience some sort of loss? Do you no longer care about the things you used to care about? Do negative thoughts cloud your mind? I know that's a lot of questions, but I'm trying to figure out if you might be depressed. Sometimes depression is situational, and it passes in a reasonable amount of time. Other times depression can be clinical and needs to be treated by a professional. One thing I can't stand about depression, though, is that it's very sneaky.

Depression is rude because it creeps up on people. Half the folks who are depressed still don't even know that they're actually depressed! Depression is like a thief that is coming to steal your joy, but first it cases the joint. At any given point depression can be found lurking around and peeking in your windows like a thief trying to figure out how it can get in and what it can take from you. If we aren't careful, depression will break in, tie us up, and steal our joy and peace. That is why when you feel depression coming on, you cannot allow it to linger. Having God's Word inside of you is like having a sniper sitting on the roof of your heart to guard it. If depression does try to creep up, you can shoot it down quickly with God's Word, "Pow! nobody now…" and kill it at the do'.

READ TODAY: PROVERBS 4:23

FEBRUARY 27

"EVERY TIME I COME AROUND YOUR CITY, BLING BLING."
-LIL WAYNE

Have you ever been in a situation where you were trying to impress someone? Maybe it was your girlfriend's parents. Maybe it was a person you were interested in dating. Perhaps it was a job interviewer. Whatever the case may have been, you went beyond yourself trying to make people believe that you were great. In today's social media culture, there are a lot of people seeking to impress others. The old saints used to call this "flossing" or "stunting." The even older saints would call it "showing out." It's all about coming around with the newest, freshest, shiniest, and bling blingiest thing. We have learned, however, that everything that blings ain't Balenciaga. There are a lot of people out here doing it simply for the "likes," but why?

The problem with going beyond yourself to impress others is the fact that you went beyond yourself to impress others. Why would you feel the need to appear to be something that you're not, unless you're unhappy with what you really are? People have gone to the greatest lengths, have lived beyond their means, and have gone into debt simply trying to bling in the eyes of others. Why do the others matter so much? Why put so much effort into **appearing** to be dope, if you really **are** dope? Maybe it's time to stop spending so much energy trying to look like you got it, and just get it. You don't have to work so hard trying to impress people when you are simply an impressive **person**. Let's work on our hearts. You may or may not gain approval from people, but you will certainly gain it from God.

READ TODAY: 1 SAMUEL 16:7

FEBRUARY 28

"OH BABY YOU, YOU GOT WHAT I NEED."
-BIZ MARKIE

Have you ever been in a situation where you needed something? Maybe what you needed was something that somebody else had. Maybe it was a study guide to a test. Maybe it was money. Maybe it was a reference letter for the job you really wanted to get or for an organization you were hoping to get into. If you're like me, you're going to do everything possible to get what you need on your own. I actually do this to a fault. I would much rather do things for myself, but in everybody's life there will come a time when you have to swallow your pride, humble yourself, and ask for what you need. We often fear rejection or just hate being a burden to others. Sometimes we are worried that the person will want something unreasonable in return. Thankfully, that is not the way of our Father.

God has everything that we need, and that means everything. I'm not sure why we do this, but sometimes we forget to ask. We will literally sit there having an anxiety attack, yet never stopped to say, "Lord, may I have…" The Bible tells us that often times we have not, because we ask not. The great thing about God is that He already knows what we have need of. Some of the things we think we need, we do not actually need. On the other hand, there are things that we have no clue about that we actually do need. God knows those things, and God cares. God's got what you need.

READ TODAY: MATTHEW 6:8-11

MARCH 1

"WELCOME TO ATLANTA, WHERE THE PLAYERS PLAY."
-JERMAINE DUPRI

Have you ever been in a situation where you felt the need to escape? I'm not talking about a little weekend getaway or even a 3-week vacation. Perhaps things around you seemed to be stagnant. Maybe you've struggled to find the kind of job you're looking for. Maybe you've struggled to find the type of friendships or romantic relationships you're looking for. Maybe you've dated so many people that you can't find anybody who isn't already close friends with one of your many exes. Perhaps you have already ruined your reputation, and it's hard to get fresh opportunities with new acquaintances without being pre-judged. People know too much about you. This is usually when black people get the hardly original idea that moving to Atlanta will solve all of their problems. Y'all know exactly what I'm talking about.

My old pastor used to say, "Wherever you go, there you are." He was saying that you cannot run away from yourself. Is the problem really your location, or is the problem with you? Sure, Atlanta might welcome you with open arms, but if you were playing around in Detroit, you're still going to play around in Atlanta. You're still going to play because you're still a **player**. You did absolutely nothing to address what was going on with you internally. Now if the Holy Spirit leads you to make a move, please move, but at what point do you decide to quit running and do the real work that needs to be done inside of you? If you think external changes will fix internal problems, you're sadly mistaken.

READ TODAY: 2 CORINTHIANS 5:17

MARCH 2

"BUT THAT'S OKAY, CUZ I'M STILL FLY."
-BIG TYMERS

Have you ever been in a situation where you didn't look like what you had been through? Perhaps you had been in an abusive relationship. Maybe you had been in a bad storm that destroyed your home. Perhaps you had been through a serious illness where you had to spend a lot of time in the hospital. Maybe you struggled through a season of depression and barely wanting to live. Perhaps you were addicted to drugs or alcohol for quite some time. Whatever the situation was, it was bad, but we wouldn't be able to tell by looking at you now.

One dope thing about God is that He is big on restoration. He's so good at restoration that if we didn't tell our stories, nobody would have ever guessed that we had one. You don't look anything like what you've been through. This just underscores the importance of our personal testimonies. If you have been through hard times and God has restored you, please don't forget to **share** what He's done. Allow the Holy Spirit to guide you on when to share and who to share it with, but know that it is needed. Somebody needs to know where God brought you from and how you overcame. They need to know that you went through a lot, but that's okay, because of God, you're still fly.

READ TODAY: JOEL 2:25-26

MARCH 3

"AIN'T GOT NO JOB, BUT I STAY SHARP."
-BIG TYMERS

Have you ever been in a situation where you didn't have a job? I'm not talking about choosing to be a stay-at-home parent. I'm talking about a situation where you really needed a job and didn't have one. Bills were due, mouths needed to be fed, and you were unemployed. You looked for a job and would have taken almost anything, but it seems like you were always either over-qualified or "not a match." Do you know how defeating it can feel to be a grown ash man or woman and feel that you can't provide for yourself or your family?

Did you notice something weird though? During that time when you didn't have a job, you never truly went without. How Sway? You may not have had everything you wanted, but you still had food to eat, you still had a place to lay your head, and you didn't have to wear tattered clothes. You didn't have a job, but somehow you stayed sharp. That was actually a really good spot to stop and praise Him, but I digress. That's because the job was never the **source** of your provision. God is your one and only source, and the job is just one of many resources He can use to get provision to you. Jobs can come and go, but Jehovah Jireh (God our Provider) remains the same.

READ TODAY: PSALMS 23:1

MARCH 4

"A YES, YES Y'ALL, AND YOU DON'T STOP."
-DJ KOOL HERC et al

Have you ever been in a situation where someone you cared about stopped caring about you? It could have been a friend, a family member, or a significant other. Perhaps you did or said something to offend them, and they decided not to forgive. Maybe you are no longer useful to them and they have moved on to someone who is. Maybe they simply listened to what somebody else had to say about you that was negative or false. Maybe you have absolutely no idea what you did, if anything. All you know is that a person, who once claimed to love you, decided to fall back.

This can lead to feelings of hurt, pain, confusion, and rejection. One of the most amazing facts of life, however, is that God is **not** like man. As humans, we are quick to cut people off and to fall back. It doesn't take much for **us** to say "Aight, I'm gonna head out..." and to go "ghost" on someone who doesn't meet our expectations. Thankfully, God's love is for us is unconditional. Of course He wants us to live a life free from sin, but He refuses to let our mistakes stop Him from loving us the **exact same way** He loved us before we messed up. When others say no to loving us, God says "A yes, yes y'all, and it don't stop." Today on March 4th, we are grateful that God's love continues to march forth.

READ TODAY: ROMANS 8:38-39

MARCH 5

"TO ALL THE LADIES IN THE PLACE WITH STYLE AND GRACE..."
-THE NOTORIOUS B.I.G.

    Have you ever been in a situation where it seemed like the floozies were winning? Maybe you're a woman trying to carry herself in a certain way, but everywhere you look it seems like the looser women are the winners in today's society. It seems like they get the man, the money, the dream wedding, the house, the trips, and even the baby. Maybe you went to college and now you're working a nine to five job, but feel that you could be doing much better financially if you could just learn a couple of good pole routines or take that sugar daddy up on his kind offer. Maybe if you went to Dr. Miami for plastic surgery and then started posting half...well three-fourths naked pics of yourself on the gram, you could land yourself a baller too. Sometimes this world seems upside down.

    I just want to encourage you that there **is** still a place in this world for ladies with style and grace. First of all, never look at what someone else has, because you never know what they have had to do or what kind of peace they gave up in order to have it. Social media has caused us to look at other people and declare them to be our #goals. You never know what is going on with people or what demons they have to fight when the cameras are off. Continue to carry yourself with style and grace knowing that when it's time, God will hook you up with something amazing that you didn't have to sell yourself short to get. Oh, and brothers, don't underestimate the level of favor and peace that this type of woman can bring into your home.

READ TODAY: GALATIANS 6:9

MARCH 6

"GET BACK! GET BACK! YOU DON'T KNOW ME LIKE THAT." -LUDACRIS

Have you ever been in a situation where somebody thought they knew you? Maybe it was somebody who you used to run with in high school or college. Perhaps you were a mess back then. Maybe you were lying, cheating, and stealing back then. Maybe you made your money selling drugs back then. Maybe you were living the heaux life back then and letting just about anybody hit. Maybe you were insecure back then and had no sense of self-worth. Maybe you were a narcissistic jerk back then and didn't care about anybody but yourself. Maybe you were drunk or high every day back then...but that was then, and this is now.

Thank God for deliverance! I am so grateful that growth is a thing, but there are some people who do not seem to understand this concept. They feel that you will always be the same old you. They see you doing better for yourself and refuse to acknowledge that maybe you have legitimately improved. The truth of the matter is, they preferred you when you were dysfunctional because it was better for them. Now that you are (as Marvin Sapp would say) stronger, wiser, and better, it makes them uncomfortable. Those types of people **always** want to remind you of what you used to do and love make claims that they know the **real,** lesser you. Preposterous! You don't need those types of people in your life or in your ear because their goal is to get the old you to rise back up. Rebuke them by telling them to get back, get back, because they no longer know you like that!

READ TODAY: EPHESIANS 5:11

MARCH 7

"MOVE! GET OUT THE WAY!"
-LUDACRIS

Have you ever been in a situation where something or someone was in your way? Perhaps it was something that seemed really big and hard to overcome. Maybe it was a health issue. Maybe it was a boss who was a hater. Perhaps it was a credit card balance that seemed like it would never go away. Maybe it was your demonic student loans. Whatever it was, you needed it to move and get out of the way.

Alright, so boom. As believers, we have this thing called faith. Faith is the ability to believe in the existence of something that you have not yet physically touched or seen. Faith is so powerful that even just a little bit of it allows us to be able to make things happen in the world. Our faith is something that is built up stronger and stronger as we spend time getting to know God and the ways that He moves within our life's experiences. Just a small amount of faith enables you to speak to whatever mountain is in your life and tell it to move. Because of your faith in God, that mountain will have to get out of the way.

READ TODAY: EPHESIANS 17:19-21

MARCH 8

"YOU GOT IT...YOU GOT IT BAD."
-USHER

Have you ever been in a situation where you couldn't get your mind off of something? It was weird. It was like no matter how hard you tried to put your mind on something else, you could not seem to think of anything but that. Over and over again, all day long, you were consumed with those thoughts. Maybe it was a huge crush you had on somebody. Maybe it was a mistake you made or something you wished you could take back. It's almost like you were obsessed. Perhaps you felt like you were being tormented. You had it. You had it **bad.**

What do you do in these situations? First and foremost, don't do anything crazy. Sometimes obsessive thoughts can cause you to take extreme actions. Don't show up to that man's house and hide behind the bushes for 12 hours waiting to see who pulls up when he doesn't even know your name yet, sis. If given time, many of your obsessive thoughts will pass, but you have to help them by intentionally **placing** your mind on higher-level thoughts. The Bible tells us that our minds have to be "set," meaning you will have to pick your mind up and move it to a specific place. This is actually called meditation. When you've got it bad, go to your Word and find something **good** to begin meditating on. Eventually there will be no space left for the disruptive thoughts.

READ TODAY: PHILIPPIANS 4:8

MARCH 9

"YOU SHOULD LET ME LOVE YOU."
-MARIO

Have you ever been in a situation where you felt like you didn't deserve to be blessed? Perhaps you had sown so many bad seeds in the past that you felt you didn't deserve a good harvest. Maybe you were trash to someone else, so you felt that you only deserved to be with someone who would be trash to you. Maybe you had been a side chick in the past, so you felt that you didn't deserve a faithful husband. You felt as if you simply did not deserve to be happy and blessed, and so your guilty conscious wouldn't let you. This is one of Satan's trickiest tricks.

I will let you in on a secret. **None of us** truly deserve all of the blessings that God gives us. He does it because He loves us. There is absolutely no way we can work hard enough or be perfect enough to deserve the level of good that God is to us. If that were the case, we'd be able to take credit for the blessings that are only coming from Him anyway. Any time you are feeling guilt, shame, or condemnation, you can be certain that these feelings are coming directly from the devil. He can't do anything to make God stop loving you, but he can fool you into allowing your own guilt to make you reject God's love. God is standing with open arms saying, "You should let Me love you." Go ahead honey, take a chance! (It's really not a chance though, God's love is a sure thing.)

READ TODAY: REVELATION 3:20

MARCH 10

"I GOT A MAN. WHAT YOUR MAN GOT TO DO WITH ME?"
-POSITIVE K

Have you ever been in a situation where you had a new boo? Aww that's so sweet! Look at you! Cuffing season rolled around, and you got "chose." Perhaps you got a new boo right before Thanksgiving, so when your nosey aunt asked why you were still single, you were able to proudly declare, "I got a man!" Christmas was just around the other corner and having a man meant you could expect to actually get some good Christmas gifts this year. Soon enough, Valentine's Day rolled around and you're no longer the poor girl in the office who didn't receive any flowers or candy. Your Edible Arrangement arrived just in time for everybody to know you got a man!

It's so sweet. Your mama likes him, and all your friends are excited for you! Meanwhile, God is looking at the whole situation and asking, "What your man got to do with Me?" That's a literal question. What, if anything, does your man have to do with God? Does he do anything **with** God? Does he pray? Is he in his Word? Does he ever fast? Does he know how to lay hands on you and anoint you with oil when you're sick? Does he have **anything** to do with God? Heck, did God even send him? The holidays have passed now, cuffing season is ending, and these are the questions that need answers. Men, if you are still reading this and you are that guy who hasn't had anything to do **with** God, today is a good day to join Him for a walk.

READ TODAY: MICAH 6:8

MARCH 11

"THE SUN DON'T SHINE FOREVER, BUT AS LONG AS IT'S HERE, WE MIGHT AS WELL SHINE TOGETHER."
-DIDDY

Have you ever been in a situation where you were worried? Maybe you were worried about the future. How am I going to make it? Who's going to pay for it? Where am I going to get it from? Am I going to be laid off soon? How will I survive? Is my spouse getting ready to leave me? Are my loved ones going to die? Am I going to die? The worries consumed your mind so much that perhaps you were unable to enjoy the good things that were going on.

I am in no way attempting to minimize the very real issues taking place in your life. Clearly, we do not live in a fantasy world. I just don't want you to let worry and anxiety ruin your life. We know that the sun doesn't shine forever. There will be days of sunshine as well as days of rain, but how will you know the difference if you are so busy worrying about **tomorrow's** weather? Everything in your life may not be perfect, but don't miss out on the times and places where the sun is still shining. Enjoy every day to the best of your ability. Pull your loved ones close, and y'all shine together while you still have time. Trust God enough to quit worrying so much.

READ TODAY: MATTHEW 6:25-34

MARCH 12

"I DON'T WANT NO CAKE ON MY BIRTHDAY. I WANT MY CAKE ERRRDAY."
-FLO RIDA

Have you ever been in a situation where it was your birthday? Oh okay, that's nice. Today is my birthday!! There will be no message today. Just kidding! Have you ever been in a situation where you cried on your birthday? And I'm not talking about the "tears of joy and gratitude for another year" type of cry. I'm talking about the "It's my birthday, and I'm not even happy. If I can't even be happy on my own birthday then what am I really doing with my life?" kind of cry. That was me on my 30th birthday. I was literally on a beautiful beach resort in Montego Bay, Jamaica and crying **that** type of cry.

There is something about it being your birthday that makes you feel like you **should** be happy. If your birthday rolls around and you are still unhappy, it's a particularly hard pill to swallow. You feel like you should eat cake and be happy **at least** today. The truth is, if you're not happy on a regular and daily basis, your birthday changes nothing. Maybe it's a good time to start reassessing some things in your life. What changes need to be made on behalf of your peace? What is it that God has been trying to get you to do that you have not yet done? Seeing your next birthday is a major blessing, but so is every single day. Birthday cake is not the only type of cake, ya know. Go to any grocery store or bakery and I can guarantee they will have "everyday" cake that you can get just for G.P. (General Purposes)...no special occasion needed. Yes, I want to enjoy my birthday, but I also want to enjoy my **life** every day.

READ TODAY: JOHN 15:11

MARCH 13

"I SEE YOU WINDING AND GRINDING UP ON THE FLOOR."
-AKON

Have you ever been in a situation where you were a hard worker? Maybe you work your fingers to the bone every day. Perhaps you have two jobs or more. Maybe you have a full-time job and a side hustle that you're hoping to one day make your main hustle. Maybe you pay your dues and take good care of your family. Maybe you have child support payments, and you make them. Maybe you are a mom and you get up earlier than everybody else **and** go to sleep later than everybody else. Maybe you selflessly volunteer your time in your church or in your community.

I just want to say that I see you. I see you winding and grinding. I see you up on the floor working and doing what needs to be done. A lot of the things that you do go unnoticed, and people rarely say thank you, so I want to say thank you. People like you make the world go around. Although you may feel like you're invisible to others, I want you to know that God sees it all. He sees. He knows. He cares. If you're waiting around for **people** to make you feel special, you may be waiting around until your funeral. Instead, I want you to understand that everything you do should be done as if you are working for the Lord. Whatever is right, God promised to pay. I assure you that He's good for it.

READ TODAY: COLOSSIANS 3:23-24

MARCH 14

"IT AIN'T TRICKIN' IF YOU GOT IT."
-LIL WAYNE/T-PAIN

Have you ever been in a situation where people thought you were winning, but you were actually losing? Maybe you wanted them to think you were winning too, so you played it up a little bit. Maybe you spent a little extra and went beyond your means to look like you had it, and now you are short for your actual bills. Maybe you went to New Orleans, and you broadcasted live on social media to show people how much fun you were having. In reality it was too crowded, and the drunk people throwing up and fighting around you was rather boring. Maybe you went to the club and bought bottles because you wanted people to know that you got it like that, but you don't. This phenomenon is called "trickin'."

There was a man in the Bible known as the prodigal son. He took his inheritance (while his father was still living, which is just rude) and tricked it off. He wanted people to think he had it, so he spent all of his money turning up and making it rain on his so-called friends. When his money dried up, so did they, and he was left alone with nothing. He eventually realized that he didn't have to trick because his father **really** had it. He returned home and his father welcomed him back with open arms and a party that he had no problems affording. Have you been trickin' social media into thinking you're happy and fulfilled? Have you been trickin' your friends into thinking you're a baller? Why not return to the Father, the One who really has it all, so that you too, can get it for real? It ain't trickin' if you got it.

READ TODAY: PSALMS 24:1

MARCH 15

"AND I JUST CHECKED MY ACCOUNT, TURNS OUT I'M RICH! I'M RICH! I'M RICH!"
-CARDI B

Have you ever been in a situation where you were broke? Maybe your friends were planning a trip. You had to pretend like you were going to be at your cousin's wedding that weekend, but really you just didn't have any money to put down. Perhaps you wanted to get your hair done, but because you were broke, you had to do it yourself. Sadly, it came out looking like James Brown's hot comb job. You were so broke that you had to split the Cup O' Noodles into two servings…one for lunch and one for dinner. Did you notice something though?

In the midst of being broke, you kept your peace. You had no money, but your joy was still intact. You had no coins, but your spirit was thriving, and you were solid in your walk with the Lord. Newsflash: You were rich. In my personal walk, I learned that sometimes God would use money struggles to test and develop me. Would my so-called peace go away when the money gets low? What does that say about my spiritual account? True wealth is when you realize that the things that make you rich cannot be touched or taken away by external circumstances. If you check your "account" some of you will discover that you are **already** rich, and the money hasn't even come yet!

READ TODAY: 3 JOHN 1:2

MARCH 16

"WHEN I DIP, YOU DIP...WE DIP."
-FREAK NASTY

    Have you ever been in a situation where you needed to go? Maybe you were in a club and noticed all the classic symptoms of somebody-is-about-to-get-to-shooting-up-in-here-itis. Maybe you were at a house party when you saw them breaking out the syringes, tourniquets, burnt spoons, and lighters. Maybe you were in a relationship with someone who you realized was drinking more Hennessey before lunchtime than most would drink in a whole year. Either way, you knew that it was time to (as black folks like to say) dip. You stood up and said, "Imma head out."

    "Dip" in the Afro-American translation means to exit a place suddenly. "Dip" in the Chicken Nugget translation means to dive or submerge into a substance. I don't know who this is for, but some of you need to dip **out of** that destructive situation, and dip **into** the very substantive Word of God. Dive into your prayer, into your praise, and into your worship. Yes, in some situations, you will have to be the first person to dip. But if you pay attention, once that first person dips, others realize that they can dip too. Lead by example, because when I dip, you dip, and we can dip. What are the areas of your life where you should chuck the deuces and dip out? What are the areas where you need to dip in?

                                              READ TODAY: 1 TIMOTHY 6:11

MARCH 17

"DUST YOURSELF OFF AND TRY AGAIN."
-AALIYAH

    Have you ever been in a situation where you were dusty? Nobody wants to admit to being dusty huh? In the Black community, being called "dusty" is one of the most cruel insults you can receive. This insult generally refers to one's appearance. A dusty person looks as if they don't take any time to care for themselves. Their clothes look dirty, their shoes are covered in dust, their hair is unkempt, and in extreme circumstances they smell as if they have not bathed or bazed. Are you sure you've never been dusty?

    I would like to submit to you the following idea: some of you are dusty right now. We said that a dusty person does not take time to take care of themselves. Do you take the time to take care of yourself like you should, or are you too busy taking care of everyone else? Some of you run yourselves ragged for others and barely ever do anything for **you**. You will literally take everybody else to their doctor's appointments but haven't scheduled one for yourself. It's starting to show too. Just look in the mirror. Are you starting to look worn out? The Bible commands us to love others **as** we love ourselves, but how can you do that if you don't love yourself **first**? Self-care is probably one of the best buzzwords to come out of the last decade, because it is so needed. You can't be the best husband, wife, mom, dad, brother, sister, son, daughter, or friend if you don't begin to take better care of yourself. Please dust **yourself** off and try that again

READ TODAY: MATTHEW 22:37-40

MARCH 18

"MY CHICK ON THE SIDE SAID SHE GOT ONE ON THE WAY."
-USHER

Have you ever been in a situation where your actions finally caught up with you? Maybe your chick on the side called and said she had a baby on the way. Perhaps you were the side chick yourself and the pregnancy test came back positive. Maybe you kept eating honey buns from the vending machine and finally got diagnosed with diabetes. Maybe the person you bullied in high school turned out to be the interviewer for the job you really wanted. Maybe you have been driving under the influence for years and getting home just fine, but you finally wrecked your car and ended up in the hospital or with a DUI charge. These are called consequences.

For each action we take, we should consider the possible consequences associated with it. Sometimes those consequences are delayed, and that makes us feel like we are "getting away" with something. The truth of the matter is that as long as you are sowing bad seeds, you have no idea when a bad harvest could pop up. It's like sleeping in your contact lenses. One person may sleep in the same pair of contacts for 225 nights with no problem (gross), and another person may sleep in their contacts for one night and wake up the next morning with a terrible eye infection that threatens to permanently damage their vision. The person sleeping for 225 nights will begin getting comfortable with their dysfunction until the 226th night comes along, and they wake up blind in one eye. What actions are you taking that need to be stopped **before** irreversible consequences show up?

READ TODAY: GALATIANS 6:7-9

MARCH 19

"PUSH IT. PUSH IT GOOD. PUSH IT REAL GOOD."
-SALT N' PEPPA

Have you ever been in a situation where you were ready to give up? Maybe you were in school, and it just seemed like too much. Perhaps you were married and tired of arguing, so you began contemplating a divorce. Maybe you were trying hard to quit smoking, but the nicotine kept calling you back. Maybe you started your own business, but it seems like you've bitten off more than you can chew. Giving up is usually a means of taking the easier way out.

Some things in life come easily. Other things must be powered through. Too often, we give up and tell ourselves that if it was meant to be, then it wouldn't have been so difficult. There's a difference between forcing something and pushing it. Breakthrough is that moment when all of your pushing and pressing finally pays off. Things in life always get harder when you are standing near a door that you are on the verge of breaking through. The devil can't actually stop you from going through the door, so he starts throwing things at you and trying to trick you into changing your mind about wanting to go in. God has already unlocked it, so let this be your reminder to get up to your door and push it. Don't just push it, but push it good. Push it real good, amen? Amen.

READ TODAY: 1 CORINTHIANS 16:9

MARCH 20

"THROW SOME D'S ON THAT..."
-RICH BOY

Have you ever been in a situation where you had trouble staying focused? Perhaps you were in class, and your mind kept wandering off while the teacher was lecturing. Maybe you were trying to complete an assignment, and the next thing you knew you were laughing at funny videos on Instagram. Perhaps you were trying to get some work done, and your co-workers kept walking up to your desk and talking about their personal lives. Perhaps you were trying to remain faithful to your significant other, but it seems like as soon as y'all made it official, everybody and their mama wanted slide in your DMs.

Now that Spring aka Sundress Season is upon us, I want to caution you. Distractions will be all around. This is one of Satan's most common strategies. When he sees you making progress, he gets nervous and tries to throw some d's (distractions) on that which you are trying to accomplish. A simple distraction can cause you to lose **everything** you have worked so hard to get. You, however, have an advantage. The Bible tells us that we are not ignorant about Satan's devices or tools. If you already know that the distractions are coming, you will be able to recognize them more easily. The next time something randomly pops up in your life, be sure to squint your eyes, give it a good side-eye, pray, and ask, "Who sent you?" If it wasn't God who sent it, him, or her, then it is called a distraction. Don't let the devil throw some d's on your purpose. Stay focused.

READ TODAY: 2 CORINTHIANS 2:11

MARCH 21

"IT'S JUST ONE OF THEM DAYS THAT A GIRL GOES THROUGH."
-MONICA

    Have you ever been in a situation where a menstrual cycle was trolling your life? Perhaps you are a woman, and your period comes on at the most inopportune times. Maybe you are a man living with a woman whose PMS has wreaked havoc on the relationship. Perhaps you said one wrong thing, and because she was on her period, she reacted by threatening to end your whole entire life. Maybe you are a woman, and once your period came on, you were an emotional wreck. You were just fine one moment, and before you knew it, you were crying, angry with your man, and missing your ex all at the same time. Once the period was over though, you felt much better.

    May I submit to you that period and even menopausal hormones are a part of Satan's strategy to defeat us? I know it sounds crazy, but hear me out. When Satan tricked Eve into messing up in the garden, she was cursed as a consequence. That curse included sorrow that would be associated with bearing children. Alright, so boom! Periods are associated with reproduction and therefore sorrow. Do you know how much drama, how many fights, and how many households have been turned upside down by a woman's unchecked period hormones? You probably wouldn't have sent that 3-page long text message if PMS wasn't involved, huh? This is just practical. Be intentional about knowing **when** your hormones are out of balance and when you don't feel like yourself. Men, y'all have hormones too. Do not let temporary physiological changes trick you into making unwise moves with permanent implications. Pause and remind yourself that it's just one of them days.

READ TODAY: 1 PETER 5:8

MARCH 22

"DON'T TAKE IT PERSONAL."
-MONICA

    Have you ever been in a situation where somebody was rude to you for no apparent reason? If you've ever been to the DMV, any (non-Chick-fil-A) drive thru, or the Financial Aid Office at an HBCU, then you know exactly what I'm talking about. Maybe it was in your own home. Maybe your own child or your significant other was crabby and rude when you were just asking a simple question (see yesterday's lesson on PMS). It's very easy to take these things personally and allow someone else's bad attitude to ruin your day.

    Do not lose your peace over someone who does not know how to maintain theirs. More times than not, it's really not about you anyway. There is something going on inside of that person which causes them to be unhappy. Sadly, they have not developed to a place of maturity where they can continue to function and separate their personal problems from how they treat others. Pray for these people because you never know what is **really** going on with somebody. When I pull up to Taco Bell at 1:00am (don't you dare judge me, TB is the only vegan-friendly place open at 1am) and the lady at the window is rude, do you think I let that bother me? I just pray over my food, pray for her, and keep it pushing. Some circumstance in that woman's life has caused her to be handing tacos out of a window at 1:00am. There's nothing wrong with that, but I'm not oblivious to the fact that she may be doing it out of some sort of necessity and is probably exhausted. Her attitude is not about me. Before you take something personally, take it to God prayerfully. I challenge you to take it one step further by asking God to bless those who try to curse you.

    READ TODAY: MATTHEW 5:44

MARCH 23

"I'M SORRY THAT YOU SEEM TO BE CONFUSED. HE BELONGS TO ME. THE BOY IS MINE."
-MONICA/BRANDY

Have you ever been in a situation where you saw a child going in the wrong direction? Perhaps it was your own child, a family member, or a neighbor. Maybe he used to be the sweetest little boy, but now that he's hanging around with the wrong crowd, he's become disrespectful and unmotivated. Maybe he's been skipping school, hanging out on the corners, and has already started to smoke, drink, and have sex. You see this child going in the wrong direction, and it pains you greatly because you know that the path he's taking will only lead to death and destruction. Satan is so lowdown that he doesn't mind trying to attack someone who is still just a boy.

Don't give up so easily. The devil is the one who seems to be confused. "The boy is mine," saith the Lord. That boy belongs to the Lord and has good seeds planted inside of him. He really needs you praying for him just like somebody prayed for you. Many of us had praying mothers and grandmothers. These women loved us and refused to stop praying even when we went astray. It's our turn now. The devil can't have him. What boy or young man in your life can you become more intentional about praying for? You can start today.

READ TODAY: LUKE 22:31-32

MARCH 24

"HOW CAN ONE BE DOWN? TELL ME WHERE TO START." -BRANDY

Have you ever been in a situation where you had just turned your life around? Maybe it was literally just yesterday or this morning. Perhaps you finally decided that you were going to quit running, and you were going to get right with God. It can seem a bit overwhelming, especially when you have lived so many years in dysfunction. Sometimes the dysfunction begins to feel like your comfort zone, and anything outside of that seems scary. Maybe you know what you want to do, but you are just unsure of how to do it. How can one be down? Let me tell you where to start.

First of all, do not compare your walk with God to anybody else's walk with God. The Bible tells us that when you first give your life to Christ, you are only a babe. There will be some things that you just don't know yet, and that's okay. This is why it's not wise to go and get saved today and then start your own church tomorrow morning. Give yourself time to learn and grow. Start by developing a prayer life where you communicate with the Lord on a very regular basis. Also, find a good Bible reading plan for new believers. You can actually Google "New Believer Bible Reading Plan," and several options will come up. You will also need a good church. They aren't all good, so make sure you pray and ask God to lead you to the right place with the right pastor. Oh, and reading this book isn't a bad idea either! *shameless plug*

READ TODAY: 1 PETER 2:2

MARCH 25

"BE SITTING UP IN MY ROOM...
BACK HERE THINKING 'BOUT YOU."
-BRANDY

Have you ever been in a situation where you were placed in a quarantine? Perhaps there was a global pandemic that was killing people left and right, and just about everything got shut down. Perhaps schools, churches, stores, nail salons, hair salons, and barber shops were all closed. Maybe you couldn't even go and visit your friends and family. Perhaps you had to cancel your vacation. The world around you was going crazy. The pandemic was actually creating pandemonium, and the country's poor leadership was only making matters worse. All you could really do was sit up in your room in isolation for months.

When the world seems to be going crazy, you have two options. You can go crazy right along with it, or you can hold on to your peace. There is an amazing way in which believers can maintain inner peace. The Bible tells us that if we keep our mind **intentionally** focused on God, that He will be responsible for keeping us in perfect peace. Of course this isn't just limited to global health crises, but any time there seems to be pandemonium all around you, go sit up in your room and be back there **thinking** about the goodness of the Lord.

READ TODAY: ISAIAH 26:3

MARCH 26

"IS IT WORTH IT? LET ME WORK IT."
-MISSY "MISDEMEANOR" ELLIOTT

     Have you ever been in a situation where you weren't sure if you were on the right path? Maybe you are tired of going to work every day to make money. Perhaps you have friends or family members who don't work at all but seem to be doing much better than you are with your job. Do you ever get tired of paying $1000 a month for rent when your homegirl on Section 8 gets to pay literally $8? What about the lady in front of you at the grocery store with the food stamp card? She has crab legs, salmon, and T-Bone steaks in her cart, while you're stretching your money thin with Hamburger Helper, Bologna, and Vienna Sausages. Her kids have the new Jordans, and your kids wear Jordache. You begin to ask yourself where you went wrong and if all of your hard work is actually worth it.

     It's a very taboo topic, but the truth of the matter is that many of the Americans who look down upon those getting government assistance are actually **envious** of them. Many feel that it's unfair how hard they have to work when others don't seem to have to do the same thing. Is it even worth it? First of all, you don't know those people's story or what they have been through, so it's not a good idea to be jealous. Secondly, yes, it is worth it. You have chosen a path that does not have to have any limitation. Be creative, be strategic, and work it. If you are not satisfied with where you are, don't give up. People have done more with less. Pray and ask God to give you a plan that will help you to create an enjoyable daily life that will also be rewarding.

READ TODAY: GALATIANS 6:9

MARCH 27

"I PUT MY THANG DOWN, FLIP IT, AND REVERSE IT."
-MISSY "MISDEMEANOR" ELLIOTT

Have you ever been in a situation where you gave up a bad habit? Perhaps you used to be a lowkey alcoholic, but you got your drinking under control. Maybe you used to be a smoker, but you got on the patch or quit cold turkey. Maybe you used to live that heaux life, but now you're sleeping in your own bed every night until the Lord says otherwise. Perhaps you used to curse like a sailor, but you cleaned up your mouth. Maybe you were addicted to porn for a while. Whatever it was, you finally decided to put that thang down!

Congratulations on changing your mind and your life! That's big, but do you know what's even bigger? After you've put your thang down, you've got to flip it and reverse it into a testimony that will be a blessing to others. When God has delivered you from something, you can use that experience to show others the way. There are people in your immediate circle who are struggling with some of the same things that you used to struggle with. Don't be overbearing with it, but don't be ashamed to tell your own story. If anyone can understand what they are going through, it's you. They need to know how God worked in your life, because it will give them the confidence to believe that they too can put their thangs down, flip them, and reverse them. Amen.

READ TODAY: PSALMS 66:16

MARCH 28

"SHAKE EM UP, SHAKE EM UP, SHAKE EM UP, SHAKE EM…"
-ICE CUBE

Have you ever been in a situation where you lost friends? Perhaps you prayed and asked God to show you who was really down for you, but you were surprised by what transpired next. Maybe you prayed and asked God to remove the fake people from your life, and it shocked you to see some of the people who actually dropped off. Some of these were people who you would have never imagined, but it turned out that they meant you no good. Perhaps they had been jealous of you the whole time. Maybe you found out that they had been speaking badly behind your back and telling everyone your business. Perhaps it was your own significant other who had been lying to your face for months. Your entire circle of trusted friends got completely shaken up.

I know from experience how much this can hurt, but I say shake em up, shake em up, shake em up, shake em, Lord! I'd rather God reveal the truth, than to be somewhere confiding in untrustworthy people. As hard as it is to lose people who you have known for years, understand that God is able to bring **new** people into your life who will add to you and not subtract. When you pray and ask God to show you the truth about people, just be ready for things to get shaken up because this is one prayer that He doesn't mind answering **quickly**. You may even get same-day results, so go ahead and let Him shake that tree. Just don't let it shake you.

READ TODAY: PROVERBS 10:18

MARCH 29

"JUST WAKING UP IN THE MORNING, GOTTA THANK GOD."
-ICE CUBE

Have you ever been in a situation where God woke you up? Perhaps someone you know didn't wake up this morning. We all know by now that tomorrow isn't promised. If you woke up this morning, that means that God still has a purpose for you on this earth. The fact that God saw fit to wake you up this morning is a good enough reason to stop and say, "Thank You." We should do our best to make the most out of every day that we are given.

How do you start off your mornings? When I was growing up, my mom would wake up as early as 4:00am just to have alone time with God. I've mentioned before that her morning routine **had** to include communing with the Lord or else her day wouldn't be right. She was (and still is) very intentional about how she starts her days. Do you just hop out the bed in a rush to get your kids off to school and go to work? I have young children, so I am still guilty of that sometimes. (Y'all pray for me saints. He's still working on me in that area, but I'm getting better. The Lord knows my heart!) Even if you have to wake up a few minutes early, try pulling out this book, reading the daily scripture, and saying a little prayer. Even that little bit of time with God will be a blessing to your day.

READ TODAY: PSALMS 63:1

MARCH 30

"TEACH ME HOW TO LOVE. SHOW ME THE WAY TO SURRENDER MY HEART." -MUSIQ SOULCHILD

Have you ever been in a situation where you wanted to be great, but didn't know exactly how? Maybe you wanted to be a great musician, but it wasn't something that you came out of the womb knowing how to do. You'd be surprised to know that some of your favorite musicians were actually classically trained. Perhaps you wanted to be the best in your career, so you got a mentor who was already at the top of the field and was willing to teach you a thing or two. Maybe you wanted to be able to make your mac and cheese taste just like the mac and cheese of your ancestors. If you were smart, you got your mother or grandmother to teach you exactly what to do while you still had the chance.

It's been said a million times that knowledge is power. By default, then, the ability to teach is one of the most important and powerful gifts given to mankind. When we need to learn something, we must humble ourselves and seek instruction. It's no different when it comes to learning how to love. If you have God in your heart, you are going to be a lover by nature. Just because you have love in your heart, however, doesn't mean that you will always know the best ways to translate that love into your words or actions. You can love your kids and still not know how to be the best parent. You can love your spouse and still not know how to be the best husband or wife. Just as we would seek instruction from any other expert, when it comes to learning how to love, we must go to God who is the stand-alone expert of love. As a matter of fact, God **is** love. He assigned us the **best** teacher for this…the Holy Spirit. Today let's pray and ask God to teach us how to be great lovers and to show us how to surrender our hearts to His way.

READ TODAY: PSALMS 25:4-5

"SOON AS I STEP ON THE SCENE, I'M HEARING HOOCHIES SCREAMIN'."
-2PAC

Have you ever been in a situation where you felt tempted? Perhaps as soon as you decided to go on a diet, there was free cheesecake in the breakroom. There's never free cheesecake in the breakroom. Maybe as soon as you decided to stop drinking, your cousin's wedding had an open bar. Your cousin barely makes rent. How are they even affording an open bar?! Perhaps as soon as you said "I do," the hoochies started screaming at you in the gym and trying to holler in your inbox. Nobody was even checking for you before. As soon as you started trying to do right, temptation popped up out of nowhere.

Get used to it. Unfortunately, temptation is a part of life. As long as you live in a body made of flesh, there will be certain things that come to tempt you. Jesus Himself was tempted, but you have to look at how He handled it. Jesus handled His temptation by knowing His Word, rebuking the devil, and refusing to give in. We can do the same. As soon as you step on the scene of trying to do the right thing, you will hear all kinds of temptation screaming loudly in your ear. Yielding to temptation has the potential to make you lose **everything** you've worked so hard for. It's not worth it. Resist the devil, and he will flee!

READ TODAY: JAMES 4:7

APRIL 1

"HA, SICKER THAN YOUR AVERAGE."
-THE NOTORIOUS B.I.G.

Have you ever been in a situation where you were sick? I'm not talking about seasonal allergies and a little congestion sick. I'm talking about sick sick. I'm talking about sicker than your average sick. Perhaps it wasn't even you that was sick. Maybe it was your child, parent, spouse, or best friend. Having to deal with sickness is one of the most difficult things in the life of a believer. Actually, it's not just difficult for believers. It's difficult for humans period.

Tomorrow isn't promised to anyone. Some sickness is unto death, and some is not. We don't always know which is which, but we do have the right to ask God to heal us and our loved ones. Sometimes God will perform miracles on your behalf simply because you asked. In the Bible, however, David's son was sick and dying. David prayed day in and day out, crying out to God to heal his son. He fasted and would not get up from the floor. His son died anyway. Once David learned of his son's death, he basically said "Oh, ok then." David hopped up, cleaned himself, anointed himself, changed clothes, went to go **worship**, fixed a plate, and slept with his wife. When asked why he responded this way, David said that he didn't know whether God was going to do it or not, but that He had to go **all in** just in case. Sometimes our prayers for the sick don't get answered in the way that we want. You should definitely pray and go all in while you have the chance, but no matter the outcome, pick yourself up and continue to walk this thing out with God as you hold on to your faith. Many have turned away from God in anger when the healing didn't come. That anger is a part of Satan's strategy to defeat us. Stay the course. We'll understand it better as we go.

READ TODAY: JEREMIAH 17:14

APRIL 2

"YOU BETTER LOSE YOURSELF IN THE MUSIC, THE MOMENT. YOU OWN IT."
-EMINEM

Have you ever been in a situation where you went to a church where they had "Praise & Worship"? Praise and worship is a time where "praise and worship leaders" stand before the people singing and encouraging them to begin to praising God too. P&W really gets mixed reviews. Some people love it, and others can't stand it. Some people will arrive to church late on purpose to miss it. It can be uncomfortable at times when the leader is telling you to lift your hands and praise God out loud. Some people view it as a performance, and all they can hear is that one note that's off or the person whose microphone is a bit too loud. If their favorite voice isn't leading the songs, they can't really get into it that day. Then there are those of us who prefer to bless the Lord at all times.

Praising and worshipping God in a group setting can be a very powerful thing. The key is that you must mentally drown out the distractions and focus on the **point.** The point is that God has been good to us, and He is worthy of our praise and adoration. The more you praise and worship God at home, the more comfortable you will become doing it publicly. Start off by thinking about a time that God came through for you. Focus on that, and forget about the distractions. Eventually, you will lose yourself in the music. It's your moment to shower praise, worship, and gratitude on to your Creator. Praise and worship time isn't just for the people on stage. It's **your** moment, and I want you to own it.

READ TODAY: PSALMS 147:1

APRIL 3

"TIME FOR NEW FLAVA IN YA EAR."
-CRAIG MAC

Have you ever been in a situation where you listened to somebody gossiping in your ear? Maybe it was some really good tea, and you couldn't resist taking a sip. Maybe somebody told you that your ex got his car repossessed and was living back at his mama's house. Oh, and that he had two girls pregnant at the same time, but that his first baby's mama was taking him to court for unpaid child support. Maybe the pastor of the church down the street was caught stealing from the collection plate and cheating on his wife, and when the sex tape came out online, you watched it.

I'm not going to lie to you…gossip can be quite tempting. It's like watching an exciting TV show when you're bored. Yeah, gossip is real fun until it gets turned around on you. If you've ever been the subject of gossip, you already know that a lot of it is fake news. As the stories spread, people will add and subtract theories that then become stated as facts. Gossip is basically a form of bullying and has caused so much detriment that people have taken their own lives because of it. When you look at it from that angle, you realize that it's not so harmless. When I am tempted to gossip, I think about the seed that I am sowing for myself later. How would I feel if it was me? The next time someone tries to come to you with gossip, you **can** decline to listen. Tell them that it's time for **new** flava in ya ear, the Word of God.

READ TODAY: PROVERBS 17:4

APRIL 4

"SO WHAT, SO WHAT, SO WHAT'S THE SCENARIO?" -A TRIBE CALLED QUEST

Have you ever been in a situation where you were going to a new place? Perhaps it was a new job, and it was your first day. Maybe you went off to college and had just arrived on campus. Maybe you just had a baby, and it was your first day as a parent. Maybe you were going on a date with somebody for the first time. Did these scenarios make you nervous?

Whenever you are entering a new place in life, it can be very intimidating. Everyone there is already oriented and acclimated to the environment, and you are simply hoping to blend in and not to mess up. You must remember that God has already gone before you and prepared the way. The Bible tells you that **every place** that the sole of your foot treads, He has **already** given you. This means that not only are you going to the new place, but the new place is **yours**. It may be your first day on the new job, but so what? Go in with confidence knowing that it's only a matter of time before you're running the place. God is with you. So what, so what, so what's the scenario that's got you nervous? Not today, Satan.

READ TODAY: JOSHUA 1:2-5

APRIL 5

"MY MIND IS PLAYING TRICKS ON ME."
-GETO BOYS

    Have you ever been in a situation where you thought something that wasn't true? Perhaps you were beautiful and thought that you were ugly. Maybe you are one of those skinny people who think that they're fat. Maybe you were dumb and thought that you were smart. Oh, my bad, I meant to say that maybe you were smart and thought you were dumb! Maybe you thought people were talking about you, but nobody was even thinking about you. Was your mind playing tricks on you?

    I am the captain of #TeamOverAnalyze, so I totally get it, but we must remember that our minds and our thoughts are extremely powerful. There is a condition in optometry called psychogenic amblyopia. The patient comes in with decreased vision and sometimes complete blindness. Upon examination, we find that there is nothing wrong with their actual eyes or their visual system. The problem is in their mind. They have some sort of psychological issue that is going unaddressed, and so the brain decides simply not to see anything else clearly until the person deals with what they've already seen. Glasses and contacts do nothing for psychogenic amblyopia. These people must seek therapy. Their vision returns as they **resolve** their issues. Crazy right? This just goes to show you how important it is to take on the mind and mentality of Christ instead of depending on your own. Study up on Jesus for yourself. He's not who a lot of people make Him out to be. Begin learning His mind so that you can adopt it as your own.

READ TODAY: PHILIPPIANS 2:5

APRIL 6

"BEAUTIFUL, I JUST WANT YOU TO KNOW."
-PHARRELL WILLIAMS

Have you ever been in a situation where you were ugly? Maybe you had big coke bottle glasses in grade school. Perhaps you were in need of orthodontic appliances for your teeth. Maybe you were overweight in middle school and were forced to shop in the plus sized section at JCPenney. Maybe you had a long neck. Maybe you had no neck at all. Was your head too big for your body? You were ugly, right? Wrong! I'm about ready to punch you for believing that mess. Who told you that you were ugly? Why did you believe it? I'm going to choke you! Don't you know that's a slap in the face to our Creator?

If you have ever believed that you were ugly, you believed a whole entire hot mess of a lie. Do you know how low-down the devil is? He will literally plant this evil seed in a little **child**. Now we have grown men and women still suffering with all kinds of false insecurities because the seed continued to grow inside of them. First off all, "beauty" as we know it in America is a man-made social construct created by people who want to use it as a means to oppress those who do not display the most coveted Eurocentric physical features. For generations, we as a people have bought into this lie and have turned around and used it to oppress each other. Wow, my lil' woke side came right on out didn't it? What I want you to know is that God says you're beautiful. I just want you to **know** that. I decided a couple years ago to "self-identify" as fine. Who is going to check me boo? If you look at TV, magazines, and even fashion shows now, you will see plenty of others who did not fit the traditional mold, but self-identified as beautiful, and so they were. Self-identify today, because what **they** think about you ain't none of your business! That's one less thing to worry about, huh?

READ TODAY: PSALMS 139:14

APRIL 7

"IT'S LIKE A JUNGLE SOMETIMES. IT MAKES ME WONDER HOW I KEEP FROM GOING UNDER." -GRAND MASTER FLASH & THE FURIOUS FIVE

Have you ever been in a situation where you were an adult? Whew chile, it's the ghetto! All you wanted to do was live, but apparently there are requirements. Apparently you have to pay bills to have things, and apparently you have to work to pay bills. We thought adulthood just meant that we'd have a car, our own place, and the freedom to do whatever we want with nobody telling us what to do. We were sadly mistaken! Between rent/mortgage, utility bills, car payments, car insurance, health insurance, license/tag renewals, and taxes, (I won't even get started on what happens when you become a parent), this world is like a jungle sometimes. It makes us wonder how we keep from going under.

How do we keep from going under? The world is like an ocean, and sometimes it feels like the weight of all these responsibilities will cause us to sink. Thankfully, Jesus told us that we can take the pressure and the weight off of ourselves and put it on Him. That is the only way we will stay afloat. The world will make you tired and weigh you down. Jesus promised that if we come to Him, He will give us rest and replace our burdens with something much lighter. Let Jesus keep you from going under today.

READ TODAY: MATTHEW 11:28-30

APRIL 8

"DON'T PUSH ME, 'CAUSE I'M CLOSE TO THE EDGE."
-GRAND MASTER FLASH & THE FURIOUS FIVE

Have you ever been in a situation where you felt on edge? Maybe you had had all that you could take that day, week, month, or year. Things at work were crazy, your kids were acting up, and your spouse or significant other wanted to be a jerk. Maybe your money was funny, and you were coming down with a cold too. You were so close to the edge that you could feel it. Perhaps some rude cashier (who had no idea how close you were to the edge), pushed you. Perhaps he or she had a bad attitude and didn't ring up your groceries correctly. Maybe you went slap off and cut the fool in those people's store. You went completely off the deep end, but once it was over and you calmed down, you realized that maybe you did a little too much. Perhaps you got a papercut and retaliated with an AK-47.

What do you do when you feel close to the edge? Do you lash out at people who don't deserve it? Are you an emotional wreck? Here's an idea. When you feel like you're close to the edge, find a secret place and go there instead. Moms and dads, I know you may be asking yourself how you will ever find a secret place when you can barely go to the bathroom without a young one banging at the door. I don't care if you have to wait until everybody goes to sleep or get up super early in the morning to lock yourself in the laundry room. I need you to find a secret place and go cry. When you cry, though, cry out to God. Tell him all about everything and ask for **help**. Having a moment to cry gives you a release valve for the pressure, and crying out to God puts you in contact with the One who can fix it all and back you away from that edge.

READ TODAY: PSALMS 34: 17-19

APRIL 9

"HOTEL, MOTEL, HOLIDAY INN..."
-THE SUGARHILL GANG

    Have you ever been in a situation where you spent the night at a hotel? Maybe it was a hotel. Maybe it was a motel. Maybe it was a Holiday Inn. All I know is that you probably shouldn't have been there. Of course hotels are not inherently evil, but throughout the history of our nation, some really terrible things have happened within the confines of a hotel room. For some of us it starts in high school when that one kid's parents let them have their birthday party unsupervised in a hotel room. Next comes prom night, and it's all downhill from there. Drugs, alcohol, sex, cheating, rape, prostitution, and even death can go down in a hotel room.

    I know you're expecting this to be some really deep message, but it's not. The thing about going to a hotel room is that you have to **go** there. This means that you have **time** and opportunity to change your mind about what you **know** you're getting ready to do. The next time you're on your way to a hotel room to do something that you know isn't right, I want you to think of this song and this message and then turn around. If it's your room, and somebody wrong is on the way over, I want you to think of this song and this message, and tell **them** to turn around. Don't play yourself. That's all I got.

READ TODAY: PROVERBS 4:14-18

APRIL 10

"YOU EVER WENT OVER A FRIEND'S HOUSE TO EAT, AND THE FOOD WAS JUST NO GOOD?" -SUGARHILL GANG

Have you ever been in a situation where you were hungry? Maybe when you're hungry, you really don't like to play around with it. You want to get something that you know is going to be good so that you can be satisfied. For many years, I found myself in a Cheesecake Factory rut. Their menu is huge, and although I like to try new things, I would always be starving by the time we finally got a table. To be on the safe side, I'd always order the same thing because I **knew** it would hit the spot for sure. Have you ever been hungry and went over a friend's house to eat only to discover that the food was just no good? What a bummer.

You should probably know by now that this is where we flip it. There is one particular friend, by the name of Jesus, whose food is always good. The food that He offers is so fulfilling that once you eat it, you will never even be hungry again. His food completely hits the spot every time. All you have to do is come to Him. Even more convenient is the fact that you don't have far to go. He literally stands right outside of your door (the door to your heart) and knocks until you let Him in. Once you allow Him in, not only does He bring the food, but He will also sit and eat it with you. That food is the Word of God. His bread is the Bread of Life. Who doesn't love a good friend who shows up with good food when you're hungry?

READ TODAY: JOHN 6:33-35

APRIL 11

"I AIN'T GOT NO TYPE."
-RAE SREMMURD

Have you ever been in a situation where you knew exactly what you wanted? Maybe you were dating and knew exactly what you wanted in a man. If you were like so many women, you had a whole list of qualifications. You wanted a man who was tall, dark, handsome, smart, funny, and educated. Said man also needed to have his own place, a nice car, make good money, and be well-dressed. You had a type.

Sometimes in life, knowing exactly what we want can be problematic. Sometimes we get so attached to our ideas of what would constitute the perfect life, that we don't leave any room for God to blow our minds. We are so focused on getting everything on our list, that sometimes we miss out on what could be better, simply because it does not **look** like our type. The amazing thing about God is that He knows us better than we even know ourselves. This is why He is able to give us something that is much better than anything we could ever think to put on our cute little list. I don't know about you, but I ain't got no type that will be worth going against His will. These days, I just want whatever God has for me. Don't you?

READ TODAY: EPHESIANS 3:20-21

APRIL 12

"I AIN'T CHECK THE PRICE."
-RAE SREMMURD

    Have you ever been in a situation where you weren't sure how much something would cost? Perhaps you were in a store and picked up some jeans in your size. You were in a hurry and forgot to check the price. Once you got up to the cash register, however, you quickly realized that you somehow picked up the most expensive jeans in the store. Maybe you were at a restaurant and ordered some seafood that was listed as "Market Price." You didn't want to sound like you were worried about money, so maybe you neglected to ask what that price actually was. When you got the check, however, you realized you were going to have to pay the bill with two different cards just to keep from getting declined.

    We do this in life. Sometimes we take an action without first considering what it may cost us. This is unwise because some things may cost more than we realized. For example, the Bible says that the wages of sin is death. *Insert that wide-eyed, lowkey freaking out emoji.* Ask the man who lost his wife, his house, custody of his kids, and half his paycheck for some one-time booty. He didn't check the price. A **wise** person takes time to consider what they buy before making the purchase. Stop trying to flex by acting as if the price is no big deal. Be wise and check the price, beloved.

READ TODAY: ROMANS 6:23

APRIL 13

"SHE SAID 'LOOK MA, NO HANDS,' AND NO DARLING, I DON'T DANCE."
-WALE

Have you ever been in a situation where you got into a fight? I'm not talking about an argument. I'm talking about an actual altercation where hands were thrown. Perhaps earrings had to be removed, hair had to be tied back, and Vaseline had to be applied. Perhaps you had to knock somebody out for running up to your sister Alicia and grabbing her booty at recess on a $1 bet. Either way, somebody crossed you in some kind of way, and so you put your dukes up, said "let's dance," and proceeded to throw hands.

Well praise God from whom all blessings flow! Just look at you now. You haven't fought in years! Look Ma! No hands! And darling, you no longer "dance." Well at least I hope not. One of the greatest signs of maturity is when you can walk away from a fight. When you're angry, do you know how to go "saddown" somewhere and chill out instead? Why would you let these mere mortals get under your skin to the point of violence? Why go down to that level when you have a God who is perfectly able to fight and win **every** one of your battles for you? Let God do it with no hands.

READ TODAY: EXODUS 14:14

APRIL 14

"WORKIN' ON THE WEEKEND, AS USUAL..."
-DRAKE

Have you ever been in a situation where it was the weekend? Soon as 5:00 hit on Friday afternoon, you felt like your shackles had been broken and you were free to live your best life for the next couple of days. Who am I kidding? You probably left work early at 3:00. By the time 5:00 hit, you had already gotten your hair cut or your nails done in preparation for the weekend's festivities. Weekends are the absolute best.

We work hard all week long, and so we feel that we deserve to let loose on the weekends. Work hard and then play hard, right? While it's great to rest, relax, and have a good time, just make sure that the Holy Spirit inside of you is still working on the weekend as usual. During the week, we are generally focused on work and school, but for some reason the weekend has been known to call forth the ratchet person who is apparently still living inside of us and ready to turn up. Don't act like you don't know what happens when you hear "Cash Money Records taking over for the '99 and the 2000." Again, there is nothing wrong with enjoying yourself on the weekend, but make sure that you are still listening to that small voice telling you how to live a life that is pleasing to God. Wherever we go, He goes with us, and He is **there.** We just have to stop pretending that He isn't. The Holy Spirit is still working on the weekend, as per usual.

READ TODAY: PSALMS 139:7-12

APRIL 15

"NOW, WHO'S HOT? WHO'S NOT?"
-MASE

      Have you ever been in a situation where you weren't hot, but you weren't cold either? Gather around children. I want to tell you a story. Once upon a time, we had four completely different seasons. They were called Winter, Spring, Summer, and Fall. Then the big bad polluting humans started doing too much and created some things called global warming and climate change. Now, where I live, we only have about two and a half seasons. It's usually either cold (Winter) or hot (Summer), sometimes all in the same day. We still have to endure the most extreme seasons, but the most comfortable ones (Spring and Fall) headed out with climate change. At the most, we might get a couple weeks of nice Spring weather before it gets hot. WE MIGHT. We might get a week or two of Fall weather before the temperatures drop down and get their eagle on. WE MIGHT.

      When it comes to extreme temperatures, we don't generally prefer them, but God does. He says that He would rather us to be hot or cold towards Him than to be "lukewarm." Lukewarm is what it's like when the hot water starts running out in your shower. It's not fun. If you're going to love God, you might as well **love Him** love Him. If you're going to believe God, you might as well **believe Him** believe Him. If you're going to obey Him, you might as well **obey Him** obey Him. If you're going to walk with Him, you might as well walk **with Him** with Him. If you're going to do it, do it for real for real. Now, who's hot? Who's not?

      READ TODAY: REVELATION 3:15-16

APRIL 16

"ME LOSE MY TOUCH? NEVER THAT."
-THE NOTORIOUS B.I.G.

Have you ever been in a situation where you got busy? Perhaps you thought you were busy before, but now you're actually busy, busy. Maybe you thought you were busy in high school until you got to college. You probably thought you were busy in college until you got to grad school. You probably thought work was really busy until you got promoted. You probably thought married life was busy until you had kids. We didn't appreciate the simple days when we had them.

In life, there will always be things that make you feel as if you are one of the busiest people you know. Something will then come along that makes you long for the days when you **thought** you were busy. It seems to be a part of our culture to fill up our lives to capacity with things that we think we **must** do. We get so busy that it is very easy to lose touch with some really good people in our lives and with God. It's not that we were meaning to lose touch, but over time, it just happened. I challenge you to put checks and balances in place in your life to be sure that all of your other "things to do" aren't becoming tyrannical and causing you to lose touch with God and with the people who matter most. What practical thing can you start doing to ensure that you never lose your touch with God?

READ TODAY: LUKE 10:38-42

APRIL 17

"IT'S LIKE THE MORE MONEY WE COME ACROSS, THE MORE PROBLEMS WE SEE."
-THE NOTORIOUS B.I.G.

      Have you ever been in a situation where you had money, but you still had problems? Perhaps in your head it seemed like if you could just get more money, everything would be straight. I know personally I could use an extra 50K in my bank account right now, but that's neither here nor there. Surely you have seen the stories of people who came into a lot of money, and all it did was lead them down a path of destruction, right? It was like the more money they came across, the more problems they saw. Why was that?

      The more money a person has, the more their true character can come out. When you feel as if you don't need others' help for anything, you start feeling like you can do whatever you feel and treat people however you want to treat them. This can be very problematic if you never did the work internally to establish good character. There is nothing wrong with having money. As a matter of fact, it is God who gives us the power to get wealth. Be intentional about working on your character now so that when you do come across more money, you won't come across more problems along with it. Make that money. Don't let it make you. Amen.

READ TODAY: 1 TIMOTHY 6:17

APRIL 18

"I THOUGHT I TOLD YOU THAT WE WON'T STOP."
-DIDDY

Have you ever been in a situation where God told you to do something, and you started doing it? Perhaps He told you to write a book. Maybe He told you to go back to school. Maybe He told you to find a church home. Maybe He told you to eat better, exercise, and take control of your health. Maybe He showed you the right person that He wanted you to marry, and you married them. If you **know** that the instructions were sent from God, why would you give up?

I'm not talking about something that you just got a bright idea about and did on your own. I'm talking about something the Lord put in your heart and even opened a door for you to do. Sometimes we get confused into thinking that because something came from God, it should be super easy, but this is not always the case. As a matter of fact, when Satan sees you trying to do something that is God-ordained, he gets scared and starts throwing darts at you in an attempt to make you stop. This isn't the time to give up. This is the time to double-down on your commitment. If it's ordained by God, don't give up on that assignment, that book, that health goal, or that marriage. Tell the devil to save those tricks for some kids. I thought I told you that we won't stop.

READ TODAY: PHILIPPIANS 1:6

APRIL 19

"GET IT RIGHT. TWO-STEP, AND LET YOUR SHOULDER LEAN."
-YOUNG DRO

Have you ever been in a situation where leaving was the best option? Perhaps you were living at your mama's house when she had just started menopause and was losing her mind. Maybe it was a dead-end job that was barely providing enough for you to live, stressing you out, and preventing you from doing anything better for yourself. Maybe it was a toxic relationship that was standing between you and your peace. Did you stay six months longer than you should have stayed? A year? More? What's up with that?

Sometimes we get comfortable in a situation, and even when it's dysfunctional, we stay longer than we should. Sometimes we **know** good and well that it's time for us to leave a bad situation, but it seems like we just can't get it right. It's like you heard it from the Holy Spirit, your friends, your mama, your doctor, your therapist, your pastor, and even your kids. It's like every time you go to read the Bible it says something about moving forward. What else do you need? I mean even if you've just been reading this book, this is like the 3rd message on leaving, and there will be more! That's because we tend to get so nervous and scared to make transitions in our lives even when we have all the confirmation in the world that it's time. Whenever you **turn** to face a new direction, your shoulder literally leads the way. Try it. Get it right. Two-step out of that old place, and let your shoulder lean you into a new season.

READ TODAY: ISAIAH 43:19

APRIL 20

"CAN'T YOU SEE WHAT YOU DO TO ME? OUR LOVE WAS MEANT TO BE."
-TOTAL

Have you ever been in a situation where things started to hit different? (Yes, I know this is grammatically incorrect, but go with me for a second since this has become a popular colloquial phrase.) Perhaps you used to enjoy some nice little gossip, but now it agitates you. Maybe you used to enjoy the club scene, but now it seems repetitive and boring. Maybe you used to enjoy heauxing around, but now you just want to be that freak for one person the rest of your life. Perhaps you used to be caught up in name brands and logos, but now you just enjoy quality things even if nobody knows the maker. Stuff started hitting different(ly).

Sometimes stuff starts hitting so different that you'll surprise your own self. Your friends and family may shake their heads at you and tell you that you're missing out. But what they don't see is that the things that you used to enjoy are replaced with better things that bring about joy, peace, and fulfillment instead of guilt, shame, regret, and drama. Have you ever been in prayer and asked the Lord, "Can't You see what You do to me?" It's so obvious that our love was meant to be. It's crazy the way that His presence in our lives takes us, grows us up, and is **always** seeking to take us higher. We must learn to be unapologetic about the changes that we experience. Things will never "hit" the same again, and for this we give God praise.

READ TODAY: 2 CORINTHIANS 5:17

APRIL 21

"DON'T BE TRIPPIN' WHEN YOU SEE US IN THE CLUB, JUST SHOW A LIL' LOVE."
-JAGGED EDGE

Have you ever been in a situation where you got saved and your friends didn't? Perhaps you finally decided to quit running, and you gave your life to the Lord. Maybe you even got fancy with it and went up to the altar to publicly confess that you had accepted Christ. Maybe you were extra fancy and got baptized too. Perhaps you started going to church on a regular basis, praying, and reading your Bible. Now if you wanted to really do it big, maybe you joined a Sunday School class or a small group. I see you boo. But as TLC might ask, what about your friends?

When you make major moves in your life like accepting Jesus, you are excited and want to share it with the people you love. Sometimes these people will be receptive, but many times they will not. Here's what I want you to understand: you are still no better than they are. You have simply chosen a better **way**. Do not get the big head. So many times, we see people get a little revelation and a little knowledge and as the Bible says, their knowledge "puffs them up." They go to treating people differently and turning their noses up at others. Don't be trippin' when you see those people whether it be at home, work, the grocery store, or in the club. Just show a lil' love. A lil' love goes a long way and helps them to see the Jesus in you.

READ TODAY: EPHESIANS 4:32

APRIL 22

"OH I NEED TO KNOW WHERE WE STAND."
-112

    Have you ever been in a situation where you were Black in America? Perhaps you have indeed been Black in America, so you're probably going to understand everything we're about to discuss. If you just so happen to be here from another culture, welcome! Listen, if you have never been Black in America, there are some things we need to talk about really quickly. Why is it that when innocent Black people, or Black people who have allegedly committed misdemeanors, are murdered by the police in cold blood, it seems as if men and women of God from other races have absolutely nothing to say? No, seriously, I'm asking for a friend.

    Your silence in matters like this is very disheartening. You explain them away as weekly isolated incidents and try to convince yourselves and others that systemic racism isn't a thing. You say that Black people are just blaming their problems on others and that everyone has equal opportunities now that slavery is over. Yet the systems we operate under were literally set up to benefit from racism. The education system, the justice system, and even the election systems, all have biases built into their infrastructure to ensure that black people as a whole are less educated and therefore more criminalized, and as a result, disenfranchised. If you really have Jesus in your heart, how do you sleep at night knowing this **evil** exists and is being perpetuated by you, your family, and your friends? I know you don't want to feel like you aren't a nice person, but hear me out. Stop being so silent. The Bible says that the Lord **requires** us to do **justly**. We need to know where you stand. We're supposed to share this special thing called love. Where is it?

READ TODAY: MICAH 6:8

"REAL GIRLS GET DOWN ON THE FLO'."
-DAVID BANNER

Have you ever been in a situation where things just weren't right? Ladies, perhaps you had the career you wanted and the man you wanted. Maybe all of your bills were paid, and you had some money left over to enjoy. Perhaps your natural curls were popping, and your edges were yet present and accounted for. Maybe you were drinking water and minding your own business. You were smashing all of your goals, so why was it that you still didn't feel right? Things were good, but for some reason you still felt like something was missing.

Have you considered that the missing piece is your prayer life? Having a prayer life is literally like having a whole different life. It keeps you connected to God and the spiritual realm in a way that is even more important than you realize. Without a solid prayer life, your spirit is suffering and starving. You can do everything else in life perfectly, but without prayer there will always be that void. Real girls get down on the flo' and pray. Real girls get down on the flo' and worship. Brothers, if you're single and looking for a good woman, make sure the girl knows how to get down on the flo'.

READ TODAY: 1 THESSALONIANS 5:17

APRIL 24

"I GO ON AND ON. CAN'T UNDERSTAND HOW I LAST SO LONG."
-TOO SHORT

Have you ever been in a situation where you loved someone unconditionally? Maybe it was your significant other. Perhaps it was your child or grandchild. Could it have been your mother or father? Whoever it was, it seemed that your love for them was not dependent on anything. You loved them. You kept on loving them, and you're going to keep on loving them as long as you are in this world. No matter what they did, no matter how they treated you, and no matter how many times you bumped heads, your love for them was unchanged.

You may ask yourself why your love goes on and on. You may not be able to understand how you last so long and why you continue to forgive. It would seem as if you truly love this person with the love of the Lord. Perhaps someone in your life has shown you this kind of love as well. God's love for us is like this, but even better. His love for us is known as "agape love." Agape love means that there's nothing **we** can do to get Him to change His mind about loving us. Even when we are wrong, the Bible says that He is faithful and just, forgives us of our sin, and cleanses us from our unrighteousness. Let's take a moment to be grateful for His love that goes on and on forever.

READ TODAY: ROMANS 8:38-39

APRIL 25

"BLOW THE WHISTLE."
-TOO SHORT

Have you ever been in a situation where you had to tell someone the truth? Maybe it was your own child asking you a difficult question about Santa Claus, where babies come from, or why mom and dad live in different houses. Perhaps it was a friend who needed to hear the truth about their toxic ways. Maybe it was your wife asking whether she was getting fat. Telling the truth to someone you love can be uncomfortable and downright painful at times.

Sometimes we do a great disservice to the people that we love by lying to them. We do it because we don't want to see them hurting, but we fail to consider that a lie may hurt them more in the long run than the truth. We also withhold truth because we're not sure how they will respond. The truth can be offensive, and if your loved one takes it personally, it can affect how they treat you in return. We will sometimes lie to keep from losing someone or making them angry, but if you truly love someone, there will come a time when you have to blow the whistle on the lie, and shine light on the truth. It's so much easier said than done, but pray and ask God for wisdom on **how** and **when** to blow your whistle. The truth must always be spoken in love.

READ TODAY: EPHESIANS 4:15

APRIL 26

"GIRL YOU LOOK GOOD, WON'T YOU BACK THAT THANG UP?"
-JUVENILE

Have you ever been in a situation where hindsight was 20/20? Perhaps you thought that guy looked like Prince Charming, but in hindsight he was clearly a court jester the whole time. Maybe you thought that girl looked like your Michelle Obama, but in hindsight she was clearly a chickenhead the whole time. Perhaps you thought your mama was just trippin' about everything, but in hindsight she was simply trying to love and protect you the whole time. Whatever the case may have been, you did not see the situation for what it was while you were still in it.

Why is it that we have problems seeing things clearly? Sometimes our proximity (how close we are) to the situation prevents us from seeing the whole picture. It's like standing with your nose against a 50-inch television. There's no way you will be able to see all that's playing on the screen until you back that thang up. If you want to see things more clearly, don't be afraid to put a little distance between yourself and the situation. Just as Jesus went up to a high mountain alone to pray at times, you will occasionally need to isolate yourself in a place of prayer. Go up to your "high mountain," and you will have a bird's-eye view. From there you can take a good look, and look at it real good as you back that thang up to the Lord.

READ TODAY: MATTHEW 14:23

APRIL 27

"GIRL YOU LOOK GOOD, WON'T YOU BACK THAT THANG UP?" (2) -JUVENILE

     Have you ever been in a situation where you were in a committed relationship or marriage? Perhaps you are a part of #TeamFaithful, and you are one of those amazing people who refuse to fall into the trap that is known as cheating. Maybe you fell in love early, have been with the same person since high school, and never really got any attention from other men or women. Perhaps you lost 50lbs and started to realize how fine you were, and so did they. Do y'all remember that episode of *Martin* where he took his ring off at the gym just to see if he still had it? What happened? The women were all up on him. Well brothers, nowadays it doesn't matter if you have a ring on or not, certain women will **still** be all up on you. Although you are indeed off-limits, some don't see it that way.

     Thanks to modern-day technology such as contouring makeup, Spanx®, lace-front wings, and photo filters, many of these girls look good, but you still need to tell them to back that thang up. Ladies, this goes for you too. Some men don't care about your lil' wedding ring or your lil' husband. Baby, Joe told us a long time ago that he wanted to do all of the things that your man won't do! You have to be very no-nonsense about telling these people to back up. If you entertain them even in the slightest, it will only be a matter of time before they find a way to slither into your space. Some people are slick and will **pretend** to be your friend, but they are really just waiting on that day when you are upset with your significant other so they can "comfort" you. I don't care how good they look. You know who they are, **tell them** to back that thang up.

READ TODAY: MATTHEW 5:27-28

APRIL 28

"NOW AFTER YOU BACK IT UP AND STOP, WHA...WHA...WHAT, DROP IT LIKE IT'S HOT."
-LIL WAYNE

Have you ever been in a situation where you finally stopped doing something? Perhaps you finally stopped ordering the 20-piece lemon pepper hot wings with the ranch cheese bacon fries and peach tea on the side. Maybe you stopped smoking cigarettes. Maybe you stopped snorting cocaine. Maybe you stopped taking tequila shots every morning before work. Whatever it was that you were doing, you finally backed it up and then stopped.

There's another step, however, that you still need to take. After you back it up and stop, you still need to drop it like it's hot. Drop it like it's hot, and then run in the opposite direction like you stole something. Backing it up a little bit is good, but it's simply not enough because it means that you continue to remain in the same vicinity of the thing that you are hoping to separate yourself from. If you continue to hang around the things that tempt you, when a weak moment comes, you are still within arm's reach of the thing that you are trying to drop. It's like being a recovering alcoholic and hanging out at the bar with your alcoholic friends. It's like trying to lose weight but hanging out at the buffet and convincing yourself that you're just going for the salad bar. Don't fool yourself. Don't continue to talk to, entertain, or hang around it or them. Don't just back it up, and stop. You've got to **completely** drop it like it's hot and **go**. #blocked

READ TODAY: EPHESIANS 5:11

APRIL 29

"GET IN THERE! YEAH, YEAH."
-V.I.C.

Have you ever been in a situation where you didn't know what to do? Perhaps you were having trouble on your job with your boss. Maybe you had a child who was completely out of control. Perhaps you had a problem in your marriage. Maybe you had money problems or trouble sleeping at night. Perhaps you struggled mentally with depression or anxiety. You had some problems, but you didn't know how to solve them.

Well you've got questions, and the Bible has answers, but you've got to get in there! Yeah, yeah! Get it there. God speaks to us in more than one way, but Bible-reading is critical in the life of the believer. It is truly an underrated tool in our daily lives. There are so many situations, circumstances, and problems that we come across on a daily basis that the Bible has already spoken on. You would be surprised how accurate the whole "nothing new under the sun" cliché really is (probably because it's actually a Bible verse). The point is, the Word of God **works**, but you've got to get in there!

READ TODAY: 2 TIMOTHY 3:16-17

APRIL 30

"NOW WALK IT BY YOURSELF, NOW WALK IT BY YOURSELF."
-CUPID

Have you ever been in a situation where you got left? Perhaps you got left at an early age by your mother or father who went out to check the mail and never came back. Maybe you got left by a boyfriend or girlfriend who found somebody that they liked better. Maybe you got left by your friends who all went away for school while you stayed in town. Perhaps you got left by your husband or wife who wanted a divorce. Maybe you felt like you were left by a loved one who unexpectedly or expectedly died. Having someone to leave you is one of the most painful things someone can experience. Abandonment issues are real.

So, what do you do when you are left to walk it by yourself? If you've ever experienced the death of a close loved one, it truly feels as though they have left you to navigate this cold, cruel world all on your own. I want you to understand that there will be some seasons where you do have to walk it by yourself. It seems like a scary thought at first, but God promised to always be with you. People will leave you, sometimes without warning. Do not allow feelings of abandonment to paralyze you. If you needed that person to make it, God wouldn't have allowed them to leave. So you must walk it by yourself **with God** until He decides to bring another person into the picture. Pray and ask God to first prepare you and then to send you the people that He wants to walk along with you. He will send them when the time is right.

READ TODAY: PSALMS 23:4

MAY 1

"BACK IT UP...AND JUMP."
-DJ TWILIGHT

    Have you ever been in a situation where you experienced a setback? Perhaps you were doing good with managing your money, but then a major bill popped up out of nowhere. Maybe you had been working out regularly, but then you injured your knee. Perhaps you had been eating right, but then Thanksgiving and Christmas hit real back-to-backish. Perhaps you had stopped smoking, but something stressed you out, and you lit up again. Perhaps you were doing a good job keeping it tight, but then you messed around and got yourself a lil' some on one lonely night.

    Setbacks can be very deflating, especially when you felt like you were on a roll or that you had overcome that particular struggle. A setback, however, can show you that your true dependence is on God. Sometimes when we start doing well, we feel like we are doing it in our own strength. A setback can humble you very quickly. If a setback does happen to occur, just take a moment, back it up, and jump. When you get set back, allow it to remind you of your dependence on God. Use it as the motivation to spring forward back into action. If you've ever had to jump over a hurdle, you know that it's a lot easier to make the jump if you back it up and get a running start. Allow your set back to give you a running start towards your victory.

READ TODAY: JAMES 1:2-4

MAY 2

"REVERSE! REVERSE!"
-MR. C THE SLIDE MAN

Have you ever been in a situation where one or both of your parents were triflin'? Let's start off with the most triflin' one possible. Perhaps they were never there. Maybe they were there physically, but completely absent mentally or emotionally. Perhaps they were addicted to drugs or alcohol, and you were left to fend for yourself most of the time. Maybe they were too busy worrying about a boyfriend or girlfriend to pay any attention to you. Maybe they still wanted to run the streets and had other people watching you all the time. Perhaps your dad was cheating on your mom and vice versa. Maybe you have several siblings that you have never even met. If you grew up in a wholesome environment, a lot of this may sound extreme to you, but it's not as uncommon as you may think.

Over the past couple of decades, the phrase "generational curse" has risen to popularity. This is usually referring to the problems in your family that tend to **repeat** themselves with every generation. For instance, if your mom was a single mom, your grandmother was a single mom, and your great-grandmother was a single mom, we might call that a generational curse. If your family has been operating with a "generational curse," you have the opportunity to **reverse** that curse. It **can** stop with you. Do not assume that just because it is normal in your family, that you must fall into the same pattern. Think about your children and grandchildren. Do your best not to sow bad seeds for which they will reap the harvest. Reverse!

READ TODAY: DEUTERONOMY 30:19

MAY 3

"DON'T BELIEVE ME? JUST WATCH."
-BRUNO MARS OR TRINIDAD JAMES

    Have you ever been in a situation where you were underestimated? Perhaps it was your middle school teacher who told you that you weren't going to amount to anything. Maybe it was your own mother or father who told you that you were just a screw-up. Maybe you experienced discrimination at school or at work, and you were expected to fail based on the color of your skin. Someone estimated your value to be low.

    When someone underestimates you, it is tempting to become discouraged. It's also tempting to believe what they say about you, especially when it is an adult or an authoritative figure in your life. They tell you that you are not good enough, and even when you try to tell them otherwise, they don't believe you. That's fine. It's okay if they don't believe you. All they need to do is watch. Sometimes you have to block out all of those negative words spoken over your future and focus on God and His ability to take you from point A to point B in life. They may not believe in you, but I do. You will exceed every expectation, maybe even your own. Just watch.

    READ TODAY: EXODUS 14:13

MAY 4

"U CAN'T TOUCH THIS."
-MC HAMMER

    Have you ever been in a situation where somebody tried to come in between you and someone you loved? Perhaps there was someone who was jealous of the close friendship you had with one of your co-workers. Maybe that same person began to talk badly about you behind your back in order to drive a wedge between you and that person. Perhaps you were married, and your in-laws weren't too fond of you. Maybe they started trying to get in your spouse's ear to talk down about you in hopes of causing some sort of discord between the two of you. Perhaps someone even tried coming on to your spouse romantically in hopes of drawing them away.

    According to the Bible, one of the things that God literally hates is someone who sows discord among the brethren. In other words, God ain't here for messy people. Never allow a messy person to gain access to your ear, because you never know what their true motives are. Furthermore, you must make sure that you're not one of the messy people yourself. Be sure to protect not only your relationships with your loved ones, but also your relationship with God. Let the messy people know that they **can't touch this**. Set boundaries, keep your head on a swivel, and never allow someone to mess up a good thing. Pray and ask God to reveal to you anybody who needs to be removed from arm's reach.

                                         READ TODAY: PROVERBS 6:16-19

MAY 5

"HOW YOU GONNA ACT LIKE THAT?"
-TYRESE

Have you ever been in a situation where you were worried? Perhaps you were worried about how you were going to pay a large and unexpected bill. Maybe you took a test at the doctor's office, and you're having to wait for the results. Maybe you're actually battling an illness or worried about a loved one who is sick. Maybe you are worried about your business staying open. Perhaps you are worried about your relationship and whether it will survive. Either way, your mind has been pre-occupied with worry and anxiety. You haven't been eating or sleeping like your normal self. You haven't been thinking clearly, and perhaps you've even been taking it out on others.

How you gonna act like that? I know that the problem is a real problem, but how you gonna act as if God has never made a way for you before? Do you not **remember** who God is in your life? Resolve within yourself that you will be fine no matter what, even if things get hard or if you lose something or someone. God has promised never to leave nor forsake us. Not knowing **how** God is going to work it out, is not a good enough reason to start acting like you don't remember who He is and what He has done for you over and over again. Please don't act like that.

READ TODAY: PHILIPPIANS 4:6-7

MAY 6

"I GOT MONEY IN THE BANK. SHAWTY, WHAT YA DRANK?"
-LIL SCRAPPY

Have you ever been in a situation where you were doing alright? Perhaps the money wasn't even funny. Maybe your bills were good and paid, and you and the kids had fresh new clothes and shoes. Maybe y'all had some king crab legs and jumbo shrimp for dinner. Maybe you even took the whole family on a nice vacation and bought the over-priced souvenirs. You had money in the bank.

snaps fingers Yasssss boo, I'm here for it! What a blessing it is to **not** be struggling for money. Am I right? You have actually accomplished something that eludes so many people around the world. You are able to provide for yourself and for your family. Looks like you have money in the bank and a cup that is full, but who else's drank have you checked on lately? If you're doing alright, do you find ways to give to somebody who may not be? If your cup is full and overflowing, you have the awesome opportunity to pour into someone else's empty one. To be honest, even if your cup is not full and overflowing, there are still ways that you can be a blessing to others. How can you be more intentional about checking on others who may need a little bit of help?

READ TODAY: ACTS 20:35

MAY 7

"...GOT ME IN MY FEELINGS."
-DRAKE

      Have you ever been in a situation where you got your feelings hurt? Maybe you went to see your grandmother and the first thing she said was, "Baby you done got so fat! I almost didn't recognize you!" Perhaps you were hoping you'd get a chance to spend Friday night with bae, but he decided to go out with his homeboys. Maybe she left your text message on "read" a little too long. Maybe you posted a picture that you thought was cute, but he put a "like" instead of a "love." Now you are "in your feelings."

      We are all humans here, and it's almost inevitable that at some point in time, you will have feelings that get hurt. The problem, however, comes when you get "in" your feelings. When you are in your feelings, it means that you are allowing hurt feelings to submerse and potentially drown you. Pay close attention to the times when you are in your feelings. You don't interact with people the same because you are often short, cold, attitudinal, dismissive, and sometimes irrational. How does that help? A bit of practical advice would be to recognize when you are in your feelings, and allow yourself a small window of time to get **out** of them. When the shock of the initial offense occurs and your emotions are driving the car, you are more likely to "react" irrationally than to "respond" calmly. Get out before you go in!

READ TODAY: JAMES 1:19

MAY 8

"KIKI, DO YOU LOVE ME?"
-DRAKE

Have you ever been in a situation where you just wanted to be loved? Maybe it started early with your own parents. Maybe you did things hoping to gain their love and attention. Maybe it was a sibling like in the movie *Frozen* when Anna wanted Elsa to help build the snowman. Maybe you had a crush on a person and could not stop thinking about them and wishing that they loved you back. It's a part of the human nature to want to feel loved.

The question you must ask yourself, however, is what are you willing to do to gain that love? Sometimes our desire to be loved can turn into desperation. That desperation can cause us to take actions that are honestly beneath us. It can also cause us to accept things that are beneath us to accept. If Kiki doesn't love you, and she's not riding, then why are you losing **yourself** to ride for her? People begin to change into something that they are not in an attempt to become "worthy" of someone's love. If you have to manipulate someone into loving you, is any of it really real? First and foremost, you must always remember that you are loved perfectly by God. Secondly, you must understand that if someone doesn't love you, it's not the end of the world. Pray and ask God to help you to move on and to send people into your life whose love you don't have to question.

READ TODAY: MATTHEW 10:14

MAY 9

"DESIGNATED DRIVER, TAKE THE KEYS TO MY TRUCK."
-MONTELL JORDAN

Have you ever been in a situation where you needed to take a backseat to someone else? Perhaps you were working on a group project at work, and you knew that your colleague was better qualified to lead this particular effort, so you let them lead while you became a team player. Maybe you were the lead singer in a group, but you knew that the lead part on this particular song was out of your range. You knew it would be best for the group if you sang backup on this number. Maybe you were leaving a party where you knew you had too much to drink. Even though it was your truck, you knew that the designated driver needed to take the keys.

As qualified as we think we are to steer the affairs of our own lives, the truth is that we're not. The problem is that we don't know how to hand over the keys to our Designated Driver. God is far more qualified to be in control of your life because He already knows what obstacles will be down the street and around the corner. He is well acquainted with the destination and knows the best route to get you there as efficiently as possible. On our own we are the staggering, drunken, incapacitated individuals with slurred words who don't even know the way home. We make wrong turns, we speed, and sometimes we even slide off the road into a ditch. In what ways can we take a backseat to our own understanding and allow God to take the lead in our lives?

READ TODAY: PSALM 23

MAY 10

"IT FEELS SO GOOD IN MY HOOD TONIGHT."
-MONTELL JORDAN

Have you ever been in a situation where you gave somebody some advice that you needed to take yourself? Perhaps you advised your homegirl to let that lying dog go, but you kept hanging on to yours. Maybe you told somebody they need to eat healthier foods but stopped at McDonald's on your way home. Maybe you told your homeboy not to cheat on his girl when you were actually cheating on *your* girl with *his* girl. Maybe you told somebody that honesty is the best policy, but you lie like a rug. There is a fancy word for this. You are being hypocritical.

The world is full of hypocrites, and to be honest, most of us have been hypocritical at some point or another in our lives. That's because there is a huge difference between **knowing** what's right and **doing** what's right. Sometimes we are so immersed in other people's business that we neglect to take care of our own. We are all up in other people's lives and homes and neighborhoods, when our own dwelling place is a mess. It feels so good in **my** own hood when I use that same energy to "sweep around my own front door" first. What good advice have you given to someone else that you should be taking yourself?

READ TODAY: MATTHEW 7:3-5

MAY 11

"IF YOU WERE FROM WHERE I'M FROM, THEN YOU WOULD KNOW."
-MONTELL JORDAN

Have you ever been in a situation where you prejudged somebody? Maybe you saw a homeless person on the street and assumed that they had been on drugs. You had no idea that they actually had a college degree and a good job, but an unexpected illness, an extended hospital stay, and a series of ridiculously high medical bills caused them to fall on hard times. Maybe you saw a young teenage mother and assumed she was out there being sexually irresponsible, not knowing that she had actually been a straight "A" student who endured a sexual assault. Perhaps you saw a kid who had behavior issues but had no idea the horrors that the child was witnessing at home every day.

Although these are some extreme examples, many of us are guilty of prejudging people and never attempting to get to know where they have actually come from. It's like seeing a person who is 350lbs and not knowing that they came from 600 and are still working to lose more. How do you feel when people who don't know you make assumptions about why you are the way you are? Let's do a better job of extending the same grace that we want extended to us. Our ultimate goal should be to help those who need it, right? How can you help someone when you haven't taken the time to understand who they are, where they come from, and where they wish to go? As the saying goes, "People don't care how much you know until they know how much you care." Never underestimate the importance of understanding.

READ TODAY: PROVERBS 4:7

MAY 12

"I PROMISE...I'M SO SELF CONSCIOUS."
-KANYE WEST

Have you ever been in a situation where you were worried about how you looked? Perhaps your boyfriend back in high school told you that your neck was long, and now you wear turtlenecks in summertime. Maybe a few of your teeth are crooked, so you always smile with your mouth closed. Maybe your skin is a bit bumpy with dark spots, so you don't leave the house without a face full of makeup. Perhaps your hairline is in a recession, and so you don't feel right without a hat or a little Bigen to make up the difference. Being so self-conscious means that there is something that you know about yourself that you don't want other people to know.

The amazing thing about God is that He already knows and cares about everything concerning you. He sees and knows the things that no one else does. When we are so self-conscious, it is because we are worried about whether people will accept or reject us. There is absolutely nothing about you that God does not already know, and yet you can't pay Him to stop loving you! Do not allow someone else's opinion of you to change how you see yourself. God's opinion of you is what truly matters.

READ TODAY: PSALMS 139:14

MAY 13

"I MAY BE YOUNG, BUT I'M READY."
-BEYONCÉ

Have you ever been in a situation where you were more mature than other people your age? Perhaps they were reading Dr. Suess and you were reading Black Enterprise Magazine. Maybe they were playing on the playground, and you were planning world domination. Perhaps they were giving each other wedgies, and you were writing out your ten-year plan. Maybe they were running the streets, and you were filling out scholarship applications. Everyone says that kids will be kids, but you didn't subscribe to that. You may have been young, but you were ready.

All throughout your life there will be people older than you trying to make you feel that your age somehow disqualifies you. In a nursing home somewhere, there is a 100-year-old person calling a 90-year-old person "young." You will always be a baby to somebody, but the truth of the matter is that God can do great things in your life no matter your age. We spend so much time thinking that we're not ready because we're young. Don't put off until tomorrow what you can accomplish today. I encourage you to pray and ask God to show you what purpose He has for your life and to help you to begin working towards it no matter your age.

READ TODAY: JEREMIAH 1:7

MAY 14

"BUT YOUR LIES AIN'T WORKIN' NOW. LOOK WHO'S HURTING NOW."
-SUNSHINE ANDERSON

Have you ever been in a situation where you believed a lie? Perhaps someone told you that you were ugly, and you believed it. Maybe somebody borrowed some money and told you that they'd pay you back, but that was 19 years ago. Perhaps somebody said they'd never cheat on you, yet you found yourself getting a "woman to woman" phone call from some lady named Shirley. Maybe somebody told you that they'd make child support payments, but to this day, you'd receive better support at a skinhead rally.

When we fall for someone's lie, it is very tempting to blame ourselves. Why were we so stupid to believe them? Why weren't we a better judge of character? Is my Holy Spirit not working properly? Don't feel bad, some lessons we simply needed to learn. The truth is that we sometimes ascribe our own good character to others, which is unwise. Just because **we** wouldn't do somebody like that, we **assume** that others are the same way, which is not always the case. Don't assume. Lean on the Holy Spirit for guidance in **all** things, even when they seem small. Don't ignore that recurring feeling that something isn't right. Reading God's Word helps you gain an understanding of Satan's tactics so that they won't continue to take you by surprise. The next time he tries it, you'll be able to say "Sorry, not sorry, devil. But your lies ain't working now. Look who's hurting now..." and you'll be able to shut him down.

READ TODAY: PSALMS 101:7

MAY 15

"I'M STARTING TO SEE SPACESHIPS ON BANKHEAD."
-D4L

Have you ever been in a situation where something seemed impossible? Perhaps no one in your family had ever finished high school, and you wanted to become a surgeon. Maybe every marriage in your family ended in divorce, but you wanted a healthy and happy marriage separated only by death. Maybe everyone around you was overweight and unhealthy, but you wanted to go vegan even though it was the week of Thanksgiving. Maybe you wanted to start your own business, but your credit was bad. All of these things can seem impossible to someone who has never witnessed them happening firsthand.

The funny thing about God is that sometimes He will give you a vision for something that clearly cannot be accomplished without His supernatural help. If you know anything about Bankhead Highway in Atlanta, you know that it has not traditionally been one of the wealthiest places to live. The Bankhead neighborhood itself has been known for some of the highest crime rates in Atlanta. A spaceship seems out of place. How is it possible that a spaceship, one of the most expensive items in the world, would find itself in such a neighborhood? That's none of your business. It's God's business. He knows just how to make things happen that we deem impossible. When God gives you a vision for something big and you start seeing spaceships on your Bankhead, stop worrying so much about **how**. Just do your part, and let God do His.

READ TODAY: LUKE 1:37

MAY 16

"DON'T WANNA BE A PLAYER NO MO'."
-JOE

    Have you ever been in a situation where you were a player? Perhaps you were Jeromie-romie-rome and you were in the ha-e-a-e-ouse. Maybe you were a player whose hometown was in the Himalayas. We always talk about getting played, but raise your hand if you've ever been the player. Perhaps you were on the phone with one guy, texting with another guy, and chatting with another guy in your DMs all at the same time. Perhaps you were the office player and had a different boo on every floor of the building. Maybe you had 7 different dates in 3 days with 8 different women. You had everybody thinking they were the one. Ahh, the glory days.

    There comes a time in life (hopefully) when you realize that you no longer want to play games. This means that you've reached a place of maturity in which you no longer desire to play with people's time and with people's hearts for your own selfish pleasures. You realize that lying to people is wrong, and you also realize that being a player forever is not the life you want to live. You begin to value true love, stability, and loyalty. If you've been a player for a long time, it may be challenging to change your ways, but do it anyway. You don't want to watch the one that you truly love walk down the aisle to someone else because you kept playing games. It happens every day, so tighten up. Talk to God and ask for help. Ask Him to cleanse your heart and tell Him that you don't wanna be a player no more.

READ TODAY: PSALMS 51:10

MAY 17

"ELEVATOR TO THE TOP, HA! SEE YOU LATER! I'M GONE."
-BIG PUN

Have you ever been in a situation where you wanted to take things to another level? Perhaps you looked good but wanted to look amazing, so you turned it up a notch at the gym. Maybe you were making good grades, but you wanted to make all A's, so you turned up the intensity of your studying. Maybe you had a bachelor's degree and a decent job, but you decided to go back to earn your master's degree or your PhD. Maybe you were already in decent health, but decided you wanted amazing health, so you became a vegetarian or a vegan. You simply wanted to go higher.

Some people are content just to ride the elevator up a couple of floors and get off, but not you. You want to take the elevator **all the way** to the top. I am the same way, so I'm with you. It goes without saying that when you decide to make your way to the top, there will be people who are unhappy about your efforts. They enjoy you on the level that you are on and want to remain in your company, but they are not willing to do what it takes to rise along with you. Be very careful with these people. If you sense that they are trying to hate on your elevation or even sabotage it, you will need to tell them "see you later," and get gone.

READ TODAY: PHILIPPIANS 3:13-14

MAY 18

"YOU DON'T WANT NO PROBLEM, WANT NO PROBLEM WITH ME."
-CHANCE THE RAPPER

Have you ever been in a situation where somebody was messing with you? Perhaps it was a supervisor who took their personal problems out on subordinates. Maybe it was a co-worker who was spreading lies or gossip about you around the office. Maybe it was an ex of yours who was salty about the breakup and went around trying to turn your own friends against you. Perhaps it was the lady at the DMV who was rude and attitudinal for no apparent reason. It may seem like they got away with it, but I've got news for you. They didn't get away with it.

What people fail to realize is that you are a child of God, which means they don't want no problems with you. When somebody is evil towards you, they have no idea that they now have a problem with God. We are not orphans in this world. We have a **Father** who is looking out for us at all times. We don't have to seek out revenge when we are wronged because God promised that He would handle all of that for us. This is why it's so important to pray for your enemies. I know it sounds backwards, but God really doesn't like it when somebody messes with one of His. The problem that they had with you has now become a problem that they will have with God. Needless to say, they really need your prayers. When somebody is evil towards me, I don't trip out. I just shake my head and say this simple prayer. "Lord, go easy on em. They didn't know I was Yours."

READ TODAY: ROMANS 12:17-19

MAY 19

"ONE MORE CHANCE…
BIGGIE, GIVE ME ONE MORE CHANCE."
-FAITH EVANS

Have you ever been in a situation where God woke you up this morning and started you on your way? Perhaps He put food on your table and brought joy to your day. Last night was not your last night on this earth, and for this we give God praise. Tomorrows are never promised to us, and far too often we take this fact for granted. No one really knows how many days they have left on this earth, but you do have today.

If our big God woke you up this morning, then Biggie gave you one more chance. Every morning that we wake up, we receive new mercies from God. This is another opportunity to walk in your purpose and fulfill your destiny. We should wake up not only grateful for another chance, but also prayerful. Pray and ask God to help you get the most out of your day and for a day that is filled with purpose. Pray that temptation will not get the best of you today. Pray that sin will not triumph over you today. Try not to waste your day by idly scrolling through social media or engaging in empty conversations that produce nothing. Ask God to give you a strategy for each day of your life, and then walk it out by faith. In case no one else tells you today, I love you.

READ TODAY: LAMENTATIONS 3:22-23

MAY 20

"SO WHAT'S IT GONNA BE? HIM OR ME?"
-THE NOTORIOUS B.I.G.

    Have you ever had to choose between two options? Perhaps you had a very simple choice such as chicken vs steak for dinner. Maybe the choice was a little more complicated such as whether to attend Hampton University or Howard University. Perhaps the choice was a lot more complex like whether you should marry a particular person. You had some time to weigh your options, but at some point you had to decide what it was going to be.

    For many followers of Christ, especially those of us raised in church, there comes a time when we have to decide what it's going to be. Are we going to continue toggling back and forth between our love for God and our enjoyment of sin and the things that Satan uses to distract us? God is asking us what it's going to be…him or Me? At what point are you going to choose to accept the calling that's on your life in **full**? What are you supposed to be doing (pertaining to your purpose) that you have delayed in doing? How many people are not getting the help that they need because you refuse to decide which master to serve? What's it going to be? Don't shoot the messenger. Whew! This message was pretty loud huh? Time for me to Bankhead Bounce my way out of your business and let you handle this one my G.

READ TODAY: MATTHEW 6:24

MAY 21

"I'M CLOCKIN' YA', VERSACE SHADE WATCHIN' YA."
-THE NOTORIOUS B.I.G.

Have you ever been in a situation where you didn't trust somebody? Perhaps it was one of your gossiping co-workers. They were always telling everybody else's business, so you were careful not to share any of yours with them. Maybe somebody was working overtime trying to holler at you. They looked good and said all the right things, but for some reason you just didn't trust him or her. Maybe it was someone offering you a business deal or selling you something. All the numbers seemed to make sense, but something just didn't settle right in your spirit.

Sometimes people like to take followers of Christ for fools. Some will try to take advantage of the fact that we're all about things like love, kindness, peace, and forgiveness. But the Bible instructs us to keep our heads on a swivel. We are supposed to **watch** as well as pray. Don't get caught off guard. When you aren't sure about something or someone, don't make any rushed decisions. There is nothing wrong with pulling off to the side of the road with your Versace shades and your radar gun to silently clock and watch the situation first. We are to be as wise as serpents, and at the same time, we are to be as harmless as doves.

READ TODAY: MATTHEW 26:41

MAY 22

"A T-BONE STEAK, CHEESE EGGS, AND WELCH'S GRAPE..."
-THE NOTORIOUS B.I.G.

Have you ever been in a situation where you used food to comfort your feelings? Perhaps you had a tough day at work, so on your way home you stopped for a double bacon cheeseburger with a strawberry milkshake to wash it down. Maybe you were dealing with the loss of a loved one, so you ordered a pizza and ate it all by yourself before moving on to the donuts. Perhaps you had just gone through a breakup, so you ordered a T-Bone steak, cheese eggs, and Welch's grape juice to-go and demolished it all alone in your car while you cried.

If everything else in life is trash, at least you can have some good food and be happy while you're eating it, right? That's how I used to think. "I don't know what to do about my problems, but I bet these chili-cheese fries finna hit the spot tho'." Did the chili-cheese fries hit the spot? Absolutely. But after the chili-cheese fries were gone, the problems were still there, and I was one step closer to being featured on *My 600lb Life*. Turning to food as a means of comfort is lowkey one of the slickest little tricks of the enemy. It seems harmless, but it actually just serves as a distraction from the truth. Everything Satan tries to do in your life is nothing but a perversion and a cheap knockoff of what God can **actually** do. God sent us a **true comforter** in the form of the Holy Spirit. The Holy Spirit comforts you not with a distraction, but with the truth. He brings the truth of God's Word to your remembrance and uses it to remind you exactly who you are and how you can have peace in the middle of every storm.

READ TODAY: JOHN 14:26

MAY 23

"CONVERSATE FOR A FEW, CUZ IN A FEW, WE GONE DO WHAT WE CAME TO DO."
-THE NOTORIOUS B.I.G.

Have you ever been in a situation where you were tired of talking about what you wanted to do? Perhaps you had been saying for years that you were going to start your business, yet you were still going to work for "the man" every day. Maybe you had been talking about going back to school for over a decade, but by now the few credits that you did earn have expired. Perhaps every time you went to the all-you-can-eat buffet, you would tell your friends how you were getting ready to go on a diet soon…as you went back for thirds.

There comes a time in life, however, when our conversations must come to an end. Our conversations have been lasting for way too long when they should only be lasting for a few. At some point, we've got to do what we came to do. We've got to do whatever it is that God purposely designed us to do. What's the one thing that you've talked about so long that your own folks are tired of hearing about it? Let's not be lazy or slow when it comes to the vision that God has given us. Write the vision down and ask God to show you what your strategy should be. Anyone can talk about it, but let's make up in our minds right now to **be** about it. What is there in your life that needs to be done not only in word, but also in deed?

READ TODAY: 1 JOHN 3:18

MAY 24

"IN A FEW, WE GONE DO WHAT WE CAME TO DO. AIN'T THAT RIGHT BOO? TRUE."
-THE NOTORIOUS B.I.G.

Have you ever been in a situation where you knew you had an assignment to complete? Perhaps you went off to college and got distracted for a couple of semesters before you realized what you actually came to college to do. Maybe you joined a seemingly great church, but somehow got sucked into the church drama and forgot what it was you came there to do. Maybe you joined a sorority or fraternity fully intending to serve your community and focus on sisterhood or brotherhood but soon realized all the popularity it afforded you. You dropped the ball on what it was you came there to do. We are all guilty of sometimes losing focus. Ain't that right boo? True.

Not only do we sometimes lose focus on our earthly assignments, but many of us lose focus on our heavenly assignments. Jesus, our example, had a specific mission when He came to earth. He came to seek and save those who were lost. Do you know what your assignment is? What are some of the things that God has shown you that you do not want to leave this earth not having done? Are you supposed to start a school? Are you supposed to be a wealthy philanthropist? Are you supposed to adopt a child? Are you called to the preaching ministry? Should you be writing a book? If you are unsure, spend some time asking God for **clarity** about your assignment and for the grace to complete it. Yes, I am trying desperately to hammer this point home, because we must be done with simply talking about it. In a few we're going to actually **do** what we came to do.

READ TODAY: JOHN 9:4

MAY 25

"I SEE SOME LADIES TONIGHT THAT SHOULD BE HAVING MY BABY, BABY." -THE NOTORIOUS B.I.G.

Have you ever been in a situation where you had a baby with someone? Perhaps you have and perhaps you haven't. If you have already had a baby with someone, I pray for your sake it was someone decent. For those of you who hope to have a baby someday, perhaps you have identified a person with whom you would like to have said baby. Hopefully, you want to also marry that person, but let's talk about how important it is to identify the right person for all of these jobs. Having a baby with the wrong person can bring entirely too much drama and stress into your life. You don't want to become inextricably tied to a toxic person for 18 years. Let's be honest, it's more than 18 years. You are tied to that person for life through your child, and that's **if** they are decent enough to even stick around. Some do not.

The first thing you want to understand is that you must use more than your physical eyes. Do not assume that just because you see a pretty lady tonight that she should be having your baby. Looks can be deceptive, and they also fade. Do not let someone's nice outer appearance distract you from the character that they are showing you otherwise. How does this person treat you? What kind of friends do they keep around? Do they love the Lord? How do they treat their mama? What kind of childhood traumas have they not dealt with? Before marrying someone and before having a baby with them, please **be sure** that God sent them. This is one of those things worth fasting and praying about...hard.

READ TODAY: PROVERBS 31:30

MAY 26

"...GIVING ENDS TO MY FRIENDS, AND IT FEELS STUPENDOUS."
-THE NOTORIOUS B.I.G.

Have you ever been in a situation where you were able to bless someone else financially? Perhaps it was someone less fortunate than you. Maybe it was family member, and the Lord placed it upon your heart to pay one of their bills. Perhaps it was a friend who you saw just grinding, working, and always giving to others. You took it upon yourself to be the one person who gives back to them. Maybe it was that broke college student, and when you dapped them up you passed them a $50 bill with the handshake.

If you've ever been in a position to give ends to your friends, I'm sure you know that it feels stupendous. The Bible says that it is more blessed to give than to receive, and I have to co-sign on that fact. Being a giver is rewarding on so many levels. And even though it's not something to be done for selfish reasons, one can't help but notice how good it feels to sow good seeds into the lives of others. It's also humbling to know that the Lord has blessed you to be in a position where you can be a blessing to those around you. Are you a giver? You may think that you have nothing to give, but start small and it will grow.

READ TODAY: ACTS 20:35

MAY 27

"BELIEVE ME SWEETIE, I GOT ENOUGH TO FEED THE NEEDY." -THE NOTORIOUS B.I.G.

Have you ever been in a situation where you had more than you really needed? Perhaps you paid off your student loan or car note, and now you have a surplus in your check. Perhaps you live below your means, put a reasonable amount away for savings, and still have some left. Maybe you recently got a raise and are currently making more than you've ever made in your life. You have something that church people like to call "overflow."

Overflow is a blessing, but so many people who have overflow do not realize it. In the society we live in, unfortunately, we always find ways for our bills and our spending to equal up to our money. Perhaps you made it 10 years just fine without cable TV, but as soon as you got a little raise, you got all the channels known to man and yet you still only watch Netflix. Perhaps you had a nice car that ran well and was almost paid off, but as soon as you realized you could afford it, you ran out and got a newer model with a higher car note. Believe me sweetie, many of us **already** have enough to feed the needy. Unfortunately, we are too busy making our personal expenses rise to the level of our income, that we never experience true overflow. This applies to our money as well as to our time. Every moment is already spent before it even comes. How can you be more intentional about freeing up time and resources to help those in need?

READ TODAY: ROMANS 15:1

MAY 28

"WHEN I WAS YOUNG, ME AND MY MAMA HAD BEEF."
-2PAC

    Have you ever been in a situation where you didn't get along with your mama? Perhaps when you were young, your mama didn't let you do some of the things your friends were doing. Maybe she didn't let you go to sleepovers at houses where she wasn't familiar with the parents. Perhaps she wouldn't let you run the streets and do hoodrat things with your friends. Maybe she wouldn't let you watch certain shows or movies that other kids were allowed to watch. When you are young, it is very easy to have beef with your mama.

    I won't neglect to mention that some mamas really are toxic, but so many mamas are simply doing the best that they know how to do. If there are any young people reading this book (God bless you, because I know you don't really get the references) just know that when you move out of the house for the first time, you will begin to realize that your mama was right about a lot of things that you just didn't understand. If you go away to college, the first thing you will notice is that half the kids there have no home training whatsoever, and you will be grateful that you do. I encourage everyone reading this book, no matter your age, to do your best to squash whatever beef you have with your mama. They are not perfect individuals, and for some of them, if they knew how to be better, they would. Don't carry around all of those old offenses in your heart. Grow up and forgive your mama before it's too late.

READ TODAY: PROVERBS 29:15

MAY 29

"YOU ARE APPRECIATED. DON'T YOU KNOW WE LOVE YA?"
-2PAC

Have you ever been in a situation where somebody did something for you? Perhaps there was a friend who helped you get a job when you were unemployed. Maybe there was a church that paid your light bill when your lights got cut off. Perhaps it is your next-door neighbor who watches your house when you are away. Maybe it was your parents who worked overtime to get enough money to pay for your extracurricular activities. Maybe you had a Sunday School teacher who selflessly volunteered time to help teach you as a kid.

So many times, especially when we are younger, we take it for granted when people do things to bless us. Everyone is so busy claiming to be "self-made," and sometimes we forget to acknowledge the little or big things that people have done for us. We do this not only with people, but also with God. We have had all kinds of supernatural help along the way, and it's only right that we let God and others know that they are appreciated and loved. Start by thanking God, and then think of someone who did something for you (big or small, old or new) and let them know how much you appreciate and love them.

READ TODAY 1 THESSALONIANS 5:18

MAY 30

"AIN'T NOTHING BUT A GANGSTER PARTY."
-2PAC

Have you ever been in a situation that required a quick exit? Perhaps you were invited to a place that you were not very familiar with. When you got there, something seemed off in the atmosphere. Maybe you looked around and realized that this party was nothing but a gangster party. Gangster parties have been known to get out of hand. There are copious amounts of drugs and alcohol, and unfortunately some of these events can end in death. Alcohol causes some people to become violent and to start fighting. Perhaps you peeped the scene and knew you didn't need to be there.

That voice telling you to leave was the Holy Spirit. Too often, people will have the desire to leave a place but will stay anyway not to ruffle feathers with their friends who aren't ready to go. If the Holy Spirit is telling you that this ain't nothing but a gangster party, you need to get your stuff and get out of there fast, even if you have to call an Uber to pick you up. There are so many testimonies of people getting that urge to leave a party only to find out that moments after they left someone was shot and killed or that the cops came and arrested people. Y'all be safe out there and listen to that voice.

READ TODAY: JOHN 10:27

MAY 31

"I AIN'T MAD AT CHA."
-2PAC

Have you ever been in a situation where you held a grudge against someone? Perhaps they borrowed some money from you and never paid you back. Maybe they made a derogatory statement about your mother's weight. Perhaps they stole your woman. Maybe they pretended to be your friend but talked about you behind your back. Maybe somebody bailed out on your travel plans at the last minute or didn't show up for you as promised. Maybe you tried to move in with a friend and ended up getting into a dispute about the rent payments. Were you mad?

Here's a better question. Are you **still** mad? No one can deny the realness of human emotions. Certain situations evoke certain emotions for which no one would fault you for having. In a perfect world, we wouldn't even let such things get under our skin and make us mad, but how long did you stay mad? Hours? Days? Weeks? Months? Years? Did you stay mad until you died? Sure, somebody did something foul to you, but what about all the times that we have done things that were foul towards God, and He forgave us? Forgiveness is important because it allows you to clear things out of your heart that will prevent you from moving forward in your own life. Let's stop wasting energy on being mad at people who probably don't even remember what they did. If you think about it or them and still get tight up in your chest area, you're still mad. Ask God to help you to release it and to move on from the anger.

READ TODAY: ECCLESIASTES 7:9

JUNE 1

"HOW DO YOU WANT IT? HOW DO YOU FEEL?"
-2PAC FT. K-CI & JOJO

Have you ever been in a situation where you wanted your life to go a certain way? Perhaps you played football in high school and wanted to one day play for the NFL. Maybe you wanted to be like Claire Huxtable. Claire was practicing law, married to a doctor who would rub her feet, a mother of five, had a snatched waist, and was only in her 40s. Claire was hashtag goals. Did you just get in your feelings reading that? I certainly got in mine writing it. Lord my life is nothing like that, but I digress!

How did you want your life to go? How do you feel knowing that things may be different from what you originally hoped for? Do you live your life regretting the decisions that you have made that got you to where you are? First of all, there's no point in looking backwards. Sure, things may not have turned out how you wanted, but don't let that affect how you feel about yourself and how you feel about what's possible in the future. Put your future in God's hands and take comfort in the fact that some of the things you wanted may have actually made your life miserable. God knows what to give you and when. Instead of feeling bad, spend that energy preparing yourself and becoming a good steward over your current blessings so that God may trust you with more.

READ TODAY: PROVERBS 13:12-14

JUNE 2

"CHECK BABY, CHECK BABY ONE, TWO. CHECK BABY, CHECK BABY, ONE."
-WRECKX-N-EFFECT

Have you ever been in a situation where you acted on an impulse? Perhaps you woke up one morning and decided to go buy a new car. Maybe you're super adventurous and ran off and eloped with someone you had only known for a week. Maybe you quit your job because your boss tried it with you that day. Maybe you went back to the hotel with that random guy or random girl you met at the homecoming tailgate. Maybe you really threw caution to the wind and allowed your sexual impulses to get you pregnant one night.

Acting on an impulse can be reckless. Sometimes it works out alright, and sometimes it doesn't. Let's not beat around the bush here. You need to check with God baby! If you're not sure after one check, heck, do two checks or however many it takes. God does not mind you continually seeking wisdom and guidance from Him. If all of us would slow down and check with God **before** acting on our impulses, the world would be a much better place. It doesn't matter if it's a big step or a little step. God has promised that if we would simply check with Him, He would direct us on which way to go. Next time you feel an impulse, check baby check baby with God to see if that's the Holy Spirit leading you or just another distraction.

READ TODAY: PROVERBS 3:6

JUNE 3

"ALL I WANNA DO IS ZOOM A ZOOM ZOOM ZOOM AND A BOOM BOOM."
-WRECKX-N-EFFECT

Have you ever been in a situation where you didn't see something that everyone else saw? Perhaps you were in a bad relationship with a narcissist. Maybe that person was deceitful, controlling, and manipulative. Perhaps you began to change in negative ways as a result of being with them. Maybe your relationship with them caused you to be insecure, to be distant towards your family and friends, and to neglect your own personal ambitions for theirs. Maybe it was a friend who was simply using you. Perhaps you were there whenever they needed you, but when you found yourself in need, you had no one. The crazy thing is that everyone could see what was going on in your situation except you.

How does this happen? Sometimes we are simply too close to a situation to judge it properly. We are so zoomed in to the picture that we can't even tell what it is. Our friends and family are standing across the street hollering, "It's a duck! It's a duck!" but our focus is so zoomed in that we don't believe them and claim that it's just a few pretty yellow feathers. We even take it as far as cutting off the people who attempt to tell us differently. Dearly beloved, we are gathered here today to tell you that **everybody** ain't wrong. **Everybody** ain't hating on you. If you want your life to begin to boom boom (grow and expand), then you need to zoom a zoom zoom zoom **out** and take a good **look** before you **leap**.

READ TODAY: PROVERBS 12:15

JUNE 4

"JUST SHAKE YOUR RUMP."
-WRECKX-N-EFFECT

      Have you ever been in a situation where you were just too fat? Perhaps you went off to college and gained that "Freshman Fifteen" and just kept on going and going like I did. Fried Chicken Wednesdays and Fried Fish Fridays in the cafeteria of an HBCU eventually begin to catch up with you. At first you get a little thick. Thick isn't so bad, but then it goes from thick to swollen. Perhaps you had some traumatic event to happen in your life that caused you to take comfort in food. Sometimes you feel that if nothing else in your life seems to be good, you can go and eat some good food and feel happy for those few moments. Well now you're overweight, obese, or morbidly obese, and your health is starting to be affected by the extra weight.

      Some things are super deep and spiritual, but some things are **not**. Eating right and exercising is something that we all know is right, but many never accomplish. Maintaining a healthy diet as well as a good workout regimen requires discipline and a changed mind. We have a responsibility to take good care of our bodies which are the temples of God. It is God's will for us to prosper and be in health even as our souls prosper. This includes eating right and yes, shaking our rumps. Get up, get out, and get moving. Oops, I was preaching to myself again and forgot y'all were here. Have a blessed day!

READ TODAY: 3 JOHN 2

JUNE 5

"CHOPPA STYLE...CHOP, CHOP, CHOPPA STYLE."
-CHOPPA

Have you ever been in a situation where you had to cut somebody off? Perhaps it was a friend who you found out was not a true friend. Maybe it was one of your social media acquaintances from high school who wanted to get on your posts talking crazy, and you had to block them. Maybe it was your favorite fast food restaurant that you cut off once you realized they were contributing financially to some very questionable organizations or political campaigns. Maybe it was someone you were dating, and you determined them to be a lying, cheating, selfish, narcissistic, manipulative, and toxic individual.

"Cancel" culture and "Cut You Off" culture have made huge surges in the past decade or so. Everyone encourages you to simply cut off and cancel anything and everything that is problematic in your life. Let's be clear, some cut offs are **more than** necessary and need to be enacted like yesterday! However, be careful about cutting off things or people if God didn't say so. There are people cutting off lifelong friends and family members just for telling the uncomfortable truth. Sometimes forgiveness and mature communication need to take place and things can be salvaged. Cutting off all who disagree with you allows you to create an echo chamber full of fake people who agree with whatever you say just to keep from being let go. We had a President like that once. Ask God for **wisdom** on how and when to chop.

READ TODAY: JAMES 1:5

JUNE 6

"THESE ARE MY CONFESSIONS."
-USHER

 Have you ever been in a situation where you said something, and it came true? Perhaps you always said that you were going to marry a woman with a big booty and y'all were going to have a couple of kids. Look at you know! Your wife has a big booty, and y'all have two beautiful kids! Maybe you always said your boss makes you sick, and now you have high blood pressure to deal with. By 15 years old, I had started telling people that I was going to be an optometrist and that I was going to have my own eye clinic. I'm now an optometrist, and I have my own eye clinic. Shout out to my friend Laura Watkins who would always **say** she would live to be 100. She lived to be 100.

 I believe that if Laura Watkins had been saying that she'd live to be 105, she would have lived to be 105. That's because the words that we speak with our tongues are very powerful. Whether you realize it or not, these are your confessions. We must be very careful about the things that we claim or confess over our lives. If you claim negative things about your life and your day, don't be surprised if that's what you get. It costs nothing to **speak well** of your life. I recently (recently as in since I've been writing this paragraph) realized that for decades I've been saying that nobody really understands me and that nobody truly gets me. To this day, that claim has not proven to be false. Coincidence? I think not. Let me stop claiming that. What inadvertently negative things do you say that need to be stopped?

READ TODAY: PROVERBS 18:21

JUNE 7

"MY GIRLS CAN'T TELL ME NOTHING. I'M GONE IN THE BRAIN."
-BEYONCÉ

Have you ever been in a situation where you didn't listen to anybody? Perhaps you were a high school student, and everyone told you to quit playing and take school seriously. You didn't take it seriously, so once you graduated, all of your friends moved on to bigger and better things while you were stuck at your mama's house. Maybe it was the classic example of a man or woman in your life who meant you no good. All your friends tried to tell you that he or she was only using you, but you called them haters. So now that he or she has lived at your place rent free for six months, torn up the transmission in your car, got put onto your phone plan, and lays up in **your** bed while you are at work, you are beginning to wonder where you went wrong.

Sometimes we get so caught up in our current situations that we fail to see the bigger picture. Not only do we fail to see the big picture, but we reject wisdom from those around us who **can** see it. It's good to be an independent thinker, but it's also good to have wise counsel in your life. Who are the people who can't tell you anything? Are they your girls? Are they your friends and family? If these are people who care about you, then maybe their words are worth earnest consideration. Don't let anything or anybody cause you to be gone in your brain.

READ TODAY: PROVERBS 11:14

JUNE 8

"GIVE IT ALL TO HIM, AND MEET HIM AT THE FINISH LINE."
-BEYONCÉ

Have you ever been in a situation where you weren't fully convinced about something? Perhaps someone was attempting to sell you a used car, and you weren't fully convinced that the car wasn't a lemon. Maybe your son tried to tell you his teacher was unfairly singling him out. Perhaps you were on your way up to the school to cuss out the teacher, but something in your spirit wasn't fully convinced that little Ray-Ray was giving you the full story. Maybe you went to the doctor to inquire about your symptoms, and you were told that everything was normal. Perhaps they rushed you in and out of the office and spent less than 5 minutes in the exam room with you. You weren't convinced of the doctor's opinion.

There are a lot of people in this world who don't mind trying to get over on others. There's nothing wrong with having a bit of healthy skepticism. Skepticism, however, does not work with God. He asks that we give it **all** to Him and meet Him at the finish line. This requires that we have faith and that we **trust** Him. When trouble shows up in our lives, we do all that we can do, and when we don't know what else to do, we give it to God. That is bass ackwards. The **first thing** we should do is to put everything about our lives and our situations in God's hands. We must remain fully convinced that He will win the race for us. All we must do is **stay in the race** so that we can meet Him at the finish line.

READ TODAY: PROVERBS 23:26

JUNE 9

"I SEE IT. I WANT IT."
-BEYONCÉ

Have you ever been in a situation where you saw something and just had to have it? Maybe it was a pair of shoes that you instantly fell in love with. Fellas, perhaps there was a woman that you laid your eyes on, and you just knew you had to have her. You weren't concerned with whether she already had a man or not, because you were not going to stop until she was yours. Maybe there was a dream home that seemed to be calling your name. Every time you looked at the house, you knew it was meant to be yours. Whatever it was, you saw it, and you wanted it.

There is nothing wrong with seeing something and wanting it, but what happens when the thing you want is not supposed to be yours? Are you able to discern which things caught your eye simply out of lust? The devil is really good at placing things in your path that look good to your eyes but may be detrimental to your spirit. I now give major side-eye to any tall chocolate man with a nice beard who pops up in my life. My God Today! If the devil was trying to throw me a distraction, Lord knows that's the way to do it! Who sent you sir? I need to know who sent you! I digress. When you see something and you want it, don't forget to ask God whether or not it is something you should actually pursue.

READ TODAY: 1 SAMUEL 30:8

"I LIKE MY NEGRO NOSE WITH JACKSON FIVE NOSTRILS."
-BEYONCÉ

Have you ever been in a situation where you didn't like something about yourself? Perhaps you were the only black girl in your class and got picked on because your hair was of a different texture, and so you began to dislike it. Perhaps you begged your mother for a relaxer so you could also have straight hair. Maybe you had a gap in the middle of your teeth and got made fun of for it in school. Perhaps you begged your parents to get you braces to close the gap. Maybe your nose was wider than anyone else's nose. Perhaps you had a "negro" nose with Jackson Five nostrils and vowed to get a nose job as soon as you could afford it.

Isn't it crazy how people's experiences can cause them to dislike the same thing that others actually love about themselves? There are people who absolutely love their curly, kinky, and nappy hair, and wouldn't trade it for the world. There are others who absolutely adore the gap in between their teeth and would fight you if you tried to make them close it up. There are others with non-European-looking noses, who like their nose just the way it is. Honestly, this page is just another quick reminder that God did a really good job in making you, but you have to see it for yourself. Beauty is truly in the eye of the beholder. Be your own beholder.

READ TODAY: PSALMS 139:14

JUNE 11

"OKAY LADIES, NOW LET'S GET IN FORMATION."
-BEYONCÉ

Have you ever been in a situation where you got along better with people of the opposite sex? Ladies in particular, perhaps you noticed that being around guys has always been more comfortable for you. There seemed to be less drama, less jealousy, and less petty grievances. Maybe the guys seemed to understand your sense of humor better and you felt more comfortable laughing with them than with other ladies. Perhaps the ladies that you came in to contact with seemed way too superficial, and you felt that you could engage in much deeper issues with the men that you knew.

So this message is an attempt to get women to see that there is value in sisterhood. I know you won't identify with every woman nor want every woman to be a part of your circle. But we need to be more intentional about forming better bonds with each other. Instead of tearing each other down and always running to the men, we should be building each other up and getting in formation. A proper formation is important because it allows us to present a united front when faced with adversity. Make no mistake about it. Women are not always treated fairly and are often seen as "less-than." Misogyny is **alive** and **well**. If we continue to throw each other under the bus, progress will be difficult. Pray and ask God to send you some good ladies with which to get in formation.

READ TODAY: PROVERBS 3:17

JUNE 12

"LET ME UPGRADE YA."
-BEYONCÉ

    Have you ever been in a situation where you needed an upgrade? Perhaps you had a bandage on your index finger because you kept trying to swipe on your old, cracked phone screen. Maybe you had to open your car door and lean out the car to order at the drive-thru because your window no longer rolled down. Maybe you had to back into every parking space just in case your battery needed a jump, and really you just needed a new car all together. Maybe your computer was so old that it could only connect to dial-up internet, and the only games you were capable of playing on it were Solitaire and Minesweeper. You needed an upgrade.

    What about spiritually? God wants to supply you with free spiritual upgrades for your life. God's Word is filled with amazing upgrades that we are eligible for if we would simply be willing and obedient. Could you use an upgrade to your peace? Perhaps an upgrade to your joy would be nice. How would you like an upgrade to your health, wealth, and relationships? Many of us could use an upgrade to our love and definitely to our patience. Upgrade the amount of time you spend walking and talking with the Lord, and He will begin to upgrade your spirit with some amazing add-ons.

READ TODAY: 2 PETER 1:5-8

JUNE 13

"I DON'T THINK YOU'RE READY FOR THIS JELLY."
-BEYONCÉ

    Have you ever been in a situation where somebody else had something that you wanted? Perhaps you were 16, and all you wanted was a Honda Civic for your birthday. Maybe you didn't get a Civic, but your best friend did. Perhaps you had a huge crush on someone, and just when you got up the nerve to tell them how you felt, you discovered that someone else had beaten you to the punch. Now you're left to watch the person you're crazy about be crazy over someone else. Maybe you really wanted a new home in a certain neighborhood, but you didn't get approved for the loan. The next time you logged in to social media, however, you saw someone holding up a "Sold" sign in front of a new home in the same neighborhood.

    The word "jelly" has become colloquially known to mean jealous. When other people get something that you've been wanting, do you feel excited for them, or do you feel jealous? Do you trust God regarding when, where, and how your blessings come? Have you ever considered the fact that maybe you're not even ready for the thing that you're jealous of? Are you truly ready for the Mercedes Benz if you don't even know how to take good care of your Geo Metro? Spend less time being envious of others, and use that time to become a good steward over what you already have. When the blessings come, you'll be **ready** to receive them.

READ TODAY: PROVERBS 14:30

JUNE 14

"NEVER TRUST A BIG BUTT AND A SMILE."
-BELL BIV DeVOE

Have you ever been in a situation where you were distracted by someone's looks? Perhaps someone came into your life that was so extremely gorgeous that you couldn't stop staring at them. Maybe every time you looked into their eyes you just melted. Maybe their booty was so perfectly formed that you hated to see them go but loved to watch them walk away. Perhaps every time they flashed that million-dollar smile, their wish was your command. Were their good looks a distraction to your otherwise well-functioning brain?

Psychology research has shown that with no additional evidence, we are more likely to ascribe good character traits to people who are physically attractive. As a nation, we spend billions each year on beauty. Think about all the money that is spent on things like hair, nails, makeup, clothes, braces, and weight-loss measures. Yet none of the things mentioned have anything to do with the kind of person we are on the inside. Far too often, we spend so much time and energy trying to improve our outward appearance, but we don't keep that same energy when it comes to improving our **inward** appearance. This is exactly why it's not wise to trust someone with a big butt and a smile simply because they have a big butt and a smile. With enough money, anyone can get their fat surgically transferred from their stomach to their behind. A beautiful smile can be created perfectly with veneers. Don't let someone's outer appearance cause you to ignore the red flags that they display. Stay woke.

READ TODAY: 1 SAMUEL 16:7

JUNE 15

"THAT GIRL IS POISON."
-BELL BIV DeVOE

 Have you ever been in a situation where you were involved with a "toxic" individual? Perhaps it was your boss. You hated to see them coming because you knew that whatever they had to say would put a damper on your day. Perhaps it was a judgmental family member who always had something to say about you and your life but had absolutely nothing to show for their own. Every time you had to be around them, you left more stressed than when you came. Perhaps it was someone you were in a relationship with. Their narcissistic ways made you feel as if you would never be good enough to satisfy them, which wreaked havoc on your self-esteem.

 I don't believe that people should be labeled as toxic as a final judgement on who they are, but I do believe that a person can be toxic **for you** and **to you**. This just means that a person's presence in your life can be poisonous to your well-being. Do you always feel angry, sad, inadequate, lonely, insecure, hurt, or taken advantage of after dealing with a particular person? The first thing you need to do is to begin praying for this person, that they would allow God to come into their hearts. The next thing is to pray and ask God for direction on how to remove any poison from your life. If circumstances won't allow you to remove someone who has become poisonous to you, ask God to help you set proper **boundaries**. You may not be able to change a poisonous person, but you can choose not to ingest.

READ TODAY: PROVERBS 22:24

JUNE 16

"MR. TELEPHONE MAN, THERE'S SOMETHING WRONG WITH MY LINE." -NEW EDITION

Have you ever been in a situation where you had trouble communicating with someone? Perhaps you wanted to communicate with a teenager, but it seemed as if there was a generational barrier that prevented you from getting through. Perhaps you were at a nail salon owned by people of a different nationality, and you had trouble understanding the nail tech due to the language barrier between you. Perhaps you were in a relationship and attempting to communicate with someone of the opposite sex, but it seemed as if they were wired so differently that they could not see things from your viewpoint. After so many failed attempts at communication, you begin to wonder if there is something wrong with the actual line.

In order to effectively communicate with each other, we have to identify potential barriers and address them. The same thing can happen with God. There are things that we allow into our hearts that can create barriers to communication even with Him. Sometimes we lack faith. God says that those who come to Him must first **believe** that He exists and that He is a rewarder of those who diligently seek Him. Sometimes we have unforgiveness in our hearts. We are instructed to forgive others in order to receive forgiveness and to have our own prayers heard. Sometimes there is sin or disobedience in our hearts which can also keep God from hearing us. If you feel that your prayers are not working, there may be something wrong with your line. Is there anything preventing your prayers from being heard?

READ TODAY: PSALMS 66:18

JUNE 17

"SUNNY DAYS, EVERYBODY LOVES THEM, BUT TELL ME CAN YOU STAND THE RAIN?" -NEW EDITION

Have you ever been in a situation where your life was in a storm? Perhaps it seemed as if trouble was all around you. Maybe everything seemed to be going fine one day, but the next day you lost your job, went through a break up, lost your dog, got a message from your doctor saying they need to discuss your test results ASAP, and found out you owed $10,000 to the IRS all before 10am. There was a stark difference between this day and the sunny day that preceded it.

Have you ever been to a family reunion picnic at a state park? It seems like everything is always going just fine until all of a sudden there is thunder and lightning. What's the first thing we do when the rain starts to fall? We run under the picnic pavilion for shelter and protection until the storm passes. The name of the Lord is the picnic pavilion of our lives. Sadly, when rain comes, some people are not able to withstand. They lose their faith in God and their hope for a brighter day. That's because it's hard to stand the rain when you continue to stand **in** the rain. As believers, we were never promised that rain wouldn't come, but we were promised that we wouldn't be left out in the elements to fend for ourselves. Instead of being angry and disappointed at God when storms come, run **quickly** to Him to find safety and covering just like you run to that picnic pavilion. The Bible tells us that the name of the Lord is a strong tower. The righteous run inside of it, and they are safe.

READ TODAY: PSALMS 27:5

JUNE 18

"IF IT ISN'T LOVE, WHY DO I FEEL THIS WAY?" -NEW EDITION

Have you ever been in a situation where you thought you were in love, but you were not? Perhaps you were in a really intense relationship with someone. There was a lot of arguing and a lot of fighting. Maybe there were even some physical altercations, but somehow you always managed to stay together and have great make-up sex. Sure, you were unhappy for the majority of the relationship, but you figured that your ability to stay together despite all the drama was a sign of true love.

Our feelings can make us confused about what love really is. Make no mistake about it, love is not always easy, but it's not supposed to be terrible either. Love isn't supposed to bring you down nor cause you to become a lesser version of yourself to maintain it. I'll be the first to admit that sometimes our feelings can make it hard to determine whether what we are experiencing is love or something else. If you are ever confused about your situation, the Bible gives us some characteristics to compare it with. Is your situation patient and kind? Does it offer protection, trust, hope, perseverance, and truthfulness? This is love. Is your situation filled with envy, boastfulness, pride, selfishness, or quick tempers? Are past wrongs always being brought up? Do you have to engage in sin in order to enjoy yourselves? I'm sorry, but this **isn't love**, no matter how it feels.

READ TODAY: 1 CORINTHIANS 13:4-7

JUNE 19

"KNUCK IF YOU BUCK."
-CRIME MOB

Have you ever been in a situation where you were being discriminated against? Perhaps you were a woman in a male-dominated industry and were treated as if you were not as smart as everyone else. Maybe the company you worked for didn't value diversity, and as the only black person in your department, your ideas were never heard. Perhaps your ancestors were violently taken from their homeland and sold into a nation where they were treated as property for several centuries. Perhaps an entire nation was built, and many were made wealthy from the free labor and inhumane treatment of your ancestors. We interrupt this week's tribute to New Edition to honor Juneteenth.

Do you ever wonder what might have happened if our ancestors hadn't been buck enough to knuck? Slavery went on for a **really** long time y'all. If no one had been buck enough to knuck, the enslavement of African-American people could still be going on today. We are grateful today for our ancestors who were abolitionists, those who participated in slave revolts, and those who ran for their freedom. Rev. Dr. Martin Luther King, Jr. famously stated that "Freedom is never voluntarily given by the oppressor; it must be demanded by the oppressed." In other words, if we aren't buck enough to knuck for justice, it will never come. Today we pay homage to all who played a part in doing what was right on behalf of our freedom. We thank God for them, and we shall learn from their examples of greatness.

READ TODAY: ISAIAH 1:17

JUNE 20

"EVERY LITTLE STEP I TAKE, YOU WILL BE THERE."
-BOBBY BROWN

      Have you ever been in a situation where you went somewhere that you weren't supposed to go? Perhaps you snuck out to a party that your parents strictly forbade you from going to. Maybe you were in college and took a road trip to D.C. for Howard's homecoming while leading your parents to believe you were safe and sound on your own campus and studying for a big test. Maybe you slid down to Miami with that guy or girl you met on Tinder after only knowing them for 3 weeks. Perhaps you were living on the edge and didn't even tell your friends or family where you were going or who you were going with because you didn't want to hear their mouths. Your people may not have known where you were in these particular situations, but God did.

      Sometimes we attempt to convince ourselves that God isn't with us. When you are laid out at the altar in prayer, praise, and worship, God is with you. When you are out there "living your worst life," God is with you. God doesn't just disappear whenever we are being ratchet. **Every** little step you take, He will be there. God sees. God knows. God cares. We should be grateful that God did not desert us in our times of ratchetry, because many times we were putting ourselves in harm's way, and it was nothing but His grace and mercy that brought us home in one piece. When you are in love with God, you will want to honor Him. Let the knowledge of God's holy presence positively influence which steps you decide to take in your life.

READ TODAY: PSALMS 139:8

JUNE 21

"IT'S MY PREROGATIVE."
-BOBBY BROWN

Have you ever been in a situation where you changed your mind about something? Perhaps you told your friends you'd go out with them Friday night, but after a long day of work you decided to stay home with some frozen pizza, a glass of wine, and the *Law & Order: SVU* marathon. Maybe you recklessly told someone that if you ever broke up with your current boo, they would definitely be the next person on your list to call. Well now you're all broken up and have realized that there are several more options to consider first. Much to the dismay of others, you decided to change your mind.

As an individual, changing your mind is your right or privilege, also known as your prerogative. When we decide to give our lives to Christ, it requires a mind change. There will be some who are not happy with your changing mind, because it is not to their benefit. Some will even try to make you feel bad for it. They will remind you of the ratchet things you did or said just last week, but you need to remind them that change is your prerogative. There is so much freedom in Christ. When God transforms your mind and your life, do not let anyone hold you hostage to the things you used to do or the person you used to be, even if it was just this morning. That's your prerogative! *shrugs*

READ TODAY: ROMANS 12:2-3

JUNE 22

"MY MY MY MY MY MY MY MY…"
-JOHNNY GILL

Have you ever been in a situation where you had the hook up? Perhaps you had a shoe plug who could get you the new Air Jordans the day before they were even released. Maybe you had a connect who worked for the airlines and could always let you use their buddy pass to fly for free. Maybe you had a homegirl in HR who hooked you up with that job at the bank. You were able to gain access to certain things simply based on who you knew.

Aht, aht! When it comes to your relationship with God, nobody can do it for you, and there are no hookups. My relationship with God has to be my, my, my, my, my, my, my, my relationship and mine alone. It doesn't matter how close your mama was to the Lord. It doesn't matter if you are best friends with the Pope. Your relationship with God is one of the things in the world that you must work out on your own. It's not just meant for the pastor to study the Bible. We have to study on our own too! It's not just for the people on the prayer team to have a solid prayer life, we must have one too. It's not just for the praise and worship team to bless the Lord, we need to praise and worship too. We must take **full** ownership of our own spiritual journey, because there will come a day when we all have to stand before Him and give an account for ourselves.

READ TODAY: PHILIPPIANS 2:12

JUNE 23

"IF YOU WANT IT, YOU GOTTA SEE IT WITH A CLEAR-EYE VIEW."
-MEEK MILL

Have you ever been in a situation where you kept seeing something in your head? Maybe you kept seeing yourself as a family man even though you had no family of your own yet. Maybe you could see yourself walking down the aisle to the man of your dreams even though your phone was as dry as a bone, and nobody was even checking for you. Perhaps you kept seeing yourself as an amazing mom or an amazing dad even though you didn't have any children yet. Maybe you kept seeing yourself completely out of debt even though you still had bills for days. Perhaps you kept seeing yourself as a homeowner even though you still lived at home with your folks. Maybe you saw yourself with washboard abs even though you currently had a beer belly. You had something called vision.

If you really want something in life, it helps to first visualize it. God will sometimes give us visions wherein we see ourselves in a better place than where we are currently. In order to get that vision to become a reality, however, there are a few steps we need to take. First, we need to write the vision down. Writing it down helps it to become plain and allows us to see it with a clear-eye view. After you have written your vision, place it in an area where you will see it pretty frequently, like on your refrigerator. Next, begin to pray and ask God for His supernatural strength as well as the strategy to help you get from point A to point B. Vision + Strategy + Obedience = **Victory.**

READ TODAY: HABAKKUK 2:2

JUNE 24

"WHEN I BOUGHT THAT ASTON MARTIN, Y'ALL THOUGHT IT WAS RENTED."
-MEEK MILL

Have you ever been in a situation where someone started a rumor about you that wasn't true? Perhaps you had gotten a little reckless with the chili cheese fries and gained a little weight. The next thing you knew, word was going around that you were pregnant. Maybe you decided to divorce someone, and they made you pay by spreading rumors that you had cheated when you hadn't. Perhaps you quit your job, and someone spread the rumor that you had gotten fired for stealing. Maybe you bought your Aston Martin with cash, and someone went around telling people that it was rented. Maybe your name was Jesus and you were God's only begotten son, and someone went around telling people that you weren't really Him…okay, not you…but it did happen to someone.

I'm not sure what it is about the human experience that causes people to assume the worst and then spread it like truth. Honestly, a lot of people who are eager to spread negative rumors do so because it makes them feel better about some of the **true** things that they **know for sure** about themselves. If they choose to believe that your new Aston Martin is rented, it makes them feel better about the fact that their credit was so jacked up that they couldn't even get approved for a used economy car. If you have ever been on the other side of a false rumor, you know how terrible it can be. Let's all do a better job of recognizing gossip and refusing to take part. This requires self-discipline. If you find yourself taking enjoyment in gossip and slander, begin to ask yourself why hearing something negative about someone else would make you feel good.

READ TODAY: EPHESIANS 4:29

JUNE 25

"SHE'S IN LOVE WITH WHO I AM. BACK IN HIGH SCHOOL I USED TO BUS IT TO THE DANCE." -DRAKE

Have you ever been in a situation where someone thought you were a good catch? Perhaps they looked at the fact that you had a good job, your own house, your own car, and a good reputation. If you've been on the dating scene any time in the last couple of decades, then you already know that people are obsessed with knowing "what you bring to the table." What a person brings to the table has become, for some, more important than the actual person themselves. Everyone wants to be impressed, so there is a lot of pressure to make sure you come across as impressive. Sadly, many of the measures we take to impress people are not sustainable and are therefore temporary. It's a blessing to find someone who loves you for who you are.

That's the wonderful thing about God. He literally knows everything about us and still loves us for who we are. He has seen our past. Sure, we may be driving a Porsche today, but He knew us back in high school when we used to take the bus just to get to the dance. Sure, we may have a perfect smile now, but he knew and loved us back when we had crooked teeth before the braces. We may have a house and a car now, but God knew and loved us even when we were sleeping on a friend's air mattress and struggling to find a ride to the store. Since God's love for us has **always** been consistent, regardless of what we do or do not bring to the table, let us also be consistent in our love for Him. When blessings come and you are living your best life, don't forget that you still need God just the same as you did when you had to bus it to the dance.

READ TODAY: HEBREWS 13:8

JUNE 26

"HAD ME OUT LIKE A LIGHT, LIKE A LIGHT... LIKE A LIGHT, SLEPT THROUGH THE FLIGHT."
-DRAKE

Have you ever been in a situation where you slept all the way through something? Perhaps you were a kid riding home in the backseat of your parents' car one minute, and the next thing you knew you were waking up at home in your own bed not even knowing how you got there. Perhaps you were at home sleeping when an entire tornado swept through your town. You had no idea that it had even rained until you woke up and saw the news. Perhaps you took a long flight and were out like a light before the plane even reached cruising altitude. Before you knew it, you felt the bumpy landing and realized that you had slept through the entire flight.

If you can go to sleep in a situation, it means that you have a certain level of trust that all will be well. You fall asleep in the backseat believing that your parents have things under control in the front seat. You fall asleep in your home believing that the structure of your house will reasonably protect you from the elements. You fall asleep on the plane trusting that the pilot knows how to fly. This is how we should be able to rest in Jesus. As humans, we sometimes have difficulty relinquishing control. There are times where we can barely get to sleep at night because our minds are going 100mph worrying about every single detail of our lives and about how things will work out. We forfeit so much of our own peace simply because we refuse to take our burdens to the Lord, leave them there, and rest.

READ TODAY: MATTHEW 11:28

JUNE 27

"I CAN'T KEEP UP WITH YOUR TURNING TABLES."
-ADELE

    Have you ever been in a situation where you had to deal with someone who was inconsistent? Perhaps you needed a workout buddy, but the person you chose would be on point one week and full of excuses the next week. Maybe you were co-parenting with someone who would drop in and out of your child's life when it was convenient for them. Perhaps you were in a relationship with someone who was loving and kind one minute, but cold and distant the next. It's so draining to deal with an inconsistent person, because you never know how to mentally prepare yourself for them.

    Satan specializes in being inconsistent. He absolutely loves to turn some tables. One moment you're drunk and having the time of your life, and the next moment you're ruining perfectly good relationships with drunken text messages. One moment you're living your "best" life and throwing it in a circle, and the next moment you're alone, pregnant, scared, and preparing to be a single mom. One moment you're enjoying the thrill of an extramarital affair, and the next moment you've lost your spouse, your children, your house, and half of your paycheck. Meanwhile, Satan is somewhere rubbing his hands together like Birdman and/or Stevie J and saying, "Myyy my my, how the tables have turned!" You may think you've got it all under control when you're playing with sin, but I'm here to tell you that you can't keep up with the enemy's turning tables, so you may as well stop trying.

                                         READ TODAY: ROMANS 6:23

JUNE 28

"LOOK ME IN MY FACE. I AIN'T GOT NO WORRIES."
-LIL WAYNE

Have you ever been in a situation where you were minding your business, and somebody asked you what was wrong? Perhaps you were super confused because you hadn't said anything to anybody. You did, in fact, have some things on your mind, but you make it a habit not to complain or to go around telling folks all of your business. How did this person even know something was wrong? Maybe you wondered if that person was some sort of prophet.

Can I tell you something? It was probably your face. If left to its own devices, your face will be one of the first things to betray you. Have you ever tried to lie to someone? Maybe you tried to tell someone that their outfit looked good, but your face didn't get the memo. When you're stressed out, anxious, or worried about something, it shows on your face. Imagine someone trying to convince you that they are happy in Jesus, but their resting b**** face consistently says otherwise. Would you be interested in trying their brand of Jesus? Probably not. Let us be more intentional about seeking true peace and trusting the Lord with all of our fears and worries. When we verbally tell people how good God is, we want our face to tell the same story.

READ TODAY: NUMBERS 6:24-26

JUNE 29

"I ONLY THINK OF YOU ON TWO OCCASIONS. THAT'S DAY AND NIGHT."
-THE DEELE

Have you ever been in a situation where you couldn't get something or someone off of your mind? Perhaps you had a huge crush on someone, and no matter what you were doing, your thoughts would always circle back around to them. You could literally be brushing your teeth, and the next thing you know, you're thinking about how perfect Leroy's smile is. Maybe you were waiting until grades came out, and you weren't sure whether you were going to pass that one course. All you could think about all day long was the snowball effect that failing would have on your life. You would literally be sitting in the drive-thru line on the verge of tears, because you had calculated in your head how you would have to work the fry basket once you had officially failed out of school.

Whether you knew it or not, you were practicing something called meditation. Meditation is the act of mentally giving your attention to one particular thing. We don't talk about it as often here in the Western Hemisphere, but meditation is actually very important in the life of a believer. The Bible tells us to **set** our minds on things that are "above." This means that we are to be very intentional about where we allow our minds to go. If you allow your mind to wander off on its own, you are more likely to struggle with thoughts filled with things like fear, doubt, lust, envy, and anger. Let's start off each day **deciding** that we will meditate on a positive thought or a scripture. Take that thought and purposely think of it on two occasions: day and night.

READ TODAY: PSALMS 1:1-2

JUNE 30

"CHOOSEY LOVER, GIRL I'M SO PROUD OF YA."
-THE ISLEY BROTHERS

Have you ever been in a situation where you lowered your standards? Ladies, perhaps you wanted to be with a man who was a provider, strong spiritually, and had no vices. How in the world did you end up in a relationship with a guy who was in between jobs, says "I mean...I do believe there's probably a God or whatever," and is a chain smoker? Fellas, maybe you wanted to be with a woman who was sophisticated, well-cultured, and independent. How did you end up with this girl whose Instagram page is nothing but booty on the sink pictures, who acts a fool in nice restaurants, and is asking you to pay for her nails after only knowing you for one week? How Sway?

In theory we are all choosey lovers, but in practice many of us miss the mark. Why is there such a disconnect between the things we say we want and the things we are willing to accept? This is where we have to check our faith and our patience. Do we not believe that God is **able** to provide us with more than what is in our face at this very moment? Are we scared that if we don't accept what's right here, right now, that we'll end up with nothing? I'm not talking about the shallow things we wrote on our "list" when we were struggling with immaturity (at least 6'4, wears name brand clothes, drives a foreign car). I'm talking about the things that you know are God's will for your life. Allowing the wrong person into your life can be the death of you, but the right person can be life-giving. It's okay to be choosey. Look at you...I'm so proud of ya.

READ TODAY: DEUTERONOMY 30:19

JULY 1

"PACK IT UP. PACK IT IN. LET ME BEGIN. I CAME TO WIN, BATTLE ME...THAT'S A SIN."
-HOUSE OF PAIN

Have you ever been in a situation where you had to fight? Perhaps all your life you had to fight. Maybe you had to fight your daddy. Perhaps you had to fight your brothers. Maybe you had to fight your cousins and your uncles. Maybe your name was Sophia, and you were a girl child who wasn't safe in a family of men. Maybe you've gotten so used to fighting that it has become normal to you. Perhaps it's not physical fighting. Perhaps you're accustomed to shouting matches. Either way, you've normalized it to the point that if someone wants a fight with you, you tell them to pack it up, pack it in, and put on a seat belt, because you are surely about to begin and win.

What if I told you that instead of fighting your enemies, you should pray for them? That almost sounds insane, but as children of God, this is exactly what we are instructed to do. When people try to battle you, they don't even realize that what they are doing is a sin, and that's why they need your prayers. You don't go attacking a child of God and expect there to be no spiritual consequences. The person who is antagonizing you is picking a fight in the spiritual realm that they simply cannot win. Most of the time they don't know what they are getting themselves into and are simply allowing themselves to be used by Satan. Meanwhile, it is our job to recognize that our fight is not against some mere mortal. We are not fighting against flesh and blood, so we must mount our defense on our knees while we watch God win our battles for us in real time. Which silly rabbit will you pray for today?

READ TODAY: MATTHEW 5:43-44

JULY 2

"JUMP AROUND. JUMP AROUND."
-HOUSE OF PAIN

Have you ever been in a situation where you felt unstable? Perhaps you had moved 7 times in 3 years. Maybe your kids had trouble making friends because you never stayed in one place long enough. Perhaps every job you got seemed like it wasn't a good fit, and you bounced around from position to position trying to find some peace. Perhaps you had to invest in a storage unit, because you weren't really sure where else to put all your stuff. Maybe every time you thought you had found "the one," the relationship somehow went awry, and you found yourself having to learn the favorite color of yet another new person *(insert deep sigh)*.

Some people actually enjoy the thrill of jumping around, while others are depressed by the fact that everything in their life seems to be so temporary. We all have to endure life's uncertainties to a degree, and (nobody likes to hear this, but) our sufferings can actually help to build our character. The good news is that after you have suffered a while (there's a time limit on your instability), God is able to establish, strengthen, and settle you. This is another one of those things that require faith in God and patience. Your assignment, if you choose to accept it, is to do whatever you have to do to hear God clearly concerning your life. Sometimes we continue to jump around because of our own disobedience. If God told you to do something, go somewhere, stop something, or start something, and you have not done it, do not be surprised when your ship begins to toss and turn or if you end up in the belly of a huge fish like Jonah. Your obedience will help to settle you.

READ TODAY: 1 PETER 5:10

JULY 3

"GIVE ME A PROJECT CHICK. GIVE ME A HOODRAT CHICK." -JUVENILE

Have you ever been in a situation where you grew up in the hood? Perhaps you took it to the next level and actually grew up in the projects. Maybe you were raised in an environment where gunshots were the norm, and you knew to stay away from windows at all times. Perhaps you grew up in an environment where you had to walk past gang members and drug dealers just to get home. Maybe blue was your favorite color, but you couldn't even wear it because you didn't want to get mistaken for a Crip in Blood territory. Maybe you were zoned for a failing school district that didn't do a good job of making sure you were ready to advance.

Does your upbringing make you feel insecure or unqualified? I'm here to remind you that the devil is a liar! As a matter of fact, in some ways your difficult upbringing qualifies you even more. All throughout the Bible, you will see that God chose people who were looked down upon by others. He used some of the most unlikely people in a mighty way. That's just how God is. He does things that seem foolish to other people, just to demonstrate how powerful He is. He doesn't need someone who fits **society's** list of qualifications to get the job done. All He needs is a heart that is **willing** to be obedient. While you are busy being timid and unsure, God is saying "Give me a project chick! Give me a hoodrat chick! Give me a thug! Give me a gangster!" and I'll show you just what I can do!

READ TODAY: 1 CORINTHIANS 1:27

"SHE GOT HER OWN THANG. THAT'S WHY I LOVE HER...MISS INDEPENDENT. -NE-YO

Have you ever been in a situation where you just did what everybody else was doing? Maybe all of your friends were losing their virginity, and even though you weren't ready, you didn't want to be left out of the club. Perhaps it was Super Bowl Sunday and you didn't even know which teams were playing. You were really just there for the chicken wings, but everybody else was cheering for the Eagles, so for a few hours one Sunday in January, you became a die-hard Eagles fan. We are all guilty of doing things in an attempt to fit in. Blending into the crowd just seems so much easier than standing out sometimes.

We must be careful, however, about always following the crowd. Groupthink can be a very dangerous thing, and we have seen this time and time again in our society, on Twitter, and even in church. There are several instances in the Bible where the majority was flat out wrong. Thankfully, God has given us our **own thing** and allows us to think and operate independently from the masses. We all know the person who always has to be disagreeable for the sake of being disagreeable. We're not talking about that. Simply put, we move based on the Holy Spirit and not based on the crowd. Sometimes you will be in good company, and other times you will have to go it alone. Don't be afraid to think and move independently from the rest when necessary.

READ TODAY: MATTHEW 7:13-14

"AND IF YOU DON'T KNOW, NOW YOU KNOW."
-THE NOTORIOUS B.I.G.

 Have you ever been in a situation where you learned your lesson? Perhaps a family member convinced you to put them on your phone plan and said you'd save money by splitting the bill. Most months you ended up paying the whole bill to keep your own phone from getting cut off. Maybe you told somebody at the office some of your personal business in confidence. The next thing you knew, your business was all in the office streets. Perhaps you opened a credit card with a really high interest rate. It took you 3 years and $3000 to pay off a $1000 purchase. These situations may have caught you slipping once, but you can bet money that they won't happen again. Tuh! You learned your lesson.

 Whenever I would tell my dad (a very sarcastic fella, God rest his soul) that I didn't know something, he would say, "We could fill up a whole library with all of the things **YOU** don't know Lori." I would (internally) roll my eyes and walk away, but my dad had a solid point. There are so many things that we don't know and won't know until life teaches us. Whenever things happen in life, especially things that don't seem to make a lot of sense, do you use the experience to learn and grow? When you're truly walking with God, one of the questions you'll find yourself asking Him **a lot** is, "Alright God, what do you want me to get out of this? What is it that you want me to **know** that I didn't know?" With every situation we face, we must be like miners seeking out the golden nuggets of knowledge buried within it. That's how you live life with no regrets!

READ TODAY: PROVERBS 4:7

JULY 6

"I GOT 5 ON IT."
-LUNIZ

    Have you ever been in a situation where you didn't know how you made it? Perhaps you were well over the legal limit to drive, but somehow you made it home safely. Maybe you went against the cardinal rule of not drinking something given to you by a stranger at a party, but somehow you didn't get taken advantage of. Maybe you spent the night with somebody you barely knew, but somehow you didn't end up pregnant, and you didn't contract an STD. Perhaps you got let go from your job, but somehow you never missed a meal or a bill. Maybe a pandemic shutdown your business for two and a half months, but somehow you didn't go out of business. There are certain situations that you can look back on and realize that it was nothing but the grace of God that kept you.

    Biblically, five is the number of grace. When 5,000 people forgot to pack a lunch, Jesus multiplied five loaves of bread to feed them all **anyway**. How gracious! If you grew up in church, you were probably taught that grace is God's "unmerited favor" towards us. In more simple terms, grace is when God helps us out even though we've done absolutely nothing to deserve it. As a matter of fact, we are more likely to have done something **not** to deserve it. Some of us deserve to be dead by now, but God had five on it. Some of us deserve to be in a jail cell, but God had five on it. Some of us should have lost our minds by now, but God had five on it. Let's spend some time today thanking God for His grace that has kept us along the way.

                    READ TODAY: LAMENTATIONS 3:21-22

JULY 7

"ME AND YOU, YO MAMA AND YO COUSIN TOO..."
-OUTKAST

Have you ever been in a situation where you were the good one? Perhaps you made all A's in school and had a 4.0 GPA. Maybe you were the star football or basketball player who was adored by all because you were just such a great young man. Perhaps you were that kid in church who did the most. Maybe you sang in the youth choir, attended youth Bible study, ush'd on the usher board, always knew your Easter speeches, and were the one they always put on program to do the Welcome & Occasion on Youth Day. Maybe you spent your weekends volunteering your time to those less fortunate than yourself in the community.

Wow! You sound like a really on-point person, but you need Jesus! No, I mean you **really** need Jesus. Sometimes when on-point individuals perform at high levels, we assume that their spirits are in order. We think the people who need Jesus "the most" are the troubled kids, the adults who are strung out on drugs, or the criminals locked behind bars. Churches even tend to concentrate ministry efforts on them because those are the people who **really** need Jesus right? Guess what? We all need Jesus just the same. Me and you, yo mama, and yo cousin too...we all **really** need Him. The millionaire CEO, the most beloved celebrity, and the successful philanthropist need to have the gospel shared with them just the same. Believers are called to be the light, not to make judgements on who needs light and who does not.

READ TODAY: MARK 16:15

JULY 8

"...I'M SUPPOSED TO REPRESENT. I'M NOT ONLY A CLIENT, I'M THE PLAYER PRESIDENT."
-THE NOTORIOUS B.I.G.

Have you ever been in a situation where God completely changed your life? Perhaps Jesus was literally the best thing that ever happened to you. If you could take a before and after picture of your actual spirit and post it on Instagram, you'd probably get a million followers all wanting to know how you did it. Perhaps God took you from constant turmoil to peace that surpasses all understanding. Maybe He rescued you from all sorts of darkness, and now you're walking in the light. Perhaps He took you from near death to life everlasting.

It sounds to me like your decision to follow Jesus was the best thing you ever did. Alright, so now that it worked for you, you're supposed to go and represent! If it was so good to you and for you, wouldn't you want others to experience the same thing that you did? It's so funny that if we find anything else that works for us, we don't keep it a secret. Ask anybody who is vegan or on the keto diet what they did to lose weight, and I bet you they won't stop talking about it. But when it comes to Jesus, sometimes we are ashamed to represent. Sadly, many people before us have given Jesus a bad name and made it socially unacceptable now to represent for Him. Most people don't want to hear you preaching to them, but what they will do is look at your example. Be transparent enough to allow people to see what Christ's work on the cross has done in your life. When they inquire, be sure to let them know that not only are you a client of God's transformative grace, but you are also the president of His fan club. Represent!

READ TODAY: 1 PETER 3:15

JULY 9

"I KNOW YOU SEE IT."
-YUNG JOC

Have you ever been in a situation where you ignored a red flag? Perhaps a guy asked you on a date to a fancy restaurant, ordered the most expensive things on the menu, and conveniently left his wallet at home. Maybe she told you she was single but could only talk to you during the day and was never available on weekends. Perhaps he was so conveniently called in to work overnight on Valentine's Day and had to move your plans to February 15th. Maybe when you went in to interview for the job, everyone working there looked like a zombie. On your first day, someone even left a card on your desk that read, "Welcome to Hell."

Are you currently ignoring a red flag? I **know** you see it. Why do we see these big and bright warning flags waving directly in our faces, only to pretend that they aren't there? For some reason, we speed past the red flags and eventually end up in a fiery crash that may be days, months, or even years down the road. How many times have you gotten to the end of a thing and realized that so much hurt and pain could have been avoided had you simply heeded the warning flag that you saw at the very beginning? Consider red flags to be the Holy Spirit's way of trying to help us make good decisions. Don't allow your desperation to sweep a red flag under the rug. I know you see it.

READ TODAY: EZEKIEL 33:3-5

JULY 10

"I LEFT HOME TO BE WITH MY SIDEPIECE."
-THE LOUISIANA BLUES BROTHERS

Have you ever been in a situation where you just didn't care anymore? Perhaps your doctor had been encouraging you to eat healthy foods, exercise, and lose some weight. You tried for a while, but eventually you gave up and said, "If I die, I die. I don't care! I just want to enjoy my life and my ribs." Perhaps you had a husband or wife and some kids. You started out doing right by them, but eventually you let temptation get the best of you. You tried to honor your wedding vows, but when things got tough, you stopped caring, gave up, and left home to be with your sidepiece.

When it comes to sin, there is a point in time where your conscious begins to shut down. You know that it's wrong and you know that it's not good for you, but you've done it so much and for so long that you simply do not care anymore. You think about the consequences that you may face, and you feel that your sin is worth it. And you know what? After a while, the Holy Spirit will even step aside, stop bothering you, and let your mind make that poor choice. But what happens when you have a stroke at age 60 and have to live 25 more years unable to talk and severely paralyzed? What happens when you realize that your sidepiece wasn't worth losing your spouse, your children, your house, your car, and half of your paycheck? If you are on the verge of not caring anymore or giving in to that unhealthy desire, I just want to encourage you to stop, exercise some self-control, think about the consequences, and pull yourself away. Once you get driven away by sin, it can be difficult to find your way back to the crib, so don't leave home to be with it.

READ TODAY: ROMANS 1:28

JULY 11

"I'M SLIM SHADY, YES I'M THE REAL SHADY."
-EMINEM

Have you ever been in a situation where you did or said something that was shady? Perhaps you saw your ex living their best life with their new boo on Instagram, so you subliminally posted a meme that said, "If you're so happy, why are you still in my DMs?" Maybe your competitor posted a promotion offering the same service for cheaper and you tweeted, "You get what you pay for. I'm just saying." Perhaps someone else was asked to make the Thanksgiving mac and cheese this year, but you made yours and brought it anyway "just in case people wanted more options." Actions such as these have become affectionately known as "throwing shade."

Almost all of us have been guilty of a good shade throw in our day, but what happens when throwing shade becomes your way of life? What happens when we begin to identify you as a shady person in general? Shady people are passive-aggressive people, which makes them hard to deal with. Instead of confronting an issue head on, they employ micro-aggressions to make their feelings known. This is a quick and easy way to alienate would-be friends and family members. We talk about Jesus as the meek and lowly Lamb, but we often forget that He was also the **Lion** of Judah. If you read through the gospels, you will see several instances of Jesus in His "I said what I said..." mode. He said everything with His chest. The reason why Jesus could be so savage though, was because everything He said was coming from a place of His love for us. If you are tempted to photograph this page and send it to someone in particular as opposed to just having a grown folks' conversation with them, you might be just as passive-aggressive and shady as they are.

READ TODAY: PSALMS 55:21

JULY 12

"THEY HOPIN' THAT THEY GONE CATCH ME RIDIN' DIRTY. TRYIN' TO CATCH ME RIDIN DIRTY."
-CHAMILLIONAIRE

Have you ever been in a situation where people were waiting for you to mess up? Perhaps you were recently released from prison and have a parole officer whose job it is to literally catch you messing up. Maybe you simply have a hater who refuses to believe that you have really changed from your old ways. Perhaps there is somebody who is jealous of you. Maybe they stalk your social media or are constantly trying to bring your name up in their conversations. We live in a society where people really don't like seeing others on top. We live in a society where people take pleasure when other people fall. Do you know how many people would throw a block party if Steph and Ayesha Curry were to get caught up in some kind of scandal? Their lives seem to be too happy and drama-free for some people's liking. Sadly, there may be people, even in your immediate circle, who would love nothing more than to catch you ridin' dirty.

As unfortunate as this may be, there is a pretty simple solution. Stop ridin' dirty. I know it sounds wild, but hear me out! If you're not ridin' dirty, it makes it really hard for people to **caaaatch** you riding dirty. *insert gif of that man who taps at his temple* Will we ever be perfect? Absolutely not, but there's a difference between accidentally driving into a muddy puddle and intentionally taking your 4-Wheeler to an off-road mudding trail every weekend. Can we do it with our own strength? No. We aren't strong enough, so we have to depend on God's strength, or we will fall every time. In your prayer time today, ask God to help you to ride and walk with integrity.

READ TODAY: PSALMS 26:11

JULY 13

"I DON'T WANT TO MEET YOUR DADDY. I JUST WANT YOU IN MY CADDY."
-ANDRÉ 3000

Have you ever been in a situation where you felt like you couldn't be yourself? Perhaps you were the only black person in your class or in your department at work. There were so many *Martin* or *Living Single* references you wanted to make, but you knew no one would get them, so you stuck to *Seinfeld* and *Friends*. Maybe you went to college, took an African American Studies class, and became "woke." When you went home for the holidays you had to pretend you were still "sleep" because you didn't want to cause a stir or come off as the know-it-all after one semester. Maybe you were in a relationship with someone that conflicted with your relationship with God. Perhaps you had a whole entire spiritual side that your partner wasn't interested in getting to know. Maybe you went to church alone, prayed alone, and read your Bible alone. They didn't want to meet your "Daddy." They just wanted you in their Caddy.

The truth is, if someone doesn't want all of you, they don't really want **you** at all. Too often we conceal a certain part of ourselves for fear of rejection. Sure, sometimes it's not appropriate to give people the full-frontal view of yourself, but this shouldn't be your normal way of life. Are you afraid of losing someone if they find out you pray and maybe even pray in tongues? Are you afraid of losing someone if you tell them you **don't** want to fornicate? Are you afraid of losing someone if they find out that you can actually hear the Holy Spirit talking to you about stuff? If someone doesn't want to meet your "Daddy," maybe you shouldn't be riding in their Caddy.

READ TODAY: PSALMS 1:1-3

JULY 14

"OOH I THINK THEY LIKE ME. BETTER YET, I KNOW."
-YUNG JOC

    Have you ever been in a situation where you wanted people to like you? Perhaps you begged your mom to buy you the new Jordans for the first day at your new school because you thought it would help your image. Maybe you got to college and joined a fraternity or sorority because you felt that you would be big on the yard, and people would respect you. When my little sister was in first grade (forgive me Alexandria for telling this story), she stole the candy bag from her teacher's desk and distributed the candy to all her classmates in order to make new friends.

    Today we see on social media where people will do just about anything to gain "likes." There are people getting naked, jumping from rooftops, slapping their mamas, and pretending to care about justice simply to get views and likes from strangers. The phenomenon has become so pervasive that we have coined a term for people who do this. We call them "clout chasers." Apparently, there is something about our human nature that causes us to want to know that we are well-liked. Life has taught me, however, that no matter what you do, there will always be some who don't like you. I got this revelation when a friend of mine (April!) called Krispy Kreme donuts "trash." Krispy Kreme ain't never did nothin' to nobody but be delicious! That's when I realized that if everyone doesn't like Krispy Kreme, there's **no way** everyone will like me. That being said, there is a Biblical way to "gain likes," if you will. Write this down because it's very deep. Be **friendly**. If you want to have friends, you must be a friend. Maybe Alexandria was on to something. She got in trouble, but she got the friends.

READ TODAY: PROVERBS 18:24

JULY 15

"HAVE YOU EVER SEEN A CHEVY WITH THE BUTTERFLY DOORS?"
-YUNG JOC

Have you ever been in a situation where you tried to be something you were not? Maybe you were one of the only black kids in a predominately white school. You pretended to enjoy country music, but deep down all you really wanted was to hear that Cash Money Records would take over for the 99 and the 2000. Maybe you found yourself in a fancy restaurant where the menu was written in French. You pretended to enjoy the escargot, but honestly you would prefer a 10-pc lemon pepper hot with ranch cheese fries and a peach tea. Do you remember the bougie character Regine Hunter from *Living Single?* Well her real name was Regina, and she grew up in the hood. She found herself constantly losing because she insisted on presenting herself as something she was not. The Chevy with the butterfly doors isn't fooling us. Anybody with one good eye can tell it isn't a Lamborghini. The Chevy is **clearly** still a Chevy.

What's wrong with being the person God made you to be? When God designed you, He did it very intentionally, so do not despise it. You have a unique personality and skillset that is meant to impact a certain audience of people. Every detail about you, including where you grew up and who your parents are, was no accident. Embrace the things about you that make you unique. Along the way, we can all pick up wrong thinking and toxic ways. I'm not talking about those. Feel free to drop those at any time, but continue to strive to be the best version of **you** possible instead of trying to be someone else. If you're a Chevy, gosh darn-it, you hold your head up high and be the Corvette ZR1.

READ TODAY: EPHESIANS 2:10

JULY 16

"STUNTIN IS A HABIT, LET 'EM SEE THE CARATS."
-YUNG JOC

      Have you ever been in a situation where you saw somebody stuntin' for the 'gram or the 'book? Perhaps you were standing right next to them at the club, which was boring, empty, and not popping at all. The next thing you knew they were going live on social media filming themselves dancing with a bottle of champagne in their hand and the caption "VIP all the way baby...it's litty." Maybe they posted a picture of a private jet with the caption "Travel Day." How awkward was it that you were sitting right next to them on a commercial flight in coach? Maybe your homegirl got proposed to, posted a gorgeous picture of her diamond engagement ring, and claimed to be the happiest woman alive. So strange how she let 'em see the carats, but didn't mention the part where she had to pay for the ring herself, caught her man cheating last month, misses her ex, and cries to you on the phone every night.

      Y'all, stuntin' is a habit that you do **not** want to pick up. When someone feels the incessant need to show off, it makes you wonder why. If you're truly busy enjoying life, why do you care **so much** about who knows it? Why do you go out of your way to make things look better than they are? Who are you trying to impress? What void are you filling with the likes? Are you really happy? These are all questions that need answers. There's nothing wrong with sharing life's moments on social media, but when you are truly **an impressive person**, you don't have to go out of your way or make things up to impress anyone. It just happens. God says that if you humble yourself, He will exalt you in due time.

      READ TODAY: PROVERBS 25:14

JULY 17

"WORK THEM HIPS. RUN GIRL."
-DAVID BANNER

    Have you ever been in a situation where you were overweight? Perhaps you went to the doctor thinking you were good but just a little thick. The next thing you knew the doctor compared your height and weight to the BMI chart and told you that you had surpassed "overweight" and were actually considered "obese." Whew chile…the devil. Maybe you were minding your business at a grocery store when an older lady came up to you and said, "Oh, when's the baby due? You look like you're ready to pop any day now hun!" As sweet as it was, it really hurt your feelings because you weren't pregnant. Perhaps you have that older relative who says whatever they want to say at Thanksgiving, and nobody stops them. As soon as you walk in the door they exclaim, "You done got so big, I almost didn't recognize you! Come give me a hug!"

    I know from experience that it's never fun to "realize" that you've gotten big. It happens to the best of us, especially when we are not paying attention to our own self-care. The Bible tells us that our bodies are the temples of the Holy Spirit. It also tells us that **whatever** we do, even down to what we eat or drink, should be done for the glory of God. So maybe it's time to eat right, exercise, work them hips, and run! I don't know about you guys, but I'm trying to be healthy, fit, and fine. Don't you dare judge me! I can be fine for the glory of God. You never know, God might want to use my fineness to bring one of you gentlemen to the cross! Yup, let them follow me on IG to see how good I look, and then bloop…catch this Word! Goteeeem.

READ TODAY: 1 CORINTHIANS 10:31

JULY 18

"DANGER! GET ON THE FLOOR."
-MYSTIKAL

Have you ever been in a situation where you were in danger? Perhaps you were in danger of failing a class because your grade was already borderline, and your teacher was a real jerk with that final exam. Maybe you were in danger of being evicted or having your home foreclosed on because you had missed too many payments and weren't sure if you could catch back up. Maybe you were in danger of being diagnosed with something serious because your doctor saw some "abnormalities" and wanted to bring you back for some extra testing. Maybe you were in danger of losing your job because they just announced that there would be a wave of layoffs this month.

What do you do when you're in danger? Do you panic or do you get on the floor? In the model prayer that Jesus prayed, we see where He asked God to "deliver us from evil." We should always be praying, but when danger arises, the first thing we should do is run to our "Rock" for safety. Get on the floor, talk to God about everything, and don't forget that we also have this wonderful thing called fasting. Fasting is when you temporarily give up something that feeds your flesh such as food, social media, or television. When you fast and deny your flesh its cravings, it allows your spiritual senses to be heightened and gives you the opportunity to hear God even more clearly. Your time of fasting and prayer also serves to calm your spirit and helps you to **remember** how God came through for you the last time you thought it was the end of the world. God's got **this**, and God's got **you**.

READ TODAY: PSALMS 4:8

JULY 19

"BOOTY BOOTY BOOTY BOOTY ROCKIN' EVERYWHERE."
-BUBBA SPARXXX

Have you ever been in a situation where you were tempted? Perhaps you were as single as a dollar bill for a really long time, but as soon as you found that special person and changed your status to "in a relationship" or "married," it seemed like booty booty booty booty was rockin' everywhere all of a sudden. Who sent these people? Maybe you were wondering how and when you got so popular. You were probably wondering how you obtained so much juice when you hadn't even been to the grocery store. Why was everybody shooting their shot all of a sudden?

This one is a little deep, so brace yourself. A strong family unit is one of the things that the devil fears the most. This is why he attacks our marriages and committed relationships. He knows that a strong, God-fearing couple can produce strong, God-fearing children and make a difference in this world. The attacks on families or potential families has to be strong. If the devil can get you distracted or deceived, he can defeat you. The key is preparation. Don't let all of those booties rocking everywhere catch you by surprise. Let's not be ignorant about Satan's tricks, because they aren't new. Be vigilant, be faithful, and be loyal to your family. Don't let someone's nicely shaped booty cost you everything you have worked so hard to build. It's not worth it.

READ TODAY: 2 CORINTHIANS 2:11

JULY 20

"I FOUND YOU, MISS NEW BOOTY."
-BUBBA SPARXXX

      Have you ever been in a situation where you were fine? Perhaps you have always been fine and have had people telling you how good you look for as long as you can remember. Maybe you didn't realize that you were fine until a little later when you got those contact lenses, had your braces taken off, and finally grew into your head. Perhaps you're like me and had to work hard to be fine. Maybe you changed your diet, started working out every day, and began doing squats. I see you Ms. New Booty. I see you Mr. New Six-Pack Abs. I'm so glad that you found yourself.

      Let's talk about what to expect if you're new to the "fine" life. First of all, it is very important that you **self-identify** as fine. This means that you are fine because **you** believe you are fine and not because of what anybody else thinks. This is crucial because it means that someone else's comments will not be able to make or break you. When you're not used to being told that you are beautiful, it doesn't take much for a snake to slither up with compliments and turn you into some putty in their hands. Be especially careful if you are married or in a committed relationship. Don't allow the new attention to go to your head and mess up what you have at home. Secondly, do not become vain. Do not allow your beauty or your new booty to define you. We've all seen the person who starts acting brand new (in a bad way) when they drop a few pounds. There's nothing wrong with being fine if you can handle it, but always remember that God is more interested in what your heart looks like.

      READ TODAY: PROVERBS 31:30

JULY 21

"GET IT RIGHT! GET IT RIGHT! GET IT TIGHT!"
-BUBBA SPARXXX

Have you ever been in a situation where you kept messing up? Perhaps you said you were going to do better with your diet, but you keep accidentally eating cookies. Maybe you said you were going to stop heauxing around, but you keep accidentally waking up in somebody else's bed. Perhaps you said you were going to stop cussing, but the people at work just won't stop trying you. Why does it seem so hard to get it right?

We all have areas in which we need to tighten up. If there is something that you are attempting to get right, there's really only one way. You must realize that you cannot do it in your own strength. The only true righteousness we have is the righteousness that we have through Christ because of our faith in Him. If it were left up to us, we'd continue to fail over and over again because we are no match for sin without supernatural help from God. It doesn't matter how big or small you consider the matter to be, if you really want to get it right and get it tight, you must ask God to **show you** how. The amazing thing about God is that He can help us transform by renewing our minds. He can also give us practical strategies to avoid pitfalls. Sometimes the answers are complex, and sometimes they are as simple as, "Verily, verily I say unto you my daughter, removest thou the Cookies-To-Go Delivery App from thine phone and make haste to blockest thou that man's cell phone number from thine contact list this very day."

READ TODAY: PHILIPPIANS 3:9

"SHE THOUGHT IT WAS THE OCEAN. IT'S JUST THE POOL."
-TRAVIS SCOTT

    Have you ever been in a situation where you didn't know any better? Perhaps you grew up thinking souse meat (hog head cheese) was a delicacy. I know I did. My dad would give me some of his souse meat, and I'd put it on a cracker with some cheese and go to town! I had no idea that it was literally made from leftover parts of an actual pig's head and then congealed into a blob using gelatin. Historically, souse meat was used as food for the peasants in the Middle Ages, but maybe you thought it was great until you tasted prime rib cooked to perfection. Maybe you thought that spending the night at WeHaveBeds Motel was really living it up, until you stayed at the Four Seasons. Because of your limited experiences, you thought you were swimming in an ocean when in reality, it was just a pool.

    Sometimes our own limited experiences cause us to have limited **expectations** of what God can do in our lives. There is absolutely nothing wrong with being content and at peace with the state that we are in, but we should not allow that contentment to make us stagnant. In Christ, there is always room for growth. As much peace as you have right now, can you believe that there is more? As much joy as you have right now, can you believe that there is more? You have enough to pay all your bills now, but what if I told you that God can bless you with enough to send one of the neighborhood kids off to college? Sometimes we assume that God wants us to stop at good when He actually has plans for great. I have news for you. That's not the ocean you're swimming in. It's simply a pool. Think bigger.

READ TODAY: EPHESIANS 3:20

JULY 23

"CAUSIN' CONFUSION, DISTURBIN' THE PEACE..."
-LUDACRIS

Have you ever been in a situation where you were confused? Perhaps you were really confused about what you wanted to do with your life. On one hand, you thought you were really good with kids, so maybe you could be a pediatrician. On the other hand, you didn't really like science classes...or school for that matter. Maybe you were confused about your relationship. On one hand, it seemed like this person really loved you. On the other hand, you argued all the time and you had to distance yourself from family and friends just to keep your partner happy. Maybe you had several dating prospects and were confused about which one to choose. On one hand, this woman was amazing, fun to be around, and seemed perfect. On the other hand, she lived in another city, and neither of you wanted to move.

There is one thing that all confusion has in common. Anything that is causing confusion and disturbing your peace was not sent by God. The Bible tells us that God is not the author of confusion, meaning that He didn't write it into your script. The Bible also tells us that God wants us to live in peace. When you are confused about something and your peace is disturbed, it is because Satan is trying to fool you into making the wrong decisions. If you have a narcissist in your life, pay attention to how they purposely try to make you feel confused. It is one of their slickest tools. When confusion and turmoil rear their ugly heads, that's the perfect time for you to go into a fast. Fasting allows you to push aside distractions, gain clarity, and strengthen your connection to the Holy Spirit whose job it is to guide you into all **truth** and away from confusion. What confuses you? What disturbs your peace?

READ TODAY: 1 CORINTHIANS 14:33

JULY 24

"IT'S UNDERSTOOD, I DO IT FOR THE HOOD."
-YOUNG JEEZY

      Have you ever been in a situation where you wanted to make a difference? Maybe the neighborhood you grew up in seemed less than ideal. Perhaps you were one of few people who left the neighborhood and became successful. Maybe you went to school and majored in business and learned about economics. Maybe you majored in Health and Nutrition Sciences and learned all about what causes health disparities among people of color. Maybe you went to prison for a while and learned about how the school-to-prison pipeline is set up specifically to allow certain industries to benefit from the free labor of incarcerated black men.

      When God allows us to learn, grow, and advance in this world, we should remember that it's not just for selfish gain. It should be understood that there are certain things we must do for our hood. We must give back. As much as we like to claim that no one helped us or that we made it on our own, that's not true. Someone along the way either took care of you, taught you, or gave you a chance. Giving back doesn't have to always be on the grand scale that we imagine in our heads. We may not go back to the hood with a bag full of money, but we can go back with a bag full of knowledge. You may not be able to open a whole school yet, but can you take one kid under your wing and mentor them? You may not be able to open a neighborhood credit union, but can you show Ms. Lucille how she can be better prepared for her retirement? The hood would be a much better place if we all did just a little.

READ TODAY: ACTS 20:35

JULY 25

"LEAN A LITTLE BIT CLOSER, SEE ROSES REALLY SMELL LIKE BOO BOO." -OUTKAST

Have you ever been in a situation where you gave something that you really didn't want to give? Perhaps a transient person approached you on the street, and you really didn't want to give them any money, but you gave it anyway so that they would leave you alone. Maybe an unstable family member had their water cut off and asked you for the money to help get it cut back on. You didn't really want to give it, but you gave it anyway so that they would leave you alone. Maybe it was Father's Day and the man wasn't there for you or the kids. You didn't really want to give the gift, but you did it anyway to keep from hearing anybody's mouth. Maybe you were at church and the pastor asked everybody to give more than their usual amount to help with the budget. You didn't really want to give it, but you gave it anyway in hopes that the pastor would just stop talking and give the benediction.

As gracious as you may have assumed yourself to be, if you lean a little closer, you'll see that your roses really smell like boo boo. Giving is honestly more about the spirit that's behind it than the actual gift itself. Back in the Old Testament Bible days, people would give burnt offerings as sacrifices to God. They would literally take perfectly good things and burn them up to show God that they were grateful and that they trusted Him enough to provide them with more. The smoke and the "smell" of the offering was said to go up to heaven. A good offering would present itself as a sweet-smelling aroma unto God, but when people brought damaged goods or gave begrudgingly, the smell was foul and unacceptable. God loves a cheerful giver whose roses really smell like roses.

READ TODAY: EPHESIANS 5:2

JULY 26

"I GOT EVERYTHING IN MY MAMA NAME."
-BIG TYMERS

Have you ever been in a situation where you had bad credit? Perhaps you were in college when you opened your first credit card and simply didn't understand the importance of making timely payments. Maybe you helped a friend or family member by co-signing for a car that ultimately got repossessed for non-payment. Maybe you had a student loan that you couldn't afford to pay back because the degree that you earned was not helping you find a good job. Perhaps your credit was so jacked up that you had to put everything in your mama's name.

Having bad credit means that at some point, you did not do what you had agreed to do. People use this information to determine the likelihood of whether or not you will keep your word in the future. In other words, if you have bad credit, you have a bad name. It's very unfortunate to have a bad name financially, but what's even worse is having a bad name in life. The best way to avoid having bad "life" credit is to be a man or woman of your word. When you have a good name, it really comes in handy when people try to lie on you and spread false rumors concerning you. Have you ever heard something about someone and just laughed at how absurd it was? Have you ever heard the same thing about someone else and believed it right away? When it comes to life, there's only so far your mom or dad's name can take you. Be very intentional about how you treat people, how you keep your promises, how you carry yourself, and how you take care of your reputation. You never know when you will need it.

READ TODAY: PROVERBS 22:1

JULY 27

"EVERYDAY I'M HUSTLIN.'"
-RICK ROSS

Have you ever been in a situation where you were always working? Perhaps you had two jobs and worked every day of the week. Maybe you had a main gig but also had a side hustle that you did on nights and weekends. Perhaps you dreamed that with enough hard work and dedication, your side hustle would one day be able to stand alone. Maybe you were a single parent. As soon as you got off work you had to rush to the school or daycare to pick up the kids. Once you got them home, you had to cook dinner, help with homework, do bath time, and get them ready for bed. Once they were down for bed, you had to start cleaning up, washing clothes, ironing things for the next day, and preparing tomorrow's lunch. Day in and out, it seemed like all you did was work. Every single day you were hustlin'.

As honorable as work is, hustlin' every single day is not God's will for our lives. Did you know that God actually designed our bodies and our minds to require rest? When you neglect the call for rest coming from your mind or your body, you're putting yourself in danger. Lack of rest is very closely linked to high stress levels which trigger the onset of sickness and disease. That correlation is **very** strong. Sometimes it seems impossible to be able to rest and still survive. The truth is that there are some things you may have to sacrifice in order to prioritize rest. I deactivated my account on "Tha Book" for two and a half years once simply because I needed those moments back to use for rest. Being lazy is clearly not an option, but neither is hustlin' every day without resting. What can you do to find a balance?

READ TODAY: MATTHEW 11:28-30

JULY 28

"I CAN MAKE YOU A CELEBRITY OVERNIGHT."
-TWISTA/KANYE WEST

Have you ever been in a situation where you were tempted to take the easy way out? Perhaps you are like me and wonder why you are struggling to eat right, exercise, and go to work every day when a good surgeon can make you rich and famous on Instagram or OnlyFans almost overnight. Maybe you're wondering why you're going the extra mile at work in hopes of a promotion, when that Eartha Kitt-looking lady from upper management has been trying to get at you ever since day one. It seems like everyone else takes shortcuts, so why shouldn't you?

I'm glad you asked. Whenever you are offered something that requires you to sell your soul for a chance at advancement, you can believe that the door is being opened by Satan and not by God. There was a moment in the Bible where Jesus was in the wilderness alone and fasting for 40 days when Satan pulled up and tried to tempt Him. Satan showed Jesus all the glorious kingdoms of the world and told Him that if He would bow down and worship him, all of it could be His. What a joke. All of it was **already** His because it belonged to His Father. Jesus told Satan to get the hell away from Him, and chose to complete the more difficult assignment that would ultimately make Him the G.O.A.T. Let us follow the example that Jesus set. Satan's way may offer temporary satisfaction, but his ultimate plan is **always** to steal, kill, and destroy our lives. Sure, God's way to success may require more patience and more discipline, but you can be sure that His way leads to a life filled with love, joy, peace, and the ability to sleep at night.

READ TODAY: MATTHEW 4:8-11

JULY 29

"I'M YO' PUSHER..."
-CLIPSE

    Have you ever been in a situation where somebody kept you in line? Maybe you were a kid and it was your grandmother who had you in church every Sunday and wouldn't allow you to run the streets with the other guys. Maybe it was your own mother who made sure you were doing your schoolwork and behaving in class. Perhaps it was your dad or even one of your coaches who helped you focus on sports rather than chasing girls all day or getting caught up in a gang. Maybe you are an adult and you have a friend, therapist, or pastor, who always calls you out on your foolishness and doesn't let you get away with your own nonsense. These are your pushers.

    A pusher is any person who tries to help push you into greatness by holding you accountable to your own dopeness. Pushers are commonly known as "accountability partners." If you don't have an accountability partner, pray and ask God to send you one. These are people who aren't afraid to offend you by telling you the truth. Your accountability partner **cannot** be a yes man or a yes woman who agrees with everything you say in order to remain in your good graces. There are times in life when you are on the right path but want to give up. Your pusher will say, "Aht! Aht! Keep going." There will be times when you want to let bitterness into your heart. Your pusher will say, "Aht! Aht! Keep your heart pure." There will be times when you are the one who is wrong. Your pusher will say, "Aht! Aht! Go apologize and make it right." Like iron, they keep you **sharp** and **on point**. Put some "respeck" on yo' pushers.

READ TODAY: PROVERBS 27:17

JULY 30

"YOU KNOW I GOT IT. IF YOU WANNA COME GET IT. STAND NEXT TO THIS MONEY LIKE AYE AYE AYE!"
-LUDACRIS

Have you ever been in a situation where you needed some money? Maybe you had a large and important bill that was due and had absolutely no idea how you were going to pay it. Perhaps you were trying to stay in school, and you needed money for tuition but did not have it and did not know where to get it. Maybe Christmas was coming up, and you wanted to get the things on your children's wish lists, but you didn't know how you were going to swing it. Maybe you were trying to purchase a house, but at the last minute, they told you that you would need an additional $5,000 to close. Maybe you were honestly just hungry and had to choose between putting gas in your car or eating.

When a need for money arises, what is the first thing you do? Do you get back on the pole at the "skrip" club for a couple of nights? Do you make a few drug runs for somebody? Do you go to the payday loan company that offers you a few dollars in exchange for your arm, leg, kidney, and soul? Why not go to God instead? You know He's got it. Everything on this earth belongs to Him, so of course He's able to supply your monetary needs. The Bible tells us that if we want it, we've got to come get it, meaning we have to **ask**. There are some things that we don't have simply because we have never **asked** in prayer. Before you sell your soul for money, talk to the One who has it, and trust that He **will** supply. Before you know it, you'll be standing right next to that money like, "Aye! Aye! Aye!"

READ TODAY: PHILIPPIANS 4:19

JULY 31

"I LIKE THE WAY YOU DO THAT RIGHT THURR."
-CHINGY

Have you ever been in a situation where you needed some encouragement? Perhaps you never really gave your parents any trouble, made it through high school, and even went on to college. Maybe you never got into any fights and never had to be bailed out of jail. Perhaps you work to make your money instead of depending on other people to take care of you. Maybe you do a really good job at raising your children and taking care of them. Maybe you selflessly give of your time and talents in your community or local church. These kinds of people are often overlooked or taken for granted.

This message isn't about anything other than encouragement. I like the way you do that right thurr. I like how you handle business. I like how you do right by people. I like the fact that you have a good heart and that you are there for people when they need you. I like how you are consistent, dependable, and a keeper of your word. Keep going sister. Keep going brother. I know it gets hard sometimes, and I know it seems like nobody sees you or appreciates what you do. I want you to know that God sees what you do, and it means **a lot** to Him. I want you to know that your family sees the example that you set, and it means more to them than they even know yet. Please continue to sow your good seeds even when you think no one is looking. You are truly making the world a better place, and your rewards are coming.

READ TODAY: PSALMS 126:5

AUGUST 1

"NOW EVER SINCE I CAN REMEMBER, I BEEN POPPIN' MY COLLAR."
-THREE 6 MAFIA

Have you ever been in a situation where you were cool? Perhaps you were the person that everybody loved to be around. Maybe you got invited to every single party, and the party wasn't live until you arrived and got it started. Maybe you were the smart, funny, and witty one who could sing, dance, play sports, and do backflips. Maybe you have always been the fashionable one, and ever since you can remember, you've been poppin' your collar.

The pop of the collar is an action that has traditionally been reserved only for those who are cool enough to pull it off. When the cool guy pops his collar one day, everyone shows up the next day with popped collars. When the unpopular guy pops his collar, people laugh, assume it was a mistake, and help him fix it. If you have ever been fortunate enough to be one of those naturally cool people, just understand that God made you that way on **purpose**. We should use everything about ourselves to the glory of God. If God has blessed you with leadership skills, do not be ashamed to use them in a way that will help bring others closer to Him. Cool people have the ability to lead by example.

READ TODAY: MATTHEW 5:14-16

AUGUST 2

"WHO RUN IT? WHO RUN IT? WHO RUN IT? WHO RUN IT?"
-THREE 6 MAFIA

Have you ever been in a situation where you were involved with a controlling person? Perhaps it was your mama. Maybe she told you which college to attend, what to major in, and what organizations to join. Perhaps it was your own little baby who hollered at the top of their lungs unless you gave them exactly what they wanted, exactly when they wanted it, and exactly how they wanted it. Maybe it was someone you were dating or married to. Perhaps they told you how to dress, where you could go, what you could buy, and who you could be friends with.

When it comes to your life, who run it? That's a question I really want you to ask yourself. We only have one life to live, and I'm worried that some of us are being controlled by any and everything but the Holy Spirit. Are you spending your life being and doing what everybody else wants while neglecting what God wants? People have even gone as far as using church and religion as a means of control, which is actually one of the things that Jesus came to free us from. Please don't be naïve. There are people **actively** seeking to manipulate and control others simply for their own pleasure or benefit. Don't you be that person, and don't you fall victim to a situation in which you are more concerned with fulfilling someone else's desires than you are concerned about God's will for your life. Man's control leads to bondage, but God's control leads to freedom and liberty. Ask God for wisdom and strength today.

READ TODAY: GALATIANS 5:1

AUGUST 3

"I'M NOT THE TYPE TO GET INVOLVED IN LONG RELATIONSHIPS."
-THREE 6 MAFIA

Have you ever been in a situation where you were single? Perhaps all of your friends were in long-term relationships and going on bae-cations while you were trying to figure out which "wyd" text message to respond to and which ones to leave on "read." Maybe you kept being a bridesmaid or groomsmen in all of your friends' weddings, and for each one of them you are pictured with a different plus-one on your arm. Maybe during cookout season, you had one lil' friend for Memorial Day, another for Juneteenth, and yet another for Labor Day. Maybe you're just not the type to get involved in long relationships.

Maybe that's true, but maybe it's a cop out. Have you classified yourself this way because it helps you to lower your expectations and therefore prevents you from being too disappointed when a relationship doesn't work out? This goes beyond just dating relationships and applies to friendships as well. It's time to ask yourself some hard questions. Why can't I sustain a lasting and healthy relationship? Could there be a problem with how I treat people or how I communicate? Am I still dealing with the hurt of past relationships? Am I bitter? Am I a narcissist? Am I controlling? Am I too selfish to tolerate another individual for more than a short period of time? In the words of my pastor, could my "picker" be broken? Am I not a good enough judge of character to pick the right people to allow into my life? Ask God to search your heart and remove anything in there that prevents you from having healthy relationships. Ask God to teach you how to love.

READ TODAY: PSALMS 139:23-24

AUGUST 4

"YOU GET THE BAG AND FUMBLE IT. I GET THE BAG AND FLIP IT AND TUMBLE IT." -GUCCI MANE/MIGOS

Have you ever been in a situation where you had a God-given gift? Perhaps you had one of the more coveted gifts like being able to dance, sing, act, or play sports. Maybe you were a gifted cook, hair stylist, or seamstress. Perhaps you were an excellent speaker or had the ability to lead. Maybe you were good at solving problems or counseling people. Maybe you were a great teacher, preacher, or writer. Perhaps you were a good listener or knew how to encourage people who were sad. Maybe you were a visionary or a creative thinker. Perhaps you were good with hospitality, organization, or administration. There are so many gifts that I cannot name them all.

God has given each of us a gift bag. In your bag you may find one gift, two gifts, or five gifts. Unfortunately, what happens all too often is that we start looking around at other people's gift bags and feel as if what we received is inadequate compared to them. We even make excuses for our own lackluster performances in life by citing that we are not as gifted as others. By doing this, you are fumbling your bag. There are people who would take the same bag that you got, and instead of fumbling it, they can **find a way** to flip it and tumble it into something greater. When God assigned us our gifts, He knew the potential that we would have. Instead of comparing your bag to someone else's, ask God to show you strategies on how to take the bag and make the most out of it in life. Pray and ask God to show you how to flip and tumble your bag for His glory.

READ TODAY: MATTHEW 25:14-29

AUGUST 5

"IF YOU TALK BEHIND MY BACK, NO NEED TO DAP ME WHEN YOU SEE ME."
-GUCCI MANE

Have you ever been in a situation where you knew somebody was being fake with you? Perhaps they didn't know that the person they had talked to behind your back was actually a loyal friend of yours. Maybe they didn't know that the person they were texting would screenshot the whole conversation and send it to you. Perhaps you worked with a racist who talked bad about you to upper management because they didn't want to see you advance. For whatever reason, this person did not like you, but whenever they saw you, they acted like you were their best bud.

In a perfect world, everybody would be real. If you talk behind my back, there's absolutely no need to dap me, hug me, or even smile at me when you see me. However, people resort to being fake when they know that they're wrong and therefore do not have the courage of their convictions to stand upon. Sometimes fake people are so good at being fake that it's hard to tell who's who. This is where the Holy Spirit comes in handy. He helps you to discern the difference between what's fake and what's real. Everyone who is nice to you isn't your friend. Pray and ask God to show you the truth and to protect you from perpetrators.

READ TODAY: 1 JOHN 4:1

AUGUST 6

"IT AIN'T MY BUSINESS. IT AIN'T MY BEEF. I AIN'T ON NO SIDE."
-GUCCI MANE & LIL BABY

Have you ever been in a situation where somebody wanted you to take their side? Perhaps your sibling was beefing with your mom and each of them wanted you to agree that they were right, and the other was wrong. Perhaps some friends of yours were going through a nasty divorce and each of them wanted to get you on their side so that they could "win" the battle for mutual friends. Maybe it was your own children who were embattled in a bitter dispute over whose turn it was to pick what to watch or to sit in the front seat. Maybe it was your sister and brother-in-law fighting over petty things within their marriage.

There are times when you must tell people that it ain't your business, it ain't your beef, and you ain't on no side. When people come to you trying to get you to take their side, they are often trying to get you to see why what someone **else** is doing is wrong or bad. When you get in someone else's business, you can take on beef against a person who has done absolutely nothing wrong or bad to you personally. What happens when the people who were at odds kiss and make up, as they often do? You're left to deal with angst in **your** heart towards someone. That angst is based on the feelings that were encouraged by someone who has long since forgotten all about it and moved on. There may be times when the Spirit is leading you to get involved to help or protect someone, but don't jump in on your own or even just because someone invites you in. If you are unsure of what to do, pray and ask God if this business belongs to you.

READ TODAY: PROVERBS 26:17

AUGUST 7

"I CAN'T STAND THE RAIN."
-MISSY "MISDEMEANOR" ELLIOTT

    Have you ever been in a situation where it was raining? Perhaps you were driving down the freeway and out of nowhere, a tsunami seemed to hit. Maybe you had just gotten your hair done and had to tie a plastic bag around your head to protect it from the torrential rain fall. Maybe you were trying to hold an umbrella and get two young children out of their car seats and into the house because you didn't have a garage or a man. Maybe you were sitting on your balcony underneath a covering with a good book and a bottle of wine while the rain fell. Perhaps you were safe and sound at home while it was storming outside, and the sound of the rain lulled you to sleep. There are times where we can't stand the rain, yet there are other times when we can.

    Your tolerance of the rain has everything to do with your location **in** the rain. Your location in the rain determines your perspective **of** the rain. If you are exposed to the elements, rain is a problem. If you are sheltered in safety, the rain can be a comfort and a blessing. You never know exactly when you will have to experience figurative "rain" in your life. That's why it's best to remain in your proper location at all times, which is near to God. Just like in the natural, the presence of rain can be either tragic or a blessing to your life. Perspective is truly everything. You will be able to stand the rain of life much better when you view it from your safe place in God while knowing that He is only using it to nurture the things in you that need to grow.

READ TODAY: PROVERBS 18:10

AUGUST 8

"DIPPIN' ON YA NINJA HONDA WITH TANISHA AND RHONDA. WHAT?!"
-LIL KIM

Have you ever been in a situation where someone was a bad influence in your life? Perhaps you were actually a smart kid with the potential to make good grades but started hanging around people who didn't care about school at all. Perhaps you were sweet, innocent, and respectful, until you made friends with the girls who were guests on the "My Teenage Daughter is Out of Control" episode of Maury. Maybe you were in college and were focused on your major, until you started hanging around with the functioning alcoholics. Perhaps you were focused on your relationship with God, until you got all boo'd up with someone who wasn't.

Bingo! Yup, let's go there. Have you allowed your romantic relationship to make you get on your spiritual motorcycle and "dip" away from God with somebody else? Before you met Tanisha and/or Rhonda, were you praying more consistently? Before you met Terrence and/or Robert, were you reading your Bible more than you do now? When you were single, were you going to church every Sunday and actively serving in ministry? What?! We have to be much more intentional about setting boundaries around our spiritual walk and making it non-negotiable. We should want to link up with people who will challenge us to go farther spiritually, and not those who will cause us to shrink back and dip away from God. Let's be honest, sometimes it's not even the other person being a bad influence. Sometimes it's just **you** forgetting that God can love you better than he or she can.

READ TODAY: MATTHEW 6:33

AUGUST 9

"IT'S LIKE THE SUMMER'S A NATURAL APHRODISIAC." -THE FRESH PRINCE

Have you ever been in a situation where it was hot? Perhaps you live in the south or some place where the summer is ridiculously warm. Maybe when you step outside, it feels so hot and humid that you could have sworn somebody was literally attempting to choke you. Perhaps when you got in your car you burned yourself on the leather seats. Maybe your power bill was so high that you started fussing at your kids because they kept opening your door and letting air out of the house.

When summer comes around, it is very important to remain hydrated because the thirst is real. Pause. I'm really proud of that double entendre. I see what I did there. Play. When summer comes around, people start getting naked. Summertime brings about less clothes, less fabric, more skin, and more thirst. Sun's out...buns out. Sky's out...thighs out. While summer may be a natural aphrodisiac, it's no excuse for you to abandon your self-control. If you have two functioning eyes, you may see some things that are tempting to your flesh, but if you are prepared, you will be less likely to get caught off guard. Lust is one of the oldest tricks in Satan's book. Summer is known as the time to take things off, but I challenge you to put something **on**. Put on the whole armor of God so that you will be able to withstand the heat today.

READ TODAY: EPHESIANS 6:11-18

AUGUST 10

"CUZ I'M NAUGHTY BY NATURE, NOT CUZ I HATE CHA."
-NAUGHTY BY NATURE

Have you ever been in a situation where you were naughty? Perhaps you went somewhere that you knew you weren't supposed to be going. Maybe you went there with someone who you knew you weren't supposed to be going with. Perhaps when you got there you did something that you knew you weren't supposed be doing. Maybe when you got back home you shook your head and asked yourself, "Why did I even do that? I knew better."

The Apostle Paul, one of our OGs, struggled with the same issues. He said that all of the good stuff that he wanted to do, somehow, he didn't do. Yet all of the ratchet things that he really **didn't** want to do, somehow, he kept on doing. He concluded that his mess ups weren't because he hated God. He truly loved God but realized that his flesh was simply naughty **by nature**. Many of us can relate to this. Our human nature is constantly at war with our spirit. The Bible tells us that if we walk in the Spirit, however, that we won't fulfill the lusts of our flesh. Walking in the Spirit means that we are in **constant** and **intentional** communication with the Holy Spirit **daily**. Doing this helps us to be consciously aware of how the things we do naturally will translate spiritually. For example, when you walk in the Spirit, it's not just sleeping with someone. It's opening yourself up to lust. It's an unhealthy and potentially demonic connection that may be hard to break. It's opening yourself up to the consequences of sin and disobedience. See how it hits differently in the Spirit? Let's walk in the Spirit today and every day.

READ TODAY: GALATIANS 5:16-26

AUGUST 11

"HERE WE GO NOW. HOLLER IF YOU HEAR ME THO'. COME AND FEEL ME FLOW." -NAUGHTY BY NATURE

Have you ever been in a situation where God used you to encourage someone? Perhaps you were a single mom whose kids were older, and you saw a young single mom with babies who was struggling to make it. Maybe you stopped to tell her that she was doing a good job, not to give up, and that things would get better. Perhaps you were a divorced dad and saw another dad who was depressed and going through it. You stopped to tell him that it wasn't the end of the world, that God was able to bring restoration to his life, and that things would get better. Maybe you were a successful business owner and saw a discouraged young entrepreneur. Maybe you stopped to tell them how you were just like them once, how you refused to give up, and how God brought you through.

If you've ever been in one of these situations, you probably already know that sometimes the words come out of nowhere. You're just minding your own business and suddenly the Holy Spirit begins to flow through you. When you allow God to use you in this way, it's very obvious that you're not doing it on your own. You never know what your flow might mean to somebody else. They may not holler. They may even give you a blank stare, but they certainly do hear you tho'. The words you speak could be the difference between life and death for somebody. If you feel the Holy Spirit tugging at you to speak, do not ignore that. You may not even know what words you're getting ready to say, but if you would just be obedient and open your mouth, you will feel His power flowing through you like a current.

READ TODAY: ISAIAH 6:8

AUGUST 12

"THE LAST P? WELL...THAT'S NOT THAT SIMPLE." -NAUGTY BY NATURE

Have you ever been in a situation where you were easily flattered? Perhaps you weren't used to getting attention from boys, so the first boy who told you that you were pretty had you hook, line, and sinker. Maybe you weren't used to getting attention from girls, so the first girl that batted an eye at you had you completely wrapped around her finger. Maybe you weren't used to getting attention from men, so even though he had no job, no car, no teeth, and lived with his mama, he had you at "Good Morning Queen." Perhaps you weren't used to getting attention from women, so even though she had multiple personalities, clearly wasn't over her ex, and only called you when she wanted something, you continued to let her use you because she would put heart-eye emojis under all of your pictures.

There was a word that the older generation would use to describe women for whom it didn't take much. They would call you "easy." Easy is not an adjective limited only to women, however. Brothers, you can be easy too. Allowing someone to get to that "last P," should not be so simple. Ladies and gentleman, you both know which "Ps" I'm referring to. Now according to the Word, the wedding bed is undefiled. A person who **values** you enough to date you, respect you, be loyal to you, and marry you? TURN UP I say! CUT UP I say! Make it **extra** easy for your husband or for your wife to get that last P. Okay cool, I'm glad we've established that. Now...who are all these other people getting it, and why are you making it so simple for them? If **you** don't understand your own value, how will they?

READ TODAY: PROVERBS 14:15

AUGUST 13

"YOU DOWN WITH O.P.P?"
-NAUGHTY BY NATURE

Have you ever been in a situation where you didn't really know what you were talking about? Maybe you were like me. I was six years old when the song O.P.P. came out, and I had no idea what it really meant. I was a good 34 years old when I found out that it did NOT stand for "Other People's Property." For reference, I'm only 35 right now as I'm writing this. I was shook. I had no business singing this song in elementary school, and my recent revelation caused me to side-eye my own parents' supervision skills. In their defense, they referenced it on *Sister Act 2* for crying out loud! I digress. The point is, I was declaring with my mouth that I was down with something, but I had no idea what I was talking about because I lacked knowledge.

Alright so boom. This page is about knowledge. We all know that knowledge is powerful, and I know y'all can't say this, so I will say it for all of us. (If they come for me, y'all gotta promise to ride for ya girl okay?) Church folks can be some of **the** most ignorant people on the planet. Whew chile, I got that off my chest! Listen to me my beloved church people (don't trip, I'm church people too, on Crip okay?), there is nothing wrong with gaining knowledge on a subject **before** we speak on it. There's nothing wrong with saying, "I don't know, but I can try to find out." Social media is overrun with church people spouting completely uninformed **opinions** that have nothing to do with God's Word, and we're all out here looking crazy for it. I've got one more word of caution before you go. The Bible also teaches us that knowledge puffs people up. Be careful not to get your knowledge and get the big head. Know what you're talking about, but always express it in love and humility.

READ TODAY: HOSEA 4:6

AUGUST 14

"COME ON RIDE THAT TRAIN."
-QUAD CITY DJs

Have you ever been in a situation where you saw somebody's kids cutting the fool? Were they your kids? Oh wait, that's too personal. Perhaps you were in the store and saw an eight-year-old boy throwing a temper tantrum and telling his mom that he hates her. Maybe you were at the doctor's office and you saw a three-year-old girl running around the waiting room with Cheeto fingers, drinking a mountain dew, and breaking things. If you are a member of the African diaspora, you probably shook your head and said these three words to yourself: No Home Training.

One of the most helpful things you can do in your lifetime is to raise your child (or a child in your life) in such a way that they can be a healthy, productive adult. The Bible tells us to train up a child in the way that he should go. We cannot take a hands-off approach with our children because Satan is sneaky, and I promise he is **not** taking a hands-off approach in attacking even a child. We must train them on more than just good behavior. We assume so often that because a child is well-behaved, that they are good. Listen, some kids are simply good at balance. They can be on the "A" honor roll and doing more drugs and having more sex than Rick James. We also have to train them on how to survive spiritually. Teach them how to pray and how to fast. Show them how to live a Godly life, but do it with your own non-hypocritical example. Practice what you preach, so they can come on and ride that training train to success.

READ TODAY: PROVERBS 22:6

AUGUST 15

"GOT ME SOME SEAGRAM'S GIN. EVERYBODY GOT THEY CUPS, BUT THEY AIN'T CHIPPED IN." -SNOOP DOGG

Have you ever been in a situation where you worked hard to get what you wanted? Perhaps you were a kid who worked at MickeyD's until you finally had enough money to buy yourself a little car. It seemed like as soon as you got your car, everybody wanted a ride somewhere. Maybe you worked hard to get good credit, save up a down payment, and buy yourself a house. It seemed like as soon as you got your new house, everybody needed a place to crash for a while until they got back on their feet. Maybe, like today's psalmist, you walked all the way to the likka sto and spent your hard-earned money for some gin and/or juice. By the time you got back to the spot, everybody had their cups out ready to receive but had not chipped in on the drank acquisition process.

The Bible is very clear in telling us that we should be givers. It's a blessing to be in a position to do so. If you are a believer who doesn't have a heart to give to others and help those in need, you may have some serious soul searching to do. If you've lived on planet earth, however, you have probably discovered that there are those who will take advantage of your kind spirit and attempt to use you until there is nothing left to use. How do you draw the line? Where is the balance between helping someone versus enabling them to be a user? You guessed it. One of the things that the Holy Spirit can do is grant you discernment on when, where, and what to give. Pro Tip: Never give out of guilt or because someone has manipulated you into it. A cheerful giver is one who obeys the Holy Spirit's leading.

READ TODAY: 2 CORINTHIANS 9:7-8

AUGUST 16

"JUMP ON IT! JUMP ON IT! JUMP ON IT!"
-THE SUGARHILL GANG

Have you ever been in a situation where you kept putting something off? Perhaps you know you need to go make peace with someone, but you haven't done it. Maybe you are supposed to be losing weight and getting fine and healthy, but you always tell yourself that you'll start tomorrow. Perhaps the Holy Spirit is telling you that you need to take some time to rest, and here you are taking care of everyone but yourself. Perhaps you need to break up with someone who you aren't supposed to be with, but you haven't gotten around to telling them.

Listen, I need you to jump on it! If you know there is something that you are supposed to be doing that you are not doing, peace will be hard to come by. Some wonder why they have trouble sleeping at night, but they haven't considered that leaving things undone can affect your ability to rest your mind. You may not know every single step in detail, but if you keep trying to analyze the situation before you move, the window could pass you by. I once knew a man who didn't know his father for most of his life. He became connected with him as an adult, and they had sporadic communication here and there. They each made a few attempts to reach out to each other, but neither going above nor beyond to try. The father died suddenly, and the son, although he didn't know his dad well, was hit with a surprising amount of grief. He just assumed that he had more time to get to know his father. What is something you need to jump on ASAP?

READ TODAY: PROVERBS 27:1

AUGUST 17

"BLAME IT ON THE ALCOHOL."
-JAMIE FOXX

     Have you ever been in a situation where you had too much to drink? Perhaps you began to get super sentimental and wanted to hug everybody all of a sudden. Maybe you began to cry because your homie Rico got smoked 13 years ago, and he didn't deserve it. Maybe you thought it was a great time to start telling people how you **really** feel about everything and everyone. Maybe you thought it was the perfect time to have a one-night stand and go half on a baby with someone you locked eyes with in the club. Perhaps you drunk texted your ex about how much you missed the good times and wanted to work things out.

     Blame it on the alcohol, right? Well that's one way to look at it. You can go about blaming things on the alcohol, but that's not really helpful when you realize that the seeds that you sow when you are drunk have to be harvested when you are sober. I want you to ask yourself the hard questions. Why does getting drunk seem more appealing than my sober mind? Is there a problem with my sober mind that explains why I can't enjoy myself just the same with it? Are there things about myself that I need to change so that being drunk isn't so appealing to me? Blaming things on alcohol gets old.

READ TODAY: 1 PETER 5:8

AUGUST 18

"BACK IN THE DAYS, WHEN I WAS YOUNG... I'M NOT A KID ANYMORE."
-AHMAD

Have you ever been in a situation where you had to grow up? Perhaps you had a parent to leave or pass away at an early age. Maybe you had to grow up quickly to take on the role that they left vacant in your family. Maybe you became a parent yourself, and it caused you to have to grow up. Having a baby is one of the quickest ways to realize that life isn't all about you anymore. It's hard, and dare I say impossible, to be selfish and a good parent at the same time. Maybe it was your own ambitions that caused you to grow up and get your stuff together. If you wanted to be a doctor, lawyer, stand-out athlete, or successful entrepreneur, you knew it was time-out for child's play.

The interesting thing about growth is that it happens at different times for different people. Age is not even the best indicator of growth. That's why some of the people you used to kick it with may not understand yet why you have changed. Their record is stuck on what you used to do back in the days when you were young, but they can't grasp the fact that you're not a kid anymore. The awesome thing about growth is that it is a continual process all throughout life. You never want to get to the point where you feel like you know too much to be taught something new. The Holy Spirit is the best teacher known to man because He teaches us how to put away childish things.

READ TODAY: 1 CORINTHIANS 13:11

AUGUST 19

"BUT SOME DAYS, I SIT AND WISH I WAS A KID AGAIN."
-AHMAD

    Have you ever been in a situation where you wished you could start over? Maybe you played around in school and now you feel like your options are too limited in life. If you could just go back, you'd take it more seriously and make better grades. Maybe you got into drugs which caused you to lose some good relationships and gave you a criminal record. If you could go back, you'd listen to the *D.A.R.E.* officer, and just say "no." Perhaps you treated a really great person badly and lost them. If you could go back, you'd do right by them next time. Maybe you had a baby with someone who is extremely hard to deal with. If you could go back, you would've stayed home and boiled rice one grain at a time and waited for the person you were actually meant to be with.

    How dope would it be if we could go back and tell our younger selves what pitfalls to avoid? It's understandable to sit and wish that you were a kid again, but that's honestly just a waste of time. You can't hop back into your mother's womb, but you can be born again. When you find new life in Christ, it helps you to find new meaning in all of your life's experiences. There is absolutely nothing you've done that God cannot use to make you better, faster, wiser, and stronger. The wisdom and knowledge that you have gained in less-than-ideal situations can be used to impact the life of another person who is going through something similar. This is the key to living your life without regrets.

READ TODAY: JOHN 3:3-7

AUGUST 20

"I WISH I WAS A LITTLE BIT TALLER."
-SKEE-LO

Have you ever been in a situation where you wished you had more than what you did? Perhaps you wished you could grow longer hair. Despite your best efforts and those expensive hair growth vitamins, your short hair wouldn't budge. Maybe you really wanted a luxurious beard, but even with the best beard oils, your struggle beard refused to connect. Perhaps you wanted a bigger booty. You did all the squats, but it seemed as if "flat" was just in your genes and in your jeans. Maybe you wished you were a little bit taller, but the growth spurt that they promised never came.

As much as you desire physical improvement and growth, do you have that same energy when it comes to spiritual growth? Are we spending time worrying about looking better and getting stronger physically while weak and dying inwardly? You may not be able to grow any taller physically, but every day you can get a little taller spiritually if you desire to do so. You are already off to a good start by spending time in daily devotion, by reading the scriptures, and by maintaining a solid prayer life. Your booty or beard may or may not grow, but your spiritual fruit certainly will. The Bible tells us that the fruit of the Spirit is love, joy, peace, patience, gentleness, goodness, faith, meekness, and self-control. These are the things that will truly make you taller.

READ TODAY: 2 CORINTHIANS 4:16

AUGUST 21

"POP, LOCK, AND DROP IT."
-HUEY

Have you ever been in a situation where you felt guilty for something you did? Perhaps you lied to your sweet old grandmother, and it's just eating you up inside. Maybe you stole some money from the church collection plate, and now you can't sleep at night. Perhaps you stole your poor children's birthday money and gambled it away in Atlantic City. Maybe you were the best man in a wedding party, but you had been messing around with the bride behind the groom's back. Goodness, it sounds like you were really wildin' out there for a minute huh?

It's very common to experience guilt over some of the foul things that we've done. The Holy Spirit actually uses something called "conviction" to help us know when we are wrong and needing to get back on the right track. Some like to say that conviction is a guilty conscious. This is a bit of an oversimplification. Conviction by the Holy Spirit not only makes you aware of where you went wrong, but it also guides you into a greater awareness of the **truth**. Satan is the one who uses guilt, shame, and condemnation in an attempt to freeze your forward motion. God is different. When it comes to your sin, He knows how to pop, lock and drop it. To **pop** something is to "burst its bubble" and render it powerless. Sin has no more power over us because Jesus burst that bubble with His work at Calvary. When we repent and ask God to forgive our sins, He also forgets them and **locks** them away for good. So now that your sins have been popped and locked, the only one still hanging on to the guilt and shame is you. Go ahead and **drop** it.

READ TODAY: ROMANS 8:1-2

AUGUST 22

"DON'T SAVE HER. SHE DON'T WANNA BE SAVED." -PROJECT PAT

Have you ever been in a situation where somebody you cared about wouldn't listen to you? Maybe your daddy was diabetic and stubborn. You kept telling him to chill out on the honey buns, but he wouldn't listen. Maybe your homegirl was in a relationship with a man who was still trying to slide in your DMs too. You kept telling her that he was no good, but she always explained it away as "men gone be men" or "he just likes to flirt," and wouldn't listen. Maybe your homeboy got together with a girl who was a known gold digger. You tried to tell him, but he was too whipped to hear anything you had to say.

What do you do when you see someone you love going down a destructive path? What do you do when someone who needs to be saved doesn't want to be saved? What do you do when someone has already determined that if loving _____ is wrong, they don't want to be right? If you really care for someone, you don't give up so easily. Of course the first thing you want to do is pray for that person. If the Holy Spirit leads you to do so, you should attempt to speak the truth to them in a loving way. If they don't want to hear you at first, don't look down upon them, and don't incessantly nag at them. Continue in prayer and ask God to open their eyes to see the truth. You may have to hit a fast or two or four. Speak only when guided by the Holy Spirit. Lastly, continue to live your life as an example, because some people have to be **shown** what to do instead of being told.

READ TODAY: COLOSSIANS 4:2-6

AUGUST 23

"LOVE LETTER CAME THROUGH THE MAIL. IT SAID, 'I MISS YOU.' I RIPPED IT UP AND FLUSHED IT WITH THE TISSUE."
-LIL BABY

Have you ever been in a situation where you were hustling backwards? Perhaps it was Christmas Day and an ex who you hadn't spoken to in years was feeling jolly enough to send you a "Merry Christmas" text message. In the midst of so much Christmas cheer, maybe you responded to the message and y'all have been talking every day since. No, your ex hadn't changed, and no they didn't apologize for the way they treated you. No, they hadn't grown or matured. Perhaps you were simply tired of being the single cousin at all of the family gatherings, and you figured that having somebody was better than having nobody. Maybe that realization was coupled with your willingness to forget just how toxic that relationship was to your life and just how much work you had to do on yourself to recover from it.

It's rare that someone will actually send you a letter in the mail these days, but a well-placed "I miss you" text message can certainly do the same damage. Forgiveness is good. Forgiveness is right. Forgiveness is required. To repeat an old mistake, however, is not good, not right, and not required. Take your past mistakes and use them to your advantage. Don't let your loneliness or the fact that you miss someone or something, cause you to forget what you **know** and have **learned**. Be sober, be vigilant, and just don't play yourself like that. It's okay to flush it with the tissue and/or leave it on "read." Take a look at today's scripture and let it bless your life. Good talk.

READ TODAY: PROVERBS 26:11

AUGUST 24

"DRIP TOO HARD, DON'T STAND TOO CLOSE."
-LIL BABY

Have you ever been in a situation that changed once you showed up? Perhaps your co-workers were gossiping in the breakroom, but once you sat down, they got quiet. Maybe you walked past some winos, and when they saw you, they straightened up long enough for you to pass by. Perhaps Negative Nancy and Dwight Downer even perked up and cracked a smile when you greeted them. Maybe as soon as **you** stepped outside, it stopped raining and the sun came out.

It's the anointing of God on your life. There is a proverbial oil that God has anointed you with, and it is powerful enough to break chains and destroy yokes. When your oil drips hard, anyone or anything that gets too close is going to have to straighten up. Even people who aren't necessarily spiritual can recognize the oil on your life. Demons can hardly even demon when you're around, because they recognize that God's power is with you. This is why you see some people freeze up when you come around. Those demonic spirits are real, and they figure if they can just be still and keep quiet, maybe you'll leave without rebuking them and casting them out...withcho ol' powerful and anointed self. Don't feel bad when you walk into a room and everything changes. Pray and ask God to show you how you can use your anointing to be a blessing to someone who needs it.

READ TODAY: PSALMS 23:5-6

AUGUST 25

"I DON'T CARE WHERE I GO, LONG AS I GET PAID."
-LIL BABY

Have you ever been in a situation where all you cared about was getting paid? Perhaps you accepted a terrible job all the way out in East Djibouti because they offered you a good salary. Maybe you were subcontracted to run a suspicious package to a suspicious person in a dangerous neighborhood, but you didn't care where you went as long as you got paid. Perhaps you went to Junior's bachelor party to dance and that's it. It looked sketchy upon arrival, but you pressed on anyway because you were getting paid.

It's an unfortunate fact of life that making money will require many of us to do some things that we don't actually prefer to do. Adulting is apparently synonymous with having bills to pay. *Insert massive eye roll here.* Unfortunately, many people have placed themselves in compromising and even hazardous situations for no other reason than to make money. People have gone places that they shouldn't have gone just to make a dollar. The first thing you need to know is that anything you do **only** because of the money, has the potential to make you miserable over time and distract you from your true purpose. Secondly, there is no dollar amount that is worth your soul or your peace. I'm not just talking about running drugs or turning tricks. I'm talking about that job offer too. Did you pray and ask God whether that open door was for you? Before you agree to do anything or go anywhere just to get paid, make sure you have the green light from your actual Provider. He is the One who gives us the power to get wealth anyway.

READ TODAY: PSALMS 37:23

AUGUST 26

"EVERY OTHER NIGHT ANOTHER MOVIE GETTING MADE."
-LIL BABY

    Have you ever been in a situation where you had to deal with someone who was overly dramatic? Maybe it was your husband who caught a little cold. He turned into a complete invalid on the brink of death who had to be waited on hand and foot. Whenever you get a cold though, you are forced to power through it and continue to perform at the highest levels as a wife, mother, and career woman. Maybe it was your sister who was the drama queen. Perhaps she called you crying and completely inconsolable when she discovered that her new love interest prefers his grits with sugar instead of butter, salt, and cheese. How could she build a future with a man who is clearly a psychopath? When you are dealing with an overly dramatic individual it seems as if they are filming a movie or soap opera almost every other night of their lives. If you don't know anyone fitting the description of this paragraph, tag...you're it.

    If you are in any field that deals with patient care, you have no doubt learned that there is a huge difference between pain and suffering. Pain is what it is. Suffering is based on the individual's **interpretation** of what they are going through. On a scale of 1 to 10, Karen and I could both have the exact same pain level of 5. Dealing with the exact same pain, however, I could suffer at a level 2 while Karen dramatically suffers at level 2,000. The Bible tells us that we don't have to glorify our suffering, because what we are going through now is minor compared to the glory that is on its way. Pain is inevitable in life, but if we continue to lift our eyes to the hills, we can find help for our suffering.

READ TODAY: ROMANS 8:18

AUGUST 27

"MAMA TOLD ME NOT TO SELL WORK."
-MIGOS

Have you ever been in a situation where you were disobedient? Perhaps you started out at a young age by touching the hot stove that your parents told you not to touch. Maybe your teacher had to separate you from your friends because you wouldn't stop talking. She didn't realize that you were friends with everybody in the class, and no matter where you sat the results would be the same. Perhaps your mama told you not to sell "work" aka drugs, yet you skipped school to stand on the corner in a long white tee.

Although disobedience always seems free in the moment, it usually comes with a price. When we are disobedient to God, we are faced with the resulting consequences. Many of the amazing promises that we find in scripture are actually linked to an act of obedience from us. If you ever find yourself in a situation where you need God to come through for you (which is every day), one of the first things you will want to check, is how you are doing with your obedience. In what areas of life are you currently disobeying? Check everything, no matter how big or how small it may seem. It could be as simple as apologizing to someone or as difficult as refusing to buss it open when you've gotten so used to getting some. Obedience often feels scary because we are worried about what or who we may lose by listening to God. Spoiler alert! Anything you lose by obeying Him...needed to be lost.

READ TODAY: LUKE 6:46

AUGUST 28

"OH MY GOSH, BACK AT IT AGAIN."
-YELLA BEEZY

Have you ever been in a situation where you looked just like your family? Perhaps you and your whole family had that same hook head. It's so characteristic that even strangers know who your folks are without asking. "I know you must be a Johnson boy. You got that Johnson hook head." Maybe your family is like my family. Apparently, we all have the same "Croom chin." When a couple has a new baby, it's always interesting to see which parent's genes won the fight for dominance. The physical features that get passed down are obvious, but we get way more from our folks than we actually realize.

What is your family's legacy? When a family expands, Satan looks at the new generation and exclaims "Oh my gosh, back at it again!" Now the "it" is highly variable. Is Satan **excited** to see that we are back at poverty, alcoholism, divorce, and poor health choices? Or is he **frightened** to see that we are back at faith in God, wealth building, strong marriages, good health, and long life? Even if the legacy you were left to inherit was less than ideal, please understand that you can break any cycle. You don't have to be back at it again if it was whack. You can establish a new legacy for your children, grandchildren, and beyond. One of the most important legacies you can pass down is faith in God. What legacy would you like to see continue, and how can you be intentional about winning the fight for generational dominance?

READ TODAY: JOSHUA 24:15

AUGUST 29

"COOK IT UP RIGHT. THEY DONE GAVE ME THE RECIPE." -MONEYBAGG YO

Have you ever been in a situation where you didn't have any instructions? Perhaps you had a baby, and even though you read all the books and attended a parenting class, there was nothing that could have prepared you for the brutal underground hazing process known as a newborn baby. Maybe you bought a bookshelf from eBay that didn't come with directions for assembly. Sure, it may be leaning to the left, but hey it holds books, right? Perhaps your grandmother passed on before you could get her recipe for perfect fried chicken. You didn't know exactly how much seasoning to use, so you just kept sprinkling until the ancestors whispered "that's enough child" in your ear. When we don't have the proper instructions, it can be a real toss up. Sometimes it works out, and sometimes it doesn't.

When it comes to the gourmet dish of life, we **can** cook it up right because God done gave us the recipe. God's Word should be the recipe book of our lives. We should keep it in our hearts, and always refer back to it with every step we take. Some recipes are more involved, and even though you may have cooked that dish dozens of times, you know not to rely on your mind to get you through it. You refer back to the recipe **over and over** while cooking, to make sure that you're not leaving out any important steps. This is how we should be with the Word of God. We should keep referring back to it, no matter how much we think we already know. God's Word is not only written, but it is also spoken to us through the Holy Spirit. God gives us the recipe we need as we study the scriptures and listen for His voice.

READ TODAY: 2 TIMOTHY 3:16-17

AUGUST 30

"LEVEL UP."
-CIARA

    Have you ever been in a situation where you weren't doing your best? Maybe you were a beautiful and talented pop star who got tied up in a relationship with a popular rap star playboy. Maybe the two of you were the talk of the town and even got engaged with a 15-Carat diamond ring. Perhaps you later had a baby with the same man but called off the engagement after allegations of cheating. Maybe he dragged you through the mud on Twitter, and the two of you fought a very nasty, very public legal battle over child custody and defamation of character. Perhaps you then met a successful NFL player who shared your love for life and your faith. The same man treated you like a queen and was willing to love your son as his own. Maybe he then proposed to you with a ring of 16 Carats, and you realized that you had gotten onto the elevator of life and gone up several levels from the floor that you once thought was the top.

    We should all challenge ourselves to examine our current situations to determine whether the level we find ourselves on is truly the top. When I was in school, my parents would always tell me that they didn't care what grade I made as long as I had done **my** best. If I made a "B" and did my best, they would be **more** proud than if I had made an "A" but stopped short of doing what I knew I could have done. Following that model, I became the first Black valedictorian of my high school. In short, we should strive for mastery in every area. Settling doesn't always feel like settling in the moment though, so let us pray and ask God to show us where we need to mentally level up.

READ TODAY: 1 CORINTHIANS 9:24-25

AUGUST 31

"THEY TELL ME I'M ON TIME EVEN WHEN I'M LATE. EVEN IF IT'S A LIE, THEY SAY EVERYTHING IS GREAT."
-BIG SEAN

Have you ever been in a situation where no one told you the truth? Maybe you were the person who shows up late to everything, and no one ever told you how rude you were actually being. Perhaps you put on some extra weight that was (let's be honest) not flattering to your personal appearance. Your friends told you that you were just thick (a lie) and looked like a snack (another lie). Maybe you got engaged to someone that everybody knew was bad for you. When you announced the engagement, everyone "liked" the post and congratulated you with heart-eye emojis and praise hands and such. They even showed up to the wedding and told you that everything was great.

When people lie to you, they aren't doing you any favors. It may seem harmless, but what happens when the pigs come home to roost? I'm pretty sure I butchered that farm analogy, but y'all know what I'm trying to say. What happens when you lose your job because you never learned how to be on time? What happens when the extra weight you put on causes diabetes? What happens when that nonsensical marriage ends in divorce? If **everyone** around you feels the need to lie or tiptoe around your feelings, the problem may be with you. Do you know how to listen to wisdom? Do you take everything personally and cut anyone out of your life who doesn't agree with you? The Bible tells us multiple times that those of us who have ears to hear, should use them to hear the truth.

READ TODAY: MATTHEW 13:9

SEPTEMBER 1

"BLESSINGS ON BLESSINGS ON BLESSINGS."
-BIG SEAN

Have you ever been in a situation where you were blessed? Maybe you received the infamous "unexpected check" in the mail just when you had a bill that was due. Perhaps you got an e-mail stating that you had gotten the job that you interviewed for last month. Maybe you got home and your significant other cooked dinner and rubbed your feet "just because." Maybe your team (The Alabama Crimson Tide in my case) won the National Championship game, and you're feeling on top of the world. Maybe you played the lottery and your numbers hit, you little heathen. Ahem...if anyone is running the state line, I need some numbers played. *cough, cough* Just kidding Pastor Bryant, if you're reading this sir. If someone were to ask you how you were doing, perhaps you'd say that you were blessed.

Some days it seems like everywhere you turn there are blessings on blessings on blessings. Why is it, however, that we only feel blessed when things are going our way? Does this mean we are cursed when things don't go how we want them to go? There was a lady in the Bible named Mary. Sis had just found out that she was pregnant with a baby that didn't belong to her fiancé. She was scared and had absolutely no idea how her man would respond to the sketchy scenario, but somehow she was supposed to believe that she was blessed and highly favored. The moral of the story is that even when you don't **feel** blessed, God is still lining the difficult pieces up to work in your favor.

READ TODAY: LUKE 1:28

SEPTEMBER 2

"LOOK AT MY LIFE MAN. THAT'S LESSONS ON LESSONS ON LESSONS." -BIG SEAN

Have you ever been in a situation where you spit some serious knowledge that changed someone else's life? Perhaps you saw a young man getting into the drug game, and you were able to show him where the bullet had grazed you and talk to him about the 10 years you spent in prison. Maybe you saw a young single mother depressed and struggling to make it. Perhaps as a college graduate and successful businesswoman, you were able to share with her how you started out as a teenage mother with very little support. Maybe you met someone who was overweight and had recently been diagnosed with diabetes. Perhaps you were able to share with them how you lost weight, got your health together, and got off the meds.

Sometimes your own life will be the greatest lesson that **you** can teach. Many of us have learned life's lessons the hard way, but if we can turn around and teach those same lessons to someone else, we can give them the upper hand. If you look at your life, you will see lessons on lessons on lessons. Too often, we are ashamed of the things that we've been through, and we sweep our experiences under the rug. The lessons get swept away right along with them. How tragic is that? We like to look like we've always had it together, but a person who hopes to quit smoking isn't trying to listen to someone who has never picked up a cigarette. Don't hide behind that mask of perfection. Someone out there needs to look at your life and get those lessons. When you become strong, strengthen someone else.

READ TODAY: LUKE 22:31-32

SEPTEMBER 3

"HEARD YOU GOT A NEW MAN. I SEE YOU TAKING A PIC. THEN YOU POST IT UP THINKING THAT IT'S MAKING ME SICK."
-BIG SEAN

Have you ever been in a situation where you knew somebody was trying to get a rise out of you? Perhaps it was some miserable soul who decided to troll you in a comment section. Maybe it was your own mother who knew exactly which buttons to press to get under your skin. Maybe it was an ex of yours who had moved on to their next and was hoping to make you jealous by posting up pictures with their new boo. Some people would love nothing more than to see you unhinged and your blood pressure elevated.

For the love of all that is holy and righteous, I beg you not to feed the trolls! The best way to respond to people who are trying to bother you, is to simply remain unbothered. How do you remain unbothered when someone is clearly poking at you? You have to build a protective fortress around your peace. Peace is one of the most valuable things that we will ever obtain, and it should be protected like the Fabergé Egg that it is. The Bible calls it "holding" your peace. We hold on to and protect our peace by allowing God to fight all of our battles for us, even the petty ones. When peace is lost, it is replaced by anxiety and stress. These are things that will make you sick not just mentally, but physically as well. That's why proving your point to some instigator, is not even worth half of an iota of your peace. They love to see that you care enough to be bothered. Not today, Satan.

READ TODAY: EXODUS 14:14

SEPTEMBER 4

"I AIN'T WORRIED, DOING ME TONIGHT. A LITTLE SWEAT AIN'T NEVER HURT NOBODY." -BEYONCÉ

Have you ever been in a situation where you had to do what was best for yourself? Maybe it was Friday night, and you were supposed to go to a friend's birthday dinner. Honestly, this was more like a friend of a friend or a "F.O.A.F." if you will. After a long day at work, you sat down on your bed, turned on that *Dateline,* and it was a wrap. You knew you were in for the night. Maybe one of your friends or relatives asked you to watch their kids so that they could go out for the night. You wanted to help, but you were beginning to feel under the weather, and honestly those kids don't have good home training. Sometimes you just have to look out for yourself.

Some of us are really sweet people, and we just hate disappointing others. Lean in close to the book, because I want you to hear me whispering this to you in the Spirit. Are you ready? You're doing way too much to keep from disappointing people who don't mind disappointing you. Whew! There are some nights when you just aren't good to go, and you've got to do **you**. Will you feel a little nervous letting someone know that you cannot or will not? Sure, but a little sweat ain't never hurt nobody. Will they potentially be inconvenienced or have to rearrange their plans? Yes, but a little sweat ain't never hurt nobody. What hurts is running yourself into the ground, stressing yourself out, and making yourself sick trying to be a people-pleaser or letting people use you without sticking up for yourself. Do your best not to overcommit to things in the first place. You don't want to be a selfish, unreliable, and habitual flaker. You just need to exercise wisdom.

READ TODAY: 2 TIMOTHY 1:7

SEPTEMBER 5

"I HAD IT UP TO HERE. I GOT NO CEILINGS TO GO." -BIG SEAN

Have you ever been in a situation where you felt like you just couldn't take it anymore? Perhaps you were unemployed, and it seemed like you couldn't find a job to save your life. The bills were piling up, and it felt like everything was caving in on you. Maybe you had to face some health challenges where you had to deal with a lot of physical pain. You were in and out of the hospital so much and felt you couldn't take another nurse poking needles into your arm. Maybe you had been in a toxic relationship that left you feeling empty, alone, and worthless once it was over. Perhaps you cried each night when you thought of how that person was no longer going to be in your life.

Sometimes when people have had it "up to here" and feel as if they can't take it anymore, they consider suicide. When I was younger, we had a relative who committed suicide. He had just purchased a new home for his family, but apparently lost his job right after that. My dad was saddened by the news and said that he had chosen a permanent solution for a temporary problem. I just want you to know that although it seems as if you've had it "up to here" and have no more ceilings to go, God is able to raise the roof of your life and relieve any pressure that you face. No matter how big it may seem in that moment, it's **not** bigger than God. Satan wants you to elevate your problems above God and feel as if you have to end it all. Remember Satan's number one goal is to steal, kill, and destroy your life. God created trained professionals both secularly and spiritually. Some counselors even do double-duty as both. If you are dealing with the urge to give up on life, don't. There is help, but you must seek it out.

READ TODAY: PSALMS 13:1-6

SEPTEMBER 6

"GRIND TILL THE SUN SET, TILL MY GRANDSON SET."
-BIG SEAN

Have you ever been in a situation where had just enough to make it? Perhaps your car was telling you that you had about 35 miles worth of gas left until empty. You didn't have any gas money, but you were only 34 miles away from home. You had just enough to make it. Perhaps you needed to make an 80 on the final exam in order to pass the class and avoid failing out of school. You made an 80.5, and it gave you just enough to make it. Maybe you were down to your last two dollars. You planned to use one for your bus fare and the other you planned to use for a nearby jukebox. You had just enough to make it.

Almost all of us have been in a situation where we made it by the hair of our chinny chin chin. When it comes to taking care of our children, however, we can't do that. It's definitely not okay to have just enough for ourselves. What's worse is when a parent passes away and the children are not left with a blessing, but they are left with a bill. Now they have to scramble or borrow money to take care of everything, and your leaving actually put them in a **worse** position in life than they were in before. We can't go out like that y'all...literally. We should work to build an inheritance that we can pass along to our children and grandchildren at the **very least.** We know that it is God who gives us the power to get wealth, so we should pray and ask Him for strategies that will allow us to have much more than "just enough."

READ TODAY: PROVERBS 13:22

SEPTEMBER 7

"NOTHING IS STOPPING YOU."
-BIG SEAN

Have you ever been in a situation where you blamed your problems on someone else? Perhaps you brought home a bad grade and insisted it was because the teacher didn't like you. It's cool how you conveniently left out that part of the story where you didn't bother to turn in three of your assignments. Maybe when you picked up all that weight, you blamed it on your significant other who was always "making" you eat out. Perhaps you had a great business idea but never did anything about it. You blamed it on the fact that you knew no one would support you anyway.

Playing the blame game may have worked when we were kids, but as adults we really need to cut it out. Let's be honest. Nothing is stopping you. Sure, there may be obstacles or difficulties that need to be addressed in order for you to move forward, but nothing is actually **stopping** you. I was once in a situation that I needed to get out of. I stayed there for a long time playing the blame game and claiming that there was no solution. I was convinced that there was nothing I could do until a friend called me to the carpet and kept it real. "There *is* something you *can* do about it, but you just don't *want* to do *that*." I realized in that moment that the things which paralyzed me were only in my head, and that nothing was **actually** stopping me in reality. Is that thing or person really stopping you, or do you just need something/someone to blame for your paralysis? Jesus once asked a sick man, "Wilt thou be made whole?" Think about the fact that the question even **needed to be asked**. Now you put that in your Big Green Egg and smoke it.

READ TODAY: JOHN 5:5-8

SEPTEMBER 8

"WE OUT HERE DRIPPIN' IN FINESSE."
-BRUNO MARS

    Have you ever been in a situation where you didn't know how to tell somebody something? Perhaps you were going out with your friends, and one of them had on a hideous outfit that did not complement them at all. Maybe you said, "OMG what are you weeearrrrrring?! You look a mess! Go change ret nii!!" You could have just said, "Do you happen to have another shirt? I think that one is doing something weird on you." Maybe your co-workers were having a potluck luncheon, and you just don't fool with potlucks. You said, "Oh unh unh, I'm not eating anything y'all cooked! Some of y'all keep your desk nasty, so I already know your kitchen ain't clean! Then Susan got all them cats too? All these dishes look a mess, and I can tell there is no seasoning!" You could have just said, "Oh I'm good love, but y'all enjoy."

    To finesse, by definition, is to handle a sensitive situation delicately. The ability to finesse something is actually considered a skill that not everybody has taken the time to hone. My mom states that when trying to communicate, she always says either too much or nothing at all, with no in between. Finesse is the in between. There will be times when the butt-booty-naked truth will stir up anger, but failing to say anything at all would be gross negligence on your part. The Bible tells us that a soft answer can de-escalate a situation. Always remember that it's not just **what** you say, but it's also **how** you say it. Is this something that you need to work on?

                                      READ TODAY: PROVERBS 15:1

SEPTEMBER 9

"IT DON'T MAKE NO SENSE."
-BRUNO MARS

Have you ever been in a situation where you couldn't figure out why something happened? Perhaps you lost a loved one tragically and unnecessarily, and you couldn't wrap your head around why this would be the case. Maybe you were convinced that you had found the love of your life, but they dumped you without really explaining why. You couldn't figure out how someone who had claimed to love you so much could walk away so easily without looking back. Perhaps you lived in a country with a president who claimed to be a Christian conservative, but instead was this petty, crass, vitriolic, narcissistic, racist, misogynistic, and divisive man who was clearly in bed with a foreign dictator. Everyone knew it, but people voted for him anyway. You couldn't figure out why people who claimed to follow Christ would blindly follow him. Somebody please make it make sense!

When it comes to this life, there will always be things that don't make sense. When things happen, we like to figure out why, so we can tie them away in a neat little box that we can understand. Even the Bible tells us that getting an understanding should be a top priority. What happens when we still fail to make sense of why things are the way they are? The first thing to know is that God's ways are higher than our ways and His thoughts are higher than our thoughts. We have to accept the fact that as humans we are operating with a limited capacity compared to God and that we only have a partial understanding of life. Secondly, we must trust Him. Some things will make sense with time. Other things we may have to ask face to face.

READ TODAY: 1 CORINTHIANS 13:9-12

SEPTEMBER 10

"RAINDROP...DROPTOP."
-MIGOS

     Have you ever been in a situation where you sensed that you were in danger? Perhaps you lived in a tough neighborhood and had to pass through gang territory just to get home from school each day. Maybe you had to go to the store late at night, and there seemed to be a man following you to your car. Maybe they had just announced a round of layoffs at your job, and you weren't sure whether or not you would be affected. Maybe you looked up your medical symptoms on the internet and determined that it could be anything from a hangnail to having only 8 hours to live.

     Sometimes when we are minding our own business and riding down the freeway of life in our spiritual droptops, we begin to feel some raindrops. If you were in a droptop and you saw clouds gathering and rain drops beginning to fall, what is the first thing you would do? You'd make sure that you were covered. You'd do whatever you had to do to ensure that the impending storm would not ruin whatever is inside of your vehicle. Usually this involves un-dropping the droptop. The Bible tells us that God is a "very **present** help" in the time of trouble. Just like the roof of your car was present **all along** to cover you, so is God. The Bible also tells us that the **name** of the Lord is a strong tower where we can go to find covering and safety. The Lord has several names, and when you find yourself in danger, don't hesitate to drop (top) the name that you need most, and run under it for cover. Need healing? Run to Jehovah Rapha. Need a provider? Run to Jehovah Jireh. Need to defeat an enemy? Run to Jehovah Nissi. The list goes on. Raindrop...name drop...droptop.

     READ TODAY: PROVERBS 18:10

SEPTEMBER 11

"BAD AND BOUJEE..."
-MIGOS

Have you ever been in a situation where you were too stuck up? Maybe you met a guy who wanted to take you out to Applebee's or Red Lobster, but you turned him down because you felt like you were too good to eat at a chain restaurant. Maybe one of your friends gave you a bag of gently worn clothes for the kids. The clothes were actually nice, but your children aren't allowed to wear anything that's not name-brand and new. Maybe you were one of those iPhone snobs who looked down upon people who prefer Androids. You actually let a good one get away because their text messages popped up green. Maybe you're like me and feel that Jesus didn't die on the cross for you to go to that one big-box retail giant who shall remain nameless.

The trouble with being bad and bourgeoisie is that it's the exact opposite of how Jesus taught us to be. If anyone on this earth had the right to be bad and/or boujee, it was Jesus. Think about it. There was absolutely nothing being done on earth that Jesus hadn't seen being done better in Heaven. He was royalty for crying out loud! Jesus knew the scriptures better than anybody, but instead of being a highfalutin snob, He humbled Himself to walk amongst us and to be an **effective** leader. He didn't get on a high horse and look down on those who didn't have their ish together. Instead of being bad or boujee, He was **good** and **down to earth**. Jesus was able to do this because He had genuine love in His heart for all of God's children and wanted to see us free from the chains of sin and death. Are you too busy being bad and boujee to be a reflection of Christ?

READ TODAY: COLOSSIANS 3:12

SEPTEMBER 12

"WHY MEN GREAT TILL THEY GOTTA BE GREAT?" -LIZZO

Have you ever been in a situation that was hypothetical? Perhaps someone asked what you would do if you were a pregnant teenage girl. Would you have the baby? Would you give it up for adoption? Would you raise it yourself? Would you let the baby be raised by its grandparents? What would you do if you found out a close relative of yours had committed a crime? Would you keep quiet? Would you turn them in? Would you advise them to confess? Would you perjure yourself for them if called to testify? What if the man you had been married to for 15 years put his hands on you one night? Would you leave him right away and take the kids? Would you stay and work it out? Would you seek help? Would you excuse it? What if you were a professional athlete being told that you would be fined, suspended, or fired for protesting police brutality against black men? Would risk your career to take the knee?

It's so interesting how we always seem to be so great and have all of the right answers until we find ourselves in an **actual** situation that challenges all of our hypothetical greatness. We so casually and judgmentally say "well if it was me, I would have…" without any **proof** of what we would have actually done. Everything is so cut and dry when it comes to somebody else's situation, but when we find ourselves in the same predicament, all of a sudden, we want people to consider all the grey areas. This is why the Bible tells us not to think of ourselves more highly than we should. Dear God, prepare us to be great when the rubber hits the road.

READ TODAY: ROMANS 12:3

SEPTEMBER 13

"YEAH I GOT BOY PROBLEMS. THAT'S THE HUMAN IN ME."
-LIZZO

    Have you ever been in a situation where you were always letting somebody's son or daughter stress you out? Maybe you were a "boss chick" who was killing it in her career. Maybe you had a nice house, a nice car, a massage therapist, a stylist, a personal assistant, a cleaning lady, a great best friend, and a cute dog. Perhaps everything seemed to be on and popping except your love life. Maybe you spent lonely nights scrolling through dating apps hoping to make a connection. Perhaps you got involved with a narcissistic jerk who tried to make you feel bad about your accomplishments. Maybe you thought you had found your soulmate until you discovered that they were cheating on you. Perhaps they had been living not just a double life, but a triple life.

    Believe me, I know how frustrating it is to see everything else firing on all cylinders while your love life looks like an episode of *The Young and The Restless.* I told my pastor that the only time I ever have anything to cry about is when somebody's son done came along and hurt my feelings. Honestly, I don't have a whole lot of advice on this subject, so this page may be a waste of time. Oh, I remember what I was going to say. You're human. Don't get down on yourself just because it seems like you can't get it right in this area. Continue to learn from your mistakes, and refuse to repeat them. Be patient, trust God, and don't settle for less. Don't put a crown on a clown, and think about the role **you** play in it. You can't have boy (or girl) problems if you refuse to entertain anything less than a man (or woman).

READ TODAY: ISAIAH 40:28-31

SEPTEMBER 14

"I WILL NEVER EVA EVA EVA EVA BE YO SIDE CHICK."
-LIZZO

Have you ever been in a situation where you disrespected yourself? Perhaps it was Thanksgiving dinner and you went back not just for seconds or thirds, but for fourths. It was straight up disrespectful how you basically smashed an entire sweet potato pie by yourself. The next day you hung your head in shame as you stepped on the scale and blew up the bathroom taking your "Browns" to the "Super Bowl." You had disrespected your own body by going too far. Maybe you got into an inappropriate relationship with someone else's man or woman. It started off as innocent flirting, and it evolved into visits and then a full-blown affair.

Secret lusters...is that what you are? When you lower your standards enough to be somebody's side chick or side dude, you are not just disrespecting another man or woman. You are disrespecting yourself as well. Aht! Aht. No buts. You are disrespecting yourself. So many side chicks fall into the trap of believing that their situation is different from all the other side chicks. Does it make you feel better that the man's marriage is on the rocks and his wife isn't treating him right at home? Guys, does it make you feel better that the man who she's with publicly isn't faithful to her anyway? When you become someone's side piece you are basically saying that you don't deserve any better and that you don't believe God can provide you with better. See that? Now you've disrespected yourself **and** God. Never eva eva eva lower yourself in that way. You are worth more than you are selling yourself for.

READ TODAY: PROVERBS 31:10

SEPTEMBER 15

"I PUT THE SI-I-I-I-ING IN SINGLE."
-LIZZO

Have you ever been in a situation that was less than ideal? Maybe you were raised in a two-bedroom house with fifty-leven kids. Things were tight. You shared clothes and beds, but you made the most of it, and those were some of the best years of your life. Perhaps you found your life being altered by a pandemic/global health crisis. You learned to cook some new recipes, realized your current dating relationship wasn't God's will for your life, started an at-home work out challenge, watched all five seasons of HBO's *The Wire* for the first time, and published a book of 365 daily devotionals.

Listen, one of the great keys to life is figuring out how to be content in whatever situation you find yourself in. Contentment is more than just being able to tolerate something. Contentment is when you are honestly happy and at peace. It has often been pitted against ambition, but that's the wrong way to look at it. You can be happy and at peace in your situation even while striving for greater. For many people, being single is one of the greatest examples of a situation that is "less than ideal." Don't let it get you down. Being sad and single is played out for real. The "woe is me" single guy or girl is sooooo 1990s *WaitingToExhale*ish. Contentment is learned, so don't kick yourself if you don't get it overnight. If you **learn** to do single right though, you'll look back at those years and realize that they too, were some of the best ever. Ask God to help you put the sing in your single or in whatever stage of life you find yourself. You can pitch a beautiful tent in your contentment.

READ TODAY: PHILIPPIANS 4:11

SEPTEMBER 16

"IF YOUNG METRO DON'T TRUST YOU, I'M GONE SHOOT YOU."
-METRO BOOMIN

      Have you ever been in a situation where it felt like something was off? Perhaps you were standing in line at a bank when a sketchy-looking character walked in. Although you hate judging people by their appearance, you felt like something was off, so you left. Your heart dropped when you saw on the evening news how that branch had been robbed at gunpoint. Maybe you met a new person on a dating app. You went on a couple of dates, and although they didn't do anything wrong, it felt like something was off. They seemed nice enough, but you stopped returning their calls. Imagine the horror you felt when you saw their mugshot on WhateverYourLocalNewsWebsiteIs.com for credit card fraud and identity theft.

      Sometimes when things are off, we will have a gut feeling that is difficult to explain. Do you trust your instincts, or do you brush them off as silly? Imagine being so utterly in tune with the Holy Spirit that if you don't trust something, there's no second guessing. Imagine being so certain that you don't even have to stick around to see how things will play out or if your feelings were accurate. Like today's psalmist, imagine being so certain that you're willing to immediately pull the trigger on whatever or whoever the Holy Spirit is telling you not to trust. Sometimes we hear the Holy Spirit warning us, but we don't move fast enough. How many times have you regretted not following the Holy Spirit's voice inside of you?

READ TODAY: JOHN 16:13

SEPTEMBER 17

"IT AIN'T SAFE. IT AIN'T SAFE. IT AIN'T SAFE. IT AIN'T SAFE."
-A$AP ROCKY

Have you ever been in a situation where the stakes were high? Perhaps you had one last class to pass in order to graduate. All of your family had already booked their flights for graduation weekend, and if you didn't pass this class, you'd have to explain to Nanna why she wasted her money. Maybe you had an interview for a job you really needed to get. You were only a few weeks away from an eviction notice, and if you didn't get back to work soon, you'd be out on the street with your kids. Maybe you had to have some type of surgery. Without the surgery, your chances of surviving were slim. The surgery itself was risky, but if successful, it would save your life.

When you are faced with a high-stakes situation, one of the first things you want to do is to pray and ask God for help. When there is a lot on the line, you want to be **sure** that your prayers are actually being heard. This is always the case, but in a time when things are critical, there is a heightened sense of urgency. Sin is one of the main things that can cause our prayers to go unheard. Do you really want sin in your life while you have so much at stake? I'm here to tell you that it ain't safe (repeat x3). IT *clap* IS *clap* NOT *clap* SAFE! Sin and disobedience are never okay, but if you know that you have an important request before the Lord, now is **definitely not** the time to be dibbling and dabbling in stuff you have no business doing. It ain't safe. Don't say A$AP Rocky and I didn't warn you.

READ TODAY: PSALMS 66:18

SEPTEMBER 18

"LOOKIN' BETTER EVERY DAY, YOU GOT THAT BENJAMIN BUTTON." -PARDISON FONTAINE

Have you ever been in a situation where you were better than you used to be? Maybe there was a time when you would cut someone down to the white meat at the slightest hint of their disrespect. Now it takes a lot more to get you to that place. Perhaps there was a time when every 3rd word you said was a cuss. Now it's more like every 10th word. Maybe you used to eat a whole pizza by yourself at one time. Now you eat half the pizza for dinner and save the other half for tomorrow's lunch. Maybe there was a time when you used to run around gossiping and spilling everyone's tea. Nowadays you may listen to some tea here and there, but you are no longer known as the town crier.

Look at you! I'm proud of you. You're looking better every day, just like Benjamin Button. Sometimes we put such an emphasis on perfection that we forget to celebrate **progress**. As long as we live here on earth, we will never attain complete perfection. Our mandate, however, is to continue pressing towards the goal of Christ's example. Don't get down on yourself if you don't get everything right overnight. The old church clichés really had this one on lock. "I'm not where I want to be, but thank God I'm not where I used to be!" One of my personal favorites was, "Please be patient with me. God is not through with me yet." The main thing is that you don't give up or lose the desire to keep growing. In what area can you plan to be measurably farther along this time next year?

READ TODAY: PHILIPPIANS 3:12-14

SEPTEMBER 19

"YOU TOO PRETTY TO BE PAUSED ON THE FACETIME."
-PARDISON FONTAINE

Have you ever been in a situation where you were undervalued? Perhaps you worked for a company that didn't really care that you had great ideas and a master's degree in computer science and engineering. They wanted somebody who could submit the TPS reports, and dassit. Maybe you were smart, witty, funny, kind, cool and good looking. Yet you found yourself constantly paused on the FaceTime conversation because the person you were talking to seemed preoccupied with everything but you. It's a shame.

It's a shame that everyone can't see your value, but it's also a fact of life. Think about the fact that Michael Jordan wasn't the first or even second draft pick in his class. As much as we'd like for everyone else to recognize how dope we are, we can't get caught up in trying to prove to people that we are worthy of their love, respect, attention, or time. I saw a meme that read, "Choose People Who Choose You." I felt that down in my soul. Do you know who chooses you more than anyone? God knows everything about you, and He still loves the hell out of you. He knows the good and the bad about you and still calls you precious and valuable. He makes Himself available to us 24/7. He's never too busy and will never have to pause your face to face time with Him. We choose Him because He first chose us.

READ TODAY: PSALMS 8:3-5

SEPTEMBER 20

"WHY WOULD I HOP IN SOME BEEF, WHEN I COULD JUST HOP IN A PORSCHE?"
-CARDI B

Have you ever been in a situation where you were being messy? Perhaps you were that messy kid in grade school who always yelled "oooooh" and "Fight! Fight! Fight! Fight!" in hopes of escalating the situation. Maybe you were that mean girl who would call somebody and talk to them while another friend was silently listening in on three-way. Perhaps when your siblings are arguing, you are the one they call in hopes of getting a co-signer for their foolishness. They know you'll jump right in the middle of the drama and may even adopt it as your own.

Have you ever stopped to ask yourself why you're so quick to hop in some beef? Do you not have better things to hop into than drama? I want to challenge all of my messy people to come up a little higher. As exciting as it may feel to hop in some beef, I want you to consider the time and energy that goes towards it. What exactly are you getting out of beefing aside from elevated blood pressure, decreased peace, and a strained relationship with one or more individuals? How far along might you be by now if you refused to engage in petty foolishness and used that same passion to advance your life to a better place? I think you have dope ideas, dreams, and goals that you could be working on instead. You're wasting your precious time and "ion like dat." Neither does God, but don't take my word for it. *RR Sound Effect*

READ TODAY: PROVERBS 6:16-19

SEPTEMBER 21

"YOU HEARD SHE GONE DO WHAT? FROM WHO? THAT'S NOT A RELIABLE SOURCE."
-CARDI B

Have you ever been in a situation where you got second-hand information? Perhaps there was a cop car outside of Ms. Susie's house. Your cousin heard from Peanut that Pig told Bri that somebody snitched on Ms. Susie. Apparently, she was cooking crack in her kitchen butt naked when the cops kicked her door in. Meanwhile, in real life, Ms. Susie's nephew is a cop, and he was just there to drop off one of his mama's pound cakes. Maybe you knew a couple that got divorced. You heard from Nook-Nook that Peaches overheard Man-Man telling Poodie that Daquan came home and caught Dee-Dee in bed with the UPS driver.

Why are we so quick to trust information that we get from unreliable sources? If you've ever been the subject of someone's misinformation, you know that it's not a good feeling. Not only is it hurtful to know that people who you thought were your friends are talking about you behind your back, but it's also hurtful to know that people would believe any and everything about you without ever coming to the source. Sometimes we are like this with God. When we are in need of help or information, do we know how to come straight to the most reliable Source? Sadly, there will always be people who use God's Word as a means of misleading or manipulating people with false doctrines. There are **absolutely** pastors and teachers who really have God's heart, but there are others who are like wolves in sheep's clothing. That's why it's so important to read the Word and talk to God for yourself. Don't believe everything that sounds good. God's Word, the most reliable source, will help you discern what's really true.

READ TODAY: HEBREWS 4:12

SEPTEMBER 22

"I DON'T WORK IN NO OFFICE, BUT THEY COPYING, AND THAT'S FAX THO."
-NICKI MINAJ

Have you ever been in a situation where somebody was trying to copy you? Maybe you went and got yourself a new sports car, so your homeboy had to go and get himself a new sports car. Maybe you showed up to work with faux locs and the very next week Brenda shows up with the same faux locks. Maybe you told everybody that you were planning a trip to Jamaica. The very next day, Tracy tells everybody that she's planning a trip to the Bahamas. Maybe you made the grave mistake of telling one of your friends which girl you were interested in. The next thing you know, he's over there flirting with her and sliding in her DMs.

Why is it that so many people feel the need to become copies when God made each of us as an original? This is one of life's greatest mysteries, and the world may never fully understand it. Since it's a fact of life though, we may as well harness it for a good cause. If people are going to be copying us anyway, instead of getting frustrated, let's just consider ourselves as the influential **leaders** that we are. Since they are watching us anyway, let's set a good example of what it looks like to live Godly in Christ. If we copy Jesus, and then they copy us...boom...goteeeem!!!

READ TODAY: 1 CORINTHIANS 11:1

"ACT UP...YOU CAN GET SNATCHED UP."
-CITY GIRLS

Have you ever been in a situation where you got snatched up? Perhaps you were a kid acting up in church, and before you knew it your mama grabbed you by the collar, snatched you up, and gave you the whoopin' of your life. Maybe you were in a swimming pool but didn't quite know how to swim. You went to flailing around and knew you were about to drown. Just before your impending doom, someone reached in, snatched you out, and carried you to safety. Maybe you ordered a waist trainer and nearly suffocated yourself wearing it. You wanted to get your waist snatched up in time for your birthday so you could act up with your friends.

There are several different ways that you can get snatched up. The most important snatching, however, will come when Jesus cracks the sky. When the final trumpet sounds and Jesus returns for all of God's children, we will be snatched up to meet Him in the air. People have termed this extraordinary event "the rapture." No one knows exactly when or exactly how it will happen, but what we do know is that in order to get snatched up, you will need to act **up**. What is the greatest, **highest**, most important, and most upwardly mobile action one can take? When Jesus knocks on the door of your heart, let Him in.

READ TODAY: 1 THESSALONIANS 4:17

SEPTEMBER 24

"AIN'T FIGHTING WITH NO RANDOM, PERIODT."
-CITY GIRLS

Have you ever been in a situation where you had an enemy? Perhaps it was somebody who was honestly just jealous of you. When they looked at you, it reminded them of all the things that they wished they could be but were not. Maybe it was somebody who was honestly just intimidated by you. They saw how on point you were, and it scared them. Let's keep it real though, you weren't always the sweet and innocent victim. Maybe you did something low-down to somebody. Hopefully you apologized, but unfortunately you may have gained yourself an enemy.

Having an enemy can be very stressful. It seems as if you're just minding your own business while someone is literally plotting ways to attack you or get under your skin. What sad and pitiful soul has the time and energy to be worried about you to that degree? That sad and pitiful soul is Satan. I know you think that Sheila is your actual enemy, but she's not. You're not fighting with some random person. It's a spiritual attack, and it's coming from Satan, periodt. The Bible tells us that we don't wrestle against flesh and blood. If you think you can win by trying to fight and get even with Sheila or Stephen, you are sadly mistaken. It's a spiritual battle that you must take on with weapons that are not physical. Don't sink to the level of fighting some random person, when your real fight is happening somewhere that your physical eyes can't see.

READ TODAY: 2 CORINTHIANS 10:3-4

SEPTEMBER 25

"GIRLS, YOU KNOW YOU BETTER WATCH OUT."
-LAURYN HILL

Have you ever been in a situation where someone took advantage of what you didn't know? Perhaps you were a woman who went to an auto mechanic for help. You went because you needed a tire alignment. They took one look at you, and before you knew it, they were saying you needed $3,000 worth of additional repairs. Had you gone in with your husband, boyfriend, or brother, the results would have been entirely different. Ladies, maybe you were talking to a guy who made you feel like a queen. He said and did all the right things. He was thoughtful, kind, and caring. The brother even bought you gifts and stopped by your job to bring you lunch. In a moment of weakness, you finally let ol' boy hit, and now you can't find him to save your life. He hasn't returned any of your texts or calls, and to be honest, you're not sure if he's even alive. He's alive alright. He just got what he was after, and now he's gone.

Girls, I hope you know that you'd better watch out. Sometimes we can be way too trusting of people who see our sex as our weakness. Sadly, the world is filled with misogynistic scammers who will see you as a target because of your (perceived or actual) lack of knowledge in certain areas. It is therefore important to apply wisdom to every situation. If you don't know something, do not be ashamed to ask for help. Use the Holy Spirit within you to discern good from evil, and if you don't have wisdom, ask God to give you some. Ever since the beginning, Satan has been trying to catch women alone in hopes of deceiving them. Watch and pray always.

READ TODAY: EPHESIANS 5:15-17

SEPTEMBER 26

"GUYS, YOU KNOW YOU BETTER WATCH OUT."
-LAURYN HILL

Have you ever been in a situation where someone took advantage of your weakness? Perhaps you had a weakness for pretty women. Maybe you crossed paths with a woman who only called you when she needed something or when her other guy was acting up. Perhaps you could have literally answered the phone, "What did he do now?" every time she called. It's like you knew exactly how she was, but no matter what she needed, you always supplied it. If she just needed a listening ear, you'd let her talk to you all night about her problems. If she needed a bill paid, you sent her the money. If she needed somebody to watch her dog while she was out of town, you were buying Kibbles and Bits. You knew that she didn't really respect you, but for some reason you were always at her beck and call.

Guys, I hope you know that you better watch out. Sadly, there are some women in this world who only see you as a tool to be used for their own pleasure. Although many women are progressive and don't mind doing things for themselves, there is still a certain percentage of women who only see men as their come up. First of all, men, I want you to do a better job at respecting yourselves. You're much more than a workhorse for the bank account and the bedroom. There are way too many women out there who would love you legitimately, for you to settle for a user with a pretty face or nice body. Ask the Holy Spirit to strengthen you inwardly so that you don't fall prey to your own weaknesses.

READ TODAY: EPHESIANS 3:16

SEPTEMBER 27

"SO I CREEP. JUST KEEP IT ON THE DOWN LOW. SAID NOBODY IS SUPPOSED TO KNOW."
-TLC

Have you ever been in a situation where you had something to hide? Perhaps you went on a bae-cation with your lil' friend but told everybody you were going on a solo trip. You had to tell your companion not to post any pics from the trip so that people wouldn't know you were down there together. Maybe you stopped to get food on the way home. You didn't get any for your significant other or your kids, so you had to scoff it down in the car and throw the evidence away in garage trash can before you went inside. Maybe you had a lowkey alcohol problem. Everyone at work thought you just really liked juice but didn't realize what you were really sipping on all day thanks to breath mints.

We are all guilty of doing things that we prefer to keep on the down low. If all of the things we did in the dark were to come out to the light, many of us would be in some **serious** trouble. While we thank God for His grace and mercy that has covered us and our trifling ways, we can't adopt creeping as a lifestyle. If you lead a different lifestyle in the dark than you do in the light, you have become nothing but the stereotype. For eons, followers of Christ have lost credibility due to the double and triple lives we lead. Instead of becoming hypocrites and praying that no one finds out, let us work diligently to get rid of anything that causes us to creep, before the chickens come home to roost.

READ TODAY: LUKE 12:2

SEPTEMBER 28

"I'LL GIVE YOU THE RED-LIGHT SPECIAL."
-TLC

Have you ever been in a situation where you just had to stop? Perhaps you were in the process of buying used a car. The salesman had a smooth tongue and talked really fast when discussing the condition of the vehicle and all the numbers. You were getting ready to sign the paperwork, but something was telling you to stop. Maybe you had interviewed for a new job and they actually offered it to you. You were planning to turn in your pink slip at your current job and sign the contract for the new one, but something was telling you to stop. Maybe you were engaged to someone. You had all the venues and vendors booked for the wedding and had sent out invitations already. As much as you wanted to ignore it, something was telling you to stop.

When God gives you the red-light special, what do you do? Do you continue to speed ahead past the red light? Let's just keep it real, sometimes the answer to our prayers is simply "no." As much as we **think** we want something, we have no idea what might be waiting for us up the road in that situation. If God is giving us an answer of no, we should trust that He is only doing so because He knows that what we are asking for will wreak havoc for us in the long run or throw us off of our purpose. As a matter of fact, if God gives you a red light, you should feel special. It means He cares enough to deliver us from evil.

READ TODAY: JOHN 10:27-28

SEPTEMBER 29

"WHAT ABOUT YOUR FRIENDS?"
-TLC

Have you ever been in a situation where you had to reevaluate some friendships? Perhaps you were generally a non-violent person, but every time you went out with a certain group of friends they would always "have to" fight somebody. Maybe you were generally a pretty chill person, but every time you spoke to certain friends, you'd find yourself in the middle of some kind of drama. Maybe you were generally a pretty sober person, but every time you got with a certain group of friends, you'd find yourself two sheets to the wind and crying in the middle of a crowd on Bourbon Street.

Listen, I know you're an on-point individual, but what about your friends? I've heard people say that you are a reflection of whatever friends you choose to keep around yourself. We've all seen the tragic story of a famous athlete or celebrity who has become wealthy and has transcended onto another playing field of life but refuses to let go of the entourage. It's always the entourage that gets them into trouble. As hard as it is to admit, every person is not meant to remain in your circle for a lifetime. There may be some people that you need to distance yourself from, and I know that it won't be easy. Ask God for wisdom on choosing your friends wisely and for the strength to do what needs to be done.

READ TODAY: 1 CORINTHIANS 15:33

SEPTEMBER 30

"BABY, BABY, BABY…"
-TLC

Have you ever been in a situation where you were immature? Perhaps you were a fully grown adult, but your mama was still the one calling to set up your doctor's appointments. Maybe you kept getting your phone cut off because you kept tricking off your money at the mall without a budget. Perhaps someone tried to give you a bit of constructive criticism, and you went completely off the deep end in response. Maybe somebody told you "no" and you literally pitched a fit until you got your way.

It sounds like you were being a baby, baby, baby. Here recently, we see that the term "adulting" has risen to popularity. Adulting is basically an action verb that means you are actually **doing** the things that an adult would do. Usually when someone says they are adulting, it is when they are doing something that they don't particularly prefer to do, but must do in order to keep things in their life from falling apart. Did you know that spiritual adulting is a thing? That's right. When you are new in your faith, you are like a baby, and that's fine. You're learning and growing, and just like a baby, no one expects you to know everything or be very strong. As a spiritual baby, even the things you learn must be simplified like milk. A baby can't eat steak, and that's okay. The problem comes, however, when we become complacent with being a baby forever. Spiritual adulting comes when you refuse to stop growing up in God. There will come a time when you will be expected to **feed** others, and babies can't do that.

READ TODAY: HEBREWS 5:12

OCTOBER 1

"GOT EVERYTHANG, I GOT EVERYTHANG. I CANNOT COMPLAIN. I CANNOT."
-DRAKE

Have you ever been in a situation where you were tired of hearing someone complain? Perhaps it was the lady in the cubicle next to you at work. It seems like she was always complaining about the job. It's crazy how she could've had all of her work done and been chilling if she didn't stop so often to complain about it. Maybe it was that one auntie at the family holiday gatherings. Whenever someone asked how she was doing, she launched into this long laundry list of things that she was unhappy about. Maybe it was that one person on social media. It seems like every day they had something fresh to complain about in their posts. They probably didn't even vote in the last election.

Then there's you and me. We aren't like those crabby complainers, are we? Okay, we can all get like that sometimes, but it's much easier not to complain when you remember that you have everything. As long as you have God, you have everything that you need. Do we spend as much time thanking God and being grateful as we do complaining about the things that we aren't satisfied with? Gratitude is a whole entire posture that you would be wise to take. Gratitude is actually pretty underrated. Most people don't realize that it's a major weapon in the battle against depression. If you intentionally allow your mind to remain focused on all of the amazing things that God **is** doing for you, there's not a lot of time or space to dwell on the things that you feel aren't going right. Just be glad it's not Old Testament Days. Back then, God was **not** here for the complaints. Whew chile, read this verse and see. I'm so glad we have grace and time to get it right.

READ TODAY: NUMBERS 11:1

OCTOBER 2

"HAVE YOU EVER LOVED SOMEONE SO MUCH YOU THOUGHT YOU'D DIE?"
-SOUL FOR REAL

Have you ever been in a situation where you were obsessed with someone or something? Perhaps you are like me. When you have a crush on somebody, you crush hard. You think about them all the time, and it's pure misery. In your head, you've made up this perfect utopian scenario in which you and the object of your affection will live happily ever after. Your refusal to see anything negative about them is rivaled only by the willful suspension of disbelief that one would employ in order to enjoy a stage play with no props. Maybe there's a goal that you are desperate to reach. Maybe it's a body goal that you're obsessed with. You eat only crushed ice and three cheese cubes per day. You also work out four times every day and therefore have absolutely no social life.

Having an obsession can be quite problematic. There's even an illness called "Obsessive Compulsive Disorder" where the obsessions can be severe enough to keep people from properly functioning in society. More commonly, you have romantic relationships where one or more parties feel as if they will die without the other person in their lives. I don't mean to go to a dark place here, but it's real. There are people who would rather kill the object of their affection and/or kill themselves than be without them. It sounds crazy to us, but to a person dealing with obsession, it makes total sense. That's why you have to be careful not to even start down that road. It's demonic, so you never know exactly how far it may take you. When you elevate **anything** over God, you have made it an idol. Stay away from idols.

READ TODAY: 1 JOHN 5:21

OCTOBER 3

"I WANNA KNOW WHAT TURNS YOU ON, SO I CAN BE ALL THAT AND MORE."
-JOE

Have you ever been in a situation where somebody new was trying to holler at you? Perhaps you exchanged numbers and texted or talked on the phone. Maybe they just slid in your DMs and chatted with you from there. Perhaps you were signed into a dating app and met them that way. It seemed as if the person liked all the same things that you liked and had all the same interests. You told them that you were a Falcon's fan, and it just so happened that they were too. You told them that you like sushi, and it turned out that sushi was their favorite food. You told them that you loved the Lord, and it just so happened that they loved Him too! What a coincidence, right? Wrong.

We have to be very careful about running our mouths too much around people that we don't really know. You will discover that there are people who want to know what turns you on, so that they can temporarily transform into that person. They will use that knowledge about your likes and dislikes in order to seem like the perfect match for you. Once they feel like they have you where they want you, however, you will notice that the mask soon comes off. Occasionally, some interested party will ask me "so, what do you look for in a man?" Aht! Aht! Sir, that's none of your business. I'll look for it, and if I see it, I see it. Satan does this too. When he gets a whiff of something that you have a strong desire for, he will send a counterfeit version that looks similar to the real thing. He is hoping that you're desperate enough to jump on it without seeking God's guidance. Be careful about bearing your soul to everyone who asks.

READ TODAY: 2 TIMOTHY 3:13

OCTOBER 4

"I KNOW I'M A LOT OF WOMAN, BUT NOT ENOUGH TO DIVIDE THE PIE."
-ERYKAH BADU

Have you ever been in a situation where you had to make a choice? Perhaps you had multiple love interests, and things had gotten to the point where you needed to choose which one to keep and which ones to let go. Maybe you were an entrepreneur. You had a day job that offered you some level of security via a steady paycheck and insurance benefits. It was getting to the point, however, that you couldn't advance your entrepreneurial dream any further without investing full-time effort and undivided energy.

Because we are humans who have finite amounts of time and energy, we often have to make tough calls on how and where we will choose to apply ourselves. There will be some areas where dividing the pie just won't be possible. One of these areas is with God. Far too often, we attempt to straddle the fence when it comes to our relationship with the Lord. We try to divide ourselves between obeying God and obeying our flesh. We are trying to look backwards and forwards at the same time, and it simply isn't possible. Ladies, you know how frustrating it is when you're trying to be with your man and all he does is play the game or watch sports on TV. Guys, you know how frustrating it is when you're trying to be with your girl, and she won't put her phone down. Sometimes all you want is for the one you love to put **it** down and **choose** you. If we are going to choose God, let's do our best to give Him the undivided attention that He sho'nuff deserves.

READ TODAY: JOSHUA 24:15

OCTOBER 5

"HOW DOES IT FEEL?"
-D'ANGELO

Have you ever been in a situation where you got what you had coming to you? Perhaps you were used to having whatever man or woman you wanted. You could jerk people around by their feelings with no regard to how it truly affected them emotionally. You would tell them that you'd call them back in a minute while knowing good and well that you probably wouldn't hit them back for days. Maybe you would ghost them for a couple of weeks and then show back up whenever you got ready. Perhaps you'd unnecessarily leave their text messages on read for hours at a time. Maybe you'd even toss them a bone from time to time by making them feel that you were more interested than you really were. You didn't really care about them, but you enjoyed their attention and wanted to keep them in the wings in case you got bored one day.

There's a word for people like you, but I won't say it because I'm trying not to cuss in here. Some of y'all know which word I'm talking about. The point is, it's all good and fun until the rabbit gets the gun. What happens when the situation turns around on you like a boomerang, and now there is someone doing the same thing to you that you have been doing to others? How does it feel? If you've ever been treated badly by someone you cared about, you will know that it doesn't feel good at all. The Bible teaches us that we should treat people how we would prefer to be treated. If you are unsure, ask yourself how you would feel if someone did the same things to you that you do to others.

READ TODAY: LUKE 6:31

OCTOBER 6

"SHAWTY GET DOWN, GOOD LORD. BABY GOT EM OPEN ALL OVER TOWN." -BLACKSTREET

Have you ever been in a situation where you were single, and nobody wanted you? Perhaps you couldn't understand what was wrong. Maybe you resigned yourself to the thought that all of the good men and women were already taken. Perhaps you told yourself that all the available men and women in your town had severe psychological issues. Maybe you told yourself that men only wanted women who looked like Instagram models anyway. Guys, perhaps you told yourself that women only wanted tall guys with money, sports cars, and muscles. Maybe you told yourself that you were too smart or too saved for anybody to want you. I'm pretty sure I've told myself almost all of these and more.

Let me tell you a story about my friend. Shawty gets down, good Lord! She literally has them open all over town. Sis has to beat the men off with a stick okay? Everyday there's a new guy vying for her attention. The one thing I know about shawty is that she get's **down**. First of all, she is one of the most "prayingest" women I know, so she gets down on her knees in prayer. Secondly, she is one of the hardest working women I know and an entrepreneur, so she gets down with her business and has business deals open all over town as well. Thirdly, yes, she has a little tinge of bougie, but she is actually one of the coolest, most down to earth women you will ever meet. Of course the men are all over her! She thinks she's my friend, but she's really my mentor lowkey. Does my friend remind you of someone? That's right. Over the next couple of days we will explore the parallels between the "No Diggity" woman and the "Proverbs 31" woman.

READ TODAY: PROVERBS 31:29-31

"GETTING PAID IS HER FORTE, EACH AND EVERY DAY...TRUE PLAYER WAY."
-BLACKSTREET

Have you ever been in a situation where you were focused on getting your bag? Perhaps you had just gone through a bad breakup and you determined that you weren't going to worry about a boy when you could be worrying about a bag. Maybe it didn't even take all that. Perhaps you were just tired of being broke and struggling. Maybe you went back to school to get a higher paying job. Perhaps you finally started focusing on that business idea that the Lord gave you a long time ago. Maybe you finally got your real estate license or cosmetology license. Maybe you sat down and wrote that best-selling daily devotional book. You resolved that you would only mind the business that pays you.

The woman in Proverbs 31 did not play about her coins. Sis was out here working hard, cutting business deals, buying real estate, farming, designing her own fashions, and making/selling her own products. In present-day terms, we would call the Proverbs 31 woman a "mogul." She was not lazy when it came to taking care of her household, her business, or herself. Although this characteristic has been ascribed mostly to women, we **all** wish to be taken care of sometimes. There's nothing wrong with having that desire, but don't let it make you lazy or dependent on someone else for the things that you should be doing for yourself. God has given us the power to get wealth, so let's get this schmoney! It's the true player way.

READ TODAY: PROVERBS 31:10-31

OCTOBER 8

"NO DIGGITY, NO DOUBT."
-BLACKSTREET

Have you ever been in a situation where you really trusted somebody? Perhaps you needed a babysitter, and you weren't the type to just throw your child off on any old person. Any person that you trusted with your baby would be someone you trusted with your own life. Perhaps you had a trusted advisor. You knew that they were in tune with God and only wanted the best for you. Whenever they spoke, you listened. Maybe you went into business with somebody who you trusted not to do anything shady.

There was this time that I had gone on a trip with my sorority sisters. I wasn't feeling too good and decided to ride back home early with a few others who also needed to get back earlier than expected. Based on the travel distance, we'd arrive home around 2am. We asked our married line sister if she was going to call her husband and tell him she was on her way home early. She said that she wasn't going to bother him. We joked that he better not be doing anything sneaky. What she said next stuck with me. "I trust that man so much that if I walked into the bedroom and saw another woman in the bed, I'd look up to the ceiling for the hole that she must have fallen in from, and then I'd help her find her way home." That's the kind of trust I want man. That's the kind of trust that the Proverbs 31 woman's husband had in her. He had no diggity, no doubt about her. So much so, that the Bible says he had no need of "spoil." I personally translate that to mean he had no need for a side chick. My God Today!

READ TODAY: PROVERBS 31:10-12

OCTOBER 9

"PLEASE EXCUSE IF I COME ACROSS RUDE, THAT'S JUST ME."
-QUEEN PEN

Have you ever been in a situation where you were just being yourself? Perhaps you are the person who always shows up late. You've done it so much that it is now expected of you. If there is a cookout, your job will always be to bring a desert. They already know they can't ask you to bring anything crucial because you won't get there on time. Maybe you have a stank attitude and a resting stank face. When your friends introduce you to new people they are constantly having to apologize and make excuses on your behalf. They have to say, "Don't take it personally, that's just how she is with everybody." You're just being yourself, right?

I'm calling bologna. Saying "that's just me..." or "that's just how I am..." has to be one of the biggest cop-outs known to man. Instead of doing self-reflection and seeking to change the things about ourselves that are whack, we would rather just tell people to excuse and accept our unacceptable behavior. This is exactly how toxic people are able to remain toxic. We do not hold them accountable because we accept the fact that this foolishness is just a part of who they are. The Bible tells us that we can be completely **transformed** simply by refreshing the web pages of our mind. Those old ways may have been cool at one point, but it's time to update your thoughts to reflect new data. Let's stop the cop-outs this year and re-examine the things that we have been calling "me" for far too long. Let's wrap up our Proverbs 31 talk by checking to see how the P31 sister likes to "come across."

READ TODAY: PROVERBS 31:26

OCTOBER 10

"IT'S 10:10. WHERE YA BEEN?"
-GINUWINE

Have you ever been in a situation where you didn't want anybody to know where you had been? Perhaps you told your boss that you were sick, but you really slid down to New Orleans for the Essence Festival. You made sure to stay out of all the group pictures and live videos for fear that someone from work might discover where you had really been. Perhaps you showed up late to a friend's birthday dinner. Your shirt was on inside out, your wig was on backwards, and you were visibly discombobulated. You were supposed to arrive at 9:00, but it is now 10:10 and your friends wanted to know where you had been. You scrambled to come up with anything but the real answer which was "Rodney's house."

And so now the attention turns to you. Today is 10/10. Where ya been? Have you been going to a place you're not supposed to be going? We're not just talking about physical places here. We're also talking about mental places. Do you go places in your mind that you shouldn't be going? How about emotionally? We are now in the final quarter of the year. I want you to think about the places that you frequent but wouldn't want anybody to know about. If someone were to ask where you had been, would you have to lie about **that** place? Would you have to lie about that person? Would you have to lie about that thinking pattern? If you can't be honest about it with the people who love you, you have to ask yourself why that is. Would going to that place be considered a "trespass?" It's 10/10 and now is a good time to ask ourselves where we've been and if God wants us to keep going there.

READ TODAY: PSALMS 84:10

OCTOBER 11

"WORK TILL YOU CAN'T WORK NO MO. I'M RICH, I CAN'T GO BROKE NO MO." -SOULJA BOY

Have you ever been in a situation where you were lazy? Perhaps you wanted to save a few steps, so you cut across someone's grass instead of using the sidewalk. Maybe you needed to shampoo and detangle your hair but got lazy and threw a wig on instead. Perhaps you were supposed to cut the grass but stayed inside watching sports and playing the game all day. Maybe you were supposed to be writing a 20-page term paper but paid someone else to write it for you instead. Maybe you called your poor child all the way from their bedroom to the living room just to hand you the remote control that was less than three feet away from where you were sitting. *triggered*

If we're honest, we all have lazy moments from time to time. The problem comes, however, when you adopt laziness as a lifestyle. I know by looking at social media, it would seem that some of these celebrities are just haphazardly rich and famous, but if they were to show what they do when the cameras are off, many of us would be stunned. Many of them are waking up early, going to bed late, and literally working until they can't work anymore. Some are hitting it hard in the gym, on the court, and on the field. Others are taking acting lessons, vocal lessons, auditioning every day, and learning lines. Some are writing songs, making beats, and editing. If you think you can be lazy and get to a place of generational wealth, you are sadly mistaken. The Bible tells us that there's no point in having faith without **works**.

READ TODAY: PROVERBS 10:4

OCTOBER 12

"THIS RIGHT HERE IS MY SWAG."
-SOULJA BOY

     Have you ever been in a situation where you were a weirdo? Perhaps you came up in the hood but enjoyed country music. Your friends would get excited about the BET Awards, but you couldn't wait to watch the CMAs. Maybe you didn't like fried chicken, Mac N' Cheese, or collard greens. Your family probably said there was something wrong with your taste buds. Maybe nobody ever understood your sense of humor, so you had to laugh at your own jokes. Maybe people thought you had no life, but you actually enjoyed being home alone, wrapped up in a blanket, eating chili, and watching your stories. Perhaps you were weird enough to write an entire book of daily devotionals based on all the times you heard the Lord speaking to you through the ratchet anthems. *shrugs*

     We live in a society where being different is often frowned upon. People are okay with you being different, but they don't like it when you're different different. (Dear Lord, please help all the readers to understand that last sentence.) I used to absolutely abhor the word "swag" when it first came out. Everyone kept using it, so to me it defeated the purpose. When you possess a unique walk or swagger, it usually denotes **confidence**. It means that you aren't concerned with blending into the crowed and aren't afraid to be different than those around you. Everyone may not understand you, but you understand yourself. Most importantly, God understands you because He created you in His own image. No matter how weird I am to others, I was made after the image of God, and that right there is my swag.

READ TODAY: GENESIS 1:27

OCTOBER 13

"I'VE BEEN DOWN SO LONG, IT LOOKS LIKE UP TO ME."
-DRAKE

Have you ever been in a situation that was dysfunctional? Perhaps you grew up in a dysfunctional family where there was a lot of arguing. Maybe there were even some physical altercations. Maybe you were the child, but you felt more like the parent in the situation. Perhaps you felt more responsible for your siblings than your own parents did. Maybe there were no men around whatsoever. Maybe you were in a dysfunctional dating relationship or marriage. Perhaps the relationship only had two settings: yelling and the silent treatment.

The crazy thing about being in a dysfunctional situation is that people often become satisfied with it simply because things are still technically functioning. Remember that the term is dysfunctional, not non-functional. This means that although things are **technically** "working," they are working very badly and at their bare minimum. It's like riding in a car in the summer with no A/C and windows that can't roll down. The car still works, and it can still get you from point A to point B. There is, however, a chance that you may have a heat stroke on the way. If you've ever been riding with someone who had car problems, you'll see where they have become so accustomed to the knocking engine or the lack of A/C that it doesn't even bother them anymore. Some of us are like that with our lives. We've been dysfunctional for so long in certain areas that they now look right to us. We've been down so long that it looks like up to us. Ask God to reveal to you any dysfunctional mindsets that you may have normalized.

READ TODAY: JOHN 10:10

OCTOBER 14

"THEY LOOK UP TO ME."
-DRAKE

      Have you ever been in a situation where you had kids or other children in your life? Perhaps you have a toddler and you can't even go to the bathroom in peace without them busting down the door to get in and watch you do number two. (Toddlers are so rude bruh, they will charge their way into the bathroom only to then clown you for how bad it smells...ugh, that's why the door was closed.) Maybe you had a child who wanted to go with you everywhere. As soon as they heard the keys jingling or the doorknob turning, they'd run all the way from the back of the house with their shoes on the wrong feet to ask, "CanniGoWitchuu? Pleeeease!"

      One of the first things I noticed when I became a mom is that these kids watch you like a hawk. You can't move a quarter of an inch without them peeping game. When they are young, it is fairly obvious that your children are looking up to you. They try on your shoes and copy everything you do. As the children grow older, however, it is easy to forget the extent to which we are being watched. They **see** what you do when you're stressed out. Do you grab a drink, or do you grab your Bible? When you're angry, do you cuss everybody out or do you go calm yourself down? Do they hear you gossiping about people on the phone? Do they see you remaining in a bad relationship? Do they see you being rude to servers in restaurants? Do they see you eating unhealthy food all the time? We all want what's best for our kids, but we have to remember that they will follow what we do more than what we say. Never forget that they look up to you, and you can show them better than you can tell them.

READ TODAY: PROVERBS 22:6

OCTOBER 15

"I GOT FAKE PEOPLE SHOWIN' FAKE LOVE TO ME STRAIGHT UP TO MY FACE."
-DRAKE

Have you ever been in a situation where somebody acted like they loved you? Perhaps it was your own kids. Every time they started acting kind, sweet, and loving, you already knew that they were getting ready to ask you for something. Maybe it was somebody who was just being nosey. They knew you were going through something like the death of a loved one or a divorce. They reached out to you as if they were genuinely concerned, but honestly, they just wanted to get some information to report back to the street committee. "Ooh girl, I'm so sorry. Well had he been sick? Aww, I hate to hear that. Did he have insurance?" Maybe you were in a relationship where your partner made you feel like they were head-over-heels in love with you. They treated you like a king/queen...knowing good and doggone well they were messing around with somebody else!

Fake love is one of the biggest elements in Satan's strategy to defeat us. He specializes in showing fake love to you straight up to your face in hopes of manipulating you into doing wrong deeds. People do crazy things for what they **perceive** to be love. Some go into debt for fake love. Others walk out on a good man or woman chasing after the fake love of another. Think of all the stories we've heard about people getting addicted to hard drugs as a result of a romantic relationship they were involved in. Don't fall for the fake love okie doke guys. Fake love is the bait, but there **is** a switch coming, and I can guarantee you that. Pray and ask God to help you discern the real from the fake.

READ TODAY: 2 TIMOTHY 3:13-14

OCTOBER 16

"REAL LOVE...I'M SEARCHING FOR A REAL LOVE." -MARY JANE BLIGE

Have you ever been in a situation where you really loved someone? Perhaps it was your newborn baby. It seemed like out of nowhere this strong mama bear/papa bear instinct just appeared and took over. All of a sudden you gave of your time, energy, sleep, and money just to make sure this little human was okay. Perhaps it was an ailing parent. You didn't want to see them go into a nursing home, so you made sacrifices, rearranged your lifestyle, and reconfigured your budget to make sure they were taken care of properly.

When you love somebody for real, you are prepared to **give** what you have to make sure that they are okay. This is what God did for us. God loved the world so much that He **gave** His only begotten Son. That level of giving and sacrifice makes God the G.O.A.T. when it comes to loving. As a matter of fact, the Bible tells us that God **is** love. If you are searching for a **real** love, you can find it, first and foremost, in God. Are you wondering if someone else's love towards you is the real deal? Do they ever give to you or are they always just taking? Is there ever a time when they would choose your well-being over their own comfort? Does it resemble 1 Corinthians 13? Most importantly, do they know God, or have they rejected Him? If we don't know God, we can't actually know real love. Cheezus Rice! Don't shoot me, I'm just the messenger! Check the scripture bruh.

READ TODAY: 1 JOHN 4:7-10

OCTOBER 17

"DON'T NEED NO HATERATION, HOLLERATION IN THIS DANCERIE."
-MARY JANE BLIGE

Have you ever been in a situation where somebody killed your vibe? Maybe you were at a family gathering and everybody was playing spades, eating, and having a good time until your cousin showed up with his bougie new girlfriend who turns her nose up at everything and everybody. Suddenly everything was awkward, and a perfectly good atmosphere was ruined. Maybe you were at Club Bella Noche' enjoying yourself and vibing with your homegirl when some idiots got to fighting and shooting. All of a sudden, there was all kinds of hateration and holleration up in the dancerie, and that was the last thing you needed. I mean, if you can't go to Bella Noche', where the heck can you go? Am I right?

One of the most annoying things about Satan is that he loves to haterate and hollerate. Whenever he sees you happy, excited, full of joy, or close to a breakthrough, he will do his best to burst your bubble. He prefers for you to be depressed and hopeless, so he will do whatever he can to steal, kill, and destroy your peace. Sometimes it's by bringing someone's negative energy into your space, but sometimes it's as simple as bringing a bad thought or memory back up in your mind. This is why we have to stay prayed up and alert not only in the bad times, but in the good times as well. Protect your peace at all times by refusing to listen to the hateration and/or holleration coming from that old jack-legged, snaggletooth, dirty microwave-having liar. Tomorrow isn't promised, and every day that you are alive is a blessing. Don't allow anyone or anything to kill your vibe today or any day.

READ TODAY: PSALMS 118:24

OCTOBER 18

"I WOULD STOP BREATHING IF YOU TOLD ME TO."
-MARY JANE BLIGE

    Have you ever been in a situation where you were a big fat dummy? Maybe someone sent you an e-mail to ask you for help. They had been awarded $500,000 US dollars, but the only way that they could claim it is if they could provide a US bank account and routing number for the deposit. Of course they'd pay you $50,000 for the assistance. It wasn't until your identity was stolen and your bank account was emptied out that you began to feel like a big fat dummy. Perhaps "the one he told you not to worry about" turned out to be more than just his homegirl. She was always over his house, and you felt like a dummy when you realized that they weren't just over there playing the game. Maybe you were a guy with a woman who was controlling. She wouldn't let you hang out with your friends anymore and even isolated you from your own family. Perhaps if she said jump, you'd ask, "How high?" Perhaps if she told you to stop breathing, you'd say...well nothing, because you'd be dead.

    Every time I listen to this line of the song, I think to myself, "Stop breeaavin'?! Naw nii sis, dat ish on you cuz." Oh, I'm sorry. Did you need that in English? "If you're dumb enough to stop breathing for somebody, that's your fault ma'am." As judgey as I want to be about someone who stops breathing at the word of another, what self-destructive things have I done to please someone else? We have got to begin taking more responsibility for our own foolish actions. If someone lowdown sees a sucker, of course they are going to lick it. The Bible teaches us to be as harmless as doves, but don't forget that it also tells us to be as wise as serpents. If you don't have wisdom, the Bible also tells us that we can ask God for it, and He will give it to us quite freely.

READ TODAY: JAMES 1:5

OCTOBER 19

"NO, I'M NOT GON' CRY. I'M NOT GON' CRY. I'M NOT GON' SHED NO TEARS."
-MARY JANE BLIGE

Have you ever been in a situation where you had to hide your emotions? Perhaps you visited someone in the hospital and were startled to see how ill they actually looked. Showing it on your face would have been extremely insensitive in that moment, so you hid your emotions and tried to make your loved one feel comfortable. Maybe someone very close to you passed away. You wanted to break down and cry, but you knew that you had to hold it together so that the rest of the family could lean on you for strength. Maybe you had your heart broken when your significant other walked out on you. You wanted to have yourself a good cry, but you had to pretend to be okay for the children.

Far too often, we do not properly process through painful events in our lives because we are so busy trying to conceal our true feelings. We all know that there may be times when it would be better not to cry. If someone starts choking on a chicken bone in front of you, the Heimlich maneuver would definitely be preferred to your tears. The problem is that many of us don't know that there are also times when crying is **needed**. Boys and men are often taught to "suck it up" at all times. Eventually all that sucking up will lead to suffocation. If we continue to bottle up our every emotion, the pressure will eventually become too much to bear. There is nothing wrong with taking a moment to grieve. The key is that we must allow the Holy Spirit to comfort us so that we won't get stuck there as many unfortunately do.

READ TODAY: ECCLESIASTES 3:1-4

OCTOBER 20

"ELEVEN YEARS OF SACRIFICE, AND YOU CAN LEAVE ME AT THE DROP OF A DIME."
-MARY JANE BLIGE

Have you ever been in a situation where somebody walked out of your life? Perhaps it was a friend of yours. Maybe you two were as thick as thieves until they jumped into a new relationship and dropped you by the wayside. Maybe it was your own father who left to get a pack of cigarettes one night, but never returned. Heck, the only reason you even know he's alive is because he has a Facebook account. Perhaps it was another family member who you fell out with. Instead of forgiving and moving on like family often does, he or she stopped talking to the family, stopped coming around, and maybe even blocked you on social media. Maybe you were in a committed relationship with someone for eleven long years, and even though it may have been gradually falling apart for a long time, it felt like they left you at the drop of a dime.

The feeling of rejection is definitely one of the most depressing feelings known to man. So many emotions are triggered by rejection. You may feel sad, lonely, angry, bitter, confused, embarrassed, regretful, and who knows what else? It's actually pretty hard to comfort a person who feels rejected. Sometimes they seem fine, but at other times they are an emotional wreck. I don't have much on this topic, but such as I have, I give to thee. Are you ready? If somebody walked out of your life, you don't need them to make it. If somebody walked out of your life, God's **plan** doesn't require their **presence** for your **prosperity**. Oh snap! Look at God y'all! Did anybody peep that alliteration?! That was exhilarating! I see why preachers do it so much!

READ TODAY: PHILIPPIANS 4:19

"I WOULDN'T CHANGE MY LIFE. MY LIFE'S JUST FINE FINE FINE FINE FINE FINE, OOH." -MARY JANE BLIGE

Have you ever been in a situation where you had regrets? Maybe your parents warned you to stop doing hoodrat things with your friends, buckle down, and go to college. Now you're in your 30s, you haven't seen those friends in years, and you're stuck with a job that doesn't seem to be going anywhere. Perhaps your mama told you not to be one of these fast-tail girls out here, but you didn't listen. Now you're 21 years old with three kids that you're struggling to take care of alone. Maybe you had a good man or good woman in your life but didn't treat them right. You took for granted that they would always be there, but now that they have moved on to greener pastures, you sit and wish that you could go back and change things.

In God's book, regret is about as useful as a hangnail. Of course we all make mistakes, but what does regret do to fix anything? I'll wait. Just kidding, no I won't. Regret does nothing but depress people. If you are a believer, you are promised that there is therefore now no condemnation for you. This means that your past mistakes no longer have authority over your life. Far too often, we allow our past to dictate our future. Any decision you make that is based in fear, shame, guilt, or regret, is a decision that the devil has tricked you into making. God does not employ those things to get the job done in you. He uses love. God has also promised us that He can take **all** the things that we've done and put them to work for a good outcome. This means that everything that you went through has a purpose and can be used to bring glory to God. If you believe this, you'll drop the regret and realize that your life's just fine.

READ TODAY: ROMANS 8:28

OCTOBER 22

"LIKE SWEET MORNING DEW, I TOOK ONE LOOK AT YOU, AND IT WAS PLAIN TO SEE. YOU ARE MY DESTINY."
-MARVIN GAYE/MARY JANE BLIGE

Have you ever been in a situation where God gave you a vision? Perhaps you saw yourself going back to your old neighborhood and making a difference. Maybe you saw yourself owning a successful business and working for yourself every day. Perhaps you saw yourself married with a beautiful home and family. Maybe you saw yourself inventing a new tool or app that would revolutionize the world. Maybe you saw yourself as a wealthy philanthropist who was making a difference in the lives of so many others.

When God gives you a vision, there are a few things that you must do, but the first thing is to write it down. Don't just write it down in a notebook somewhere, write it down somewhere that's big, bold, and plain to see. I once went to a vision board party and created an entire board that represented my vision for the upcoming year. Why a board? You want something that can be displayed conspicuously and seen continuously. Some people even put their visions in a place where they can be seen every morning like one might see the sweet morning dew. Make it obvious and make it plain to see, so that even when you're in a hurry, you can take one look at it and be re-inspired about your destiny Keep it always before you, so that it never gets pushed to the back of your mind. Every time you **see** the vision, say a little prayer, and ask God to show you the strategy that goes along with it.

READ TODAY: HABAKKUK 2:1-3

OCTOBER 23

"WE CAN MAKE WAR OR MAKE BABIES."
-METHOD MAN

Have you ever been in a situation where your relationship was on the rocks? Maybe you argued over what the other person was doing or not doing with their paycheck. Maybe you argued about why the other person was always going out with their friends. Perhaps you argued over childcare responsibilities or the cleaning. Perhaps you argued over the free-loading little brother camping out in the basement. Maybe you argued over your intrusive in-laws who thought they could tell you what to do in your own household. Perhaps you argued over their social media activity.

Relationships can sometimes seem like an endless minefield of battle. Of course some relationships are just toxic, but let's talk about the ones that are not. Most times, if you would just step back for a moment and look at what you're fighting about, you will realize that it's not something worth going to war over. Have you ever tried to explain the argument to a third party and realized how ridiculous it sounded as it was coming out? It's even worse when they repeat it back to you. "So...what you're saying sis, is that y'all are about to get a divorce because he put heart eyes under a picture of Angela Simmons on Instagram?" or "So basically bro, you're mad because she likes to spend too much time with you?" Meanwhile, Satan is smiling and happy because if you're at war, you can't be making babies. Even if you're somehow still making them, you're too busy fighting in front of them to train them up in the way that they should go. One of Satan's worst fears is that we birth another generation of great men and women of God. If you're always at war with the person that God has placed in your life to love, you're falling right into the devil's trap.

READ TODAY: MATTHEW 5:9

OCTOBER 24

"YOU WOULD RUB ME ON MY BACK AND SAY, 'BABY IT'LL BE OKAY.' AND THAT'S REAL TO A BROTHER LIKE ME BABY."
-METHOD MAN

Have you ever been in a situation where you needed some encouraging words? Perhaps you just discovered that you had lost your job, and you weren't sure how you were going to make it. Maybe you applied for a job that you really wanted and needed but just found out that you didn't get it. Perhaps you just learned that a dear friend of yours passed away tragically and unexpectedly. Maybe you just returned from a doctor's visit and got some bad news about your health. Maybe the money troubles got worse and you just had your home foreclosed on or your car repossessed. Maybe you just discovered that you didn't pass a class that was needed to move forward in your program.

In today's society, there is an unrealistic expectation that we should always be up and never down. Both men and women are always expected to be operating at 100% and doing completely fine at all times. The truth is that life has its moments when all you really need is for someone to rub you on your back and let you know that it will be okay. We don't always need the lecture or the "I told you so" speech. If you're in a relationship with a person who can use their words to strengthen you when you're feeling weak, you might have a keeper. Men especially can feel as if they are never allowed to show any signs of vulnerability. If and when he does ladies, don't make him regret it. Let's use our words to build up today and not to tear down.

READ TODAY: PROVERBS 18:21

OCTOBER 25

"WORD LIFE, YOU DON'T NEED A RING TO BE MY WIFE. JUST BE THERE FOR ME..." -METHOD MAN

Have you ever been in a situation where somebody told you a whole entire lie? Perhaps your man told you that one day he would make an honest woman out of you. All you had to do was be there for him by doing every single thing that a wife would do without actually being married. Maybe you moved in together, shared bills, and even had a joint bank account. Perhaps you helped him with his business idea and even got all the paperwork together so that he could be legit. Maybe you were even giving up the wife-like booty and had a baby by the man. Maybe he even had you saved in his phone as "wifey."

Now although it's true that you don't technically need a ring to be somebody's wife, you do have to be married. So many women have suffered over the years because they have jumped into playing the wife role without actually being cast for the part. A good man will respect you enough not to string you along while dangling marriage in front of you like some sort of prize you can win if you play your cards right. Ladies, we have to do a better job of exercising wisdom. Think about it. It doesn't take all day (aka 14 years) to see that the sun is shining. If he hasn't made you his wife after all that time, I want you to know it's because he doesn't want to. Also, if you're already running around doing all the wife-like things, what's left? Why would dude commit to you in the eyes of God or in the eyes of the law if it doesn't add any additional benefit to him? You're already giving everything away for free, and if he up and decides to leave you, it's no big deal. Let's just be **honest** and say that you lowered your standards, bought into a lie, and hoped for the best...never again.

READ TODAY: PROVERBS 18:22

OCTOBER 26

"AT NIGHT I THINK OF YOU..."
-GHOST TOWN DJs

      Have you ever been in a situation where somebody sent you that late night text message? Perhaps it was midnight and you were just getting comfy in bed when you got a text message that said, "wyd?" Umm...duh. About to go to sleep. Maybe you knew right away what that person wanted, and less than thirty minutes later you were at their door in a hoodie and sweatpants or leggings. Perhaps you really liked this person, so you hopped up and went to see them like this multiple times. Eventually you realized that this person only seems to think of you at night...late at night.

      There is nothing new under the sun, so I'm sure booty calls have been around since the Bible days. How does it feel, though, to know that you are only being thought of in that capacity? I'm sure it may have been exciting the first couple of times, but when you realize that this person doesn't seem to actually care about you beyond some reliable booty, how does it make you feel? How does it feel when you're having a tough day and **still** have no one to tell? How does it feel when you're having a great day and still have no one to tell? You are only desired at night when that person feels either lonely or horny. This goes for men and women alike. If you're honest, maybe you can admit that sometimes you relax your own standards because you feel lonely and horny too. Let this be your wake-up call. There's a void that you're trying to fill improperly. You must make room for the person who is really meant to be in your life by refusing to let just any random person park themselves in that space. It may not be easy to block that person's number, but as the old hymn says, "Ask the Savior to help you."

READ TODAY: PROVERBS 41:10

OCTOBER 27

"I'VE BEEN WATCHING YOU FOR SO VERY LONG."
-JODECI

Have you ever been in a situation where you were procrastinating? Perhaps you were supposed to be writing a term paper and suddenly realized that your refrigerator needed to be cleaned out. Maybe you were supposed to be breaking things off with someone you knew you weren't meant to be with. Every time you got ready to do it, you realized that a holiday was coming around. Nobody wants to be alone for the holidays, am I right? Perhaps God gave you a talent that you were supposed to be using or a creative business idea. It never seemed like the right time, so you kept hiding it and putting it off for one reason or the other.

Sometimes God gives us things to do or moves to make, and all we do is come up with excuses. We claim to be watching and waiting for the right time, when we are honestly just being scared or lazy. Sometimes we even blame it on God and claim that we are waiting to hear a "word" from Him. I guess maybe the 8th time that He says it will be the charm, right? We sit and watch for so very long, either trying to get our nerves up or waiting on the perfect conditions to finally obey God. Sometimes we waste so much time watching and waiting that the opportunity passes us by completely. The truth is, sometimes you will be instructed to do something that doesn't make sense to you in that moment. You may feel that you don't have all of the money, experience, or resources you need to take the leap, but if you are waiting on perfect circumstances to obey God, you are completely missing what it means to have faith. Ask God to grant you an ear that is tuned to hear His voice and for the **boldness** to move when He says it's time.

READ TODAY: ECCLESIASTES 11:4-6

OCTOBER 28

"GET MY THOUGHTS TOGETHER FOR THE VERY NEXT DAY."
-JODECI

Have you ever been in a situation where your mind was all over the place? Perhaps your car needed some new brakes, but also, your child needed some new braces. Maybe you were in school and had an exam to study for, but at the same time, your grandmother was sick in the hospital. Perhaps you wanted to plan a trip with your boo, but at the same time, you weren't sure if the relationship was going to last that far out. Maybe you needed to set up a visit with your primary care doctor, but at the same time, you really needed to see your dentist, optometrist, psychiatrist, gynecologist, dermatologist, podiatrist, chiropractor, and massage therapist. Maybe you had a big presentation to make at work the very next day, but also, you were beefing with your spouse over something that happened 10 years ago.

When you lay down to go to sleep at night, is your mind racing? Do your thoughts seem to be going in fifteen different directions? So many of us have trouble getting to sleep because we don't know how to shut off all of the competing thoughts in our mind. If your thoughts are scattered, you may want to take some time before bed to get them together for the very next day. Taking a moment to write down the things you would like to get accomplished tomorrow is a good practical way to gather your thoughts. After that, be sure to shut off competing voices at a reasonable hour so you can hear from God. This might mean cutting your phone or television off well before bedtime. Consider picking up your Bible instead. Use a physical copy if you have one. I know from experience that it's easy to get distracted with something else while reading on your phone. (Also, the blue light rays coming from screens can negatively affect your sleep cycle. Sorry, I had an optometrist moment.) Try it.

READ TODAY: PSALMS 63:5-8

"I'M A SINGLE MAN, I HOPE THAT YOU ARE SINGLE TOO." -JODECI

Have you ever been in a situation where you had a relationship that was inappropriate? Perhaps you had a real wife and a "work wife." You figured that since you had to be there for 40 hours each week, you may as well make it enjoyable right? Maybe your work wife looked out for you, brought you food, sent you flirty e-mails, visited your desk quite often, and wore things that she knew would catch your eye. Maybe you thought it was all fun and games until you brought your actual wife to the company party and noticed your work wife staring daggers into her soul. Maybe you were married in real life, but not on social media. There were no pictures on your profile that contained your spouse, family, or ring. There was no relationship status posted, but there were plenty of thirst trap pictures that would garner the attention of the opposite sex and hopefully a DM slide.

This is a warning to my single people. Don't fall for the okie doke. Are you naïve enough to think that all of these people messing around with somebody else's husband or wife **planned** to do so? Sure, you have your homewreckers who simply do not care, but there are a lot of people who "caught feelings" after engaging in things that seemed to be harmless activities at the time. It started with an extra 0.5 seconds of eye contact and a flirtatious text, and it ended with the devastation of a lot of lives. If you are single, certain interactions should only take place with someone who is single too. That means nip it in the bud. Stop the train before it leaves the station. I know you are saying, "Relax doc. I got this under control. I know where to draw the line with him/her." Oh, okay then...that's what they all said. Don't play yourself. That's a game that you will lose every time.

READ TODAY: 1 CORINTHIANS 10:12

OCTOBER 30

"COME AND TALK TO ME."
-JODECI

Have you ever been in a situation where you were scared to tell somebody something? Perhaps you had broken your mother's favorite vase while she was at work. You were so scared to tell her that maybe you hid the evidence and prayed that she would never notice. Maybe you were let go from your job and drove around for an hour trying to figure out how you would break the news to your family. Perhaps you had a little whoopsie and got yourself pregnant. Maybe you waited months to tell anybody because you were scared to see the look of disappointment and shame in their eyes. Maybe you had to be the one to share the news of someone's tragic passing and were scared about how your loved one might react.

Have you ever been scared to tell God something too? Maybe you had wandered off into the wilderness of sin and terrible decisions for a little while and were scared about what God might say when you talked to Him again. The thing about God, is that He's not like man. He doesn't react in the same ways that people do because He sees and knows everything anyhow. When you were out there doing your dirt, God saw you. He waits with open arms for us to repent and run back to Him. God says, "Come and talk to Me." He really wants to assure you, comfort you, teach you, and draw you closer to Himself. There will be times when no one else will understand your situation, but know that you can always go and talk to God about it in prayer. Tell Him all about your troubles. He's actually a great listener. Once you're done talking, spend some time listening to Him as well. His lovingkindness is better than life itself.

READ TODAY: JEREMIAH 33:3

OCTOBER 31

"I THINK I'M SCARED OF WHAT THE FUTURE HOLDS."
-DRAKE

Have you ever been in a situation where you were scared of something? Perhaps you were scared to fly on an airplane, so you've never even been anywhere that you can't get to on the ground. Maybe you were scared to fall in love and get your heart broken. Every time someone got too close to you, you pushed them away and sabotaged the whole thing. Perhaps you were scared to be alone, so instead of waiting on God, you accepted the first person with a pulse who showed interest in you. Maybe you were scared of what the future holds, so you let your anxiety and your fear of what might happen hold you hostage.

Y'all, I know it's Halloween or whatevs, but we have to stop living in so much fear. Fear is binding. It limits your movements severely, which is just how Satan prefers for it to be. The Bible says that we aren't ignorant of Satan's devices. This means we already know which tools and tricks he uses, and fear is one of the main ones. When you begin to take actions based on your fear of the future, you have played right into his hands. God operates in love which is powerful enough to cast out fear. All fear is based in a lie, so if you can discover God's **truth** for your life, you can use it to defeat fear. Yeah, I know it's Halloween, but not today Satan. We **will** be free to move about God's cabin of truth and love.

READ TODAY: 2 TIMOTHY 1:7

NOVEMBER 1

"I COULD TEACH YOU, BUT I'D HAVE TO CHARGE." -KELIS

Have you ever been in a situation where you undervalued yourself? Perhaps you had a bachelor's degree, a master's degree, and a PhD, but accepted a job that only required an associate's degree and paid you as such. Perhaps you stayed in a relationship with a person who took you for granted. You knew that you were worth more than that person was giving you, but you accepted it anyway because you were just glad to have anybody at all. Maybe you are a creative. There are always people attempting to "do you a favor" by allowing you to complete projects for them for free. They tell you that you will be paid in something called "exposure." Okay y'all, I'm back. I had to walk away and laugh for a minute!

There will always be people who will attempt to get what's inside of you for as cheaply as possible. People will take of your time, talent, and knowledge, and then turn around and use what you taught them to make money and even to become your competition. There will be times when the Holy Spirit leads you to do things for people for free, but there are also times when you need to know your worth and charge accordingly. Sadly, there are people who will try to take advantage of you because they know you love the Lord. Don't allow yourself to be flimflammed simply because you aren't self-aware. It was God who gave us the power to get wealth anyway. Apply wisdom to **every** situation. We aren't greedy, but we don't have to sell ourselves short either. Jesus paid the ultimate price for us on Calvary, and if that doesn't tell you how valuable you are, I don't know what will.

READ TODAY: 1 CORINTHIANS 6:20

NOVEMBER 2

"RAKE IT UP. BREAK IT DOWN. BAG IT UP."
-YO GOTTI

    Have you ever been in a situation where you had to throw something away? Maybe you had a refrigerator full of leftovers that were no longer identifiable, and you knew it was time to clean them out. Perhaps you had some old clothes in your closet that you knew you would probably never fit into again. They were too worn to donate for thrift, and you knew it was just time to throw some things away. Maybe you were a hoarder. Your basement was filled with everything from Chia Pets to ThighMasters to Pogo Sticks.

    As much as we hate to be wasteful, there comes a time in everybody's life when things must be thrown away. Do you know what we really need to be throwing away? We should throw away the negative words that have been spoken over our lives. There are adults walking around still holding on to something that was said to them at age 10. There are women who will only wear hairstyles with bangs because they were told at age 12 that they had a big forehead. There are men still walking around feeling lost and angry because someone told them at age 16 that they would never amount to anything good. You'd be surprised what some of us women get told. I was once told that no man would want me again because I'm in my 30s and have two children. If you aren't careful, you will allow these words to remain scattered on the lawn of your mind like dead leaves in the fall. When someone speaks a negative word over your life, rake it up like a dead leaf, break it down like a cardboard box, and bag it up like the trash that it is. If it does not line up with God's thoughts about your life, it's trash. Clear it out and make room for the truth.

READ TODAY: PHILIPPIANS 4:8

NOVEMBER 3

"BABY, WON'T YOU COME MY WAY?"
-FETTY WAP

Have you ever been in a situation where you did things your own way? Perhaps you had a special take on how you made your grits. Your way was different from everybody else's way, but they were just the way that you liked them. Maybe you never did math how it was taught in class. You had another way that you did in your head. No one else understood it, but it worked for you. Maybe you played basketball and your free throw form went against everything that was coached, but they let you do it because your shots would always go in. Perhaps you liked to drive with your seat reclined and low to the ground. Your mom hated it, but your way worked for you, and you were actually an excellent driver.

We all have unique ways in which we like to do certain things. We take after God in this area because He also has a way that He wants for things to be done. As a matter of fact, God sent His son Jesus whose nickname is literally "The Way." Although divine, Jesus walked on this earth as a natural man to physically show us God's way. God's ways are higher than our ways and His thoughts are higher than our thoughts. Although we may feel that our ways are right, they are **nothing** compared to His. That's why God asks us to come His way. Our way is to worry. God's way is to have peace even in the midst of a storm. Our way is to hate our enemies. God's way is to pray for them. Our way is to run around like a chicken with our head cut off. God's way is to be still and know that He's got it all under control. Choose God's Way today.

READ TODAY: PSALMS 37:23

NOVEMBER 4

"I'M LIKE 'HEY, WHAT'S UP? HELLO.'"
-FETTY WAP

Have you ever been in a situation where somebody ignored you? Perhaps you walked past them in the mall, and you saw them see you. You smiled and waved, but they pretended not to see and kept on walking. Maybe you had a co-worker who would walk in and literally say "good morning" to everybody but you. Maybe you were talking to someone who just seemingly disappeared. One day things seemed fine, and the next day that had gone completely M.I.A. You called them and got no answer. You text them and said, "Hey, What's up? Hello..." and there was no response. I mean you had literally just been hanging out with this person yesterday, and now they can't even respond to you. Maybe you thought that something bad had happened to them until you saw them active on social media.

I had a friend once whose boyfriend just stopped responding to her completely unexpectedly. She hadn't heard back from him in days and wasn't sure if he was okay. She had me text him pretending to be interested in his business services, and he responded in less than 60 seconds. My friend had been "ghosted." It's a horrible feeling when adults are so utterly inconsiderate, narcissistic, and immature that they can't just use their words. I know some of y'all ghost people too, but is that really necessary? If you've lost interest and want to cut someone off, that's completely fine, but let's still treat people how we would want to be treated in the situation. Lastly, can we just raise some praise today for a God who will never go ghost on us? He will never ignore us when we cry out to Him. Go holler at God today. Tell Him, "Hey, What's up? Hello."

READ TODAY: HEBREWS 13:5

NOVEMBER 5

"NO FLEX ZONE. NO FLEX ZONE. THEY KNOW BETTER."
-RAE SREMMURD

Have you ever been in a situation where you were flexing on 'em? Perhaps you graduated from high school and got accepted to college with a full scholarship. You worked hard for the accomplishment and were proud of yourself, so you had to let 'em know how you did your thing and flexed your academic muscle. Maybe you got a nice new house or a new car that you could actually afford. You pulled up to the family function flexing in your new whip and everybody was impressed with how well you were doing for yourself! Maybe while everybody was busy taking their lil' trips to Cancun, you "flewed" yourself out to Santorini, Greece for vacation. Of course you had to flex on social media, so you posted up the gorgeous photos, and everybody was impressed with your obviously luxurious lifestyle.

I'm not going to lie, when I finally reached my goal weight, the first thing I did was get on the 'gram and flex for the people. I was proud of the accomplishment, and I wanted everyone to know that I had worked hard to reach my goal. There is a zone, however, where flexing is simply not allowed. There is never a time when it's proper to take sole credit for the things that God has done in your life. Paul said that if he was going to boast about anything, it would be about how the Lord had sustained him despite all of his weakness and inability. Let's be honest, without God's help, everything we do will fail. Does God want us to have great success? Yes. Does God want us to get there and act like we did it on our own? No. Let's make sure that we always give God His props. When we do dope things, we should use that attention to point people to the One who made it possible.

READ TODAY: PSALMS 34:1-3

NOVEMBER 6

"RAN OFF ON DA PLUG TWICE."
-PLIES

Have you ever been in a situation where you fell off in your relationship with the Lord? Perhaps there was a time when you would pray and read your Bible regularly. Maybe you even kept a journal that chronicled your spiritual growth and the journey you were on with God. Perhaps you had found a good church and were attending worship services regularly. Oh snap, maybe you were even serving faithfully in one of the church's ministries. Perhaps you even had so much inner peace that you no longer felt the need to go out and get drunk or sleep with random people every weekend to fill some void. Unfortunately, something happened, and you fell off.

This is definitely not a new phenomenon. The saints of yesteryear would call it "backsliding." In essence, you ran off on The Plug. Why is it that God can literally be so good to us, supply all of our needs, answer our prayers, and still have us running off on Him not just once, but twice or maybe even seventy times? He is literally our plug and our power source for everything, yet we'll still choose to leave Him whenever something seems more appealing. As long as we live in a suit made of flesh, we will always experience some level of temptation because of it. Our physical bodies are constantly trying to do things that go against what we **know** in our spirits. We must be careful not to allow anything or anyone to come along and create distance between us and God. No man, no woman, no money, no emotion, and no busy schedule, should be able to make us back up from Him. Thankfully, He's like the father of the prodigal son who will always welcome us back home even after we ran off and got ourselves into a mess of our own making.

READ TODAY: LUKE 15:17-24

NOVEMBER 7

"HOW DID YOU GET HERE?"
-DEBORAH COX

     Have you ever been in a situation that seemingly came out of nowhere? Maybe you stepped on the scale one morning and it said you were almost 300 pounds. You stared at yourself in the mirror trying to figure out exactly how you let yourself get to this point. Perhaps you found yourself looking a hot mess and calling an Uber at 3:00am after yet another random encounter with yet another random guy who didn't give a flying flip about you. Maybe, in the middle of your life, you woke up one morning to a "crisis" in which you realized that you were not following your dreams, not happy in your marriage, and living only paycheck to paycheck. None of this was your plan, so how did you get here?

     For many of us, the answer to that question is even more simple than we think it is. We got here one questionable decision at a time. We got here one (maybe two) french fries at a time. We got here one small compromise at a time. Unfortunately, we don't always consider the long-term effects of our more immediate decisions. It's like a person who eats a daily diet high in cholesterol and "suddenly" has a heart attack. It's took years and years to form the clogged arteries, but when it's time to face the music, it seems as if it came out of nowhere. There is a Chinese Proverb that says, "The best time to plant a tree was 20 years ago. The second-best time is now." You can't do anything to change the past, but a made-up mind is all you need to begin transforming yourself for the future. Make up your mind to let every decision be a beneficial one. Remember that the little foxes are the ones that spoil the vines.

READ TODAY: SONG OF SOLOMON 2:15

NOVEMBER 8

"NOBODY'S SUPPOSED TO BE HERE."
-DEBORAH COX

Have you ever been in a situation where you made someone your number one priority? Perhaps it was your husband or wife. Your love for them inspired you to work extra hard to make sure that they were always taken care of. Whatever they needed, you were on it without any thought for yourself. Maybe it was your child. You made sure that they were always well looked-after. If they needed anything, you were on it before they could even ask. If they had a problem, you handled it like Olivia Pope. If the choice was between something that you needed and something that they needed, you'd choose their need over yours every time.

As extremely sweet and selfless all of this may sound, it's important to note that our number one priority should always be God. That top spot is a sacred place that should be reserved for God only. Nobody's supposed to be there but Him, and I do mean **nobody**. As important as our loved ones are, they cannot compare to who God is and the love that He has for us. We create an idol god out of anything that we elevate above our relationship with Him, which is dangerous. God lets us know that He is a "jealous" God and tells us not to have any other gods that we place before Him. Think about it. Are you busy running around doing things for your family all day, but too tired to spend any time communicating with God? Did you get boo'd up with somebody who likes to sleep in and go to brunch on Sunday mornings? Does that take precedence over your usual Sunday morning worship time? There are only two commandments these days. Listed in order of importance, they are 1) Love God 2) Love everybody else in the same way that you love yourself. Let's not switch the order.

READ TODAY: MATTHEW 22:35-40

NOVEMBER 9

"I TRIED THAT LOVE THING FOR THE LAST TIME."
-DEBORAH COX

Have you ever been in a situation where you were ready to throw in the towel? Perhaps you had your heart broken once or twice, and once or twice was enough. It's not that you didn't desire love or a healthy relationship, but you were just so sick of trying and failing. Maybe your love life was like playing Super Mario Bros. You started out with three lives on your way to the glorious castle, but once those three lives were gone, it was game over for you. Now if you recall SMB3, you'll remember that once your game was over, there was an option to get a "Continue." This would allow the user to pick up at the level where they left off and keep trying. Sometimes the journey and the defeat would be so exhausting that you wouldn't even use your option to continue. You'd just shut the whole thing off and walk away. (Unrelated, but in the original SMB there is a secret continue option if you press A+Start on the main screen.)

My question to you is who determines when you've tried love for the last time? I definitely believe that some of us are meant to remain single, but who is making that call for you? Is it God, or is it your broken heart? Is it your fear of failure? Is it your fatigue with the process? The Bible tells us that when the things that we hope for get delayed, it makes our hearts sick. If we aren't careful, we will allow our past experiences to make our hearts bitter, cynical, and hopeless when it comes to love. If we aren't careful, we will allow our journey and our defeat to keep us from exercising our option to continue. This applies to married couples just the same. All I'm saying is don't pull the plug on the life support before The Doctor even gets to the room.

READ TODAY: GALATIANS 6:9

NOVEMBER 10

"MY HEART SAYS NO, NO."
-DEBORAH COX

Have you ever been in a situation where you had a good heart? Perhaps someone did you dirty and you were in a position to get back at them, but your heart wouldn't let you do it. Maybe you had been dogged out by someone you were in a relationship with. Perhaps they treated you badly, cheated on you, left you, and then went about spreading rumors and dragging your name through the mud as if you were the problem. You really wanted to hate their guts, but for some strange reason, your heart wouldn't let you. Of course you have them blocked in every way possible and hope to God that you don't catch them in the street, but still, you pray for them.

Sometimes having a good heart can make you feel like a sucker, but I can guarantee you that you're better off that way. If you have a heart that says no to anger, hatred, bitterness, fear, guilt, shame, or pettiness, count your blessings. Do you knooooow how many times that petty spirit rises up in me, and my heart pushes it back down? My God today, that ain't nothin' but Jesus working in my life y'all! The truth is, when you allow these demonic spirits into your heart, you are hurting yourself way more than you are hurting the object of your displeasure. Buddha once said that holding on to anger is like drinking poison and expecting the other person to die. The truth is, it's not just anger. It's anything toxic that you allow to take residence in your heart because of another individual. It's not always easy, but we must say no to any thought, feeling, or emotion that would prevent us from having a heart that is pure.

READ TODAY: MATTHEW 5:8

NOVEMBER 11

"SO I PLACE MY HEART UNDER LOCK AND KEY."
-DEBORAH COX

Have you ever been in a situation where you had to do some time? Perhaps you did the classic movie thing where you had a house party while your parents were out of town, and they found out about it. They grounded you, and you were only allowed to go to school and come right back home for three months. Maybe you lived a little on the wild side and committed something like armed robbery. Perhaps you were arrested, charged, found guilty, sentenced, and placed under lock and key with guards to make sure you didn't escape.

Punishments are technically supposed to have a purpose. When parents ground their kids, it's in an attempt to get them to see the error of their ways and to teach them early that poor decisions do have consequences. When a person commits a crime and has to enter the penal system for a period of time, the supposed (emphasis on supposed) purpose is to reform them. Although it's not a very efficient system, we still call them "correctional" facilities because the mission is said to be that of change and betterment. When your heart has gone off the rails, do you know how to place it under lock and key? Do you know how to guard it and give it a chance to be corrected and **reformed**? Too often, we see people who have experienced heartbreak but never let their heart do its time. So many broken hearts are walking around freely and recklessly overexposed to the elements. If you are hurting and are not seeking God's healing, you are posing a threat to yourself and others. Hurt people hurt people, remember? Don't be that person. It may feel like punishment, but the heart is simply in need of some TLC. That's Tender Loving Correction.

READ TODAY: PROVERBS 4:23

NOVEMBER 12

"TO TAKE SOME TIME AND TAKE CARE OF ME..."
-DEBORAH COX

Have you ever been in a situation where you didn't take care of yourself? Perhaps you worked all year and never used any of your off days. Maybe you did use your off days, but not to rest. You used them to catch up on housework or to run errands for your family. Perhaps you haven't been to see your primary care doctor, optometrist, dentist, or gynecologist in years. Maybe if someone asked you who your doctors were, you wouldn't even have an answer. Perhaps your hair needs trimming, your feet need pedicuring, your eyebrows need waxing, and you need to get back in the gym.

Once upon a time in my life, I lived in this fairy tale dream world where I thought that at some point, someone would notice how exhausted I was and how hard I worked. They would see how burnt out I was and would be moved by some sort of compassion to take care of me like a good Samaritan who saw me wounded on the side of life's road. Y'all I was really under the delusion that because I took care of others, someone would eventually take care of me too. That erroneous thinking led me to basically ignore myself for about a decade. I ended up seriously overweight and was diagnosed with the trifecta of death: hypertension, diabetes, and high cholesterol...in my 20s! My stress levels even triggered a random autoimmune issue that didn't even run in my family. If this were a testimony service, I'd tell you how I lost the weight and how God healed me from all those diseases. But I'm Otis and y'all didn't come to see me, so I'll just say that God is good, and self-care is biblical. Our bodies are literally (not figuratively) temples where the Holy Spirit dwells. We must glorify God in our bodies so that the Spirit can have a nice place to live and operate effectively.

READ TODAY: 1 CORINTHIANS 6:19-20

NOVEMBER 13

"BUT I TURN AROUND, AND YOU'RE STANDING HERE." -DEBORAH COX

Have you ever been in a situation where you tried to run from your calling? Maybe from a young age you knew that you were supposed to be proclaiming the gospel, but that just wasn't your style. Perhaps you had a prophetic gift where you saw visions that eventually came true. You knew you were supposed to be using your gift somehow, but you didn't want people to think that you were a weirdo. Maybe you were called to be a teacher. You had a strong desire to teach children and make a difference in their lives, but since teachers are underpaid, you went to law school instead. Scratch all that complicated stuff, maybe you were just supposed to give your life to Christ, but you ran from it because you didn't want to give up your ratchet ways.

The thing about our God-given purpose, is that it doesn't just disappear because we run away from it. It doesn't matter where you go. If you turn around, God and your purpose will still be standing there. It's like the person who is from the suburbs and likes to hang out with their friends from the hood. It doesn't matter how hard you try. We know your English ain't broken for real. Double negatives don't even sound right coming out of your mouth, I'm sorry. Subject-verb agreement is just inside of you. Meanwhile, when it comes to your purpose, you're not fooling anybody either. We see it standing there, even when **you** try to act like you don't. "Minus whale" stop running from God. Just like Jonah who ended up in the belly of a fish, your life will never be quite settled until you answer the call. Pray and ask God to show you how He wants you to go about obeying Him.

READ TODAY: PSALMS 139:8-10

NOVEMBER 14

"IT'S BEEN FIFTY-LEVEN DAYS UMPTEEN HOURS."
-USHER

Have you ever been in a situation where you had to wait? Perhaps you got the bright idea to go to Popeye's Chicken and didn't realize until after you paid your money that they needed to go out to the chicken coop and wait on a new chick to hatch and become fully grown before being able to serve you the #1 combo that you ordered. Perhaps you went to the hair salon or barber shop on a Saturday morning at 8am, and although you had an appointment, there were already 90 people in front of you. You had to wait until 9:30 just to get called back to the chair. Perhaps you went to an HBCU and you needed your refund check, but when you called the financial aid office, they said, "New phone, who dis?" and you had to wait. Perhaps you wanted a husband, bless your heart...we won't speak on that.

Patience is a virtue, but it's certainly not easy to wait fifty-leven days nor umpteen hours for what you want. One of the most tell-tale signs of a person's maturity is their ability to be patient. Lord knows it's a struggle, but you've got to try. Allow me a moment to share my personal testimony. I used to be at least 10x more impatient than I am now, and so God would put me in situations to teach me patience. I used to want all things instantly and so God would make me wait for them. I used to want everything to be fast, and so God would slow things down. The moral of the story is that until you learn patience, God is going to **keep** trying to teach it to you. Learn patience so you can move on to the next lesson.

READ TODAY ROMANS 8:25

NOVEMBER 15

"IS YOUR MAN ON THE FLOOR? IF HE AIN'T, LET ME KNOW."
-CHRIS BROWN

Have you ever been in a situation where you were in a relationship? Perhaps somebody slid in your DMs and it snowballed from there. Maybe you got on one of the dating apps, and y'all both swiped right...whatever that means. Maybe y'all met at work or at church. Perhaps you met in the grocery store, in the gym, or at the bar. Maybe you met through a mutual friend. Perhaps you met at the Black Awareness rally and then began working together at the McDowell's restaurant, located at 8507 Queens Blvd. Either way, you are now in a relationship with this person and wondering if they are truly the one for you.

In a good number of dating relationships, one or both parties are involved in hopes that their dating will eventually lead to marriage. The choice to marry someone can be one of the best choices you've ever made. It can also be one of the worst. For far too often, it ends up being the latter. I'm clearly not an expert on this subject, but there is one easy question you can ask yourself. Is your man (or woman) on the floor? Does the person you're hoping to spend the rest of your life with know how to get down on their knees and **pray**? Life is unpredictable, and you never know what storms may come. It would do you well to have a partner who knows how to get on the floor and get a prayer through when needed.

READ TODAY: LUKE 18:1

NOVEMBER 16

"REAL G's MOVE IN SILENCE LIKE LASAGNA."
- LIL WAYNE

Have you ever been in a situation where somebody did you a favor and then went and told everybody how they helped you? If you've ever experienced this, you know how lame it is. When a person is in need, there is already enough on their mind. The last thing they want is to be used as somebody's PR move. We've all seen the social media posts from an individual or organization showing how they came to save the day for someone who was less fortunate. Some beneficiaries may not mind, but think about how embarrassing this could be for someone who had simply fallen on hard times.

When you are doing God's work to be a blessing in someone's life, remember to move in silence like the "g" in lasagna. Examine your motives. If you are doing good things for the applause of men, then that will serve as your reward. If you are showing love to others as a servant of God, however, you can expect for God Himself to reward you. I can guarantee you that His rewards will **always** be better than the applause of the people.

READ TODAY: MATTHEW 6:3-4

NOVEMBER 17

"BUT I WAS CAUGHT UP IN PHYSICAL ATTRACTION..."
- SHAI

Have you ever been in a situation where you let your eyes get you in trouble? Perhaps you went to Target for one item and one item only. The end caps did what they do, and eventually your hands were so full that you just gave in and got yourself a cart. Maybe you went to the car dealership for an oil change and messed around and saw the new models on the showroom floor. Before you knew it, you were trading in your almost paid-off vehicle for a newer, fancier model. Perhaps you saw a girl who had a pretty face, a thin waste, and a big ol' booty. In that moment, it didn't matter to you that she had no job, no ambition, no skills, and no common sense. You had to have her anyway.

For thousands and thousands of years, people have been allowing their eyes to get them caught up. Think about Eve with that dern fruit in the garden. The fruit looked good, so she threw everything she **knew** to the wind just to have a bite. Whenever something catches your eye and prompts you to do foolish things, that's a sure sign that you have fallen into lust. The Bible tells us that we can literally be **lured away** by our own lust, which means that it is simply used as the bait that kidnaps us away from our purpose. Kidnappers flash candy and toys to lure children into a van. Fishermen use fake worms to lure fish onto their hook. Our lust does the same thing to us. When the physical attraction fades, you realize that you walked right into a trap. The best way to fight off lust is to feed your spirit on a daily basis. If your spirit is constantly **starving** for Word and for quality time with God, you won't stand a chance.

READ TODAY: JAMES 1:14

NOVEMBER 18

"SEE FIRST OF ALL, I KNOW THESE SO-CALLED PLAYERS WOULDN'T TELL YOU THIS."
- JAGGED EDGE

Have you ever been in a situation where somebody was trying to be secretive with you? Perhaps you asked somebody where they got their outfit, and they didn't want to tell you because they didn't want you shopping where they shop. Maybe somebody posted a healthy-looking dish that you wanted to attempt. When you asked for the recipe, they just said "It's a secret" with the wink emoji as if that makes it any better. Maybe you wanted to start a business, but you weren't sure how to go about making it legit. You inquired from another business owner, and their attitude was one of, "Well, I figured it out on my own, so you need to do the same." Perhaps you had heard of Juneteenth but weren't exactly sure what it was all about. You asked a "woke" person, and all they did was roll their eyes and act appalled that you didn't already know. No education was given.

We all know that knowledge is power, but did we also know that knowledge can make people puffed up and arrogant? Does being able to say that you know something that someone else doesn't know make you feel special? Black people especially, often have the "crabs in a barrel" mentality where we don't want to share our knowledge for fear that someone will come along and surpass us in the "race." Slavery did a real number on us y'all. Do you prefer to look down on others, or do you prefer to help them reach the top? Just know that when you help someone else, you are sowing good seeds, and you will reap a good harvest. I know these so-called players wouldn't tell you this, but God is in control of your success, so you don't have to be threatened by the success of others.

READ TODAY: 1 CORINTHIANS 8:1

NOVEMBER 19

"BUT IMMA BE REAL AND SAY WHAT'S ON MY HEART." - JAGGED EDGE

Have you ever been in a situation where you just had to go ahead and speak your mind? Perhaps you had a horrible boss, and after so many years of enduring their foolishness, you finally sent an e-mail detailing all your grievances with them both personally and professionally. Maybe your mother finally pressed your button too hard and too long, and you finally said everything that you had been holding in for the past 20 years. Perhaps you had a little too much to drink and sent that long asp text message to the person you were secretly in love with. You just couldn't hold it inside anymore, so you poured your heart out and told them exactly how you felt and about your hopes and dreams of being together one day.

If you've ever done any of these things, the initial feeling is that of relief. It was like a pressure valve had finally been released and you were able to blow off the steam. That feeling is nice, but often it is quickly followed up by feelings of regret. We must be extremely careful with our words because once they are released, they can never be taken back. We see this on social media all the time where one wrong tweet can get somebody's career cancelled. Retractions do little to nothing to help those situations. Words are powerful, and it's our responsibility to discipline and then harness them in a way that is constructive and not destructive. Before you speak your mind, just make sure that the Holy Spirit is leading the way and not your own emotions.

READ TODAY: EPHESIANS 4:29

NOVEMBER 20

"SAID I DONE IT ALL, BUT FRANKLY GIRL, I'M TIRED OF THIS EMPTINESS."
- JAGGED EDGE

Have you ever been in a situation where you were not feeling fulfilled? Perhaps you used to get your enjoyment from staying out all night and drinking. For some reason, the clubs got old and waking up with a hangover was no longer fun. Maybe you enjoyed the thrill and the grind of climbing up the ladder of success in your career. Perhaps you finally made it to the top, but it didn't do for you what you thought it would. Maybe you used to enjoy messing around with different women every weekend. It was fun at one point, but maybe you've realized that you're missing that one committed relationship with an actual queen who will be your friend, hold you down in life, and love you unconditionally. Maybe you feel that you've done it all, but "all" was not enough to get rid of the emptiness you felt inside.

The truth is, we will always feel empty when we attempt to fill our voids with things or people. Until we realize that God is the only One who can truly fill us, we will be searching endlessly for something that we will never find. You can literally do it all and still feel empty without God. Think about Deion Sanders who won two Super Bowl titles and played in the World Series of baseball. He had women, fortune, fame, and worldly acclaim. Yet the anticlimactic nature of "doing it all" caused him to attempt suicide. We can't reject God in selected areas of our lives and still expect to be fulfilled. We must allow Him to fill every crease, crevice, nook, and/or cranny...even the ones we don't want Him to bother. Gaining the world but losing your soul simply ain't the move. That ain't what Jesus died for y'all.

READ TODAY: JOHN 4:13-14

NOVEMBER 21

"SO MEET ME AT THE ALTAR IN YOUR WHITE DRESS."
- JAGGED EDGE

Have you ever been in a situation where you got married? Perhaps you had a beautiful wedding day filled with friends, family, and fun. Maybe you had a beautiful custom gown or a perfectly tailored tuxedo. Maybe you had the best photographer, and your wedding pictures were bomb. Perhaps you got really fancy and had a videographer who put together the most beautiful wedding movie that anyone had ever seen. Everyone literally cried watching it, and it even went viral on social media. It was such an amazing day when you met at the altar.

Record Scratch Is that what God told you to do? I sure hope so. Marriage itself can be very difficult by nature. You are literally taking two completely different lives and attempting to mesh them together in a way that will be constructive and not destructive to either party. There is so much more to it than planning a beautiful day and meeting at the altar in nice clothes. I know it sounds random, but I was actually a wedding photographer for six years, and during that time I saw it all. One thing remained consistent though. We made the images look amazing. But images are only that...images. I have heard far too many stories of brides or grooms flipping the entire script almost immediately after the wedding day. I have learned that when it comes to having a truly successful marriage, **only God can do it**. If you are already married, make sure you place God at the center and keep Him there. If you are engaged or considering marriage, make sure you **fast, pray, listen,** and **obey** even if it means losing a deposit or facing a bit of embarrassment. I'm not trying to scare you, but hey, let the chips fall where they may.

READ TODAY: PROVERBS 3:6

NOVEMBER 22

"WE AIN'T GETTING NO YOUNGER, WE MIGHT AS WELL DO IT." - JAGGED EDGE

Have you ever been in a situation where you were getting older? Perhaps you hit 30 and out of nowhere your knee wanted to act up. I mean gahlee, you weren't even doing anything new. You were literally just walking and dassit. Maybe you turned 40 and all of a sudden you couldn't see small print up close. You went to get your eyes checked and they prescribed you reading glasses or maybe even bifocal lenses. Perhaps you turned 50 and realized that you couldn't just hop out of the bed so quickly in the mornings. You had to sit on the side of the bed for a couple of minutes so that you could get everything "in balance" before you stood up. Maybe you found a grey hair or realized that kids born in 2000 are in their 20s now. Perhaps (my personal testimony) you mentioned Whitley Gilbert & Dwayne Wayne to a 25-year-old, and they gave you a blank stare.

It **should be** a real wakeup call when we realize that we ain't getting no younger. Whatever dream or vision that God has given us to complete while we are here, we might as well do it. What are we waiting on? Anyone who has experienced any level of aging knows that as the years go by, you have less energy to expend, so it must be used wisely. We don't want to get to that point of stagnation where we look back over our lives and realize that we didn't do any of the things that were important, yet feel that we no longer have the time, energy, or opportunities that we were once afforded to get them done. It's time to stop putting things off, and it's time to stop wasting energy on things that don't produce fruit. What are some ways that you can be obedient as soon as possible?

READ TODAY: PSALMS 90:12

NOVEMBER 23

"LET'S GET MARRIED."
- JAGGED EDGE

Have you ever been in a situation that was as serious as a heart attack? Maybe you're like me and you play too much, but this particular situation made you straighten right up. Perhaps it really was a heart attack or even a situation where someone almost drowned. It was a situation where swift action had to be taken in order to save a life. Perhaps the serious situation was...a marriage proposal. You're probably wondering why we're talking about marriage again.

Well marriage is a serious situation, and it's absolutely worth hitting again for the people in the back. I got married fresh out of undergrad, thinking that all was well in the sight of God and man. I thought I had "signs" from God that I was on the right track. It just "seemed" like it was the right thing to do, but I honestly wasn't spiritually mature enough to know that I should have actually been **fasting, praying,** and **listening** to hear what God had to say. I didn't understand the gravity of the situation. My grandad (the best man I know) officiated the ceremony. At the rehearsal, he quieted everyone and told us that this was a serious matter because "marriage is the next closest thing to death." We just blank stared and thought it was a pretty morbid thing to say for such a happy occasion. Ohhh but My God Today! Granddaddy was right on the money. There are people walking around dead inside because a marriage or resulting divorce killed their spirit a long time ago. Some get physically sick and literally die from the elevated levels of stress that a bad marriage can bring to their life. Marriage can be the most beautiful thing in the world, but for the love of God, take it seriously. **Assume nothing**. Ask.

READ TODAY: JOHN 5:30

NOVEMBER 24

"LATELY YOU'VE BEEN QUESTIONING IF I STILL SEE YOU THE SAME WAY."
- MUSIQ SOULCHILD

Have you ever been in a situation where your perspective changed? Perhaps you thought marriage was absolutely ridiculous until you met that one person who was just so dope that it forced you to reevaluate your views on commitment. Maybe you never understood why anyone would want to have kids until one unexpectedly slid through on you. You never wanted kids, but now you can't even imagine your life without the love, joy, and fulfillment that they bring. Perhaps you thought you'd always be friends with a certain group of people no matter what. As life went on, maybe you saw that being connected with some of those same people was more hurtful than helpful.

As we progress through life, it's natural to have changing perspectives. If we are moving onwards and/or upwards we are literally changing geographical positions in such a way that we will not be able to see things in the same ways that we did previously. Views from the six, for instance, will be much different than views from the three (whatever that means). Sometimes when your views on life evolve, people will begin questioning you. Some will even attempt to make you feel bad for not moving in the same ways that you used to. Some may even say that you've forgotten who you are and where you came from. Of course there are some important foundations that will never change, but if you still see everything the same way that you did in high school or in your early 20s, you will miss out on these really beautiful gifts from God called spiritual growth and maturity. Y'all, that's how folks end up sitting across from Iyanla...no cap.

READ TODAY: 2 CORINTHIANS 5:17

NOVEMBER 25

"CAUSE THROUGH THESE TRYIN' YEARS WE'RE GONNA BOTH PHYSICALLY CHANGE."
- MUSIQ SOULCHILD

Have you ever been in a situation where you began to look a little differently than you used to? Perhaps you were once a brickhouse, but these days you're looking more like a whole apartment complex with some siding that's starting to peel off. Maybe you once had six-pack abs, and now you have more of a beer keg for a stomach. Perhaps you used to have a full head of hair, but now you are starting to get that Baptist deacon bald spot at the top. Maybe your "twins" used be more perky, but now they are beginning to sag like a 90s gangbanger with no belt.

If you are blessed to see many days upon this earth, it's inevitable that you will physically change. Apparently this does not apply to Angela Bassett, Pharrell Williams, or myself, but for the rest of y'all it is what it is. We always talk about what happens in relationships when looks fade, but we never really speak on what happens when our looks improve. Guys, what happens when you've gone hard in the gym to shed the fat and pick up the muscle? Ladies, what happens when you lose the weight, snatch your waist, and go to looking like a snack? When you begin to physically change, you need to be prepared to experience some things that you're not used to. You may not be used to getting as much attention or flattery from the opposite sex, and it's very important not to let it distract you. It's easy to start feeling yourself and fall into a trap where you allow your vanity and new-found popularity to give way to lust and eventually inappropriate connections. Stay woke. If these people didn't notice you before now, what does that tell you? Be careful not to ruin a good relationship or marriage because somebody sent you some looking-eye emojis.

READ TODAY: MATTHEW 26:41

NOVEMBER 26

"SO LET ME REASSURE YOU, DARLIN', THAT MY FEELINGS ARE TRULY UNCONDITIONAL."
- MUSIQ SOULCHILD

Have you ever been in a situation where you made a mistake? Perhaps you had always planned to get married one day and then have kids. It was never in your plan to have a baby with someone who wasn't your spouse, but hey it happened. Maybe you were in a bad mood and completely snapped on someone who didn't deserve it. You wanted to take the words back, but it was too late. Maybe you had taken a vow of celibacy and were doing good but had a weak moment. You found yourself waking up next to someone and regretting it. Perhaps you just lied to someone you love.

Maybe you're feeling like you failed yourself or like you failed God. When we make mistakes, they have the potential to negatively impact the strength of our human relationships. We stop talking, cut people off, and fall back like it's the end of daylight-saving time. Thankfully, God is not like man, and our mistakes do not intimidate Him. If we allow them, our mistakes can actually be used to **strengthen** our connection to Him, because His strength becomes more obvious to us when we are weak. If you've never messed up before, I hate to say it but you're missing out. Am I saying you should go mess up on purpose? Certainly not! What I'm saying is that one of the greatest feelings I've **ever** known was when God reassured me that His feelings are **truly** unconditional. I fully expected Him to be angry and dismiss me for my mistakes. Imagine my surprise when He picked me up, pulled me even closer, showed me even more favor, and reminded me that His love "don't change." God's grace is truly amazing, and His love is actually the original "I said what I said."

READ TODAY: LAMENTATIONS 3:21-23

NOVEMBER 27

"I'LL STILL LOVE YOU IF YOU GAIN A LITTLE WEIGHT." - MUSIQ SOULCHILD

Have you ever been in a situation where somebody loved you inside and out? Perhaps you had one of those bomb relationships where 50 years later you were even more in love than you were on day one. Maybe your hair wasn't done, but you had somebody who was still going to smack your booty when you walked by and tell you how fine you were. Perhaps you were working in the yard with some raggedy clothes and shoes on. You looked like a scarecrow, but you had somebody who was going to sit on the porch, have your ice-cold drink waiting, and just watch you be all fine and glistening and whatnot. Maybe your hair turned gray or you gained a little weight. Not only did they still love you, but they'd still drink your bath water, okay?!

That's an amazing kind of love. Y'all, Ossie Davis and Ruby Dee's ashes are at this very moment together in an urn that is inscribed "In This Thing Together." Okay, that's beside the point, but I just needed somebody else to know that. Getting to the point though, some of us have gained weight not just naturally, but spiritually. God sees all of that extra weight on us and continues to love us just the same way that He always has. Although His love towards us doesn't change, He loves us enough to let us know when the weight that we have picked up is **unhealthy**. Because we love Him in return, we should strive to get rid of the spiritual weight (sin) that keeps us from running our race at full speed. Sin is literally like strapping on ankle weights for a sprint and thinking they won't affect your time. God loves us, but He also wants us to be great and win.

READ TODAY: HEBREWS 12:1

NOVEMBER 28

"CAUSE I'M NOT IMPRESSED, MORE OR LESS, BY THEM GIRLS IN THE TV AND MAGAZINES." - MUSIQ SOULCHILD

Have you ever been in a situation where somebody catfished you? Maybe they told you on the phone that they were 6'4", but when you met them in person, they were really 4'6". Perhaps you got got by a photo filter that changed their eye size and color, smoothed out their skin, changed their nationality, and gave them a flower halo to cover up the fact that they had no edges to speak of. Maybe you were stuck in a basement, sitting on a tricycle. Perhaps the girl you were with got on your nerves as she removed her hair, nails, and colored contacts. At that point you didn't even know if her body was hers.

Most of what we see on TV, in magazines, and on the internet is nothing but high-level catfishing. I spent six years working as a photographer, so take it from me. Photos can be edited...a lot. These days, anybody with enough money can get a good glam squad and have the fat surgically transferred from their stomach to their booty. Voilà! You'll look like every other Instagram model. When we compare ourselves to these "perfect" images, we become increasingly dissatisfied with our own appearances...just like the companies want. Think. As a nation, we spend billions every year (and who knows how much time) trying to look just as impressive. Here's the gag, though. God is not impressed any more or less with you based on your outer appearance. I just want us to take time to ask ourselves if we spend nearly as much time and **energy** making sure that we are just as impressive inside. What's your heart looking like? Is it impressive? I mean that **is** what God looks at, right?

READ TODAY: 1 SAMUEL 16:7

NOVEMBER 29

"CAUSE HONESTLY, I BELIEVE THAT YOUR BEAUTY IS WAY MORE THAN SKIN DEEP." - MUSIQ SOULCHILD

Have you ever been in a situation where you used your looks to your advantage? Perhaps you got pulled over by a cop, and you got out of it by turning on the flirtation. The poor thing found you and tried to slide in your DMs afterwards. Whoops. *Blocked!* Perhaps you were a gentleman of a certain caliber who didn't enjoy peasant activities such as getting and keeping a job. Maybe you were able to parlay your good looks into a place to stay, a car to drive, designer clothes, fine dining, and vacations. (*point of clarity* find out if people who don't work can technically take vacations and come back to this. Consider editing the wording to say "free trips.")

Listen, I'm with Ronnie and Diamond. I understand that sometimes you have to use what you've got to get what you want. I just want you to consider that maybe you have more than what you're giving yourself credit for. Some kids are told from an early age how cute they are, but if that's the only compliment they ever hear, the effects can be just as damaging as when a child is never reminded of their beauty. There are kids who have never heard that they were smart, funny, sweet, or creative. Perhaps you are now an adult who has never heard about anything more than your physical features. Life will hit and looks will fade, so I want you to know that your beauty can be way more than skin deep. There are two simple (but important) things you can do to make sure that your beauty reaches below the surface. First, love God with everything you've got. Second, love others the same way that you love yourself.

READ TODAY: MATTHEW 22:36-40

NOVEMBER 30

"SOMEBODY'S SLEEPING IN MY BED... MESSIN' WITH MY HEAD."
- DRU HILL

Have you ever been in a situation where you weren't thinking straight? Perhaps you were with someone who had no job, no money, no skills, no place to stay, and a confusing body. You'd think that a person who has nothing going for themselves would be sweet and humble, but this person (who was clearly using you) was a narcissistic jerk who always made you feel like you would never be good enough. Maybe you were with someone who was clearly a gold digger. The only time they even paid any attention to you was when they wanted or needed something. They had a stank attitude and even found a way to drive a wedge between you and the family/friends who attempted to warn you of their subterfuge. Yet for some reason, you were head-over-heels for this person.

Once that ride was over, you probably scratched your head trying to figure out what in the heck you were actually thinking! What made you sacrifice friends, family, finances, dreams, goals, and standards to jump through hoops for someone who wasn't even all that? Holy Spirit, do you want to tell them or should I? No, let me! Okay, when somebody is sleeping in your bed, it will mess with your head! And when I say sleeping, I'm not talking about catching some Zzz's. I'm talking about throwing it in a circle, sweeping the ol' chimney, and twice-baking the potato. For real though, if your body is the temple of the Holy Spirit, how will you be able to hear Him clearly if you're too busy polluting the place? All of that smog in your temple is reducing **visibility** and clouding your judgement. Don't let cuffing season catch you slipping. We do **not** have to be slaves to that.

READ TODAY: ROMANS 6:18-23

DECEMBER 1

"FEELINGS...SO DEEP IN MY FEELINGS."
- ELLA MAI

Have you ever been in a situation where you were in your feelings? Perhaps you asked your husband how you looked in your new dress. You loved it, but he hesitated for a while before giving you a dry answer about it. "It's straight." You got your little feelings hurt, and it made you salty for the rest of the night. Maybe you're missing somebody that you used to be in a relationship with. You made the mistake of checking their social media pages and saw them happily posted up with somebody who wasn't you. Now you feel some kind of way that you can't really describe, but you just know that it hurts.

December is a month where people feel a lot of feels. It's the end of the year, and if you haven't reached all of the goals you set, it's easy to start feeling regretful about how you spent the other 11 months. For a lot of people, feelings of grief are much more intense because their loved ones are more noticeably absent around the holidays. December can be especially hard on singles. You watch your friends put on matching pajamas and wake up Christmas morning to a tree full of gifts. Meanwhile, you're somewhere still trying to figure out what the lonely do at Christmas. The voids that we feel are much more palpable this time of year. That's why I want to urge you not to get so deep into your feelings that you fill the voids in unhealthy ways. I know everybody's cuffing right now, but did God send that person? I know you miss your loved one, but will all those shots of vodka bring them back? Let us remember that Jesus truly is the reason for the season. He came that we might have life and have it more abundantly. Every void that you feel, He can fill.

READ TODAY: JOHN 10:10

DECEMBER 2

"CUT IT, CUT IT, CUT IT, CUT IT, CUT IT, CUT IT, CUT IT, CUT IT."
- O.T. GENASIS

    Have you ever been in a situation where you had a kryptonite-like weakness? Perhaps you were normally a pretty wise person, but when the Tequila shots went down, so did your common sense. Maybe you usually made pretty good decisions, but when you got around your friends from back home, you just let the chips fall where they may. Maybe you were normally a choosey lover until your HBCU Homecoming came around and you went back to your hotel room with the first person who made eye contact with you at tailgate. Maybe you liked them a certain height, a certain skin tone, and a certain build with a great smile. As much willpower as you normally have, you don't own a "no" for that.

    Don't feel bad. We all have our weaknesses. Even the Apostle Paul speaks of a thorn in his flesh (a weakness), that remained in his life to keep him humble. The key to being victorious, however, is to study yourself to learn where your weak points are. Once you have put your pride to the side and become self-aware, you can begin to remove or cut those things away from your sacred space. It's like an alcoholic who wants to recover. He or she will have a hard time if they continue to keep the liquor cabinet stocked, continue to frequent bars, and continue to hang around their alcoholic buddies. The Bible says a funny thing about this. It says if your own hand causes you to sin, just cut it off. If your foot causes you to sin, cut it off too. It even says if your eye causes you to sin, pluck it out. *Insert silent screams of an optometrist.* I sure hope that was figurative. Anyway, whatever causes you to sin, identify it and cut it.

READ TODAY: MARK 9:43-48

DECEMBER 3

"YOUR PRICE IS WAY TOO HIGH. YOU NEED TO CUT IT."
- O.T. GENASIS

Have you ever been in a situation where you got a bad deal on something? Perhaps you went to a car dealership and purchased a new vehicle. It wasn't until you got home and talked to your financially savvy friend that you realized that the interest rate was ridiculous, and your monthly payment was way too high for the kind of car you got. Maybe you saw a commercial for a "college" on TV. You went into all kinds of debt paying for these "classes," but by the time you finished, you realized that your "degree" wasn't even accredited and you still couldn't find a decent job.

A sad fact about life is that there will always be someone who is attempting to get over on you. There will always be someone trying sell you something for a price that is way too high. That someone is Satan. He will attempt to "sell you" sin. The Bible tells us that if we go to work for sin, we will get paid in death. That's a terrible deal if I've ever heard one. The truth is that the price of sin is way too high, and we need to cut it out of our lives. There are little things we do here and there, not realizing that **any** unrighteous seed can pop up at any time and yield a miserable harvest. The thing about sin, is that the devil is literally trying to re-sell you something that Jesus already paid for. We were already made free from sin, yet some of us are attempting to purchase it again at a price that's way too high. As enjoyable as it may seem in the moment, I can guarantee you that the car of sin is a lemon.

READ TODAY: ROMANS 6:23

DECEMBER 4

"PUSH IT. PUSH IT. PUSH IT. PUSH IT."
- O.T. GENASIS

Have you ever been in a situation where you lost your motivation? Maybe it was getting towards the end of the semester and your professors were showing out. You had 2 projects due, 3 reports due, and 4 exams to take. All you wanted to do was put on some Christmas music, do some Christmas shopping, watch some football, and spend some quality time with your family. Perhaps you really wanted to get healthy and go to looking like a snack. But hey, it's the holidays, right? Good food is everywhere and your boo ain't complaining about the fat rolls, so what's the point?

At this time of year, it's so easy to lose your motivation. The year has been a lot of work, and it's understandably hard to remain motivated. Listen, I'm with you. By this time, I'm about ready to put the whole thing on autopilot and soak it in some rice, but that's exactly why we should push it. Let's challenge ourselves to finish **strong**. If we do what the average person is doing right now, we are more likely to get what the average person is getting. Enjoy yourself, but remain focused on your vision for the future. Maintain your motivation in practical ways such as re-visiting your vision board or even by creating a new one. Visualize yourself being faster, stronger, better, and more accomplished. Think about the people whose hard work paid off. Do you think Beyoncé, Oprah Winfrey, Tyler Perry, Barack Obama, and Michelle Obama got to where they are by letting up? No. They were pushing when others weren't. It's not easy, but you can pray and ask God to give you a strategy on how to remain motivated and focused during this season. Remember that the end goal is to bring Him glory. Keep pushing the gas and not the brakes.

READ TODAY: PHILIPPIANS 3:14

DECEMBER 5

"THAT PART. THAT PART. THAT PART. THAT PART."
- SCHOOLBOY Q

Have you ever been in a situation where you wanted to leave something out? Perhaps you were telling your parents the story about how your teacher is rude, doesn't like you, and treats you unfairly compared to all of the other students. You so conveniently neglected to mention that one part where you routinely disrupted the class and refused to stop talking while the teacher was trying to teach. Maybe you went through a divorce and when people asked you what happened, you told them how your spouse had basically been the spawn of Satan. You so conveniently neglected to mention that one part where you had a drinking problem, didn't come home some nights, and had a whole side piece.

We always want to be seen in the best light possible, so oftentimes we leave out certain parts about ourselves that are less than glowing. This is one of the things that can make dating somewhat difficult. People only present the things that they want you to see, while sweeping the other, less noble, things under the rug so that you will like them more. The amazing thing about God is that He sees and knows everything about us, even **that part**, and still loves us just the same. You know it's real love when you can tell someone the truth about yourself and they don't throw you away because of that part. Don't get it twisted though. Real love will hold you accountable and call you up to a higher level. This is what God does for us. When it comes to Him, we should bring our full selves. We can't hide anything anyway, so we don't have to leave anything out. He will take all of our parts, clean them, and make them brand new.

READ TODAY: PSALMS 51: 6-12

DECEMBER 6

"OKAY, OKAY, OKAY, OKAY, OKAY, O-KAY!"
- KANYE WEST

Have you ever been in a situation where you weren't okay? Maybe you suffered from Seasonal Affective Disorder (aka SAD) where you literally got depressed every year around the same time. Some people struggle with this when daylight saving ends and it's already dark outside by 4pm. Perhaps you had a parent or grandparent who passed away. Once the funeral was over and everyone else returned to normal, you were left alone to deal with your grief, and you weren't okay. Maybe you had a three-year-old. I don't even have to explain that one. IYKYK. You weren't okay.

If you've lived long enough, you've gone through some days, weeks, or seasons where you simply were not okay. We are taught that no one really cares how we feel, so we must continue to carry on as if nothing is wrong. The world doesn't stop just because we are going through something, and we are still expected to perform on a certain level no matter what. I remember going through a pretty tough time following my divorce and feeling disappointed that none of my "friends" at the time were concerned enough to reach out to see if I was okay. I chalked it up to the fact that everyone was too busy with their own lives to be worried about mine. I did my best not to take it personally, but I did pray and ask God to send me new friends who would check on me instead of just talking behind my back. He did just that! I also became more **intentional** myself about checking on others to make sure they're okay. Sometimes it's as simple as a text message that says, "You good?" You never know what a person is going through, and you can't judge it by the fact that they are still "performing." Ask the Holy Spirit to show you when you need to check on someone.

READ TODAY: PHILIPPIANS 2:4

DECEMBER 7

"I HEAR HE GOT YOU ON LOCKDOWN, BUT I GOT THE MASTER KEY."
-JOE

Have you ever been in a situation where you felt trapped? Perhaps you were in a lot of debt, and it seemed as if no matter how hard you tried, you couldn't break free from it. Maybe you were in an abusive relationship and felt like there was no way out. Maybe you were addicted to drugs, alcohol, nicotine, porn, or sex and felt like you just couldn't stop. Perhaps you were in your lady's bedroom when her husband, Mr. Biggs, unexpectedly came home early, and then you ran to the closet and got trapped there like 33 times. Maybe you were working a dead-end job. You wanted to leave and better yourself but couldn't figure out how to do so and still afford to pay your bills.

Life is constantly attempting to find ways to box us into corners. The devil wants nothing more than for us to be on lockdown, enslaved by sin for as long as we live. Aren't you so glad to know that God's got the master key? God wants us to be free from sin and from anything that tries to keep us bound. Some people assume that a life in Christ is nothing but a binding set of rules to follow. Religion has misled so many people into this wrong way of thinking. As you begin to strengthen your relationship with the Lord, you will begin to experience how the truth about Christ Jesus is the master key that makes you free from everything that had you on lockdown.

READ TODAY: GALATIANS 5:1

DECEMBER 8

"TURN UP. ALL I KNOW IS TURN UP."
-ROSCOE DASH

Have you ever been in a situation that was out of your control? Perhaps a loved one was lying sick in the hospital and you felt completely helpless. Maybe you were in some legal trouble and were at the mercy of the court and the judge. Perhaps you were in a relationship with someone who decided to leave. As much as you wanted them to stay and work it out, there was nothing you could do to change their mind about leaving. Maybe you were a supervisor and were assigned the heartbreaking task of telling certain employees that they were being let go. Although you didn't think it was the right move, the decision was with the higher-ups, and it was above you now. Maybe you had an important bill that was due, but you had no money to pay it and no idea where to get that kind of cash from anyway.

When things seem to be out of your control, what do you do? Do you panic or do you turn up? God is a very present help in the time of trouble, but unfortunately many of us see prayer as the last resort. People like to say, "all we can do now is pray..." as if prayer isn't the first, second, third, and twenty-fifth thing we should be doing **anyway**. Turn up should be all we know. We get so caught up looking at the dire situation around us, however, that we don't stop to turn our eyes upward to God. We are focused horizontally when we should be focused vertically. The Bible tells us that we should turn our eyes up to the hills because that's where our help comes from. Turn up to the one who made the heavens and the earth.

READ TODAY: PSALMS 121

DECEMBER 9

"I'M SO ANXIOUS."
-GINUWINE

    Have you ever been in a situation where you felt anxious about something? Perhaps you had a big presentation to give at school or work. You practiced it over and over again, but you still felt nervous. Maybe you even had a bad dream the night before that everything turned out horribly, and you forgot to wear pants. Perhaps you were a single woman with no kids. You felt like your biological clock was ticking, and if you didn't get married and have kids soon, you'd end up like the weird lady down the street who has eight cats and sits by her window all day. Maybe your teenage child just got their driver's license, and every time they leave the house you basically have a panic attack that lasts until they get back.

    Let's examine what it means to be "so anxious." When you are overwhelmed with feelings of **anxiety**, you are allowing some sort of **fear** to run freely around your mind. Let's examine what it means to be fearful. All fear is based in a **lie**, so when you are overtaken by fear, it means that you have accepted at least one lie as the potential truth. Let's examine where lies come from. Satan is the "Father of Lies," which means that every lie you encounter was made up by him. Let's recap. Anxiety comes from fear. Fear comes from lies. Lies come from Satan. This means that the best way to overcome anxiety is with the **truth**, which comes from God. When anxiety tries to speak to you, talk over it with God's Word. Are there exceptions to this rule? Nah. The Bible tells us to be anxious for **nothing**, but to bring all of our concerns to God where we can we find peace that surpasses our understanding.

READ TODAY: MATTHEW 6:25-34

DECEMBER 10

"I'M A DANGEROUS MAN WITH SOME MONEY IN MY POCKET."
-BRUNO MARS

    Have you ever been in a situation where you had a little money and didn't know how to act? Maybe it wasn't you, but let's assume we're talking about your neighbor. Once they got a little come up, they started really trippin'. Maybe they started tricking the money off on drugs or alcohol. Perhaps they decided to make it rain in the club. Perhaps they were one of those people who get some money and forget how to treat people. Now that they have money, they go to Red Lobster and cut up on the servers and treat them as if they are slaves or something. Perhaps they have gained 50lbs and no longer cook because they can afford to eat out all the time now.

    Let's be honest, some people were better off when they were broke. Having money in your pocket is dangerous when you don't have good character or the **discipline** to go along with it. All money does is magnify who you already are and give you the freedom to do what you **really** want to do and to act how you **really** want to act. Have you ever heard the stories of people who won the lottery or came into some unexpected money but wished they hadn't? We've all seen the young athlete or celebrity who was handed a ton of cash that ruined them. I don't know about y'all, but I plan to be rich one day. Therefore, I am praying **now** and asking God to build me up in my weak areas so that when the money comes to my pocket, we won't have any problems. If you're like me and haven't come into all your riches just yet, (or if all your bills ain't on autopay just yet) make sure you are using this time to prepare your heart and mind for the increase.

                                      READ TODAY: 1 TIMOTHY 6:17-19

DECEMBER 11

"SEVEN WHOLE DAYS WITHOUT A WORD FROM YOU."
-TONI BRAXTON

Have you ever been in a situation where you went a whole week without talking to someone? Perhaps when you were younger, you got into an argument with your mom, dad, brother, or sister, and although y'all lived in the same home, you went a whole week without saying anything to them. Maybe you were mad at your spouse, and even though you shared the same bed, you literally went an entire week without saying a mumbling word to them. Maybe you were in a relationship with someone and y'all got mad at each other and "broke up" for a whole week before realizing how dumb the fight was in the first place.

If you've ever been on the receiving end of a cold shoulder, you know that it is a terrible feeling. When communication completely breaks down in a relationship, we would say that relationship is in ICU. Why then, do we so frequently give God that same cold shoulder? Perhaps you went to church on Sunday, and when the pastor said "turn your Bibles to the book of," that was the first time you had cracked it open (or clicked on the app) since the same time last week. Maybe you had not prayed, praised, or worshipped since they gave the benediction last week. Listen, my brothers and sisters, you're going to need a lot more than that. The devil doesn't take a break in his plans to defeat us, so we need our connection to God to be **consistently** strong. When your relationship with God is in the ICU, your defenses are down, which makes it difficult to withstand all of the tricks and traps that the devil sets for you. Let's rearrange our priorities to make sure that we aren't giving God the cold shoulder when He doesn't deserve it.

READ TODAY: EPHESIANS 6:10-18

DECEMBER 12

"I DON'T WANT NO SCRUBS."
-TLC

Have you ever been in a situation where you shouldn't have allowed someone into your life? Perhaps you were minding your business in the grocery store one day when someone came up to you making small talk. Six months later they left you broke, broken, bruised, bewildered, and burned out. Maybe there was somebody in your family who you were trying to help. You did everything you could to help them get back on their feet and even let them stay with you while they were trying to get their life together. As it turns out, there was a reason why nobody else in the family wanted to help them. They weren't interested in doing any better and honestly just wanted someone to take advantage of while they continued with their same foolish ways. By the time you finally kicked them out, you had lost more time, money, peace, and sleep than you could count.

When something is being scrubbed, it is being cleaned out by some sort of abrasive tool. When we are being scrubbed, we are being cleaned out by an abrasive fool. Okay, my grandmother told me not to call people fools, but y'all get the point. Are you allowing someone into your life to scrub you of your peace? Are you allowing someone into your life to clean you out of your money? Inviting a scrub into your life is like pouring cold water into a boiling pot. The added water stops the boiling and causes the process to lose progress. Don't allow anybody to come along and add cold or room temperature water to your boiling pot. Don't allow anybody to take you backwards or slow down your momentum. Pray and ask God to reveal anyone or anything that may be a scrub in your life.

READ TODAY: PROVERBS 13:20

DECEMBER 13

"YOU CALL ME YOUR FRIEND, BUT YOU ONLY WANT THE ENDS. AND I'LL NEVER SEE YOU IF I HAD NO LOOT."
-TONY! TONI! TONÉ!

Have you ever been in a situation where you had an expensive friendship? Perhaps you were a kind and generous person. You knew that your friend _____ was always on the broke side, but you wanted them to be able to go out with the group, so you covered them. Maybe that was meant to be temporary, but here you are 10 years later still covering them. Maybe it's become an assumption that any time you want to hang out with them, you'll be responsible for the bill.

Listen, maybe you and your friend have an arrangement that works for you. Maybe you've worked that friendship bill into your monthly budget, and that's none of my business. I just wonder what might happen if you had no loot. If you didn't have any ends, would that person still be your friend? If you know that person is going to ride for your regardless, by all means, carry on. But if they asked you for something and the answer was no, would they still keep the same energy towards you? One of the most difficult things for wealthy celebrities is not knowing who is there for them and who is there because they are paying. We wouldn't want someone around us who only cares about the perks, so why are we like that with God? He blesses us like crazy every single day, but does our energy change when He has to say no? A good relationship with God is one where we seek His **face**, and not just His hand. I challenge you to get to know Him for His beauty and not just for His blessings.

READ TODAY: PSALMS 27:8

DECEMBER 14

"AND I WILL NEVER EVER DEPEND ON YOU."
-TONY! TONI! TONÉ!

Have you ever been in a situation where you lost your job? Perhaps your company did layoffs right before Christmas, and you were stuck trying to figure out how you would make things happen for your family. Maybe you were unfairly targeted by your co-workers and ended up losing your job for something that wasn't even your fault. Perhaps a global pandemic wrecked the economy, and your company went completely under.

If you've ever lost a job unexpectedly, you know that it can be a very nerve-wrecking feeling. There is often a sense of uncertainty because you may not know how long it will be before you receive another paycheck. You begin to wonder how certain bills will get paid and what you will do when you run out of money. There are so many people who have been crushed under the weight of being unemployed. If you ever find yourself in that position, I want you to always remember that your job was **never** intended to be your source. It was only a "resource" that God was using to get provision into your hands. God is your **only** source, and He is literally the only One we should **ever** depend on. You should never depend on your job, on your savings account, or on another individual to be your provider. If you've ever gone for a while without a job, you have seen firsthand how God still took care of you in the midst of it all. Now you may have had to cut back on some things, but did you die though? If you're reading this, it means that you survived or are surviving the difficulty with the help of the Lord. Continue to depend on Him and watch how He comes through for you, His child.

READ TODAY: PSALMS 37:25-27

DECEMBER 15

"OH, 'ROUND HERE WE RIDIN' SLOW."
-CIARA

Have you ever been in a situation where you took shortcuts? Maybe somebody enticed you into a get-rich-quick pyramid scheme. It seemed like a great idea at the time, and the person who was trying to recruit you seemed to have it all figured out. Maybe you sunk a lot of time, energy, and resources into something that never really panned out. Maybe someone got rich off of you, but you ended up with no more than what you started off with. Perhaps you ended up with even less. You never even questioned the fact that you had absolutely no training, no education, and no real experience in weight loss or sales. Yet someone convinced you that at 600lbs, you could get rich selling weight loss supplements and getting others to do the same. You bought right into it because you wanted to get rich quickly.

There is absolutely nothing wrong with getting rich. As a matter of fact, it is God that has given us the power to get wealth. He wants us to prosper and be in good health, even as our souls prosper. That doesn't mean, however, that it will all come overnight. There are some for whom wealth will come quickly. For many of us, however, it will be a slow ride so that God has time to develop our **character** along the way. I know I say this all the time, but pray and ask God to give you the strategy to create your wealth. But also pray that He prepares you to handle it. We've seen too many times when a person got more than they could handle too quickly, and it led to their downfall. It's okay to ride slow so that when you do arrive, you'll be ready.

READ TODAY: DEUTERONOMY 8:18

DECEMBER 16

"CAN WE GO BACK TO THE DAYS OUR LOVE WAS STRONG?"
-BOYZ II MEN

Have you ever been in a situation where you wanted to turn back the hands of time? Perhaps you were having a quarter or mid-life crisis in which you realized that you had wasted a lot of time that you can't get back. If you knew then what you know now, you would have done a lot of things differently. Maybe you were seven years into a marriage that started out so much better. In the beginning, your love was strong. You were thoughtful and considerate of each other, you had fun together, and you enjoyed each other's company. Now it seems that all you do is argue and find excuses to be away from the house as much as possible.

It's not very often that I get to use my chemistry degree, so just go with it for a minute, okay? The second law of thermodynamics is about something called "entropy." Entropy has to do with order vs. disorder of a thermodynamic system. By nature, everything has the tendency to **degenerate** over time from an orderly state to a more disorderly state (or for the sake of discussion...a more powerful state to a less powerful state). Imagine a poot...yes, a poot. When someone first poots, the gas is nice and unified in one spot, and the smell is strong. As the molecules begin to lose order and spread out across the room, as they naturally do (entropy), they lose the power that they had when they were gathered together. The smell/strength fades away. To prevent entropy from taking over any system, you must apply another thermodynamic principle called "Work." You cannot turn back the hands of time, but you can be more intentional about **working** for the things you say you want. If you don't put in the work, your relationship will, by nature, lose power and get out of order. Ask God to give you the motivation to go back to work for the life you want.

READ TODAY: JAMES 2:26

DECEMBER 17

"OH GOD, GIVE ME A REASON."
-BOYZ II MEN

Have you ever been in a situation where you didn't understand why things happened the way they did? Maybe you were minding your own business when you got a phone call telling you that one of your friends had been in a tragic accident. Your friend was so full of life and potential, and it just seems like they were taken away for no reason. Perhaps your husband or wife left you for someone else. You felt as if you were good to them and did everything you could to make them happy, but they left you anyway. Not only did they leave you, but they ended up getting the house, the car, primary custody of the kids, and a good chunk of your paycheck. You felt like you didn't deserve any of this, and maybe you begged God to give you a reason.

The question of why bad things happen to good people has been around since the beginning. Our human reasoning has led us to calculate that if you are a "good" person, you deserve to have only good things come to you. I wish I could explain exactly why you suffered loss the way that you did. I wish I could give you a reason why suffering is a thing. The only thing I can tell you is that God, in His infinite wisdom, decided that suffering is something that we need to experience in this lifetime. That means that there is always a reason whether we know it yet or not. I can honestly say that most of my sufferings, while nonsensical in the moment, eventually made complete sense. Many of you were taught incorrectly never to question God. The truth is, when things happen that you don't understand, there is nothing stopping you from going to God in prayer and asking Him to show you what He wants you to gain from it.

READ TODAY: ROMANS 5:3-4

DECEMBER 18

"I'M DOWN ON BENDED KNEE."
-BOYZ II MEN

Have you ever been in a situation where you needed something, but didn't know how to get it? Perhaps your child had been accepted to the college of their dreams. The enrollment date was swiftly approaching, but you had no idea how to get the money to send them there. Maybe you needed peace in your family. Perhaps your children hated each other's guts and all you wanted was for them to have a close relationship as siblings. Maybe your child's mother or father was lowdown and trifling for no reason and always finding ways to start drama. All you wanted to do was work together to give your child the best upbringing that you could. Maybe you need your child to act right or for your marriage to get back on track.

There will come a time when you need something in life that money simply cannot buy. My pastor once said that there are certain things we must buy with our "spiritual currency." It stuck with me because there were things I needed at the time that were well beyond my control naturally. The spiritual currency at our disposal includes faith, fasting, prayer, supplication, praise, worship, meditation on God's Holy Word, and obedience. These are the spiritual big head Benjamins. Before you worry yourself to death about things that are beyond your control, go down on bended knee and purchase what you need from the spiritual realm. From there it will only be a matter of time before you begin to see these things manifest in the natural world. Sometimes you won't even have to say anything to anybody. You just go down on bended knee and watch God begin to move things around on your behalf. It works, but don't take my word for it.

READ TODAY: 2 CORINTHIANS 10: 3-4

DECEMBER 19

"I'M GONNA SWALLOW MY PRIDE... SAY I'M SORRY."
-BOYZ II MEN

Have you ever been in a situation where you had trouble swallowing your pride? Perhaps you got into an argument in the barbershop. You were 1000% sure that Joe Louis was the greatest boxer that ever lived. You argued everybody down that he was badder than Cassius Clay, Sugar Ray, Mike Tyson, and Rocky Marciano. When you finally asked Google, there it was. Rocky Marciano had whooped Joe Louis in 1951. Once you realized you were wrong, you were too proud to apologize so you just cussed everybody out before assisting the two gentlemen from Zamunda.

Pride is one of the greatest relationship spoilers of all time. Some people will literally do anything and everything to keep from admitting that they were wrong. Do you know that there are people who would rather just not talk to you ever again than to admit that they were wrong? It sounds crazy, but it happens every day. Our own pride is one of Satan's most useful weapons in his strategy to defeat us. Pride can easily destroy an entire marriage. Parents and children go completely estranged for years (and sometimes for life) simply because one or both parties refuse to admit that they were wrong. Pride is so low down that it even keeps us from taking advantage of certain opportunities for advancement because we don't want to admit that we actually need the help. Think about it this way. What's the worst thing that can happen if you humble yourself? Ooh, somebody will find out that you aren't perfect? How scary. What's the best thing that can happen? Perhaps swallowing your pride is the key that unlocks more doors than you realize. The benefits of humility far outweigh the risks.

READ TODAY: PROVERBS 29:23

DECEMBER 20

"THROW YOUR CLOTHES ON THE FLOOR."
-BOYZ II MEN

Have you ever been in a situation where you needed to change clothes? Perhaps you were going out with some friends after work and needed to run home to change into something for the occasion. Maybe you were going to the gym and needed to change into your workout attire. Maybe you had just gotten a stain on your shirt and needed to change into a fresh one so that people wouldn't stare at you all night. There's nothing like feeling that you are improperly or inadequately dressed for a situation.

Did you know that there are certain clothes that the Bible tells us to take off and throw on the floor? When you decide to live your life for the Lord, there are things that He will ask you to **take off** so that you will be able to **put on** what's coming. The Bible also tells us that any man who is in Christ becomes a new creature. This new creature needs new "clothes" to wear. We are to take off old things like anger, wrath, doubt, envy, pride, and lies in order to put on new things like mercy, kindness, humility, patience, love, and truth. When you allow Christ into your heart, He cleanses you from the inside out. Certain dirty clothes you will no longer have need of. Take those clothes, throw them on the floor, bag them up, and take them to the dumpster. Pray and ask God to show you which old clothes you need to dispose of and which new clothes you need to begin putting on.

READ TODAY: COLOSSIANS 3:8-15

DECEMBER 21

"I LONG FOR THE WARMTH OF DAYS GONE BY."
-BOYZ II MEN

Have you ever been in a situation where things just weren't the same? Perhaps you had trouble getting into Christmas like you used to. You were used to everybody gathering at Big Mama's house. For 30 years you could count on everything being the same. You knew you'd get your grandmother's dressing, your auntie's mac and cheese, and your cousin's red velvet cake. Once Big Mama passed on, everybody just started doing their own thing. Things just weren't the same, and you would have given just about anything to experience the warmth of the holidays that had gone by. Even the gifts seemed pointless.

As we discussed earlier in the month, the holidays can be a tough time for some people, and this is one of the big reasons why. When our sacred traditions are disrupted, it can really throw us off balance mentally. There's nothing that you can do to go back to the days gone by, but what you can do is make up your mind to live well in the moment. Don't you think that there was a point in which your Big Mama lost her Big Mama? Our parents and grandparents had to pick up the mantle at some point and begin to create memorable experiences for themselves and for us. So let's stop with the "woe is me," and start with the gratitude for this new opportunity that is before us. Even though it's not the same as days gone by, it's still the day that the Lord has made. We can **choose** to rejoice and be glad in it.

READ TODAY: PSALMS 118:24

DECEMBER 22

"LET'S NOT WAIT TILL THE WATER RUNS DRY."
-BOYZ II MEN

Have you ever been in a situation where you were passive? Perhaps you were passive with your health. You knew that eating all that bacon might eventually catch up to you, but since your doctor hadn't said anything yet, you felt no need to make a change. Perhaps you were passive in your relationship. It wasn't bad, but at the same time it wasn't good. Your partner wasn't doing much complaining, so you figured you were safe.

When I was in college, I got some pretty wise relationship advice from my friend Taurean. He told me that relationships are like campfires. If you sit around the fire and do nothing, it will burn for a while but eventually it will die out. In order to keep the fire going, you must do the sometimes-difficult work of chopping firewood, bringing it back, and throwing it in. You have to watch the fire and continuously stoke the flames to keep them from going out on their own. He said that just as a campfire requires constant attention and **work** to stay alive, so do relationships. Pretty good advice coming from some 19-year-old guy, huh? Well this applies to just about everything. We can apply it to our physical health, our human relationships, and even to our spiritual walk with God. Let's not wait until the water runs dry or until the flame goes out before we do what we **already know** we need to be doing anyway. Once you've let the water run dry, there's no guarantee that you'll be able to get it back flowing again. Let's not wait until that switch flips from on to off to start doing our best.

READ TODAY: JAMES 4:17

DECEMBER 23

"HOW COULD WE NOT TALK ABOUT FAMILY, WHEN FAMILY'S ALL THAT WE GOT?" -WIZ KHALIFA

     Have you ever been in a situation where you didn't get along with your family? Maybe every time you went to the family gathering, you had that one messy aunt who always wanted to know why you were still single. Perhaps you put on a few pounds and already knew that somebody was going to call it out as soon as you walked in the door. Maybe your family didn't approve of your lifestyle or maybe you didn't approve of theirs. Whatever the reason, you made it your business to stay as far away from your own family as possible.

     Every family is different, and I understand that certain environments can be downright toxic. I am definitely a proponent of protecting energies, but I am also a proponent of strong families wherever possible. I've seen too many occasions where family members stayed away too long and waited until it was too late. "Death beds" aren't promised to anyone. There's no guarantee that you'll have an opportunity to make things right, and I've seen people whose grief hit 10x worse because they felt that things were left unsettled when their family member died. Sometimes we expect perfection from people who are no more than flawed individuals just like we are. Sometimes you have to be the bigger person who takes the first step, forgives, and tries to move forward. At the very least, you will be able to say that you tried your best. I challenge you this holiday season to try to live peaceably with your family, even if it's just in very small doses.

                                           READ TODAY: PSALMS 133:1

DECEMBER 24

"WORK HARD. PLAY HARD."
-WIZ KHALIFA

Have you ever been in a situation where you just needed a break? Perhaps your job was demanding and even when you were at home, you had to respond to company e-mails that seemed to be non-stop. Maybe you were a stay-at-home parent, and it seemed as if being home was the same thing as being constantly at work. The dirty dishes never stopped piling up and neither did the laundry. It seemed as if you went to bed thinking about the work you needed to do and woke up in the morning thinking about the work you needed to do.

Oh, lighten up a bit why don't ya? While work is a very important part of life, it shouldn't be the only part. If you're not careful, work and other obligations will completely take over your entire schedule. When all you do is work, your relationships will suffer. Many marriages have ended because one or both parties became too wrapped up in work to notice that the marriage was falling apart. Even housework can put a strain on the things that are truly important in life. My old pastor's wife once told me that I was a businesswoman and that I shouldn't feel bad if I needed to hire domestic help. She said that even if I felt I couldn't afford it, that it may be worth cutting back in other areas. "You're no better of a mother to your kids because you scrubbed some toilet seats. As a matter of fact, you'll be worse to them when you're exhausted." Whew chile. That thang set me free. Working non-stop doesn't make you noble. It makes you burned out. When you work hard, it's important to be very intentional, cold, calculating, and almost savage about setting aside time to play hard as well. This Christmas Eve, I pray that you have made plans to play hard with your family and friends.

READ TODAY: ECCLESIASTES 5:18

DECEMBER 25

"HAY IN THE MIDDLE OF THE BARN." -CRUCIAL CONFLICT

Have you ever been in a situation where Jesus was born? Perhaps you were a shepherd minding your own business and watching over your flock at night when an angel of the Lord appeared, scared you a little bit, and then told you to chill out. The angel told you that He was coming with the good news that the Savior had been born, and that you could find him lying in manger. Maybe your name was Mary (Mary? Are you reading this?), and the innkeeper told you that there was no room in the hotel, but that there was this little stable-like thing outdoors, and you could have your baby there.

Y'all, Jesus was literally born on some hay in the middle of the barn. My God Today. The King of Glory entered the world in the most humble way possible. Why is this an important part of the Christmas story? The Bible tells us that Jesus was born this way as a **sign** unto us. When Jesus comes into our lives, He has to enter into a place that may be nasty, dirty, and stinky with sin. His love for us makes Him willing to humble himself to that point just to gain access into our hearts. He's so confident in His ability to wash us, that He's not in the least bit worried about the filthy situation that He finds us in. Let's take some time today to be grateful for the amazing gift that is Jesus, the Christ...Son of the Living God. Merry Christmas from me to you!

READ TODAY: LUKE 2:12

DECEMBER 26

"WANNA BE A BALLER, SHOT-CALLER. 20 INCH BLADES ON THE IMPALA."
-LIL TROY

Have you ever been in a situation where you kind of overdid it for Christmas? Perhaps you woke up this morning and slapped yourself when you checked your bank account balance. Maybe you hadn't planned to spend so much this year, but things just got out of hand. Perhaps you did the parent thing where you tell your kids that you're only getting them two things this year. You really meant it too, but before you knew it, you had gotten them everything on their list. Maybe you decided to "treat yo self" this Christmas and bought a big-ticket item to reward yourself for all of the hard work you put in this year. You probably deserved it. I won't argue with you there.

Christmas morning was such a thrill, but now you're sitting here trying to figure out which bills you can pay late this time around. What is it about Christmas that makes us throw caution to the wind to become ballers and shot callers for a day? Perhaps you even put 20-inch blades on your son's Impala just cuz. Now that you're back to reality, we need to have a little talk. There is nothing wrong with living within your means, even on the holidays. Did you wipe yourself completely out, or do you still have some stored away like a wise person would? You want to be able to start your new year off on a good note, not owing more debt. I've been guilty of this myself, but let's do a better job of applying wisdom instead of letting the excitement of the moment cause us to have regrets later on. You know the kids are just going to play with the cardboard box anyway, right?

READ TODAY: PROVERBS 21:20

DECEMBER 27

"CAN WE JUST TALK... TALK ABOUT WHERE WE'RE GOING?" -KHALID

Have you ever been in a situation where you didn't have any direction? Perhaps you were a high school senior whose school counselors were pretty sorry. You weren't sure if you should be applying to college, picking up a trade, enlisting in the Army, or going to work on the corner for a guy named Marlo. Maybe you were in a relationship with someone and weren't sure if you should be getting engaged or breaking up and never seeing each other again after today.

Not having a sense of direction can be extremely frustrating. In 2012, I was in D.C. for my sister's graduation from Howard. My brother and I left to drop someone off at the train station. On the way back, both of our phones died which meant no GPS. Our memories weren't serving us well on how to get back, so we drove around what looked like the set of *227* for what seemed like forever, just trying to get back to my sister's apartment. We even stopped to ask strangers for directions. I wondered if we'd ever make it back, and finally we did. Once we arrived and told everybody what happened, my other brother informed us that his backpack (which was laying across the backseat) was literally a phone charger. All the while, we could have plugged our phones into his backpack and gained power and thus direction. I said alllll that to say that when you are lost, you need to look no further than the Power Source that is **already** with you. Have a little talk with Jesus, tell Him all about it, and talk about where you're going. Ask Him to give you a clear vision for the future, and then allow His leadership, guidance, and direction to rule in your life.

READ TODAY: PSALMS 32:8

DECEMBER 28

"SEND ME YOUR LOCATION."
-KHALID

Have you ever been in a situation where you couldn't find someone? Perhaps when you were a kid, you got separated from your mom in the grocery store (aka your lil' bad butt wandered off when you weren't supposed to). You checked every aisle and couldn't seem to find her. I really hope it didn't end in her being called over the loudspeaker (aka an automatic whooping when you get home). Maybe the situation was more serious and one of your loved ones literally went missing. Hopefully they were found alive and well, but not knowing their location was probably pretty scary.

Although God always knows where we are, we are not always consciously aware of where He is. What we sometimes fail to realize is that God actually **moves**. Back in the Old Testament Bible days, His presence was literally represented by a moving cloud that people could follow in order to find their way. Now, we have the Holy Spirit within us to lead and guide us in the way that we should go. Sometimes we get so preoccupied with life and disconnected from God, however, that we don't recognize the instances where He has already moved. Take the church for instance. Sometimes we get caught up in old traditions that were once relevant and effective, but when God made a move, we weren't focused on Him enough to follow. Don't let this be your life. We should be constantly asking God to send us His location as we continue to refresh our screen for updates. Wherever God is, that's where we need to be.

READ TODAY: ISAIAH 43:18-19

DECEMBER 29

"GO BEST FRIEND. THAT'S MY BEST FRIEND."
-TOKYO VANITY

Have you ever been in a situation where you had a best friend? Perhaps you had a crush on somebody, and your best friend was the one who played wingman or wingwoman to put you on. Maybe you had gone through a terrible break up and your best friend was the one you could cry to. Your best friend was the one who encouraged you, told you that you could do better anyway, and helped you make fun of your ex's new love interest.

If you have someone you can call your best friend, count yourself as blessed. Some people have good friends but can't quite put their finger on a "best" friend. Thankfully, we all have a best friend in Jesus. I know it sounds crazy to call the Savior of the world "friend," but that's exactly what He is. The good thing about Jesus is that He's been here and has experienced every emotion and every temptation that we ever could. Yet He is the one person who literally did life perfectly! Ayye! Go Best Friend! That's **my** Best Friend! Listen, as you continue walking with the Lord, you will begin to appreciate His friendship even more. As amazing as your current friends are, there will be times when they can't be there for you. There will be times when they won't know what to tell you, but what an amazing friend we have in Jesus! He is literally the Prince of Peace, which means that when we take our situations to Him, He won't be that friend who gets us even more riled up and upset about it. He will be the one to calm us down and let us know that He has it all under control. Because of Jesus, we are blessed with the **best**!

READ TODAY: JOHN 15:15

DECEMBER 30

"JUST HOLD ON. WE'RE GOING HOME."
-DRAKE

Have you ever been in a situation where you weren't at home? Perhaps your parents sent you down to "the country" to spend some time with your relatives there over the summer. You were from the city, so they made fun of the way you talked. They ate differently, every day was hot, and there wasn't a whole lot to do aside from going to the general store. Eventually, you began to get the hang of it, but you were miserable at first and just wanted to go home. Maybe you had to spend the night in the hospital. The bed was uncomfortable, the food was just alright, random people kept coming in to poke you with needles, and the TV was only getting 15 stations. All you wanted was to go home.

Did you know that we aren't from here? This world...I mean we aren't really from this world. As believers we are actually citizens of heaven. That's why certain things here will never completely make sense to us. That's why we have to fight so hard. Things here may seem to be difficult at times, but just hold on. We're going home. Everything here is temporary. Everything we have here can deteriorate or be stolen, but what we have in Heaven is eternal. Let's do our best to complete our God-given assignments here on earth so that when we finally meet the Lord in Heaven, He can say. "Well done my good and faithful servant. Welcome Home."

READ TODAY: JOHN 15:19

DECEMBER 31

"ALTHOUGH WE'VE COME TO THE END OF THE ROAD..." -BOYZ II MEN

Have you ever been in a situation where a good thing came to an end? Perhaps you started some amazing little devotional book at the beginning of the year and now the year is over. Maybe you've enjoyed the daily messages and feel as if some of them really spoke to your life. Maybe you are now wondering how you're going to get "Your God Today."

First of all, let me say thank you so much for reading this book. I have truly enjoyed writing it, and I pray that it has been a blessing to you in some small or big way. I will definitely miss talking to you every day, and although we've come to the end of the road, it's just the beginning for you. The Word of the Lord will stand **forever**. Let this book be like the springboard from which you jump into a deeper relationship with God. I really hope these messages have gotten you into the rhythm of spending daily, intentional time with the Lord. If you are ready, you can begin to craft a new daily routine that keeps you accountable. I really don't want you to fall off. Heck, if you want to start the book over again, you go right ahead. Also, if this book has been a blessing to you, please don't keep it a secret. Share it with family, friends, enemies, and strangers. Please pray for me, and I will continue to pray for you. I will now leave you with my dad's favorite saying. "Oh, what a beautiful morning! Oh, what a beautiful day! I've got a wonderful feeling that the Lord is going to bless someone today, and my prayer is that that someone is you...and me."

My God **today, tomorrow, and forevermore.** Amen.

READ TODAY: ISAIAH 40:8

REFERENCES

Page No.	
3	Chad Hugo and Pharell Williams. "You Don't Have to Call." *8701*, Performed by Usher Raymond, Sony/ATV Music Publishing LLC, Warner Chappell Music Inc., 2001.
4,5	Jeremy Varnard Allen, Jonathan Reed, Torence Hatch, and Webster Gradney. "Wipe Me Down." *Trill Entertainment Presents: Survival of the Fittest*, Performed b y Foxx A Milliyone, Warner Chappell Music Inc., 2007.
6	Jeremy Varnard Allen, Mac Knight Claude III, Melvin Vernell, Torence Hatch, Webster Gradney. "Independent." *Savage Life 2*, Performed by Webbie, Boosie Badazz, and Lil Phat, Warner Chappell Music Inc., 2008.
7	Douglas B. Rasheed, Stevie Wonder, Larry James Sanders, Artis L. Ivey, Jr. "Gangsta's Paradise." *Dangerous Minds Soundtrack*, Performed by Coolio and L.V., WB Music Corp., Large Variety Music, Boo Daddy Publishing, Black Bull Music, Madcastle Muzic, Songs of Polygram Inc., Jobete Music Co., Inc. 2010
8	Anthony Paul Jefferies, Aubrey Drake Graham, and Timmy Thomas. "Hotline Bling." *Views*, Performed by Drake, Sony/ATV Music Publishing LLC, 2015.
9	Brytavious Lakeith Chambers & James Lee Baker. "Shoot." *The Purple M&M*, Performed by BlockBoy JB, Warner Chappell Music Inc, BMG Rights Management, 2017.
10	Shaffer "Ne-Yo" Smith, Tor Erik Hermansen, Mikkel S. Eriksen, Espen Lind, and Amund Bjorklund, & Beyonce. "Irreplaceable." *B'Day*. Performed by Beyonce Knowles, Warner Chappell Music Inc, 2006.
11	Jonathan Smith, Karim Kharbouch, Steve Guess, and William Gricahcine. "Turn Down for What?" *Turn Down for What?* Performed by Lil Jon and DJ Snake, BMG Rights Management, Warner Chappell Music, Inc., 2013.
12	Christopher Bridges, James Phillips, Jonathan Smith, LaMarquis Jefferson, Patrick Michael Smith, Sean Garrett, and Robert McDowell. "Yeah!" *Confessions*, Performed by Lil Jon, Ludacris, & Usher, Sony/ATV Music Publishing LLC, Universal Music Publishing Group, Kobalt Music Publishing Ltd., BMG Rights Management, Songtrust Ave, 2004.
13	Deongelo Holmes, Eric Jackson, Michael A Jones, Craig Love, Jonathan Smith "Salt Shaker." *Me & My Brother*, Performed by YingYang Twins and Lil Jon & The East Side Boyz. Sony/ATV Music Publishing LLC, 2003.
14, 19	Andre Harris & Jill H. Scott. "A Long Walk." *Who is Jill Scott? Words & Sounds Vol 1*, Performed by Jill Scott, Universal Music Publishing Group, 2000.
15, 21	Vidal Davis and Jill Scott. "Gettin' In the Way." *Who is Jill Scott? Words & Sounds Vol 1*, Performed by Jill Scott, Sony/ATV Music Publishing LLC, Universal Music Publishing Group, 2000.
16, 17, 18,	Jill Scott, Darren Henson, and Donald Thompson. "Slowly Surely." *Who is Jill Scott? Words & Sounds Vol 1*, Performed by Jill Scott, Sony/ATV Music Publishing LLC, Universal Music Publishing Group, 2000.
20	Darren T Henson, Tameka Mintze, Keith Isaiha Pelzer. "He Loves Me (Lyzell in E Flat)." *Who is Jill Scott? Words & Sounds Vol 1*, Performed by Jill Scott, Sony/ATV Music Publishing LLC, Universal Music Publishing Group, 2000.
22	Jahmal D. Cantero & Erica Wright. "On & On." *Baduizm*, Performed by Erykah Badu, Universal Music Publishing Group, 1997.
23	Erica Wright & Norman Hurt. "Tyrone." *Live*, Performed by Erykah Badu, Universal Music Publishing Group, Key Club Music, 1997.
24	Erica Wright, James Dewitt Yancey, Philip Eugene Clendeninn. "Didn't Cha Know." *Mama's Gun*, Performed by Erykah Badu, Walt Disney Music Company, Universal Music Publishing Group, 2000.
25	Isaac Hayes, Erica Wright, and Shaun Martin. "Bag Lady." *Mama's Gun*, Performed by Erykah Badu, Universal Music Publishing Group, Warner Chappell Music Inc, 2000.
26	Queen Latifah. "Living Single Theme Song." *Living Single*,. Performed by Queen Latifah, Fox Broadcasting Company, 1993.
27	Tauheed Epps, Onika Maraj, and Jordan Maurice. "Beez In The Trap." *Pink Friday: Roman Reloaded – The Re-Up*, Performed by Nicki Minaj and 2-Chainz, Universal Music Publishing Group, Reservoir Media Management Inc, 2012.
28	Aubrey Drake Graham, Noah James Shebib, & Michael Colemand. "Started From The Bottom." *Nothing Was The Same*, Performed by Drake, Kobalt Music Publishing Ltd., Sony/ATV Music Publishing LLC, 2013.
29-31	Andre Young, Tracy Curry, Calvin Broadus, Frederick Knight, and Leon Haywood. "Nuthin' but a "G" Thang." *The Chronic*, Performed by Dr. Dre and Snoop Dogg, Universal Music Publishing Group, 1992.
32	Roderick Moore & Samuel Gloade. "The Box." *Please Excuse Me for Being Antisocial*, Performed by Roddy Rich, Kobalt Music Publishing Ltd., Warner Chappell Music, Inc., Peermusic Publishing, 2019.
33, 188	Christopher Wallace, Sean Combs, James Mtume, Jean Claude Oliver. "Juicy." *Ready to Die*, Performed by The Notorious B.I.G., Sony/ATV Music Publishing LLC, Universal Music Publishing Group, Downtown Music Publishing, 1994.
34-35	Karen Lynn Anderson, Chauncey Andrae Hannibal, Roosevelt Harrell, Etterlene Jordan & Teddy Riley. "Don't Leave Me." *Another Level*, Performed by Blackstreet, Sony/ATV Music Publishing LLC, Universal Music Publishing Group, BMG Rights Management, Warner Chappell Music, Inc 1997.

36	Andre Benjamin, Patrick L. Brown, Raymon Ameer Murray, Antwan Patton, and Rico Renard Wade. "So Fresh, So Clean." *Stankonia*, Performed by OutKast, BMG Rights Management, Sony/ATV Music Publishing LLC, 2000.
37, 38	Lavell Crump, Clifford Harris. "The Rubberband Man." *Trap Muzik*, Performed by T.I., Warmer Chappell Music, Inc, Universal Music Publishing Group, Royalty Network, 2003.
39	James Scheffer, Clifford Harris, and David Siegel. "Whatever You Like." *Paper Trail*, Performed by T.I., Sony/ATV Music Publishing LLC, Warner Chappell Music, Inc, 2008.
40	Clifford Harris, Curtis Mayfield, Leroy Hutson, Donny Hathaway, Aldrin Davis, Billy Roberts, Gabriel Arillo. "What You Know."*King*, Performed by T.I., Warner Chappell Music Inc, 2006.
41	Kasseem Dean, Thomas Randolph Bell, Shawn C. Carter, Kenneth Gamble, Roland Lawrence Chambers, and Clifford J. Harris. "Bring Em Out." *Urban Legend*, Performed by T.I., Sony/ATV Music Publishing LLC, Warner Chappell Music, Inc, Universal Music Publishing Group, 2004.
42	Aldrin Davis & Clifford Joseph Harris. "U Don't Know Me." *Urban Legend*, Performed by T.I., Warner Chappell Music, Inc, 2004.
43	Aldrin Davis & Clifford Joseph Harris. "Motivation." *Motivation*, Performed by T.I. Warner Chappell Music, Inc, 2004.
44	Wayne Hardnett, Clifford Harris, & Michael Render. "Never Scared." *AttenCHUN!* Performed by Bone Crusher, Killer Mike, and T.I., Warner Chappell Music, Inc, Universal Music Publishing Group, 2003.
45	Jerry Leiber, Mike Stoller, Nathaniel Hale, & Warren Griffin, III. "Regulate." *Above the Rim*, Performed by Warren G and Nate Dogg, Sony/ATV Music Publishing LLC, Warner Chappell Music, Inc, Royalty Network, Ole Media Management LP, 1994.
46	Jonathan Smith, Eric Jackson, & Deongelo Holmes. "Get Low." *Kings of Crunk*, Performed by Lil Jon & The East Side Boyz and Ying Yang Twins, EMI Blackwood Music Inc., Greensleeves Publishing Limited, Reservoir 416, Songs Of TVT BMI, Da Crippler Music, Collipark Music, 2002.
47	Chad L. Butler, Bernard James Freeman, Willie M. Hutch, Andre Benjamin, & Antwan Patton. "Int'l Players Anthem." *Underground Kingz*, Performed by UGK, Three 6 Mafia, and OutKast, Sony/ATV Music Publishing LLC, Universal Music Publishing Group, BMG Rights Management, 2007.
48, 49	Andre Benjamin, Antwan Patton, & David Sheats. "Ms. Jackson." *Stankonia*, Performed by OutKast, BMG Rights Management, 2000.
50, 196	Andre Benjamin. "Hey Ya!" *Speakerboxxx/The Love Below*, Performed by OutKast, Sony/ATV Music Publishing LLC, BMG Rights Management, 2003.
51	Antwan Patton, Carlton Mahone, Patrick Brown. "The Way You Move." *Speakerboxxx/The Love Below*, Performed by OutKast & Sleepy Brown, Sony/ATV Music Publishing LLC, BMG Rights Management, 2003.
52	Montay Humphrey, Korey Roberson, Anthony Platt, Howard Simmons, Richard Sims Jr., Reginald Jones, Miguel Willis, and Jarvis Griffin. "Walk It Out." *Beat'n Down Yo Block!* Performed by Unk, Ultra Tunes, Universal Music Publishing Group, Tunecore Inc., 2007.
53, 56	Skip Scarborough, Gene Clark, and Lauryn Hill. "Lost Ones." *The Miseducation of Lauryn Hill*, Performed by Lauryn Hill, Sony/ATV Music Publishing LLC, Warner Chappell Music, Inc, Universal Music Publishing Group., 1998.
54, 55	Lauryn Hill, Alan Bergman, Marilyn Bergman, Marvin Hamlisch, Robert Diggs, Corey Woods, Jason Hunter, Clifford Smith, Lamont Hawkins, Dennis Coles, Gary Grice, and Russell Jones. "Ex-Factor." *The Miseducation of Lauryn Hill*, Performed by Lauryn Hill, Sony/ATV Music Publishign LLC, Universal Music Publishing Group., 1998.
57	Bobby F. Ervin, James Todd Smith, Marlon Williams, George Clinton, Gregory Jacobs, James Louis McCants, Sylvester Stewart, Walter Morrison, and William Collins. "Mama Said Knock You Out." *Mama Said Knock You Out*, Performed by LL Cool J, Sony/ATV Music Publishing LLC, Universal Music Publishing Group, A Side Music LLCL D/B/A Modern Works Music Publishing, 1990.
58	Christopher A Stewart, Bobby F. Ervin, Steven J. Ettinger, Terius Youngdell Nash, Darryl La Mont Pierce, Dwayne Emil Simon, and James Todd Smith. "I Need Love." *Bigger and Deffer*, Performed by LL Cool J, Sony/ATV Music Publishing LLC, Peermusic Publishing, Universal Music Publishing Group, Warner Chappell Music, Inc, BMG Rights Management, Warner Chappell Music Inc, 1987.
59	Cameron Gipp, Patrick Browon, Raymon Murray, Rico Wade, Robert Barnett, Thomas Callaway, and Willie Knighton, "Cell Therapy." *Soul Food*. Performed by Goodie Mobb, Universal Music Publishing Group, BMG Rights Management, Shelly Bay Music, 1995.
60	Christopher Dorsey, Dwayne Carter, Tab Virgil, Jr., Byron Thomas, Bryan Williams, and Terius Gray. "Bling Bling." *Chopper City in the Ghetto*, Performed by B.G., Hot Boys, Big Tymers, Ultra Tunes, Universal Music Publishing Group, 1999.
61	Marcel Theo Hall, "Just A Friend." *The Biz Never Sleeps*, Performed by Biz Markie, Warner Chappell Music, Inc., Cak Music Publishing, Inc., 1989.
62	Christopher Bridges, Calvin Broadus, Jermaine Dupri, Murphy Lee, Cameron Mosley, Christine Perren, Freddie Perren, and Christine Yarian. "Welcome to Atlanta." *The Source Presents: Hip Hop Hits, Vol. 6*, performed by Jermaine Dupri and Ludacris, Sony/ATV Music Publishing LLC, Universal Music Publishing Group, 2002.
63, 64 209	Bryan Williams and Byron O. Thomas. "Still Fly." *Hood Rich*, performed by Big Tymers, Universal Music Publishing Group, BMG Rights Management, 2002.
65	Clive Campbell, Anthony Martin, Cheryl James, Sandra Denton, and Michael Love. "Break of Dawn." *Very Necessary*, performed by Salt-N-Pepa, Break of Dawn lyrics © Kobalt Music Publishing Ltd., Warner Chappell Music, Inc, 1993
66	Christopher Jasper, Christopher Wallace, Ernie Isley, Marvin Isley, O'kelly Isley, Ronald Isley, and Rudolph Isley. "Big Poppa." *Ready to Die*, performed by The Notorious B.I.G.,Sony/ATV Music Publishing LLC, 1994.

67	Dominic Bazile and Christopher Bridges. "Get Back." *The Red Light District*, performed by Ludacris,Ultra Tunes, Universal Music Publishing Group, 2004.
68, 206	Paul D. Beauregard, Ricky Dunigan, Jeffery Grisby, Jordan Houston, Sean Paul Joseph, Stephanie Martin, Lola Chantrelle Mitchell, Jonathan H. Smith, and Jason Williams. "Move B**ch!" *Word of Mouf*, performed by Ludacris, Universal Music Publishing Group, Downtown Music Publishing, BMG Rights Management, Reservoir Media Management Inc, 2001.
69	Jermaine Dupri, and Usher Raymond, and Bryan Cox. "U Got It Bad." *8701*, performed by Usher, Sony/ATV Music Publishing LLC, Warner Chappell Music, Inc, Warner Chappell Music Inc, 2001.
70	Kameron Houff, Scott Storch, and Shaffer Smith. "Let Me Love You." *Turning Point*, performed by Mario, Sony/ATV Music Publishing LLC, Warner Chappell Music, Inc, Universal Music Publishing Group, Reservoir Media Management Inc, Kobalt Music Publishing Ltd., 2004.
71	Byron Miller, Darrel Gibson, Janice Marie Johnson, and Roland Bautista. "I Got A Man." *The Skills Dat Pay da Bills*, performed by Positive K, Cohen And Cohen, Music Sales Corporation, 1992.
72	Jason Phillips, Christopher Wallace, Trevor Smith, Sean Puffy Combs, Bill Conti, and Steven A Jordan. "Victory." *No Way Out*, performed by Puff Daddy and The Family, Emi April Music Inc., Justin Combs Publishing Company Inc., Big Poppa Music, Jae'wons Publishing, Tziah Music, Emi Unart Catalog Inc., Emi U Catalog Inc., Steven A. Jordan Music, Inc.,1997.
73	Andrew Harr, Jermaine Jackson, Tramar Dillard, and William Roberts. "Birthday." *Mail on Sunday*, performed by Flo Rida, Sony/ATV Music Publishing LLC, Warner Chappell Music Inc, 2008.
74	Aliaune Thiam and Calvin Broadus. "I Wanna Love You." *Konvicted*, performed by Akon, Sony/ATV Music Publishing LLC, Universal Music Publishing Group, BMG Rights Management, 2006.
75	Dwayne Carter, Shondrae Crawford, Kamaal Fareed, Charles Hester, and Ali Shaheed Muhammad. "A Milli." *The Carter III*, performed by Lil Wayne, Sony/ATV Music Publishing LLC, Warner Chappell Music, Inc, Universal Music Publishing Group, 2008.
76	Dwayne Carter, Shondrae Crawford, Kamaal Fareed, Charles Hester, and Ali Shaheed Muhammad. "A Milli." *The Carter III*, performed by Lil Wayne, Sony/ATV Music Publishing LLC, Warner Chappell Music, Inc, Universal Music Publishing Group, 2008.
77	Eric Henry Timmons. "Da' Dip." *Controversee*, performed by Freak Nasty, Sony/ATV Music Publishing LLC, 1997.
78	Stephen Ellis Garrett and Timothy Z Mosley. "Try Again." *Romeo Must Die*, performed by Aaliyah, Sony/ATV Music Publishing LLC, BMG Rights Management US, LLC, 2000.
79	Bryan Michael Paul Cox and Jermaine Dupri."Confessions Part II." *Confessions*, performed by Usher Raymond, Sony/ATV Music Publishing LLC, 2004.
80	Herby Azor and Raymond Douglas Davies. "Push It." *Hot, Cool, & Vicious*, performed by Salt-N-Pepa, © Warner Chappell Music, Inc, 1987.
81	Gregory Williams, Jamal F Jones, Marece Benjamin Richards, and Robert L. Debarge. "Throw Some D's." *Rich Boy*, performed by Rich Boy, Universal Music Publishing Group, Sony/ATV Music Publishing LLC, 2007.
82, 83	James Todd Smith, Derek Simmons, Dallas Austin, Quincy Jones, Willie Baker and Jerry Davis. "Don't Take It Personal (Just One of Dem Days)." *Miss Thang*, performed by Monica, Warner Chappell Music, Inc, Sony/ATV Music Publishing LLC, Universal Music Publishing Group, BMG Rights Management, 1995.
84	Fred Jerkins III, Lashawn Ameen Daniels, Rodney Jerkins, Japhe Tejada, and Brandy Norwood. "The Boy Is Mine."*Never Say Never*, performed by Brandy and Monica, Sony/ATV Music Publishing LLC, 1998.
85, 86	Kenneth Edmonds. "Sitting Up In My Room." *Waiting To Exhale*, performed by Brandy, Sony/ATV Music Publishing LLC, Fox Music, Inc, 1998.
87, 88	Paul Simon, Melissa A. Elliott, Darryl Matthews Mcdaniels, Joseph Ward Simmons, Curtis James Jackson, Deborah Harry, and Christopher Stein."Work It." *Under Construction*, performed by Missy Elliot, Kobalt Music Publishing Ltd., Warner Chappell Music, Inc, Universal Music Publishing Group, BMG Rights Management, Sony/ATV Music Publishing LLC, 2002.
89, 90	O'shea Jackson, Arthur Lee Goodman, O'kelly Jr. Isley, S. Robinson, Ernest Isley, Marvin Isley, Ronald Isley, Rudolph Bernard Isley, Chris Jasper, and H. Ray. "It Was a Good Day." *The Predator*, performed by Ice Cube, Sony/ATV Music Publishing LLC, Warner Chappell Music, Inc, Universal Music Publishing Group, 1992.
91	Ivan Barias, Carvin Haggins, Corey Latif Williams, Adam W. Blackstone, George Mccurdy, Randall C. Bowland, and Johnnie Ii Smith. "Teachme." *Luvanmusiq*, performed by Musiq Soulchild, Universal Music Corp., Hc 1030 Publishing, Nivrac Tyke Music, Tetragrammaton Music, My Soulmate Songs Llc, Ablack Productions, Latif Music, Melodic Piano Productions, 2007.
92	Andre Romell Young, Roger Troutman, Larry Troutman, Tupac Amaru Shakur, Christopher Stainton, Ronnie Hudson, Mikel Hooks, Joe Cocker. "California Love." *All Eyez On Me*, performed by Tupac Shakur, Roger Troutman, and Dr. Dre, Sony/ATV Music Publishing LLC, Universal Music Publishing Group, Songtrust Ave, BMG Rights Management, Music Sales Corporation, T.R.O. Inc., 1996.
93	Deric Micheal Angelettie, Sean Combs, Christopher Wallace, Andy Armer, Ron Badazz, and Ronald Anthony Lawrence. "Hypnotize." *Life After Death*, performed by The Notorious B.I.G., Sony/ATV Music Publishing LLC, Universal Music Publishing Group, BMG Rights Management, 1977.
94	Jeffrey Irwin Bass, Marshall B Mathers, and Luis Edgardo Resto. "Lose Yourself." *8 Mile SoundTrack*, performed by Eminem, Kobalt Music Publishing Ltd., 2002.
95	Combs Sean Puffy, Wallace Christopher, Smith Trevor, Smith James Todd, Harvey Osten S, Mack Craig J, and Mc Nair Roger. "Flava In Ya Ear." *Funk da World*, performed by Criag Mack, Wb Music Corp., Emi April Music Inc., Justin Combs Publishing Company Inc., Ll Cool J Music, Big Poppa Music, Alvin Toney Music, For Ya Ear Music, Tziah Music, Sony/atv Tunes LLC, 1994.

96	Ali Shaheed Jones-Muhammad, Andrew Noland, Bryan Higgins, G Webster, James Jr. Jackson, Jim Morrison, Kamaal Ibn John Fareed, Leroy Bonner, Malik Izaak Taylor, Marshall E Jones, Marvin R. Pierce, Norman B Napier, Ralph Middlebrooks, and Trevor Smith. "Scenario." *The Low End Theory*, performed by A Tribe Called Quest, Sony/ATV Music Publishing LLC, Universal Music Publishing Group, 1991.
97	Isaac Hayes, Brad Jordan, Willie Dennis, and Doug King. "Mind Playing Tricks on Me." *We Can't Be Stopped*, performed by Geto Boys, Universal Music Publishing Group, 1991.
98	Calvin Broadus, Chad Hugo, and Pharrell Williams. "Beautiful." *Paid tha Cost to Be da Boss*, performed by Pharrell Williams and Snoop Dogg, Sony/ATV Music Publishing LLC, Warner Chappell Music, Inc, 2002.
99-100	Carl Davis. "The Message." *The Message*, performed by Grandmaster Flash and Furious Five, Warner Chappell Music, Inc, 1982.
101-102	Nile Rodgers and Bernard Edwards. "Rapper's Delight." *Sugarhill Gang*, performed by The Sugarhill Gang, Sony/ATV Music Publishing LLC, Warner Chappell Music, Inc, Songtrust Ave, 1980.
103, 104	Aaquil Brown, Khalif Brown, and Michael Williams. "No Type." *SremmLife*, performed by Rae Sremmurd, Warner Chappell Music, Inc, 2014.
105	Jeffrey Lee Johnson, Christopher James Gholson, Olubowale Victor Akintimehin, and Juaquin Malphurs. "No Hands." *Flockaveli*, performed by Roscoe Dash and Waka Flocka Flame, Warner Chappell Music, Inc, Universal Music Publishing Group, 2010.
106	Aubrey Drake Graham, Darius Hill, Mathias Daniel Liyew, Nayvadius Wilburn, and Ozan Yildirim. "Life Is Good." *High Off Life*, performed Future and Drake, Universal Music Publishing Group, Sony/ATV Music Publishing LLC, 2020.
107, 108 109, 110	Christopher Wallace, Sean Combs, Mason Betha, Bernard Edwards, Steve Jordan, J Phillips, and Nile Gregory Rodgers. "Mo Money Mo Problems." *Life After Death*, performed by The Notorious B.I.G., Mase, and Sean Combs, Sony/ATV Music Publishing LLC, Warner Chappell Music, Inc, 1997.
111	Clifford Harris, Clifford J. Harris, Cordale Quinn, Darwin Cordale Quinn, and Djuan Hart. "Shoulder Lean." *Day One (Gangsta Grillz)*, performed by Young Dro and T.I., Warner Chappell Music, Inc., 2006.
112	James Brown, Fred Wesley, John Starks, Terri E. Robinson, Herb Middleton, Mark South, Joe Howell, Randy Ryan, And Sean Combs. "Can't You See." *New Jersey Drive, Vol. 1*, performed by Total and The Notorious B.I.G., Universal Music Publishing Group, Sony/ATV Music Publishing LLC, Warner Chappell Music, Inc., 1995.
113	Brandon Casey, Brandon D Casey, Brian Casey, Brian D Casey, Bryan Michael Paul Cox, Jermaine Dupri, and Cornell Haynes. "Where The Party At lyrics." *Jagged Little Thrill*, performed by Jagged Edge, Tony/ATV Music Publishing LLC, Warner Chappell Music, Inc, Universal Music Publishing Group, Kobalt Music Publishing Ltd.
114	Harry Casey, Sean Combs, Richard Raymond Finch, Daron Jones, Steven A Jordan, Michael Keith, Quinnes Parker, Marvin Scandrick, Christopher Wallace, and Dj Jr Rogers. "Only You." *112*, performed by 112, Sony/ATV Music Publishing LLC, Warner Chappell Music, Inc, Royalty Network, 1996.
115	Bernard Freeman, Chad L Butler, Eric Barrier, Jordan Houston, Jordan Stuart, Paul Beauregard, Todd Shaw, and William Lee Griffin. "Like A Pimp." *MTA2: Baptized in Dirty Water*, performed by David Banner, Twista, and Busta Rhymes, Warner Chappell Music, Inc, Universal Music Publishing Group, BMG Rights Management, 2003.
116, 117	Craig Love, James Phillips, Jonathan H Smith, La Marquis Jefferson, and Todd Anthony Shaw. "Blow the Whistle." *Blow the Whistle*, performed by Too Short, MG Rights Management US, LLC, Reservoir Media Management Inc, Roba Music, Sony/ATV Music Publishing LLC, Warner Chappell Music Publishing Group, 2006.
106,118 119, 120	Teruis Gray, Byron Thomas, and Dwayne Carter. "Back That Azz Up." *400 Degreez*, performed by Juvenile, Lil Wayne, and Mannie Fresh, Sony/ATV Music Publishing LLC, Universal Music Publishing Group, Warner Chappell Music, Inc, 1998.
121	Frank Ski, Jonathan Dumas, Jonathan Wright, Michael Crooms, Scott Pajaro, and Victor Owusu. "Wobble." *Beast*, performed by V.I.C, Sony/ATV Music Publishing LLC, 2008.
122	Bryson Bernard."Cupid Shuffle." *Time for a Change*, performed by Cupid, BMG Rights Management, The Bicycle Music Company, 2007.
123	Willie Perry and Emiliano Venturi. "Mississippi Cha Cha Slide." *Pure Instrumental: Dance, Vol . 2*, Performed by DJ Casper and DJ Twilight. 2011.
124	Marvel Thompson, Willie Jr. Perry, Capser Hudson Beaudy. "Cha-Cha Slide." *Cha-Cha Slide*, Performed by DJ Casper, Spirit Music Group, Hayrome Music Publishing, 2000.
125	Charles Wilson, Devon Gallaspy, Jeffrey Bhasker, Lonnie Simmons, Mark Ronson, Nicholaus Williams, Peter Hernandez, Philip Lawrence, Robert Wilson, Ronnie Wilson, and Rudy Taylor. "Uptown Funk." *Uptown Funk*. Performed by Bruno Mars, Sony/ATV Music Publishing LLC, Warner Chappell Music, Inc, Universal Music Publishing Group, BMG Rights Management, Kobalt Music Publishing Ltd., Concord Music Publishing LLC, New Songs Administration, Warner Chappell Music Inc, 2014.
125	Devon Gallaspy and Nicholaus Williams. "All Gold Everything." *Street Runnaz 71*, Performed by Trinidad James, Sony/ATV Music Publishing LLC, Kobalt Music Publishing Ltd.
126	Rick James, Alonzo Herbert Miller, MC Hammer. "U Can't Touch This." *Please Hammer Don't Hurt Em*. Performed by MC Hammer, Sony/ATV Music Publishing LLC, BMG Rights Management, 1990.
127	Eric Dawkins , Tyrese Darnell Gibson, Harvey Jay Mason, Damon Thomas, and Damon E Thomas. "How You Gonna Act Like That?" *I Wanna Go There*, Performed by Tyrese, Sony/ATV Music Publishing LLC, Universal Music Publishing Group
128	Darryl Richardson II and Isaac Hayes III. "Money In the Bank." *Bred 2 Die, Born 2 Live*, Performed by Lil Scrappy, Sony/ATV Music Publishing LLC, 2006.

129, 130	Adam James Pigott, Aubrey Drake Graham. Benjamin Joseph Workman, Caresha Brown, Darius Harrison. Dwayne Michael Carter, James Gregory Scheffer, Jatavia Johnson, Noah James Shebib, Orville Erwin Hall, Phillip Glenn Price, Renetta Yemika Lowe, Rex Fritz Zamor, Stephen Ellis Garrett, and Kinta Cox. "In My Feelings." *Scorpion*, Performed by Drake, Warner Chappell Music, Inc, Peermusic Publishing, Universal Music Publishing Group, Kobalt Music Publishing Ltd., Sony/ATV Music Publishing LLC, Royalty Network, Behind The Ropes Entertainment, 2018.
131, 132, 133	Montell Du'Sean Jordan, Oji Pierce, and Ricky M L Walters. "This Is How We Do It." *This is How We Do It*. Performed by Montell Jordan, Warner Chappell Music, Inc, Universal Music Publishing Group, Kobalt Music Publishing Ltd., The Bicycle Music Company, Sony/ATV Music Publishing LLC, 1995.
134	Lauryn Hill & Kanye West. "All Falls Down." *The College Dropout*, Performed by Kanye West and Syleena Johnson, Sony/ATV Music Publishing LLC, 2004.
135	Andre Benjamin, Beyonce Knowles, Dexter Mills, Douglas Davis, Jeffrey Bhasker, Kanye West and Ricky Walters. "Party." *4*, Performed by Beyonce, Sony/ATV Music Publishing LLC, Warner Chappell Music, Inc, Ultra Tunes, Downtown Music Publishing, Songtrust Ave, Kobalt Music Publishing Ltd., BMG Rights Management, 2011.
136	Michael Flowers, Rayshawn Sherrer, Sunshine Anderson. "Heard It All Before." *Your Woman*, Performed by Sunshine Anderson, Warner Chappell Music, Inc, 2011.
137	Barry Adams, Barry Lewis Adams, Lefabian Williams, Fabo, and Adrian Parks. "Scotty." *Down For Life*, Performed by D4L, Kobalt Music Publishing Ltd., Royalty Network, 2005.
138	Rodney Jerkins, Jolyon Ward Skinner, Japhe Tejeda, Joe Thomas, and Michele Williams. "Don't Wanna Be A Player." *All That I Am*, Performed by Joe, Sony/ATV Music Publishing LLC, Universal Music Publishing Group, Songtrust Ave, 1997.
139	Rodney Jerkins, Rodney Roy Jerkins, Brenda Gordon Russell, Jolyon Ward Skinner, Japhe Tejeda, Joe Thomas, and Michele Williams. "Still Not A Player." *Capital Punishment*, Performed by Big Pun and Joe, Sony/ATV Music Publishing LLC, Universal Music Publishing Group, 1998.
140	Cameron Osteen, Chancelor Bennett, Conor Szymanski, Dwayne Carter, Ivan Jackson Rosenberg, Jamie Woods, Jonathan Hoard, Lakeithsha Williams, Peter Wilkins, Rachel Cato, and Tauheed Epps. "No Problem [Carry Me]" *Coloring Book*, Performed by Chance The Rapper, Warner Chappell Music, Inc, Sony/ATV Music Publishing LLC, BMG Rights Management, Reservoir Media Management Inc, The Administration MP Inc, Warner Chappell Music Inc, 2016.
141,142 143,191	Blues Brothers, Carl Thompson, Christopher Wallace, and Sean Combs. "One More Chance." *Ready to Die*. Performed by The Notorious B.I.G. and Faith Evans, Sony/ATV Music Publishing LLC, Songtrust Ave, BMG Rights Management, Downtown Music Publishing, 1994.
144,145, 146,147, 148, 149	Christopher Jasper, Christopher Wallace, Ernie Isley, Marvin Isley, O'kelly Isley, Ronald Isley, and Rudolph Isley. "Big Poppa." *Ready to Die*. Performed by The Notorious B.I.G., Sony/ATV Music Publishing LLC, Songtrust Ave, BMG Rights Management, Downtown Music Publishing, 1994.
150, 151	Tupac Amaru Shakur, Tony Pizarro, Bruce Andre Hawes, Charles B Simmons, Joseph Banks Jefferson, Joseph Leslie Sample, Terence Thomas, and Tony D Pizarro. "Dear Mama." *Me Against the World*, Performed by 2Pac, Universal Music Publishing Group, Royalty Network, 1995.
152	Tupac Amaru Shakur, Delmar Drew Arnaud, Calvin Cordozar Broadus. "2 of Amerikaz Most Wanted" *All Eyez on Me*, Performed by 2Pac and Snoop Dogg, Warner Chappell Music, Inc, Universal Music Publishing Group, 1996.
153	Delmar Arnaud, Danny Steward, Tupac Shakur, and Etterlene Jordan. "I Ain't Mad at Cha." *All Eyez on Me*, Performed by 2Pac and DannyBoy, Sony/ATV Music Publishing LLC, Universal Music Publishing Group, Songtrust Ave, Ole Media Management Lp, Ent One Pub, Warner Chappell Music Inc, 1996.
154	Johnny Lee Jackson, Tupac Amaru Shakur, Bruce Fisher, Quincy D. Jones, Leon Ware, and Stanley J. Richardson. "How Do U Want It?" *2 Gangsta 2Die*, Performed by 2Pac and K-Ci & JoJo, Universal Music Publishing Group, BMG Rights Management, 1996.
155, 156, 157	David Wynn, Markell Riley, Anton Lamont Hollins, Etterlene Jordan, Eldra Debarge, William Debarge, AQqil Davidson, Pharrell Williams, David Porter, Teddy Riley. "Rump Shaker." *Hard or Smooth*, Performed by Wreckx-N-Effect, Sony/ATV Music Publishing LLC, Universal Music Publishing Group, BMG Rights Management, 1992.
158	Percy Miller & Choppa. "Choppa Style." *Straight From The N.O.*, Performed by Choppa, UMG (on behalf of No Limit Records); LatinAutor, BMI - Broadcast Music Inc., and 7 Music Rights Societies, 2003.
159	Bryan Michael, Paul Cox, and Jermaine Dupri, "Confessions Part II." *Confessions*. Performed by Usher, Sony/ATV Music Publishing LLC, 2004.
160, 161	Robert Shea Taylor, Terius Youngdell Nash, Wanya Jermaine Morris, Nathan B. Morris, Cainon Renard Lamb, Beyonce Gisselle Knowles, Julie Frost, Michael Bivins, and Esther Dean. "Countdown." *4*, Performed by Beyonce, Peermusic Publishing, Sony/ATV Music Publishing LLC, Warner Chappell Music, Inc, Universal Music Publishing Group, Downtown Music Publishing, BMG Rights Management, 2011.
162, 163, 164	Asheton Hogan, Aaquil Iben Shamon Brown, Khalif Malik, Beyonce Giselle Knowles, Michael Len Williams. "Formation." *Lemonade*, Performed by Beyoncé, Warner Chappell Music, Inc, Sony/ATV Music Publishing LLC, 2016.
165	Solange Knowles, Willie James Clarke, Beyoncé Knowles, Makeba Riddick, Clarence Henry Reid, Shawn Carter, Angela Beyince, and Sean Garrett. "Upgrade U." *B'Day*, Performed by Beyoncé, Sony/ATV Music Publishing LLC, Warner Chappell Music, Inc, BMG Rights Management, Warner Chappell Music Inc, 2006.
166	Rob Fusari, Beyonce Knowles, and Falonte D Moore. "Bootylicious." *Survivor*, Performed by Destiny's Child, Sony/ATV Music Publishing LLC, Warner Chappell Music, Inc, Universal Music Publishing Group, Warner Chappell Music Inc, 2001.

167, 168	Elliot Straite. "Poison." *Poison*, Performed by Bell Biv DeVoe, Universal Music Publishing Group, Sony/ATV Music Publishing LLC, BMI Broadcast Music Inc, Warner Chappell Music Inc, 1990.
169	Parker Ray Erskine. "Mr. Telephone Man." *New Edition*, Performed by New Edition, Universam Music Publishing Group, 1984.
170	James Harris III, and Terry Lewis. "Can You Stand the Rain?" *Heart Break*, Performed by New Edition, Kobalt Music Publishing Ltd., 1988.
171	James Harris III, and Terry Lewis. "If It Isn't Love." *Heart Break*, Performed by New Edition, Sony/ATV Music Publishing LLC, Kobalt Music Publishing Ltd., 1988.
172	Alphonce Tyree Smith, Brittany Nicole Carpentero, Chris Henderson, Jarques Usher, Jonathan Lewis, and Venetia Lewis. "Knuck If You Buck." *Crime Mob*, Performed by Crime Mob and Lil Scrappy, Sony/ATV Music Publishing LLC, Kobalt Music Publishing Ltd., Create Music, Reservoir Media Management Inc., 2004.
173	Antonio Reid and Kenneth Babyface Edmonds. "Every Little Step." *Don't Be Cruel*, Performed by Bobby Brown, Sony/ATV Music Publishing LLC, Karen Schauben Publishing Administration, 1998.
174	Teddy Riley, Gene Griffin, and Bobby Brown. "My Prerogative." *Don't Be Cruel*, Performed by Bobby Brown, Sony/ATV Music Publishing LLC, Universal Music Publishing Group, BMG Rights Management, 1998.
175	Daryl Simmons and Kenneth Edmonds. "My My My." *Johnny Gill*, Performed by Johnny Gill, After 7, and Kenny G, Sony/ATV Music Publishing LLC, Warner Chappell Music, Inc, Karen Schauben Publishing Administration, Unidisc Music, Warner Chappell Music Inc, 1990.
176, 177	Maurice Jordan, Jermaine Anthony Preyan, Robert Rihmeek Williams, and Anthony Tucker. "Dreams and Nightmares." *Dreams and Nightmares*, Performed by Meek Mill, Sony/ATV Music Publishing LLC, Warner Chappell Music, Inc, Universal Music Publishing Group, Warner Chappell Music Inc., 2012.
178, 179 205	Brytavious Lakeith Chambers, Jacques Webster, Khalif Malik Ibin Shaman Brown, Aubrey Drake Graham, Chauncey Hollis, Cydel Charles Young, Mike Dean, Mirsad Dervic, Ozan Yildirim, Ali Shaheed Jones-Muhammad, Bryan Higgins, Chris Wallace, Christopher Edward Martin, Chylow M. Parker, Fred Scruggs, Harry Casey, James Jackson, Kamaal Ibn Jonathan Davis Fareed, Keith Elam, Kevin Gomringer, Kirk Jones, Luther Roderick Campbell, Malik Isaac Taylor, Osten Harvey, Roget Lutfi Chahayed, Tim Gomringer, and Trevor Smith. "SICKO Mode." *Astroworld*, Performed by Travis Scott, Drake, Swae Lee, and Big Hawk, Warner Chappell Music, Inc, BMG Rights Management, Sony/ATV Music Publishing LLC, Universal Music Publishing Group, Kobalt Music Publishing Ltd., 2018.
180	Adele Laurie Blue Adkins and Ryan B. Tedder. "Turning Tables." *21*, Performed by Adele, Universal Music Publishing Group, Downtown Music Publishing, 2011.
181	Dwayne Carter, Rasool Diaz, Andre Proctor, Brian Soko, Bryan Williams, Noel Fisher, Jermaine Anthony Preyan, and Marco Rodriguez. "No Worries." *I Am Not A Human Being II*, Performed by Lil Wayne and Detail, Sony/ATV Music Publishing LLC, Warner Chappell Music, Inc, Universal Music Publishing Group, Songtrust Ave, 2013.
182	Darnell Bristol, Kenneth B. Edmonds, and Sidney De Wayne Johnson. "Two Occasions." *Eyes of A Stranger*, Performed by The Deele, Sony/ATV Music Publishing LLC, Missing Link Music, Tammi Music Ltd., 1987.
183	Christopher Jasper, Ernie Isley, Marvin Isley, O'kelly Isley, Ronald Isley, Rudolph Isley, "Choosey Lover." *Between The Sheets*, Performed by The Isley Brothers, Sony/ATV Music Publishing LLC, 1983.
184, 185	Larry Muggerod, Kal Mann, Erik Schrody, and David Appell. "Jump Around." *House of Pain*, Performed by House of Pain, Warner Chappell Music, Inc, Spirit Music Group, BMG Rights Management, Sony/ATV Music Publishing LLC, Royalty Network, Warner Chappell Music Inc, 1992.
186	Bryan Williams, Byron O. Thomas, Dwayne Carter, and Terius Gray. "Project Chick." *Baller Blockin'*, Performed by Cash Money Millionaires, Big Tymers, Lil Wayne, and Juvenile, Universal Music Publishing Group, Ultra Tunes, 2000.
187	Mikkel Storleer Eriksen, Shaffer Smith, and Tor Erik Hermansen. "Miss Independent." *Year of The Gentleman*, Performed by Ne-Yo, Sony/ATV Music Publishing LLC, Universal Music Publishing Group, 2008.
189	Anthony Gilmour, Claydes Smith, Dennis Thomas, Denzil Foster, Donald Boyce, Garrick Husbands, George Brown, Jay King, Jerold Ellis, Mike Marshall, Rick Westfield, Robert Bell, Robert Mickens,Thomas McElroy. "I Got 5 On It." *Operation Stackola*, Performed by Luniz, Sony/ATV Music Publishing LLC, Warner Chappell Music, Inc, Mike Meszy Publishing, The Bicycle Music Company, 1995.
190	Andre Benjamin and Antwan Patton. "Elevators." *ATLiens*, Performed by OutKast, BMG Rights Management, 1996.
192	Brandy Hambrick, Dwain Warren, and Jasiel Robinson. "I Know You See It." *New Joc City*, Performed by Yung Joc and Brandy B, Warner Chappell Music, Inc, Jellybean Music Group, 2006.
193	Brown Wardell and Lewis Charles Wesley. "Love on The Bayou." *My Sidepiece*, Performed by The Louisiana Blues Brother, Major Clark, Jr. and Pokey, Beat Flippin, Highwayheavywait, 2014.
194	Marshall Mathers, Andre Young, Michael Elizondo, and Thomas Coster. "The Real Slim Shady." *The Marshall Mathers LP*, Performed by Eminem, Warner Chappell Music, Inc, BMG Rights Management, 2000.
195	Juan Salinas, Oscar Salinas, Anthony Henderson, and Hakeem Seriki. "Ridin'." *The Sound of Revenge*. Performed by Chamillionaire and Sway, Sony/ATV Music Publishing LLC, Universal Music Publishing Group, BMG Rights Management, 2005.
197, 198,199	Chadron Moore & Jasiel Robinson. "It's Goin' Down." *New Joc City*, Performed by Yung Joc and Nitti, Sony/ATV Music Publishing LLC, Warner Chappell Music, Inc, Songtrust Ave, 2006.
200	Niladri Kumar and Talvin Singh. "Play." *Certified*, Performed by David Banner, BMG Rights Management, 2005.
201	Chad Hugo, Michael Tyler, and Pharrell L. Williams. "Danger (Been So Long)" *Let's Get Ready*, Performed by Mystikal and Nivea, Sony/ATV Music Publishing LLC, Warner Chappell Music, Inc, Universal Music Publishing Group, Warner Chappell Music Inc, 2000.

202, 203 204	Deongelo Holmes, Eric Jackson, Michael Antoine Crooms, and Warren Mathis. "Ms. New Booty." *The Charm*, Performed by Bubba Sparxxx, Mr. Collipark, Ying Yang Twins, Sony/ATV Music Publishing LLC, 2006.
207	Clifford Joseph Harris, Darwin Cordale Quinn, Jay Jenkins, and Lavell Crump. "My Hood." *Let's Get It: Thug Motivation 101*, Performed by Young Jeezy, Sony/ATV Music Publishing LLC, BMG Rights Management, Warner Chappell Music Inc, 2005.
208	Andre Benjamin, Antwon Patton, and Matt Boykin. "Roses." *Speakerboxxx/The Love Below*, Performed by Outkast, Sony/ATV Music Publishing LLC, BMG Rights Management, 2004.
210	Andrew Harr, Jermaine Jackson, and William Roberts. "Hustlin'." *Port of Miami*, Performed by Rick Ross, Warner Chappell Music Inc, 2006.
211	Carl Terrell Mitchell, Miri Ben-Ari, Michael Bennett, Leonard C. Sr. Williams, and Kanye Omari West. "Overnight Celebrity." *Kamikaze*, Performed by Twista and Kanye West, Sony/ATV Music Publishing LLC, Universal Music Publishing Group, 2004.
212	Chad Hugo,Terrence Thornton, Gene Thornton Jr, and Pharrell Williams. "Grindin'." *Lord Willin'*, Sony/ATV Music Publishing LLC, Warner Chappell Music, Inc., 2001.
213	Pharrell Williams and Christopher Bridges. "Money Maker." *Release Therapy*, Performed by Ludacris and Pharrell Williams, Sony/ATV Music Publishing LLC, Warner Chappell Music, Inc, Universal Music Publishing Group, 2006.
214	Howard Bailey, Shamar Daugherty, Jermaine Dupri, and Alonso Lee. "Right Thurr." *Jackpot*, Performed by Chingy, Sony/ATV Music Publishing LLC, Universal Music Publishing Group, 2002.
215	D. Pears, Darnell Carlton, Jordan Houston, Paul Beauregard, and Willie Hutch. "Poppin' My Collar." *Most Known Unknown*, Performed by Three 6 Mafia, Sony/ATV Music Publishing LLC, BMG Rights Management, 2005.
216	Paul D. N Beauregard, Thomas Randolph Bell, William Alexander N Hart, and Jordan N Houston. "Who Run It?" *Three 6 Mafia Presents: Hypnotize Cam Posse*, Warner Chappell Music, Inc., 2011.
217	Paul D. Beauregard, Darnell Carlton, Robert Edward Cooper, Ricky Dunigan, Lisa Melonie Fisher, Jordan Houston, Lola Chantrelle Mitchell, and Narada Michael Walden. "Late Night Tip." *Chapter 1: The End*, Performed by Three 6 Mafia, Warner Chappell Music, Inc, Universal Music Publishing Group, BMG Rights Management, 1996.
218	Joshua Luellen, Kiari Cephus, Kirsnick Ball, Leland Tyler Wayne, Quavious Keyate Marshall, and Radric Delante Davis. "I Get The Bag." *Mr. Davis*, Performed by Gucci Mane and Migos, Warner Chappell Music, Inc, Universal Music Publishing Group, Reservoir Media Management Inc, 2017.
219, 220	Radric Davis and Dominique Jones. "Both Sides." *Gucci Mane Presents: So Icy Summer*, Performed by Gucci Mane and Lil Baby, Universal Music Publishing Group, 2020.
221	Tyler Bryant and Will Bowen. "The Rain (Supa Dupa Fly)" *Supa Dupa Fly*, Performed by Missy 'Misdemeanor' Elliott, Warner Chappell Music Inc., 1997
222	Kimberly Jones, Carlos Broady, Nashiem Myrick, Mary J. Blige, and Rodney Jerkins. "I Can Love You." *Share My World*, Performed by Mary J. Blige and Lil Kim, Sony/ATV Music Publishing LLC, Warner Chappell Music, Inc, Universal Music Publishing Group, The Administration MP Inc, 1997.
223	Robert Bell, Ronald Bell, George "Funky" Brown, Robert "Spike" Mickens, Lamar Hula Mahone, Craig Simpkins, Jeffrey A. Townes, Will Smith, Charles Smith, Alton Taylor, Dennis "D.T." Thomas, Richard Westfield. "Summertime." *Homebase*, Performed by The Fresh Prince and DJ Jazzy Jeff, Warner Chappell, BMI - Broadcast Music Inc, ASCAP, UMPI, EMI Publishing, SOLAR Music Rights Management, Warner Chappell Music, Inc., 1991.
224	Christopher H. Jasper, Rudolph Isley, Ronald Isley, O'kelly Isley, Marvin Isley, Ernie Isley, Anthony Shawn Criss, Keir Lamont Gist , Vincent Brown. "Hip Hop Hooray." *19 Naughty III*, Performed by Naughty by Nature, Sony/ATV Music Publishing LLC, Warner Chappell Music, Inc., 1992.
225	Anthony Criss, Arthur Neville, Cyril Neville, George Porter, Joseph Modeliste, Keir Gist, Leo Nocentelli, Vincent "vinnie" Brown. "Feel Me Flow." *Poverty's Paradise*, Performed by Naughty By Nature. Warner Chappell Music, Inc, BMG Rights Management,1995.
226, 227	Freddie Perren, Alphonso Mizell, Deke Richards, Berry Gordy Jr, Vincent Brown, Anthony Criss, Keir Gist. "O.P.P." *Naughty by Nature*, Performed by Naughty By Nature, Sony/ATV Music Publishing LLC, Warner Chappell Music, Inc, 1991.
228	Barry White, Jay Mcgowan, Michael Phillips, Nathaniel (cc Lemonhead) Orange. "C'mon N' Ride It (The Train)." *Get On Up and Dance*, Performed by Quad City DJs, Warner Chappell Music, Inc, 1996.
229	Andre Romell Young, Calvin Broadus, Harry Wayne Casey, Raymond Guy Turner, Richard Raymond Finch, and Steven R Arrington. "Gin N Juice." *Doggystyle*, Performed by Snoop Dogg, Sony/ATV Music Publishing LLC, Warner Chappell Music, Inc, Ole Media Management Lp, Entertainment One U.S. Lp, 1994.
230	Lordan Jeremiah Patrick, Sylvia Robinson, Clifton "Jiggs" Chase ,Cheryl Cook, and Michael Wright. "Apache (Jump On It)." *8th Wonder*, Performed by The Sugarhill Gang, Francis Day & Hunter Ltd, 1981.
231	Brandon Melancon, Nathan Walker, Christopher Henderson, Emerson Ballard, Terius Nash, Jamie Foxx, Christopher Stewart, Najm Faheem, James Thomas Brown, John Conte, Breyon Prescott, Eric Bishop. "Blame It." *Intuition*, Performed by Jamie Foxx and T-Pain, Spiky I M IN Publishing, 2008.
232, 233	Bobby Ross Jr. Avila, Izzy Avila, James Harris III, Chaka Khan, Terry Lewis, Tony Maiden, and James Quenton Wright. "Back In The Day." *Ahmad*, Performed by Warner Chappell Music, Inc, Universal Music Publishing Group, Kobalt Music Publishing Ltd., John T. Klemmer D/B/A Remohj Music Company, Bonefish Music, 1994.
234	Anne Dudley, Archie Leroy Roundtree, Breyan Stanley Isaac, Lo Skee, Malcolm Robert Andre McLaren, Mason Levy, Michael Caren, Miles Beard, Tom Merridith, Tramar Dillard, and Trevor Charles Horn. "I Wish." *I Wish*, Performed by Skee-Lo, Peermusic Publishing, BMG Rights Management, Kobalt Music Publishing Ltd., A Side Music LLC D/B/A Modern Works Music Publishing, 1995.

235	Calvin Jermel Miller, Shad Gregory Moss, Dandre Lemont Smith, Lawrence Franks, and Faheem Rasheed Najm. "Pop Lock & Drop It." *Notebook Paper*, Performed by Huey, Sony/ATV Music Publishing LLC, Kobalt Music Publishing Ltd., BMG Rights Management, 2006.
236	Brandt Jones, Paul Beauregard, Jordan Houston, Thomas Hudson, Danell Stevens, Earl Stevens, and Marvin Whitemon. "Don't Save Her." *Mista Don't Play: Everythang's Workin*, Performed by Project Pat, Ultra Tunes, Universal Music Publishing Group, BMG Rights Management, 2001.
237	Deundraeus Portis and Dominique Jones. "Emotionally Scarred." *My Turn*, Performed by Lil Baby, Universal Music Publishing Group, 2020.
238, 239, 240	Chandler Durham, Dominique Jones, and Sergio Kitchens. "Drip Too Hard." *Drip Harder*, Performed by Lil Baby and Gunna, Universal Music Publishing Group, Warner Chappell Music, Inc, Kobalt Music Publishing Ltd., Reservoir Media Management Inc, 2018.
241	Brandon Rackley, James Bernard Jr Rosser, Kirsnick Ball, Trevon Campbell, Kiari Cephus, and Quavious Keyate Marshall. "T-Shirt." *Culture*, Performed by Migos, Warner Chappell Music, Inc, Universal Music Publishing Group, Songtrust Ave, Reservoir Media Management Inc, Tunecore Inc, Sentric Music, 2017.
242	Christopher N'Quay Rosser, Markies Deandre Conway, Quavious Keyate Marshall, and Radric Delantic Davis. "Bacc At It Again." *Baccend Beezy*, Performed by Yella Beezy, Quavo, and Gucci Mane, Universal Music Publishing Group, BMG Rights Management, 2019.
243	Demario White Jr. "Me vs Me." *Time Served*, Performed by Moneybagg Yo, Songtrust Ave, 2020.
244	Theron Thomas, J.R. Rotem, and Ciara Wilson. "Level Up." *Beauty Marks*, Performed by Ciara, Sony/ATV Music Publishing LLC, Universal Music Publishing Group, BMG Rights Management, Kobalt Music Publishing Ltd., Warner Chappell Music, Inc, Tunecore Inc, 2019.
245	Shawn Michael Leonard Anderson. "Too Fake." *Finally Famous, Vol. 3*, Performed by Big Sean and Chiddy Bang, INgrooves (on behalf of Black Out Records); Sony ATV Publishing, Create Music Publishing, 2010.
246, 247	Aubrey Graham, Kanye West, and Sean Anderson. "Blessings." *Dark Sky Paradise*, Performed by Big Sean and Drake, Sony/ATV Music Publishing LLC, Universal Music Publishing Group, 2015.
248, 250	Dacoury Natche, Dijon Mcfarlane, Dwane Weir, Dwayne Rogers, Earl Stevens, Mikely Adam, Sean Anderson, and Willie Hansbro. "IDFWU." *Dark Sky Paradise*, Sony/ATV Music Publishing LLC, Warner Chappell Music, Inc, Universal Music Publishing Group, Kobalt Music Publishing Ltd., The Administration MP Inc, Warner Chappell Music Inc, 2015.
249	Solange Knowles, Beyoncé Knowles, Makeba Riddick, Sean Garrett, Angela Beyince, and Kasseem Dean. "Get Me Bodied." *B'Day*, Performed by Beyoncé, Sony/ATV Music Publishing LLC, Universal Music Publishing Group, Warner Chappell Music, Inc, BMG Rights Management, Warner Chappell Music Inc., 2006.
251	Michael Carson, Lawrence Jenkins, and Sean Michael Leonard Anderson. "Intro (I Decided)." *I Decided*. UMG (on behalf of Getting Out Our Dreams Inc. (G.O.O.D.) Music / IDJ); ARESA, Sony ATV Publishing, Abramus Digital, LatinAutor - Warner Chappell, BMG Rights Management, 2017.
252	Pharrell Williams, Sean Anderson, Alexander Izquierdo, and Dwane Weir II. "Nothing Is Stopping You." *Hall of Fame*, Performed by Big Sean, Sony/ATV Music Publishing LLC, Warner Chappell Music, Inc, Universal Music Publishing Group, BMG Rights Management, 2013.
253, 254	Christopher Steven Brown, Bruno Mars, Jeremy Reeves, Jonathan Yip, James Edward II Fauntleroy, Philip Lawrence, Ray Charles II McCullough, Ray Romulus, Belacalis Almanzar, and Klenord Raphael. "Finesse." *24K Magic*, Performed by Bruno Mars and Cardi B, Warner Chappell Music, Inc, Universal Music Publishing Group, Sony/ATV Music Publishing LLC, BMG Rights Management, 2016.
255, 256	Leland Tyler Wayne, Kiari Kendrell Cephus, Robert Mandell, Quavious Keyate Marshall, and Symere Woods. "Bad and Boujee." *Culture*, Performed by Migos and Lil Uzi Vert, Universal Music Publishing Group, Warner Chappell Music, Inc, Reservoir Media Management Inc, Cypmp, 2017.
257, 258, 259, 260	Jesse St John, Melissa Viviane Jefferson, Ricky Reed, and Steven Cheung. "Truth Hurts." *Cuz I Love You*, Performed by Lizzo, Sony/ATV Music Publishing LLC, Kobalt Music Publishing Ltd., Warner Chappell Music, Inc., 2019.
261	Leland Tyler Wayne, Allen Ritter, Chancelor Johnathan Bennett, Cydel Charles Young, Jerome Potter, Kanye Omari West, Malik Yusef El Shabazz Jones, Mike Dean, Noah D. Goldstein, Rick Rubin, Samuel Zadoc Griesemer, Scott Ramon Seguro Mescudi, and Thomas Lee Barrett. "Father Stretch My Hands Pt 1." *The Life of Pablo*. Performed by Kanye West and Metro Boomin. Sony/ATV Music Publishing LLC, Warner Chappell Music, Inc, Universal Music Publishing Group, BMG Rights Management, Kobalt Music Publishing Ltd. 2016.
262	Allan Ritter, Belcalis Almanzar, Earl Taylor, Matthew Samuels. Rakim Mayers, Edgar Machuca, Gerald Gillum, Jay Fort, Jordan Thorpe, and Klenord Fort. "No Limit." *The Beautiful & Damned*, Performed by G-Eazy, A$AP Rocky, Cardi B, Sony/ATV Music Publishing LLC, Warner Chappell Music, Inc, BMG Rights Management, O/B/O Capasso, Cypmp, 2017.
263, 264	Belcalis Almanzar, Bryant Bell, Jorden Thorpe, Joshua Huizar, Joshua Scruggs, Ramon Russell, Rawshawnna Guy, Stuart Jordan, Stuart Lowry, and Todd Anthony Shaw. "Backin' It Up." *UNDER8ED*, Sony/ATV Music Publishing LLC, Warner Chappell Music, Inc, Universal Music Publishing Group, 2019.
265, 266, 267	Belcalis Almanzar, Francisco Saldana, Kevin Gomringer, Kiari Cephus, Kirsnick Khari Ball, Onika Maraj. Quavious Marshall, Ramon Ayala, Shane Lindstrom, Tim Gomringer, and Victor Cabrera. "Motorsport." *Culture II*, Performed by Migos, Nicki Minaj, and Cardi B, Warner Chappell Music, Inc, Sony/ATV Music Publishing LLC, Universal Music Publishing Group, 2018.
268, 269	Isaac Earl Bynum, Jatavia Johnson, and Miles Mccollum. "Act Up." *Girl Code*, Performed by City Girls, Universal Music Publishing Group, 2018.
270, 271	Lauryn N. Hill, "Doo Wop (That Thing)." *The Miseducation of Lauryn Hill*, Performed by Lauryn Hill, Sony/ATV Music Publishing LLC, 1998.
272	Dallas L Austin. "Creep." *CrazySexyCool*, Performed by TLC, Sony/ATV Music Publishing LLC, BMG Rights Management, 1994.

273	Kenneth B. Edmonds. "Red Light Special." *CrazySexyCool*, Performed by TLC, Sony/ATV Music Publishing LLC, 1994.
274	Dallas Austin, Lisa Nicole Lopes, Bootsy Collins, George Clinton, Gregory Jacobs, Lisa Lopes, and Walter Morrison. "What About Your Friends?" *Oooooohhh... On the TLC Tip*, Performed by TLC, Sony/ATV Music Publishing LLC, Mojo Music & Media Group Ltd, 1992.
275	Kenneth Edmonds, Antonio Reid, and Daryl Simmons. "Baby-Baby-Baby." *Oooooohhh... On the TLC Tip*, Performed by TLC, Sony/ATV Music Publishing LLC, Mojo Music & Media Group Ltd, 1992.
276	Maurice Yvain, Jacques Mardochee Charles, Albert Lucien Willemetz, Sean Michael Anderson, Dwane M. Ii Weir, Tauheed Epps, Aubrey Drake Graham, Anthony George Palman, Roger Perry, Tracy Lauren Marrow, Alphonso Henderson, Jason Harrow, Lawrence Parker, Domingo F. Padilla, Kevin Coley, Korry Marcus Downey, Alwyn Christopher Phillips, Everton Bonner, Sly Dunbar, John Christopher Taylor, Lloyd Oliver Willis, Clement Dodd, Dave Kelly, Barrington Levy Ainsworth, and Hyman Wright. "All Me." *Nothing Was The Same*, performed by Drake, Big Sean, and 2 Chainz, Universal Music Publishing Group, Marlong Music Corp., 2013.
277	Jean-claude Olivier, Terri Robinson, Heavy D, and Samuel J Barnes. "Candy Rain." *Candy Rain*, performed by Soul For Real, Uptown Records, MCA Records, 1995.
278	Michele Williams, Jolyon Skinner, and Joe Thomas. "I Wanna Know." *The Wood*, performed by Joe, Sony/ATV Music Publishing LLC, Universal Music Publishing Group, BMG Rights Management, Broma 16, Warner Chappell Music, Inc, 1999.
279	Samuel J Barnes, Anthony S Cruz, and Jean Claude Olivier. "Next Lifetime." *Baduizm*, performed Erykah Badu, Universal Music Publishing Group, 1997.
280	Michael D'angelo Archer and Raphael Saadiq. "Untitled (How Does It Feel)." *Voodoo*, performed by D'Angelo, Universal Music Publishing Group, Sony/ATV Music Publishing LLC, 2000.
281, 282 283, 284	Bill Withers, Teddy Riley, Lynise Walters, William Stewart, Andre Hannibal Chauncey, Richard S Iii Vick, and William Anthony Jr. "No Diggity." *Another Level*, performed by Blackstreet and Dr. Dre, Universal Music - Z Tunes Llc, Donril Music, Notting Hill Music (uk) Ltd., City Housing Publishing, Songs Of Universal Inc., Royalty Recovery Inc., 2003.
285, 345	Benjamin Bush, Stephen Garrett, and Timothy Mosley. "So Anxious." *100% Ginuwine*, Performed by Ginuwine, Warner Chappell Music, Inc, Kobalt Music Publishing Ltd., Reservoir Media Management Inc, Warner Chappell Music Inc, 1999.
286	Christian Arceo, Deandre Way, Jeffrey Lee Johnson, and Kevin Michael Erondu. "All the Way Turnt Up." *Ready Set Go!* Performed by Roscoe Dash and Soulja Boy, Universal Music Publishing Group, Warner Chappell Music, Inc, Songtrust Ave, Warner Chappell Music Inc, 2010.
287	Chadron Moore, Deandre Way, Delray Hobson, and Wilbert Martin. "Pretty Boy Swag." *The DeAndre Way*, Performed by Soulja Boy, Sony/ATV Music Publishing LLC, Kobalt Music Publishing Ltd., Warner Chappell Music, Inc, Shelly Bay Music, It's A Big E Beat, 2010.
288, 289 290	Leon Huff, Gene McFadden, John Whitehead, Adam King Feeney, Aubrey Drake Graham, Brittany Tali Hazzard, and Anderson Hernandez. "Fake Love." *More Life*, Performed by Drake, Warner Chappell Music, Inc, Sony/ATV Music Publishing LLC, Cypmp, 2017.
291	Willie James Clarke, Roy Hammond, Mark Morales, Clarence Henry Reid, Kirk Robinson, and Mark Rooney. "Real Love." *What's The 411?* Performed by Mary J. Blige, Sony/ATV Music Publishing LLC, BMG Rights Management, 1992.
292	Andre Young, Asiah Lewis, Bruce Miller, Camara Yero Kambon, Luchana N Lodge, Mary J Blige, Melvin Charles Bradford, and Michael A Elizondo. "Family Affair." *No More Drama*, Performed by Mary J Blige, Kobalt Music Publishing Ltd., Universal Music Publishing Group, Spirit Music Group, BMG Rights Management, Warner Chappell Music Inc, 2001.
293, 294 295	Kenneth Edmonds. "Not Gon' Cry." *Waiting To Exhale*, Performed by Mary J Blige, Sony/ATV Music Publishing LLC, 1995.
296	Phalon Alexander, Terius Nash, Mary J. Blige, and Christopher Stewart. "Just Fine." *Growing Pains*, Performed by Mary J. Blige, Peermusic Publishing, Warner Chappell Music, Inc, Universal Music Publishing Group, 2007.
297. 298 299, 300	Ivan A. Matias, Joseph Simmons, Darryl Mcdaniels, and Lawrence Smith. "I'll Be There For You/You're All I Need." *Tical*, Performed by Method Man and Mary J Blige, Universal Music Publishing Group, 1995.
301	Carlton Mahone and Rodney Terry. "My Boo." *My Boo*. Performed by Ghostown DJs, Sony/ATV Music Publishing LLC, 1995.
302, 303 304, 305	Donald DeGrate. "Come and Talk to Me." *Forever My Lady*. Performed by Jodeci, Sony/ATV Music Publishing LLC, 1991.
306	Aubrey Drake Graham, Pranam Injeti, Chin Injeti, Daniel Tannenbaum, and Khalil Abdul Rahman. "Fear." *So Far Gone*, Performed by Drake, Sony/ATV Music Publishing LLC, Universal Music Publishing Group, Royalty Network, 2009.
307	Chad Hugo and Pharrell L. Williams. "Milkshake." *Tasty*, Performed by Kelis, Sony/ATV Music Publishing LLC, Warner Chappell Music, Inc, Universal Music Publishing Group, 2003.
308	Mario Mims, Michael Len Williams, Onika Tanya Maraj, and Samuel Gloade. "Rake It Up." *I Still Am*, Performed by Yo Gotti and Nicki Minaj, Warner Chappell Music, Inc, Kobalt Music Publishing Ltd., Universal Music Publishing Group, 2017.
309	Angel Jr. Cosme, Aubrey Drake Graham, Dominick Eagles, and Willie Maxwell. "My Way." *Fetty Wap*, Performed by Fetty Wap and Drake, Sony/ATV Music Publishing LLC, Warner Chappell Music Inc, 2015.

310	Willie Maxwell and Anton Matsulevich. "Trap Queen." *Fetty Wap*, Performed by Fetty Wap, Gradur, and Afrostringz, Sony/ATV Music Publishing LLC, BMG Rights Management, Songtrust Ave, 2015.
311	Aaquil Brown, Asheton Hogan, Khalif Brown, and Michael Williams. "No Flex Zone." *Sremm Life*, Performed by Rae Sremmurd, Warner Chappell Music, Inc, 2015.
312	Algernod Washington and Detorious Raheem Rivers. "Ran Off On Da Plug Twice." *Ain't No Mixtape Bih 2*, Performed by Plies, Kobalt Music Publishing Ltd, 2016.
313, 314 315, 316 317, 318 319	Anthony Schapell Crawford and Montell Jordan. "Nobody's Supposed to Be Here." *One Wish*. Warner Chappell Music, Inc, Universal Music Publishing Group, The Bicycle Music Company, 1998.
320	Usher Raymond, Jermaine Dupri, Bryan Michael Cox. "Burn." *Confessions*, Performed by Usher, Sony/ATV Music Publishing LLC, Warner Chappell Music, Inc, Universal Music Publishing Group, 2004.
321	Laron L. James, Sean Garrett, and Scott Spencer Storch. "Run It." *Chris Brown*, Performed by Chris Brown and Juelz Santana, BMG Rights Management, RoyaltyNetwork, Reservoir Media Management Inc, 2005.
322	Dwayne Carter, Greg Attaway, Irvin Burgie, Peter Pankey, and Shondrae Crawford. "6 Foot 7 Foot." *The Carter IV*, Performed by Lil Wayne and Cory Gunz, 2011.
323	Carl E. Martin. "If I Ever Fall In Love." *...If I Ever Fall In Love*, Performed by Shai, Universal Music Publishing Group, Songtrust Ave, 1992.
324, 325 326, 327 328, 329	Brandon D. Casey, Brian D. Casey, Bryan Michael Paul Cox, and Jermaine Dupri. "Let's Get Married." *J.E. Heartbreak*, Performed by Jagged Edge, Sony/ATV Music Publishing LLC, Warner Chappell Music, Inc, Universal Music Publishing Group, 2000.
330, 331 332, 333 334, 335	Frank Romano, Ivan Barias, Carvin Haggins, and Taalib Johnson. "Dontchange." *Juslisen*, Performed by Musiq Souldchild, Reach Music Publishing, 2002.
336	Darryl Simmons, Ralph Stacy, and Raphael Brown. "In My Bed." *Dru Hill*, Performed by Dru Hill. Universal Music Publishing Group, EMI Music Publishing, BMG Rights Management, Warner Chappell Music, Inc 1996.
337	Dijon Isaiah McFarlane, Ella Mai Howell, Joelle Marie James, and Larrance Levar Dopson. "Boo'd Up." *Ella Mai*, Performed by Ella Mai, Warner Chappell Music, Inc, Peermusic Publishing, BMG Rights Management, Sony/ATV Music Publishing LLC, Universal Music Publishing Group, 2018.
338, 339	Adolph Thornton Jr., Itrez Beats, and Odis Flores. "Cut It." *Cut It*, Performed by O.T. Genasis and Young Dolph, Sony/ATV Music Publishing LLC, Kobalt Music Publishing Ltd., The Administration MP Inc, 2015.
340	Odis Flores and Mauricio Rosales. "Push It." *Coke N Butter*, Performed by O.T. Genasis, Sony/ATV Music Publishing LLC, 2016.
341, 342	Quincy Matthew Hanley, Kanye Omari West, Kevin Go, Ronald N. La Tour, and Daveon Lamont Jackson. "THat Part." *Blank Face LP*, Performed by ScHoolboy Q and Kanye West, Universal Music Publishing Group, Sony/ATV Music Publishing LLC, Warner Chappell Music, Inc, Kobalt Music Publishing Ltd., BMG Rights Management, The Administration MP Inc, Concord Music Publishing LLC, 2016.
343	Joe L. Thomas, Joshua Paul Thompson, and Michele Williams. "All The Things (Your Man Won't Do)." *All That I Am*, Performed by Joe. Universal Music Publishing Group, Sony/ATV Music Publishing LLC, 1996.
344	Christian Arceo, Deandre Way, Jeffrey Lee Johnson, and Kevin Michael Erondu. "All The Way Turnt Up." *Ready Set Go!* Performed by Roscoe Dash and Soulja Boy, Universal Music Publishing Group, Warner Chappell Music, Inc, Songtrust Ave, 2010.
346	Philip Martin Lawrence, Christopher Brody Brown, and Peter Gene Hernandez. "24K Magic." *24K Magic*, Performed by Bruno Mars, Warner Chappell Music, Inc, Universal Music Publishing Group, BMG Rights Management, 2016.
347	Antonio Reid and Kenneth Edmonds. "Seven Whole Days." *Toni Braxton*, Performed by Toni Braxton, Sony/ATV Music Publishing LLC, Karen Schauben Publishing Administration, 1993.
348	Kevin Briggs, Kandi Burruss, Tameka "Tiny" Cottle, Lisa Lopes. "No Scrubs." *Fan Mail*, Performed by TLC. Sony/ATV Music Publishing LLC, BMG Rights Management, 1999.
349	O'shea Jackson, John M. Bautista, Bernard Worrell, George Clinton, Anthony Wheaton, William Earl Collins, Steve Cropper, Eddie Floyd, Raphael Wiggins, and William H. Harris. "If I Had No Loot." *Sons of Soul*, Performed by Tony! Toni! Toné!, Warner Chappell Music, Inc, Universal Music Publishing Group, 1993.
350	Ciara Harris, Andre Harris, Christopher Bridges, Don Carlos Price, Balewa Muhammed, and Vidal Davis. "Oh." *Goodies*, Performed by Ciara and Ludacris, Universal Music Publishing Group, Songtrust Ave, BMG Rights Management, Sony/ATV Music Publishing LLC, 2004.
351, 352 353, 354	James Samuel Harris and Terry Steven Lewis. "On Bended Knee." *II*, Performed by Boyz II Men, Kobalt Music Publishing Ltd., 1994.
355	Kenneth B Edmonds. "I'll Make Love To You." *II*, Performed by Boyz II Men, Sony/ATV Music Publishing LLC, 1994.
356	James Samuel Harris III and Terry Lewis. "4 Seasons of Loneliness." *Evolution*, Performed by Boyz II Men, Kobalt Music Publishing Ltd.,1997.
357	Kenneth B Edmonds. "Water Runs Dry." *II*, Performed by Boyz II Men, Sony/ATV Music Publishing LLC, 1994.
358	Andrew Cedar, Justin Scott Franks, Charlie Otto Puth, and Cameron Jibril Thomaz. "Furious 7: Original Motion Picture Soundtrack, Performed by Wiz Khalifa and Charlie Puth, Universal Music Publishing Group, Warner Chappell Music, Inc, Kobalt Music Publishing Ltd., 2015.

359	Mikkel Eriksen, Tor Hermansen, Benjamin Levin, and C Thomaz. "Work Hard, Play Hard." *O.N.I.F.C.*, Performed by Wiz Khalifa, Sony/ATV Music Publishing LLC, Kobalt Music Publishing Ltd., Warner Chappell Music, Inc, Downtown Music Publishing, 2012.
360	Wandosas Martin, Marrico King, Corey Johnson, and Ralph Levertson, Grace Cook Hazel, George Clinton, Jr. "Hay." *The Final Tic*, Performed by Crucial Conflict, Universal Music Publishing Group, 1996.
361	Bruce Isaac Rhodes, Jarvis Lemon, John Edward Hawkins, Patrick L. Hawkins, Terence Glen Prejean, and Troy Birklett. "Wanna Be a Baller." *Sittin' Fat Down South*, Performed by Lil' Troy, Big T, Fat Pat, and Yungstar, Universal Music Publishing Group, Kobalt Music Publishing Ltd., 1998.
362	Guy William Lawrence, Howard John Lawrence, and Khalid Robinson. "Talk." *Free Spirit*, Performed by Khalid, Sony/ATV Music Publishing LLC, Universal Music Publishing Group, 2019.
363	Sean J McNichol, Babatunde Abiodun Balogun, and Kaila Ola Asugha. "That's My Best Friend." *That's My Best Friend*, Performed by Tokyo Vanity, Kobalt Music Publishing Ltd., 2015.
364	Aubrey Drake Graham, Noah James Shebib, Anthony Paul Jefferies, Majid Al Maskati, and Jordan Ullman. "Hold On, We're Going Home." *Nothing Was The Same*, Performed by Drake and Majid Jordan, Sony/ATV Music Publishing LLC, Warner Chappell Music, Inc, 2013.
365	Kenneth Edmonds, Antonio Reid, and Daryl Simmons. "End of The Road." *Cooleyhighharmony*, Performed by Boyz II Men, Sony/ATV Music Publishing LLC, Warner Chappell Music, Inc, Karen Schauben Publishing Administration, Unidisc Music, 1991.

Made in the USA
Monee, IL
10 August 2024

63556423R00213

SAVAGE DOM: A DARK ROMANCE

SAVAGE ISLAND BOOK ONE

JANE HENRY

PROLOGUE

FINLEY MOROSE PULLED up an article on his phone and read it one last time. His pale, too-thin lips pulled back in a smile and his gray eyes glittered like granite.

"She's the one," he said. His heavy frame, swathed in a luxurious custom-made suit, rocked in his desk chair, and he ran a hand through his snowy white hair.

"You sure?" Jay Hunter sat across from him, dressed in a neatly pressed military uniform, his face cast in shadow.

"Positive."

Morose stood from his desk, laced his fingers behind his back, and paced the room slowly, his heavy jowls swinging as he walked, his voice shaky with age and excitement. "She's so perfect for my plan—*our* plan, it's as if fate herself has orchestrated this, offered her to me for my very own." He waved a hand toward Hunter. "Read that section I highlighted in her latest article."

Hunter cleared his throat and read aloud. *"Though modern-day society's fascination with sadism glorifies the disorder, romanticizing the disease as a form of sexual fantasy, wide-spread psychological evidence is clear: sadists need mental help. Even the mildest forms of pain play can lead to a deeper need to hurt a loved one, and it's time we put an end to the glorification of such base acts."*

Morose chuckled. "Mental health indeed. Base acts. If she had *any idea*. It's so obvious, it's almost comical. She's been demonizing the alpha male in her column now for months and vilifying dominant men. She's earned widespread anger from certain crowds and applause from others. It's why you earmarked her, no?"

Hunter nodded. "Yeah. It is." He looked down at his hands.

"Then why the hesitation?"

Hunter huffed out a breath. "Because when word gets out about what you've done—and if I'm implicated in any way—"

Morose slammed his palms on the desk, his glittering eyes nearly bulging out of his reddened face. "They will laud me as a fucking genius and give you the highest honors. We will go down in *history*."

Hunter drew in a deep breath, then let it out again but didn't talk. He wasn't so sure.

People had died. People had fucking *died* because of Morose's insane plan, and he'd implicated more than Hunter. Scientists had taken the bait, padding their bank accounts with his tainted millions, actors had agreed to stage the cruise. Technicians orchestrating what he needed, valuing money over humanity.

Morose continued. "I've spent my entire life's work leading up to this moment. To this very experiment. And I won't have you backing out now. Not when I've invested everything I own in this operation."

Hunter blew out a breath, and Morose waved a hand in his direction. "Give me her specs."

Hunter opened up a file on a tablet on his lap. "Five foot five, red hair, and hazel eyes." He looked up at Morose. "She's fair and will burn easily."

Morose grinned. "That ups the stakes, though, you see. Go on."

Hunter's jaw tightened before he continued. "Never been married. Works for *The Times,* but we can arrange for that to change. I have connections. She's somewhat private, has no real friends to speak of. She's been working in investigative journalism for the past year, though right out of college she worked for a few tabloids."

"Of course, she did. Family?"

"Almost all dead," he says.

"Almost?"

"She has a younger brother she has custody of, but he's in state care."

Morose scowled and nodded. "We will arrange to take care of that situation." His eyes grew bright while he rubbed his chin in concentration.

"What did she find in her research?" he muttered. "Does she fantasize about being tied up and dominated when she's alone at night? Are the very perversions she decries publicly the ones she conjures up in bed, with the shades drawn, under the cover of sheets?"

Hunter shifted uncomfortably. "Sir, that's far outside of our interest. I don't—"

Morose interrupted impatiently. "They may not interest *you,* but they interest *me.* Are the men ready?"

Hunter sighed, then nodded. "More than ready, sir. There are three left." He shook his head, a note of sadness in his voice. "It worked better than we even hoped. They're damn near feral."

"All of them?"

"*All* of them."

Morose grinned. "Find her. You know what to do."

ONE

HARPER

"Holy *shite,*" Malorie says, walking into the break room holding a huge golden envelope. "Babe, this is addressed to you, and just arrived via certified mail."

I look up from my novel and place my fork down in my salad bowl.

"If it arrived via certified mail, why are you holding it instead of me?" I ask her, more curious than upset with her. This girl is so annoying sometimes.

"Oh, I forged your signature," she says, waving her hand at me. I grunt at her and shoot her a disapproving look, but it seems to be lost on her. "Open it!"

I take the large, rather ostentatious envelope in hand, pursing my lips and looking at it. There's no return address, and the front is embossed in thick, black letters. I flip it over, sliding my finger under the flap, but it doesn't budge easily. Malorie watches me, and I swear she's holding her breath.

"Don't you have some hot celebrity to interview or something?" I ask her.

She sighs, rolling her eyes. "Not until next Monday, and I want to see what this *is*. C'mon, don't be a stick in the mud."

I bristle. Not the first time I've heard *that* one.

"Fine," I say, finishing the final tear on the envelope. I blink in confusion at the message. "I'm sorry, but I think you got excited over nothing." I roll my eyes at her. "It's just some sort of Publisher's Clearing House thing, Mal. Like some kinda hoax."

Blinking in confusion, she takes it in her hand and reads it, her wide brown eyes growing as large as saucers.

"This is *not* a hoax, babe," she says. "It's from *Paradise Cruise Lines*."

"So?"

"*So?*" she repeats. "Is the rock you live under really that big?"

I huff out a breath and cross my arms on my chest. "Apparently. Spill."

"Paradise Cruise Lines are legit. They're one of the biggest luxury cruise lines in the country. How can you call yourself a reporter and not know this?" She waves the envelope under my nose as if I just got the golden ticket to Willy Wonka's chocolate factory.

"Of course, I've heard of them," I tell her. "But did you read this? They're saying I won an all-inclusive two-week cruise. That's *huge*. And there's no way I won that. Hell, I didn't even enter anything." I shake my head, dismissing her and turning back to my book. "It's a scam."

But she's ignoring me while she reads on. "Um, this is not a hoax," she says. She shakes her head at me, pulls out her cell phone, and dials.

"Hello? Hi, my name is Harper Lake, and I'm calling about a letter I received via certified mail?"

I glare at her, but she ignores me, plowing on. "I don't recall entering to win such an amazing prize," she says, glaring right back at me. "Can you tell me how I got entered to win?"

Her eyes go wide. "Ohhh," she says. "Can you hold just a minute?"

She places her call on mute, then hisses to me, "You went to Vegas recently, didn't you?"

"Yes," I say, giving her a curious look. It was a business trip and brief, only three days long. "So?"

"*So*? The hotel where you stayed at had a massive giveaway they were doing, and the grand prize was this all-inclusive vacation."

I blink at her in confusion, then swallow hard. "Really?"

God, I need a vacation. I *so* need a vacation. I've done nothing but work and care for my brother now for months, since that Vegas work trip she's asking me about. It was the last trip I took out of my office in San Diego, but it was rushed and cut short when I had to come home to my brother. It was hardly a vacation.

If this is actually true... if this were actually *legit*... I would *love* this.

I take the envelope from her hand while she finishes her call, not even listening to what she's saying, and pull out my phone. I type in the name of the cruise line, then add *all-inclusive cruise prize*.

Several hits immediately come up, with five-star reviews and people talking about how in previous years they won this very cruise.

"It was life-changing," one article reads. *"The most*

luxurious vacation of my life. Exactly what I needed for some respite."

I read on, story after story of people saying how amazing this cruise was. And for the first time in so long I don't even remember, something that resembles hope blossoms in my chest, and my throat tightens.

"Did I really win?" I ask Mal.

She grabs my hands and squeezes. "Babe. You *so did*. Now call them before I call them and pretend to be you and go myself!"

I sigh. "But what about Daniel?"

"Honey, your brother's in good hands. You need to let the good people who take care of him *take care of him*. Go recharge yourself and when you come back, all this shit will still be here waiting for you." She smiles sweetly and I playfully smack her arm.

"Gee. Thanks."

"I mean it, babe," she says. "He'll be fine."

He will, I guess. I mean they'll make sure he's fed and gets his rest and sees his doctors, though no one quite knows what he needs the way I do. They don't know how he likes his hot chocolate or how his bedsheets need to be tucked in just right, or how we're only on the seventh chapter of *The Prisoner of Azkaban* and we're supposed to read chapter eight tonight, or where to find the seamless socks that don't drive him crazy.

"Will I have phone access?"

She snorts. "Of course, you will. And Wi-Fi. None of these places are off the grid anymore."

"You sure about that?"

"Pretty sure," she says with so much confidence, I actually let myself believe her.

"But what if—"

"*Harper*."

I stop and look at her. "Yes?" My throat feels strangely tight, my nose a little tingly, and I'm not sure why.

"Please, honey. Do this for yourself. Don't just do it for you. Do it for all those women you write for every single damn day. You're the one championing women's rights, no? You're the one who speaks to the plight of the working mother, the overtired stay-at-home mom. You're the one preaching self-care and neglecting your very own. You're not a hypocrite, are you?"

I huff out indignantly. God, this woman knows how to push my buttons.

"Of course not," I mutter.

"Then do this. And while you're gone you can bring your laptop and write all about how important it is to take time for yourself and replenish, and how to champion rights for those of us stuck back here in the office."

I finally nod, take a deep breath in, then let it out slowly. "Okay. Alright. Okay, I can do this."

She hands me my phone, and with trembling fingers, I dial.

TWO

HARPER

I sit beside Daniel in the crowded cafeteria, reach for the straw for his chocolate milk, and remove the wrapper.

"How long, Harper?" he asks, his wide, innocent brown eyes looking at me with concern etched in the depths. Daniel, at fifteen years old, is ten years younger than I am and the spitting image of our father. Tall and thin, with a wild shock of light brown hair that frames his freckled, oval face, it's almost startling to me how much he looks like dad when I pause to think about it. But Daniel's eyes will always be innocent, his voice always childlike, and he'll never grow to mental maturity.

"Two weeks, honey. Fourteen days," I say gently. This was the part of going away I dreaded the most, telling my baby brother that I'd be gone for a little while. Since the accident, when I became his legal guardian, he's lost the ability to track time.

"But it's my birthday," Daniel says sadly, his whole body drooping in resignation.

I smile sadly. "Sweetie, your birthday's—"

But Adrianna, the petite spitfire staff member who loves Daniel arguably as much as I do interrupts me. "I bought you a cupcake with sprinkles, and we'll sing to you in a bit, okay?"

I give her a grateful smile. It isn't Daniel's birthday until December, but every day he likes to think it's his special day.

"And won't we have a good time while she's traveling? Hmm?" Adrianna says. She gives him an affectionate look while she takes his lunch tray, then leans over and ruffles his hair. Her dark hair, tied in a messy ponytail, flounces when she nods her head. A little older than I am, having just celebrated her thirtieth birthday, Adrianna came to this country from the Dominican Republic as a child, but still has the faintest trace of an accent. "Sweetheart, your sister works hard and deserves a little break. While she's gone, lucky *you*, you get to spend more time with *me*." She's fiercely independent and loyal to her core, and it gives me immeasurable relief to know she'll be taking care of him in my absence.

Daniel almost smiles, his lips turning up at the edges but his eyes still sad.

"You're not my sister," he says to her. Adrianna and I share a look and a sigh, and my own eyes water.

Maybe I shouldn't do this after all. But before I can open my mouth, Adrianna steps in. "I'm not your sister, honey," she says. "But that doesn't mean I don't love you. And I will take the very best care of you I can. Got it?" My throat tightens. God, I'm a mess.

He sighs. She continues. "I'll even play that game you love. What is it?" She rolls her eyes with mock frustration. "Chinese something?"

"Chinese *checkers,*" he says, his eyes lighting up. "And I'll win."

I glance at my watch. Maybe it was a mistake coming here on my way to my vacation. My stomach clenches with nerves, and there's a lump the size of a golf ball in my throat. *I hate this.*

"Ha! I'm not as nice as your sister," Adrianna says, whisking a rag across the tabletop. "I don't throw games."

"Hey! I do not throw the games!" I protest, but I'm only teasing, because Daniel gets a kick out of the two of us bantering. Predictably, he cracks a real smile.

Adrianna continues. "Now you sit here and wait for your dessert while I walk your sister out. Give her a big hug before she goes, and before you even blink your eyes, she'll be back."

He frowns, blinks, and shakes his head. "It doesn't work that way," he says. "That isn't true." Figurative language is sometimes lost on him.

I walk to him, marveling at how much he's grown and tousle his hair. "You're like a full head taller than I am now," I muse. "When did I tell you that was okay?"

He laughs good-naturedly, but when he leans down to hug me, he holds me so tightly in his embrace that I wince a little.

"I'll miss you," he says. "I will miss you so *so* much. Call me?"

"Of course, I will," I tell him. "Whenever I have a connection, I'll call you."

"Pinky swear?"

"Pinky swear."

Letting me go, he wraps his larger pinky around my own and shakes. I swallow hard and pull him to me again, burying my face on his chest. He wears a faded *Black Sabbath* tee that's too tight around the arms and almost too short, but it's his favorite, the memory of my dad's obsession with classic rock fading as much as the tee.

I can't bear to take it away from him. It's hard enough leaving him in the care of someone else, but with his seizure condition I have no choice. And they take good care of him here. His residency is set up like a well-furnished home, with large dining tables in the dining room, comfortable furniture in the living room, each bedroom private with its own bathroom, only there are nurses here around the clock, transportation, plus doctors and therapists who pay frequent visits. Daniel is one of the more high-functioning people here, others in wheelchairs and still others more seriously mentally disabled. But for all his innocence and abilities, leaving him makes me ache inside.

I sigh and hold him tighter. Daniel is the only one I have left after the accident, and knowing I'm leaving him almost makes it impossible to go.

But how can I champion self-care and women's rights if I don't take my own advice? Adrianna and Mal are right. I haven't had a vacation since I took over guardianship of Daniel. Still, it doesn't make it easy.

I sigh for the umpteenth time.

This vacation is *free*. It seems almost irresponsible not to take this opportunity.

It's time.

"You'll be fine," I whisper, because I'm afraid if I speak out loud, I'll cry.

I feel strong hands behind me. Adrianna, pulling me away from Daniel. She's short but feisty, and she has a no-nonsense, maternal look about her.

"Go, now," she says. "You have a ride waiting, don't you?"

I do. It's so weird. Surreal even. There's a limo outside Daniel's residence, ready to take me to the airport. We'll fly from Boston to Miami, where I'll board my ship this evening.

"Eat your dessert, and when I come back in, we'll play a game," Adrianna says.

Daniel shoots me a grin. I give him a half-smile back.

"*Go,* Harper," Adrianna says. "I promise. While you're gone, I'll be here every single day to look out for him. And remember, this is our goal, right? That he not become too dependent on you and learn some self-advocacy?"

"It is," I tell her. "I just—"

"I know, honey." She puts her arm around my shoulders as she leads me firmly to the exit, and when we reach the door, she spins me around to look at her. "You deserve this. Okay? Remember that. You deserve this."

I look outside the door to where the limo is waiting.

"It's so crazy weird," I tell her. "I mean, who the hell wins a cruise?"

She smiles at me. "It's so crazy weird," she says on a laugh. "And honey, *you* did."

I give her a quick hug, then leave before I lose my resolve. I have to get some space, or I'll change my mind and stay. I hold my head high and walk to the waiting limo. The driver, an older, clean-shaven man wearing a uniform and matching hat, stands beside the door, and he tips his hat to me when I draw close.

"Miss Lane," he says. "Ready to go?"

I draw in a shaky breath. "I am."

He opens the door and ushers me in. I manage to save my tears for when the door closes, and I'm alone in the interior of the luxurious car, then I cover my face with my hands and weep. I miss him already.

I know the driver can hear me, but thankfully, he doesn't let on. I see him lift his cell phone and watch as he presses a button. "I have her," he says. It seems a little odd, as if I'm specially acquired goods in a heist, and he's just managed to find me. I dismiss the weird thought as soon as I have it, because with a job like mine, you learn to suspect literally everyone and everything. It gets wearying after a while.

So, I lean back in my seat and close my eyes. I hope and pray the hardest part of this is over.

Vacation time.

THREE

Cy

I WAKE BEFORE THE SUN, the aches and pains in every muscle of my body screaming for attention before I open my eyes. I roll over and groan, then stifle the sound. It takes me a minute to realize that I'm still in hiding. I have to remain noiseless, so they don't find me.

I half open one eye, casting a curious glance to the opening of the cave where I took shelter last night, and shiver. Though it's warm on the island during the day, occasionally night is a different story. Once the sun sets, we occasionally have colder temps. Fortunately, it remained warm for most of last night, but it seems a cold front trickled in while I was sleeping. The good news was, I didn't have to build a fire. I didn't want to. Smoke from any fire I build could identify my location.

I'll have to eventually, though.

Christ. It was bad enough when all of us were here. Six of us, military, joining forces to survive on an island in the middle of fucking nowhere. The battle for food, water, and shelter, the three most fundamental necessities for survival, was difficult but made easier when we banded together to overcome the elements.

But that was a long, long time ago. When? I have no idea. When I try to ask myself how long I've been here, my mind grows hazy and uncertain. The man in our number who took record of the passing of time died months ago, and none of us took it up again. It unsettles me not to know the answer, so I force myself not to dwell on it.

The days, weeks, and months—hell, it could even be *years*—follow one another like the inevitable dripping of a faucet. *Drip. Drip. Drop.* Monotonous. Demoralizing. Fucking exhausting.

I asked all the questions. I got few answers. And that was when we first arrived here. Back when the other men were my allies. Back before the little we had was stripped from us and the men around me grew savage and wild.

There were six of us.

Now there are three.

I think there are three, anyway. Fuck it, who knows. While I've been holed up in this cave, we could've lost another. Maybe both of them even.

Maybe I'm all alone.

I'm not sure how I feel about that.

Does a man alone on an island eventually go mad? He would have to, wouldn't he? Humans aren't meant to live in stark isolation. I guess I'd make the most of it if I were alone, though. At least I wouldn't have to fight them for the last goddamn crab or whatever the fuck.

I sit up when the gnawing hunger in my belly

propels me forward. I haven't eaten in days—I *think*, I mean who the fuck knows—but I've adamantly insisted on staying hydrated. Still, the hunger comes in waves. When I ignore the pangs, they eventually go away again, and I feel almost empowered, because I'm still here. I'm still breathing. I didn't succumb to death.

Or did I? Have I died and this is some form of hell? No. *No.*

I close my eyes and breathe in and out. I'm still very much fucking alive.

But at the back of my mind, I do wonder.

We found the rotting skeleton of the first man we lost shortly after we landed here. He was the most selfish bastard in the group, refusing to do the hard work of banding together and finding resources that would keep us alive. He insisted he would find a way off this island. Insisted he wouldn't stop until he did.

We don't know how he died. But it doesn't matter. In the end, the human body is far more fragile than one might think.

I would know.

I look around the cave and see something flapping around to my left. Bats. If they provided any sustenance at all, I'd catch the fuckers. Hell, I still might.

I push myself to my feet and find my legs a bit wobbly. I curse under my breath. Though the man I was before I landed here fades a bit more with each passing day, I know one thing's unchanged: I despise any show of weakness and always will.

So, one more time, I push myself forward. I'll find something to eat if it kills me. I just wish the motherfuckers I'm on this island with weren't lying in wait to kill me in the meantime.

We started out strong, all of us. But bit by motherfucking bit, as everything we needed was stripped away, the men began to turn on one another, like *Lord of the Fucking Flies.*

I blink at the early morning light at the entrance to the cave and take in a deep, cleansing breath. No matter where I am or how long I've been here, one thing remains the same: the island is beautiful in the morning.

Fingertips of golden sunlight paint the miles of blue-green ocean surrounded by white sand as far as the eye can see. The faintest wisps of clouds dotting the sky like dandelions, breathe to scatter the seeds, and you can make a wish.

Like a sentimental fool, I gather in a breath and blow it out, pretending I'm earning a wish.

Get me off this island.
Find me food.

The clouds vanish as if the universe mocks me. I stretch my arms up over my head, feeling the ache in my muscles and back. I ran for miles yesterday, the only thing fueling me the adrenaline that coursed through my body.

Since I landed on this island, I've been working my body to the bone, strengthening my muscles and core and not allowing a single part of me to atrophy. That grew more difficult when food sources diminished. Yesterday's run wasn't about training, though, but survival.

I'll find both of the men today. The two remaining people on this island, if they haven't died or killed each other. After I fortify myself and fashion some weapons, I will find them. I'm not going to cower and hide anymore. The more I'm bereft of the bare necessities, the more animalistic instinct takes over. I'm doing everything I can to mentally prevent the degeneration of my mind and body.

Stay strong.

Stay sane.

Stay fucking human.

So today I'll prepare for an ambush. But first, I have to prepare myself.

After I'm sure there's no one in the near vicinity, I walk to the back of the cave and relieve myself, grateful this one most basic duty is a good indicator I haven't let myself grow dehydrated. The human body can withstand much in the way of starving, but dehydration is another story. I've been dehydrated before on this island. My mental capacities quickly downshifted to hallucinations, fever taking over. That was back when there were six of us. One of them—who knows which one, it all blurs now—saved me.

That was back when we cared for each other, when our training as soldiers made us band together as one.

If I let myself get dehydrated at this point, I'm sunk. They'd rejoice in my demise.

One less mouth to feed.

So, every day I get up, the first mission is to ensure I have enough water for the day. The second is to make sure no one's going to attack me. The third is to find food.

I outfit myself with round rocks and the makeshift slingshot I made in case I encounter one of the others by the water. I have a knife, but I don't want it to come to that. Not today.

Fortunately, there are multiple sources of fresh

water on the island. I hope they've left this one for me. But I'm mentally prepared for an ambush.

I walk quietly down the bank to where the water churns, keeping an eye out for any source of wildlife I can capture to put some food in my belly. A flutter of wings overhead gives me momentary hope, but by the time I locate the bird, it's flown too far away for my dismal excuse of a weapon to reach.

Christ. I don't know the name of it, but the large, duck-like bird makes for good damn eating on this island. The first time we found a flock it was like Thanksgiving dinner.

But that seems so long ago now.

Once I'm down to the water's edge and certain I'm alone, I splash water on my face and rub it briskly up and down my arms. I frown at my body. I've grown leaner though fought to remain muscular these past few months. My arms and upper body are still covered in the ink I earned as a fighter, before I enlisted. Navy SEAL regulations allow for tattoos that don't cover the face, neck, or hands, as long as the uniform covers every inch.

I pause, my cupped hand raised to my mouth. Droplets of cool water trickle between my fingers.

I was a fighter.

I was in the Navy.

There were rules governing the way I dressed and behaved.

I blink hard.

The memory of who I was fades in and out, and when I remember facts, I hold onto them with vicious determination.

I go through the mental gymnastics I force myself through when the memories surface.

My name is Cy Kaufman. Raised an orphan in the foster care system in America, I have no family, my own family is the Navy. But now I have only myself to depend on, and no matter how dire the circumstances, I will not fail.

This island has stripped many things from me. It won't strip my faculties.

I ignore the little voice in my head that mocks me.

It already has.

It already robbed the other men of theirs. Most of them, anyway.

I drop down again and cup more water in my hands, guzzling as much as my empty stomach can muster, when I hear a scattering through the underbrush. I turn slowly, so slowly it feels as if I'm in slow motion and see an injured duck. It's struggling in the brush. Injured somehow. And I go into autopilot survival mode.

I was born a fighter and I'll die one.

I pull back a rock in the slingshot, take aim, and let the ammo fly. It's clumsy compared to the weapons I'm used to wielding, but with hours upon hours to fill my time, I've done nothing but practice my aim. I hit the duck with the first shot, and watch it slump to the ground.

I look around me once more before I go to fetch it, but I'm all alone.

I take the bird back to the cave and clean it quickly and efficiently with my knife, then wash my hands. I have to risk a damn fire if I'm going to eat this bird, so I decide I'll do it at a good distance away from the cave.

Far enough that whoever tracks it here won't notice the shelter I've made.

My stomach aches and gnaws, my mouth watering at the mental image of roasted meat.

By the time I'm roasting the meat, the sun's high and bright overhead, beating down with relentless heat. My mouth feels papery and dry. Damn it, I need to get more water.

I turn the roasting meat over the flame, then freeze when I hear the sound of snapping twigs. I look quickly behind me, my slingshot in hand, when Will steps into my line of vision, hands raised in surrender. Fucking Will, the most selfish of the bunch, the last to agree to band with us. He's tall and lanky, with ragged black hair and a beard that would make our former drill sergeant lose his fucking mind. We were made to be clean shaven in the Navy. Here it's impossible.

I don't trust him. I put a rock in the sling and hold it in front of me, prepared to shoot. I will fucking *kill* him if he's here to attack me.

It didn't used to be like this. It didn't fucking used to be like this. When food was plentiful and we all got along, we were like brothers in arms with one another.

But now...

"What do you want?" I demand. I'm ready to kill this man if he steps one toe out of line.

"Easy," Will says. His eyes shoot to the meat roasting by the fire and he swallows hard. "I'm not here to fight," he says, taking a step toward me.

"Don't fucking move or I'll shoot you with this."

He scoffs. "As if you could really use that thing to hurt me anyway."

"Sure as fuck could. David used it to slay Goliath.

And I just used it to catch *my* dinner, which you're totally welcome to go do on your own." He doesn't know the slingshot would only bring him down, but the knife would slit his throat.

"Jesus, man," he says, shaking his head at me. "I'll help you catch more, but give a brother a little to hold him over?"

I growl, the snarling sound coming from my own throat startling in its intensity. Who the fuck am I becoming?

Son of a bitch.

"Listen, Cy," he says, his hands palm-up, his eyes wide and pleading. He's almost convincing, the son of a bitch.

"What," I bite out.

"Eugene's gone *batshit crazy,* man. I swear to fucking God he doesn't even know how to talk like a human anymore. He's a rabid animal." He shakes his head. "The only way we can survive at this point is to join together, me and you."

"Join together?" I scoff. "Right. Just like we did with the others, right? Before we lost everything and turned on each other? Before I had to sleep with one eye open, afraid that someone would slit my throat in the middle of the night, so we had one less mouth to feed? Hell no."

His eyes grow narrow on me and he swallows hard, eyeing the food by the fire. "I'll fight you for it."

What the fuck.

"Fight me for it? Are you a fucking moron?"

Though he's smaller than I am, he's ruthless and lethal, like a crazed rodent, and I swear it might be my hunger that's making me imagine this, but right then, he actually *looks* like a rat, his eyes beady and his nose twitching at the scent of the food before us.

"Get your own food." I'm standing my ground.

With a low, feral growl, he lunges, not for me, but for the fire. I leap after him and grab his leg just before he reaches the flames. Howling, he kicks his leg out and catches my jaw, pain radiating along my skin.

"You fucking bastard," I growl, my own voice vicious and snarling, and my instincts take over. I've got the son of a bitch. I drag him toward me and deck him, enjoying the satisfying feel of my fist connecting with his jaw. I hit him a second time, then a third, and actually give myself mental permission to beat him to death, until his pulse stops beating and he lies dead.

One less person on this island, one less person fighting me for survival, makes it that much easier to live.

I hit him again and again, until his lip splits open, crimson blood staining his cheeks and my fists.

"Okay! I'm sorry!" he screams, and this time he's crying, real tears falling down his cheeks like a goddamn baby. I'm kneeling above him, his wrists pinned in my fists, and his eyes come to mine. A flicker of humanity gives me pause.

"I'm sorry, Cy. Jesus, man, I'm sorry. I'm just fucking starving." Then he blinks as I stare at him. "Did you hear that?"

Oh no he does not. "You're not going to fucking distract me," I tell him. "I should kill you right now. I should fucking kill you."

"Shut the fuck up," he growls. "And *listen*."

Still pinning him beneath me, I do. But I don't hear the crash through the underbrush or sound of human life I expect, but something very, very different. The sound's so foreign to my ears, it takes me a moment to realize what's happening.

It's... people. *Chattering.*

"What the fuck is that?" I ask him in a whisper.

"If you let me up, I can help you look," he says, glaring. "Christ, I'm sorry, okay? I won't take your food."

I hold his gaze with mine and give him a warning I mean to my core. "If you step one goddamn toe out of line again, I will *end* you. You will do exactly what I say, or I'll slice your goddamn throat. You get me?"

I fucking mean it, and he knows it. I've schooled this son of a bitch with more than one beating, and it's clear he remembers. This time is different, though. This time my warning holds more weight.

He swallows, his eyes wide and a thank fuck, fearful. "Yes," he says, nodding. "I get it. I made a mistake. Now get off me."

With a reluctant growl, I do. And just to keep things quiet while we figure out where the voices are coming from, I take the scorching meat out from the flames with a stick and toss it on some clean leaves. "You get half, but not yet. Let it cool, and you don't touch it until I give you permission." I let him live but he's under my command now and he'll listen.

He swallows hard but nods. It's a good sign.

"There," he says. "On the beach. Look."

I drag Will in front of me where I can see him and look to where he points. I blink in surprise. For once, I'm glad he's with me, because if he wasn't, I'm not sure I'd believe what I see. I'd convince myself I was hallucinating or something.

There's a *ship*. A huge cruise ship or something,

anchored just off our coast. And aboard the deck are at least a dozen people dressed in clothes you'd wear on vacation... swim suits and sunglasses. It's so surreal, we both watch in amazement. My heartbeat accelerates, sweat breaking out over my body.

People.

Civilized people.

Who are they? Are they here to hunt us? Will they take the limited food we have?

"Get them off this island," I growl. I blink and shake my head. What the hell am I saying? "Get them *off*." I poise my slingshot at the ship inanely, as if somehow, I can shoot rocks at them and make them retreat.

"Maybe they have food," he says in a fevered whisper. "Cy, what if they have food? Cruise ships have... oh, God, *everything*." He swallows, and saliva drips down the corner of his mouth. "Let's go, Cy. We need to get them."

"Don't let them go. Call to them. We have to fucking call them and get off this island!" I whisper, my pulse pounding. "We need to kill them," I amend, as if this makes perfect sense.

"All of them," he agrees. "Kill them and take their food and water."

"We'll deal with killing them when we find them."

There's something off about this conversation, but I'm too desperate to care what it is. We need food and we need it *now*.

"Heyyyy!" Will shouts, screaming so loudly my ears ring.

"Up here!" I scream, louder than him. "Help!"

They've got to hear us, but no one even looks our way. But we're deep in the woods and we can't run down to them. The only way down is back to the cave, then down to the rocks, then across the beach. We can't get to them from up here.

"Go," I tell him. "Get down there. We have to *go.*"

We pause just long enough to grab the roasted carcass. I clumsily tear it in half and give him the larger portion, shoving the meat in my mouth as we run back toward the cave. I choke it down, not caring it's nearly burnt and tasteless. My stomach growls appreciatively. It's not delicious, but it's food.

"We have to get to the cave," I tell him. "If we don't, there's no way back down to the beach."

"Jesus," he mutters. We're both panting, when I stumble. I go flying headfirst, blocking my head with my arm, but he grabs my arm and yanks me back up, and we're running again, the two of us. We've been here all this time and never once seen a boat, a ship, nothing at all that would indicate human life until now.

We make it back to the cave then begin the descent toward the beach, but I don't hear any more voices. I ignore the foreboding that builds in my chest. I'm not giving up. It's the first sign of civilization we've seen since we got here and *I'm not giving up now.* But the distance is longer than I thought, and it seems we're running so much longer than we should.

"Are we lost?" Will asks. "You sure this is the right way?"

I look wildly around me but do recognize where we are.

"Left," I say, panting. There's a stitch in my side and between the water I drank and the scarcity of food in my stomach, I feel like I'm going to be sick, but I push on. We run until we make it to the beach. The stark, empty fucking beach.

I drop my elbows to my knees, panting, my lungs constricted so I can hardly speak.

"You see anything?" I say in between gasps.

"They're gone," Will says. His voice cracks and I swear he's on the verge of tears. "There's no one here."

I curse, my own throat tight, but I refuse to cry. I learned young that real men don't cry. *ever.*

And I won't cry now.

"They left that quickly? They looked like they were out for a daytime excursion."

"Jesus," he mutters, shaking his head, and he swipes his hand across his eyes. The bastard's crying. It makes me want to beat him all over again. "What the fuck? Where'd they go?"

"For Christ's sake, stop your blubbering," I mutter, but I hate myself for saying that because it was the constant refrain I heard growing up.

Real mean don't cry.
Stop your blubbering.
Man up.

I walk over to him and shake my head, my voice gruffer than I intend. "It's alright. It's a sign that we're not as isolated as we think."

Even though I hate him, even though I hate that I've become the bastard who has no mercy, it makes me feel more human than I have in days... weeks... months.

But he pushes me away. "Shut up," he says, full on crying now. "We are isolated. We've got nothing to eat and we're going to fucking die here and *you know it.*" Tears stream down his cheeks and it makes me so mad I have to breathe through my nose so I don't hurt him.

My hand clenches into a fist and I want to deck him again. He's a slow learner.

He opens his mouth to speak, then pauses with his mouth still hanging open. Wordlessly, he points behind me. I turn, half expecting to see Eugene. I'm ready to attack. But when I turn, I don't see what I expect at all.

There's a woman with her back to us, so far up on the ridge she couldn't hear us if we called her. She's curvy and gorgeous, with billows of vibrant auburn hair. I can't see much more than that but can see she's dressed in a skimpy dress and walking away from us.

"It's a woman," Will says, as if that isn't fucking obvious.

I turn to him, a different kind of hunger consuming my every thought, consuming every fiber of my being, and a ferocious need to protect what's mine rages through me.

"She's *mine*."

FOUR

Harper

THIS ISLAND IS MAGNIFICENT. Breathtakingly beautiful. I've been so taken by the sights around me for days, and even now I still can't process the vibrant blue of the ocean, the beautiful white of the sand, the endless sky and greenery that surrounds the island like icing on a cake. This is the stuff that dreams are made of. Utter paradise.

The cruise ship has been amazing, and I've indulged more in the past week than I have my entire life. Mimosas in the morning and omelets made to order, decadent desserts and chocolate fountains, filet mignon and the largest, most succulent shrimp I've ever had. And even though there are other guests on board, I somehow feel as if I'm the one they're most focused on. I convince myself that it's because I'm the weirdo that won the all-inclusive cruise.

It feels a little creepy, if I'm honest. When I enter

the dining room, all eyes are on me. At the spa, I have half a dozen women waiting on me hand and foot. The chef has paid me a personal visit when dining multiple times now, asking if there's anything at all he can do for me.

And I just can't get used to it. I'm the independent one, ready to take care of whatever or whoever I need to. I'm not used to being served like this, and it makes me a little uneasy. That's the only reason I can fathom that this whole luxurious vacation has me on edge.

When we finally dock on an island, and we're told we can roam freely for a few hours, I eagerly get off the ship. I don't trust anyone, so I take my bags with me, but I packed fairly lightly. I throw my backpack on, take my phone, and get ready to take some pictures.

I took jugs of sunscreen with me because fair girls like me burn easily, but I've gotten used to limiting my exposure to the sun and staying in the shade to avoid being burned. I have the lightest tan now, and only burned once, but on the island, there are enough trees I can hide beneath during the full blare of the sun.

I miss Daniel. And if I'm honest? I'm even missing my work. Still, I'm not going to pretend this isn't stunningly beautiful. I feel as if I've stepped foot straight into paradise.

I find a waterfall a few yards from the main beach and take a seat on a rock. Though the cruise ship's been delightful, being alone like this is more my speed. I wish I had more time to explore, but I don't want to get lost, so I get up after a few minutes and go in search of some photogenic places.

I wonder what Ben's doing right now. Is he celebrating his birthday again? I smile to myself. Though it's been devastating to see my baby brother regress after the accident, his childlike simplicity inspires me. There's an ache inside me being apart from him.

I shake my head. I'm here to enjoy myself, not pine away for home.

Since I ate a substantial breakfast, I don't even think about food or water for a while, as I explore the beauty of this island. I put my backpack down and take out my camera, marking where I put it so I don't lose it. I don't want its weight on me while I take some pictures.

The first picture I take is of a beautiful white flower with a yellow center in full bloom, the second the waterfall hidden in the woods. Birds tweet overhead, but at times it's almost silent here. I'm so focused on taking pictures, I don't hear anything but my own thoughts as I focus the lens on the beauty that surrounds me.

But after a little while, I start to feel as if I'm being watched. I look around me, but none of the other passengers have ventured this far. I look to my left and then my right.

"Hello?" I ask into the vast emptiness, but of course no one replies.

The first clue that tells me it isn't my imagination and I'm not alone is the snapping of twigs. I look all around me but see no one at all.

"Who's there?" I yell out, but my voice only echoes back to me. Then something flashes in front of me. I gasp, covering my mouth with my hands. That wasn't an animal but a person.

He passes several yards in front of me again, running.

What the hell?

It's not a passenger, though. No, it couldn't be. His clothes were torn into shreds, his hair hanging about him in wild, unkempt light brown strands.

The skin at the back of my neck prickles, little goosebumps rising on my arms.

Are there natives on this island?

Was it a man? Or an animal? He looked somewhere in between, if I'm honest.

"Who is it?" I yell. I don't see him, but footsteps draw closer. I look wildly around me for some sort of weapon, anything at all I can use to defend myself, because I know intuitively I'm in danger. My belly ties itself in knots.

Would anyone hear me if I screamed? Would I be attacked?

I need to get back to the ship, but cast one more final, wild look around me. All I see is a large stick, but it's better than nothing. I pick it up, even though I have no idea what to actually do with the thing.

"Where are you? Who are you?" I scream, but my voice echoes around me. My pulse races and the stick slips in my sweaty hands, when I hear him *breathing* behind me. I spin around with a hysterical scream. It is indeed a man, but something about him is wild and rabid.

He lunges at me, his arms outstretched, his eyes hugely wide and terrifying. I barely register what's happening, wildly jabbing my stick at him with another terrified scream, but he dodges me and yanks it from my grip.

"Leave me alone!" I scream, words are my only weapon now, but he merely tosses the stick to the side and lunges at me, his hands at my throat. I slap at him, and on instinct knee him between the legs. He easily deflects my knee and slaps me across the face, hard. My cheek stings and blood fills my mouth. I'm whimpering and flailing when he grabs me in his ferocious grasp and throws me to the ground.

I tear at him, my fingernails clawing at his arms and neck, but he only hits me again. I'm dizzy with pain, and I know I'm no match for him. He's so much stronger and more vicious than I am. I'm crying and begging, when he yanks up my dress and shoves it up higher, then to my horror, grabs my panties and tears them down my legs. I realize with terrifying, vivid awareness that he's going to assault me. Oh, God, he's going to rape me.

"Stop!" I scream, whimpering. I'm so shocked and petrified, I'm shaking and pleading. "Please. Leave me alone." I can't push him off me. He's lanky and filthy, encrusted with blood and dirt, but seems bent on one thing. He palms my breasts with a savage growl and pins me down with one hand while he tears down his zipper with the other.

"No!" I scream, flailing so hard beneath him my muscles ache, but I can't push him off me. My voice raises in pitch and takes on a note of hysteria. "Get the fuck off me! Get off me!" I'm screaming but no one's coming. Where is everyone? Why can't anyone hear me scream?

My pulse races, and right then, my mind goes to every woman who's ever been assaulted, to every act of sexual violence we women have endured. I've written in support of sexual freedom and women's rights and in criticism of the patriarchal society that seeks to strip women of their identity. But never, never in my life, have I been in a position like this.

It's paralyzing. Terrifying.

And I make up my mind. I may not be able to stop him, but I will escape, and when I do, I will *kill* him. He will pay for this.

I scream with everything I've got, until my vocal cords feel like they're bursting and my throat burns, but he isn't deterred at all. He throws his head back with a savage howl, and in my crazed, frantic state of mind, I wonder if I'm being attacked by a werewolf.

That isn't real, my mind says. But this man is little more than a beast.

He raises his hand and slaps my face. The pain radiates to my jaw and I turn to deflect him. He hits me all over the shoulders, the chest, my body, until I'm whimpering beneath him, dizzy and bloodied.

I will kill him.

I'm pinned beneath him with no help for it, too dizzy to deflect his frenzied attack. I can feel him shoving himself between my legs and bile burns at the back of my throat.

"*No!*" I scream. I gather saliva in my mouth and spit at him, but he doesn't even bother to wipe it, just glares at me and growls while he clumsily fumbles between my legs. But he isn't going to take me easily. I will make him hurt for this before I kill him. I'm squirming and twisting beneath him when suddenly, the pressure of his body lightens, and he's lifted clean off me. I scramble away, unsure of what just happened, but grateful for the momentary reprieve.

I grope for my clothes and yank them back on to cover myself. There are others. Other...men? There's a frenzy of limbs and snarls like a pack of savage dogs fighting. I scurry for the safety of cover, leaving the animals or men or whatever they are to fight among themselves.

Someone just saved me, but I'm not safe.

I'm balanced on a ledge of some sort, the men are snarling and fighting with vicious kicks, biting and tearing at one another. My mouth falls open in horror. It's the most savage thing I've ever seen. How many even are there?

I should run. I should get back to the ship and leave this place and never look back. It's cursed, maybe even possessed. My dress is torn, my face throbbing from the assault, and yet I can't bring myself to run. I'm riveted to the scene in front of me, as if I have to see how this plays out.

I manage to mentally untangle the limbs and bodies so I can decipher there are three men: one, the man with the light brown hair, the rabid savage that tried to rape me; the second, a smaller man with dark hair and a thick black beard, a third; the largest of the lot, lithe but muscled, covered in ink, with sandy blond hair and a thick beard. He's clearly the alpha, the one they fear the most, and I can see why. He takes the man who attacked me by the hair, holds him, and punches him so hard I can hear the snap of bone.

They resemble dogs fighting more than men, with growls and ferocious tearing of skin and hair. My stomach lurches as the two smaller men suddenly turn on the larger one, but he has a decided advantage. Not only is he bigger, obviously stronger, and fearless, he's the only one with a weapon. He holds a thick, club-like stick in hand and swings it with sickening accuracy across the head of the man who tried to rape me. He strikes him again and again. I turn away, not able to watch the brutality.

I have to get away.

I'm crawling toward the forest. I have to get away from these savage men. What will happen when the dust settles? Do the other people on the ship know there are violent natives on this island? It isn't safe. Someone has to warn them.

I'm trying to get away when a deep, angry voice cuts through the melee of screams and hoarse screams.

"Stay right there!"

They see me leaving, and don't want me to escape.

I move faster, but I don't get far. There's a howl and cursing behind me, a sickening *thud,* and snarled curses. I'm trying to run but I feel as if I'm caught in quicksand. My feet are too slow, my movements too labored, when a hand catches me at the back of my head, tangling in my hair.

With a scream, I fall to my knees, grasping at my hair, but I'm unable to move him. "Stop! Let me go! Leave me alone!"

I'm howling but not moving, for every movement brings blistering pain to my scalp. I look up to see the largest of the men standing over me, his violent blue eyes piercing mine.

"Who the fuck are you?" he asks.

Okay, then, so he actually is human.

"Harper," I say. "Let me *go.*"

He doesn't even acknowledge my request but grabs my elbow and drags me to my feet. "Come with me."

As if I have a choice?

"Fine, but let me go, will you? God!"

He ignores me. He drags me back through the underbrush to where they fought. The ground is stained with blood, and the man who tried to rape me is strewn on the ground, his limbs askew. Eyes vacant.

The monster of a man narrows his eyes on me. "I'll let you go while I do what I need to, but if you run, you'll regret it. Understood?"

My God, what is his purpose here?

"Yeah," I sputter, confused and shaken, but it works. He lets my hair go and kneels beside the broken body of the man who attacked me.

"You killed him," I accuse, angry at him for doing what I wanted to do, though I know I wouldn't have had the actual nerve to go through with it. "*I* was supposed to kill him."

He's holding the man's wrist between his fingers, frowning, and when I speak, he turns to me with a fierce snarl. I shiver. He's like half wolf or something.

"You had your chance," he mutters.

"He tried to rape me," I say, my voice shaking, as if I'm pleading with the universe to understand why a human life was taken. "He tried to rape me."

The savage man kneels on one knee and turns to look at me, his blue eyes piercing straight through me. "Of course, he did. He was nothing more than an animal when he saw you." He shakes his head and his eyes narrow on me. And what he says next sends a terrifying chill straight through me. "None of us are. You shouldn't be anywhere near us. You shouldn't have come here."

I blink in surprise. "Oh, this is my fault? I brought this on myself for setting foot on your precious island?"

He nods. "Yes."

I don't even know how to respond. The women I write for would have a *field* day with this line of thinking. Instead, I change the subject.

"Is he dead?"

I'm still shaking, from nerves and anger.

Scowling, he takes the man's second wrist in his hand and feels for a pulse, as if to confirm what he already knows.

"Sure as hell is." He shakes his head. "Not many survive a broken neck."

"You broke his neck?"

He just gives me a withering look and pinches his lips together.

I take that as a yes.

"So, he's dead."

"He is," he says with a sigh. "I'll have to get rid of the body."

I'm pissed he did this. I hate that he killed this man, when all I wanted was to do the very same.

"He was supposed to be for *me*," I repeat.

What am I saying? Who *am* I? I don't kill people. What is it with this place? I shudder. I can't seem to stop speaking. I'm angry at him for killing the other guy but not because it's a savage thing to do.

"*I* was the one who was supposed to kill him for trying to rape me." The more I speak, the angrier I become. "No one asked you for your help. No one asked you to save me. You did that on your own."

At first, I don't heed the way his eyes narrow and gleam with flicks of fire in them, the way his body grows taut and he flexes his fingers.

"I was going to kill him myself," I protest again, repeating the words as if somehow, it'll give them more weight. "He tried to rape me. He was *mine* to kill, not yours." I want to stomp my foot and shove him, I'm that angry, and I think the shock of it all has made me maybe a little insane. "But no. You had to swoop in here and kill him for yourself, didn't you?"

What the hell am I even saying?

He just killed a man. Maybe I should proceed with a little more caution, but a part of me wants to show him I'm not a hapless female who needs his prowess to survive.

I pause in the middle of my tirade and swallow.

Where am I? What just happened? Where the hell do I go from here?

Where did the third man go?

I have to get back to the ship.

The man doesn't say a thing, just watches me with his furious, narrowed eyes, and it makes me angrier.

I continue inanely, though my voice has lost some of its edge. "The next time someone tries to attack me, you don't have to swoop in and save me."

This might be the stupidest thing I've ever said, the stupidest non-conversation I've ever had.

Still, he doesn't respond. Instead, he grabs me by the arm and hauls me away from the dead body, dragging me toward him. My pulse spikes when suddenly I realize he could hurt me, that maybe he wasn't trying to help me at all.

Maybe he just wants me for his own.

Oh, God.

"Let me go," I whisper, but he ignores me, tugging me closer to him so that I'm standing toe to toe. He wraps one strong, sinewy arm around me as if to anchor me to him, and with his free hand, tips my chin so he can look in my eyes.

In another time and place, he'd be hot as hell, ruggedly masculine with the square cut of his jaw and vibrant blue eyes, muscular and tall, covered in ink that makes my heart accelerate. But there's a desperation in his eyes and thirst in his grip that sends warning bells clanging.

"Who sent you here?" he demands, his voice thick and snarling. "Was this a trick? Were you sent here to distract me?" His voice is angry and tight, his eyes flashing while he questions me. "To tempt me?"

Tempt him?

"What the hell are you talking about?" I say, trying to pull out of his grip, but he only tightens his hold. This man is no savior of mine, but every bit the enemy.

"Why are you here?" he demands, shaking me.

"I—there was a ship," I say, almost pleading, because his grip hurts, and I want to get away, but he only holds me tighter. Still holding my chin in his hand, his narrowed eyes tell me he doesn't trust me. "There *is* a ship—"

"And why aren't you on that ship? Why didn't you get back on before it left? Did you know I was here? Have you come to mock me?"

"I... what?" I whisper. "No, I—I just wanted to explore a little."

Is the ship still here? Oh, God, it has to be. Is he serious?

How will I find it? How will I get home? I'm going to cry, and I don't want him to see me, so I yank my chin out of his hand. He still holds me in his vicious, tight grip.

"I don't need your help," I manage to grit out. "You didn't have to kill that other man."

"Fine, then," he finally says. His voice is husky and rough. "You can kill the other one." He lets me go so quickly, I stumble, falling to the ground and skinning my knee, but I barely pay attention.

There were three men in that skirmish. One lies dead, one walks beside me, manhandling me like I'm a piece of property, and the third is missing.

I get to my feet. He's eying me as if I'm a slab of steak and he's a starving dog. I swallow hard and pretend I'm courageous.

"Where'd he go?" I snap.

He scoffs, his eyes traveling the length of my body before he answers. "Who the hell knows? Likely to the easiest place where he can hide, maybe one of the shelters we've made before. He'll need food and water, and he'll want to put as little effort into his own fucking survival as possible."

He takes a step toward me and grabs my hand, pulling me away from the forest and toward the beach.

"Let me go," I tell him.

"No."

I grit my teeth but don't fight him. I'm not so sure he won't hurt me if I argue, and if I'm honest, the terrain is rough and rocky. His footing is more sure here, and if I hold his hand I'm less likely to fall again.

I'll get away from him. I'll fend for myself. But first, I need to find out where I am and how I'm getting out of here.

He continues to drag me out of the woods to a sort of cliff that overlooks the beach. I blink. The beach is familiar. I still see the shells lined up at the water's edge where I left them earlier today. But my stomach ties in knots when I see the vast, empty shoreline with *no ship in sight.*

"Where'd it go?" I whisper. I'm suddenly cold and shaking. "*Where?*"

He raises a brow to me. "Your ship? I have no idea. The only thing I know is that it came today, when we called out to them, they somehow didn't hear us, and by the time we got to them, they were gone."

I blink. "They weren't supposed to leave without me."

He narrows his eyes and looks with hatred at the horizon. "Nor me. But here we are."

I fall to the ground in a sitting position and bury my head in my hands. "And where... where might that be?"

He scoffs. "Who the hell knows?"

FIVE

Cy

JESUS *FUCKING* CHRIST.

It was bad enough when Eugene was alive, and we didn't know where he was. This is far, far worse. As soon as he could, while I was distracted ending the motherfuckering savage, Eugene, Will took off. Where to, no one knows, but Will's selfish insistence on taking care of himself will always prevail. He likely took one of the shelters we built, the son of a bitch.

And now not only do I have Eugene's dead body to bury, I've got a riled-up girl who thinks she can protect herself on my hands, a girl who doesn't have a goddamn iota of self-preservation in her body, and Will is in hiding.

And why is she here? This was no accident. Cruise ships don't land on this island, and no random turn of events brought her here. There was something malicious and deliberate about her being here, though I can't understand how or why it happened.

Jesus, we've got to get off this island.

It doesn't make sense, though, any of it. Why the hell did they bring her here, only to leave? Why would anyone do such a thing? Did they forget her?

Or was this on purpose?

She's sitting on the ground, her head buried in her hands, and Christ, she's a mess, but even a wreck she's stunning.

I blame the island for the way my body responds. My pulse quickens and my dick hardens. It would be so easy to take her like Eugene tried. She's small and fragile, and she wouldn't be expecting it. I could pin her down and slide my cock—

God. What am I thinking? I don't rape women. I just killed a man for trying. Who—*what*

the hell have I become?

I won't let my mind deteriorate any further. I will retain whatever civility I have left if it kills me.

Still, I can't help but give her a solid, thorough once over.

She's short, and younger than I am, but not by much. With a sturdy, well-built frame and gorgeous, vibrant auburn locks, she stirs something deep and primal within me. But now her auburn hair hangs about in her in wild, scraggly curls, her face is streaked with dirt, and her clothes are torn, revealing a curvy body and full breasts. She's a mess, though if I'm honest, I'm not that much better. I look from me to her and realize the responsible thing is to get her to safety before we assess our situation.

I don't know what's affected my head since I've

been on this island. I know my hold on the civilized behavior fades with each passing day, and I become more and more uncivilized with every day that passes. But when I saw her... when I first laid eyes on her, I could see nothing beyond how beautiful she was. It awoke a hunger in me, a deep, abiding need to bury my cock between her thighs and fuck her like the savage beast I've become. I got one look, caught one glance, *and I had to have her.*

What the hell is that all about?

When I saw her, I didn't see a fellow human or someone in trouble, but a beautiful woman in need, and my instincts took over. I had to save her. I had to protect her. I was taken with the sudden, irrational need to drag her off and claim her as my own, away from the danger. Yet, she nearly slapped me for saving her from rape.

The other men likely felt and saw the same, which makes sense in retrospect. When Will and I saw her, we reacted more strongly than we did when we saw the roasted meat. We've been starved for real food and damn near ravenous for female companionship. Even now, just looking at her, sitting on the ground helplessly, her clothes hanging about her in tatters, I want to claim her, to ravage her.

But I won't let myself succumb to my base needs. I've been stripped to primal urges, torn down to the most basic needs, and I won't let this be one of them.

"Come," I command gruffly. She looks up at me with her vivid green eyes, and they immediately shutter.

Is she in shock?

"Uh, no," she says, shaking her head. "I'm not going with you. I'm going to find my ship and get out of here.

I'm not staying another minute on this godforsaken island." She shudders.

I look from her to the wide expanse of the sea, then back to her again.

"Are you, then?"

She stumbles to her feet and plants her hands on her hips, glaring at me as if I personally took her ship for my own.

"I. *Am.*"

I shake my head and against my better judgment, try to reason with her. She's being stubbornly stupid. "There were three of us. One, *as you know,* is dead, and the other ran off. You do realize that he's probably going to come after you? That he ran from *me* but was as ready to violate you as the other was?"

She blanches, and it gives me momentary hope that maybe she's coming to grips with the reality here.

I go on. "At the very least you should come with me to shelter before you make your plan." I snort mirthlessly. "And if finding a way off this island were as simple as you make it out to be, I wouldn't be here myself."

"What do you mean?" she says, her bravado momentarily slipping. She swallows hard. She looks out at the wide expanse of ocean. "They... they have to come back. We're not... stranded here..."

I shake my head. "You might say that."

"But that doesn't make any sense," she says.

Will may eventually find me—find us, if she joins me—but knowing the location and intricacies still gives me a decided advantage.

"I'm going to find my ship," she says stubbornly.

"Go, then," I say, waving my hand toward the water. "If you find it, let me know?"

Panic flits across her features, and her eyes roam over my body again, as if she's just seeing me for the first time. I don't look like she does, like someone who accidentally found their way here after getting off a cruise ship. I look like Robinson Fucking Crusoe who's been fending for himself for an eternity, because that's what I fucking am.

I have no doubt it sobers her, but she juts her chin out and squares her shoulders, then turns to head back to where the body lies.

"Where are you going?"

"My bag is down... down there." She takes off at a good clip, I watch her go.

I follow behind her, shaking my head. She isn't going to find her ship, but at least she locates her bag. My stomach swirls with hunger when I catch up with her, the half carcass I ate earlier now a distant memory. I wonder if she's eaten. I wonder if she has any food with her. She's walking away from me and I have to stop her because I know if Will finds her, there's no telling what he'll do.

But is she even safe with me?

She takes off for the shore and I follow, cursing behind her.

She paces the white sand, like if she keeps looking, she'll find the ship under a rock or something. She's wearing a thin, light green sundress with a faded brown pattern and delicate sandals that will do little to protect her from the elements, looking every bit the part of stranded tourist.

"They wouldn't just leave," she says, biting her

nails, and hell I wish she wouldn't do that. She looks vulnerable and innocent, and I don't trust myself not to lose my fucking mind, because my hold on my self-control is nebulous.

"No? They wouldn't?" I follow behind her, though my eyes are on the forest and not the shore. Will is hiding. He likely won't make his move anytime soon, but I know he will in time.

"No," she says. "I was the one who won the prize. I only went because I needed the vacation. *God!* I was the one they attended to most. I mean I couldn't even come out to breakfast without the entire staff making sure I was taken care of. *I* was the one every single member of that ship looked out for."

What the hell is she talking about? She seems nearly irrational, and her chatter borders on the frenzied.

Prize? What prize?

It doesn't matter, though. Not now. She's not making reasonable sense, but she'll have to find that out for herself.

I pace the edge of the beach to keep myself calm. To keep my instincts in check, because all I see before me is a weak, fragile creature. The rational part of my brain reminds me that she's probably capable of taking care of herself and she isn't here for *me,* and another thread of thought filters in and out of my consciousness, begging the question: *what the hell has this island done to me?*

I didn't used to be barbaric and desperate. I used to know how to talk to women. Hell—the memory is faded, but I think I once had a woman I loved, even. Did I? God. And as I pace the beach, I filter through my thoughts and try to sort memory from dream. I can't. I growl to myself, angry that I don't know who I am, why I'm here, or what to do with the girl.

The sun beats hard overhead, heading toward the peak of early morning. I look from her to the sun again. She's fair, lightly tanned and heavily freckled.

"That sun is fucking brutal," I call out to her from my position on the edge of the beach. I try to keep my tone conversational but fail. My voice is harsh, unwelcoming, and it makes her jump. I continue, trying to quell my rising temper. I hate that she's here. I hate that I am. I hate that I can't control my thoughts and barely contain my actions. My words come out heated and sharp like flames. "For Christ's sake, don't stand in direct sunlight like that for more than a few minutes at a time. You'll make yourself sick."

She pauses, looks up at the sky as if just noticing the full force of the sun's rays, then glances back my way.

"Right," she says, waving a hand in my direction. "I know, I know." She paces away from me again. What the hell is her problem? Her ship isn't coming back. She's stuck here with me.

I grunt, but don't make a move. I'm still keeping an eye out for Will, I'm starving, and I don't trust myself not to hurt her.

There was a reason why Eugene attacked her. I doubt he could even help himself. Whatever brought us to this island has contributed to our tenuous hold on civilized behavior. He probably couldn't help himself, he was that far gone. Killing him was the only way to keep her safe.

"Any food in that backpack of yours?" I ask her. I prowl toward her, suddenly nearly delirious with hunger. I've gone days without eating, but the thought of actual food right where I can grab it tempts me.

She pauses her pacing again and grabs at her bag, her eyes wide on me as if I'm about to attack her and hell, I might be. I don't trust this lust and craving inside me.

"Yeah. Protein bars and nuts, but not much else."

I can't even see straight, the need to eat the food she has is that strong. I snatch it out of her hand.

"Wait!"

I tear it open, ignoring her.

Her eyes widen when panic flits across her features. "Do you mean to tell me there's nothing to eat on this island?"

"Depends," I tell her wryly, reaching my hand in her bag with trembling fingers, like a vampire who's just smelled blood. "Do I look like I've been eating three squares a day?" The contents of her bag spills onto the beach in front of me, and when I see cellophane wrappers I fall to my knees. I grab a package of salted nuts, my mouth watering. I swallow hard and my stomach aches with hunger when she sprints toward me.

"Hey! Don't go through my things!"

"I'm not going through your things," I say in a growl.

"Eat what you want, just don't touch my stuff," she says, scowling at me.

I don't give a shit about her stuff, but apparently, she does, because she's picking things up at a frenzied pace, her cheeks flushed a vibrant shade of pink. Maybe I *should* pay attention to her things. I look down and realize she's shoving her panties and bras and something else—a thick pink vibrator in her bag. My lips tip upward for the first time in a really, *really* long time and my dick hardens.

Looks like someone really *was* taking a much-needed vacation. My mind goes to deep, dark places. Being around a woman like her tempts me in ways I haven't been tempted in ages. A different kind of hunger grows deep in my belly, and it unsettles me.

I'd give her good reason not to need that thing. I would fuck her until she screamed my name and prayed for deliverance. I would give that woman orgasms that would rock her to her very core and leave her panting for more.

What the hell has this island done to me that I'm reduced to animalistic instincts in the presence of a woman? It's fucking weird as hell.

"Give me that," she says, and her voice wavers as if she's about to cry.

I'm growing impatient, letting her do her thing while looking out for Will. I tip the rest of the nuts in my mouth, chew thoughtfully, and shake my head at her.

"You know, princess," I drawl, my casual tone belying the anger she's inspired in me. It isn't just her, though, it's the whole fucking situation. I want to break things with my bare hands. "Your ship has fucking *sailed.* Maybe you should think twice about treating me like your enemy, when you don't have so much as dinner to put in your belly or a roof to put over your head."

She looks at me in bewilderment, and I finally realize she's going through some kind of shock or denial.

"Were there others?" she whispers, wrapping her

arms around her body and shivering, holding her bag to her chest.

"Yeah," I say with a sneer. "The point is, it isn't as easy as you might think. You can fight me all you want, but in the end I'm the only one you've got here. Me, and that sneaking, selfish bastard, if he doesn't manage to get himself killed."

I hope he's close enough to hear me.

"How long have you been here?"

She's still standing in front of me, wrapping her arms around herself.

I look away. I don't like this question, because I don't have an answer.

With a forced sigh, I raise my eyes heavenward. "Too fucking long."

"Jesus," she whispers. She blinks, then clears her throat and shifts uncomfortably. "It's like you're Rip Van Winkle or something."

I sigh. "I wish. That would've been a mercy. I've been awake the whole time."

SIX

Harper

A DISCONCERTING SENSE of foreboding comes over me at his words.

Too fucking long.

He's been stranded here. How long? He says there are only three—maybe two of us—on this island.

Why am I here?

I swallow hard and try to put on a brave face, but what I want to do is bury my head in my arms and weep. I never should have gone on that cruise. I knew I should've stayed home.

"Can you... can you ballpark it?" I ask, my voice higher in pitch than normal, taking on a frenzied sort of note. "A day, a week, a month...years?"

He only polishes off the nuts, wads up the empty wrapper, and shoves it into a side pocket of my bag, but he doesn't answer my question. He stalks off away from the beach.

"Get off the fucking beach before you give yourself sunstroke," he says over his shoulder. I want to rail at him and tell him to fuck off, that he has no right to tell me what to do, but I don't want to be stupid, either. He's right, even if he's a douche about it. I will burn if I'm in direct sunlight too long, and I don't want to deal with that.

So, I follow him, with great reluctance, and mumble under my breath, "Obviously. Stop telling me what to do. I'm not the enemy here." He doesn't respond, just walks through the woods in his loping stride.

"Stay behind me," he says over his shoulder. "I don't trust the bastard to not attack us."

I grit my teeth together. Back at home, I wouldn't do a damn thing if a man like him told me what to do, but I'd be stupid not to follow his lead here. As far as I can tell, he might be my only potential friend on this island.

"Where are we going?" I ask.

"Be quiet."

I clench my fists and follow. The thick palm leaves overhead cover us enough to give me protection from the sun's brutal rays. I wish I wasn't wearing flimsy, delicate sandals. I look to his feet. They're bare, tan, and rough. He doesn't even flinch when he steps on rocks or tree roots, but my own feet are already aching.

He knows his way. He's used to the terrain. He's been here a very, very long time. I have so many questions I don't even know where to begin, and I'm not sure he'd answer them anyway. I'm not sure if he even could.

"This way," he grunts, pointing in the forest to the left, when he freezes.

I look to where he's staring. He's shaking his head, his eyes wide and mouth opened as if he's in shock.

"What?" I ask. I look to where he does but all I see is trees.

"Coconuts," he says, as if that explains anything at all. "Christ. They weren't here before. I *know* they weren't here before."

That makes no sense, though. How could a whole patch of coconut trees suddenly appear? It makes me wonder at his level of sanity.

Before I can respond, he's running to one of the trees, and he's climbing the smooth, narrow trunk.

"Catch them or let them fall, but don't get hit by one," he says, and before I can really process what he's doing, large, ripe coconuts are falling all around me. I catch a few but let the rest fall, until there's a small pile by my feet.

I look up in surprise when he swings from a branch on the tree and lands on his feet beside me.

"Open your bag."

Grumbling to myself, I do what he says. It makes sense, I just hate the way he orders me around. I unzip my bag and he shoves as many coconuts in it as he can.

"Perfect. Those will last for a little while." Without asking me, he reaches for my bag, yanks it out of my hand, and slides it onto his back. I let him. The bag is damn heavy.

"We're almost there. Keep up." He turns his back to me and starts climbing up again. I don't ask him where "there" is. I'll see soon enough.

Within a few minutes, we're at the top of some sort of hillside. I can still see the shore, but it's a good way off now. I wonder if it's a mistake being up here. What if the ship comes back? Will I be able to get there in time?

I'm hot and sweaty and thirsty as hell, and I feel like I need a really good cry.

I miss Daniel. What's he doing right now? How will I get back to him?

And God, I was almost raped today. I saw a man killed, and now I'm with another man that seems to hate my very presence, in the middle of God knows where, food scarce. I hate this.

When we reach the cave, he tosses my bag down, takes a knife from his waistband, then sits on the ground.

"Sit." He points to the ground. I sit and glare, though I'm pretty sure it's lost on him. He could try to be a bit more civilized. I've never been one of those girls that like the alpha male, the bossy guy who thinks he has to protect everyone and everything around him. I can hold my own, *thank you*. But, he's about to give me some coconut, and I'm starving, so I don't quibble.

He looks around him for something.

"Need to catch the water," he says.

"I'm guessing you have no bowl," I mutter, barely stifling the desire to roll my eyes.

"No, but I have shells." He comes back a moment later with shells the size of my head. I blink in surprise. I've never seen anything like them. I watch, rapt, while he opens my bag and takes out a few coconuts. The rest spill onto the ground around him. Placing one on the center of a shell, he takes his huge knife and whacks it along the center of the coconut with rapid, solid strikes. His muscles bunch and stretch, and he's the epitome of strength wielding the cruel weapon. I can't look away.

It's weirdly hot, seeing him bare-chested and muscled, whacking the coconuts with gusto, like some island version of a lumberjack chopping wood. I squirm uncomfortably at the raw display of strength.

Oblivious to my musings, he turns the coconut, then whacks it again until the hard, brown shell cracks. Clear liquid drips down and gathers in the base. Lifting the coconut, he carefully catches every drop, then hands me the shell.

"Drink," he orders. "It will prevent dehydration."

"Then why don't you drink?" I ask. I'm not sure why I feel such a strong urge to push back against him.

"I will," he says, his eyes narrowing. "Ladies first."

I wonder if he's testing to see if it's poisoned, and I eye it warily.

He growls.

"Drink the fucking water."

I frown at him so he knows I don't do this willingly, and he better not get used to his highhanded communication methods working, but take the shell and tip some into my mouth. It's warm, and lightly sweet, but somehow refreshing. I continue sipping it while he splits the coconut in half.

"Here," he says a moment later, handing me a shaved slice of coconut meat on the end of his knife.

I take it. "Thanks."

It's creamy and rich, and my stomach growls in appreciation. I've only had coconut it its processed form, shredded and sweetened, this is completely different. We eat in silence, then he cracks open another and another, until our bellies are full and empty coconut shells litter the ground around us.

He sits back and shakes his head. "Doesn't make

sense," he says. I look him over. He almost looks like could be on vacation, bare-chested, wearing a faded pair of jeans.

"What doesn't?" I ask. He looks at me as if he just remembered I was there, then shakes his head.

"You're here," he says. "The coconuts showed up. It's almost as if—"

He freezes when we hear something crashing through the woods. I sit still, not sure what it is he sees or hears, and I know instinctively to be quiet. I look from him to the woods again. The sounds are heavy and clumsy but light, clearly not the sounds of a man trying not to be discovered. A moment later, he's on his feet.

"What the hell," he mutters.

I look and stifle a scream when a passel of rodent-like creatures goes scurrying past us a few yards off. Mousy brown with sleek fur and tiny ears, they're almost the size of rabbits. Squirrel-like in appearance with beady little eyes and curved backs, but they don't have the fluffy tail a squirrel has.

I hate rodents so much I shudder, pulling back into the cave to get away from them, but Cy lifts his machete and goes after them.

I gasp. "You're going to kill them!" I say, my voice a squeak. Oh, *Jesus Christ on a cracker,* he's killing rodents for dinner. My stomach swirls with nausea, and I'm afraid I'm going to lose the coconut I ate.

"Stay here," he orders, then he's gone.

As *if* I'm going after him on his rodent-hunting mission? I close my eyes and whimper. How did I get here? This is torture. Am I dreaming? No, I'm not, but if I were it would definitely be a nightmare or something.

I whimper when I hear a scuffle and squealing, and I shove the heels of my hands into my eye sockets.

Oh God oh God oh God.

In a few minutes he comes back, holding several limp carcasses in his hand.

"Oh my God, you did not," I moan, covering my mouth with my hand. "I'm not eating them!"

He laughs mirthlessly and shakes his head. "You can be a princess and starve to death or eat and live. You can skip the agoutis."

Agoutis?

"Suit yourself. Don't eat them, even though half a dozen Latin American countries consider them *fine* dining." He's sitting outside the cave doing *something* with his knife, but I can't bear to look. "But don't come crying to me when you're so hungry you can't even remember your own fucking name."

"I'll find my way out of here," I insist. "I'll get back on that ship."

He doesn't reply, just continues his preparation with his knife. When he's done, he brings them to an open space surrounded by large rocks that looks like a fire pit of sorts.

"We should be safe here," he says. "Will ought to be hiding from me, not looking to attack, though we we'll take precautions."

I draw in a breath and let it out slowly. "Can you tell me anything at all about this place? How you got here?" I ask him. "I—I'm completely in the dark."

He gives me a grim smile, and I have to look away as he begins skewering the skinned animals on sticks.

"Now that I've had a little something to eat? Yes. My name is Admiral Cy Kaufman. US Navy SEAL. I, and five of my companions, landed on this island. We don't know how we got here. We have no idea how to get off. We don't know how long it's been."

"How many of you were there?"

"Six, but now there are only two. I think."

I stifle a groan. "And I take it the other guy isn't friendly."

"Yep." He turns the sticks over the fire, and to my surprise, it smells like roast chicken.

"You keep saying this doesn't make sense," I say. "What doesn't?"

He waves his hand at the forest. "All of it. The way..." his voice trails off and he points to his temple. "The way I *think*. The way I act. The fact that we had literally almost nothing to eat for days, then suddenly you show up and there's food practically falling from the sky. You come on a boat, after years and years of no one coming here at all? It doesn't add up."

It doesn't make any sense to me either. "Were you all Navy SEALs?"

A muscle clenches in his jaw as he turns the meat over the fire. "Don't remember."

I nod slowly. "What can you tell me about your life back in the states?"

His eyes meet mine, panicked for a moment, before they shutter. "I've forgotten a lot, but what I do remember comes in waves. I know I was in the military. I know I was raised in foster homes. I know my name is Cy Kaufman."

I don't respond at first, worrying my lip and looking away from him. Either he's undergone some type of trauma that impacted his memory, or someone tampered with him. And if someone's tampered with *him*...

I shove the thought away. Sometimes my imagination gets away from me. I have to stay logical.

"What about you?" he asks.

"What about me?" I frown at him. It makes me uncomfortable turning the attention onto me.

"Who are you? Why are you here? What do you do?"

I shrug. "A few weeks ago, I got notified that I'd won an all-inclusive cruise. I almost didn't take it. I have—"

No, I'm not going to tell him about Daniel. I'm not sure how much I want to tell him.

"I have a job I'm responsible for," I tell him. "But something like this doesn't come up often, so I took the opportunity."

He nods, removing the roasted meat from the fire. "And you went on the cruise. You checked it out ahead of time?"

"What do you mean?"

"It wasn't a scam?"

"Of course not. I'm here, aren't I?"

He purses his lips and slides the meat off the stick onto one of the shells. "My point precisely."

I don't understand what he's talking about. I look about the cave. It's dark and cooler than on the beach, but the back of the cave opens behind us. I shiver. I hate to think of what creatures could come join us. I want out of here. I remember my room on the cruise ship, luxuriously appointed and cozy. And my home—God, my home, that I worked so hard to furnish so it was my little haven. My house in the country, a fair drive away from the city, small but idyllic, with its wrap-around porch and swing and maples by the front yard. The interior was decorated in "modern country" design, complete with refinished wood and minimalistic decor. It was my little oasis.

He points the end of one of the sticks to the roasted meat. "Help yourself."

Oh hell no. I will starve to death before I eat a rodent. I swallow the bile that rises in my throat. "Uh, no. I'm good."

He sits beside me, tears off a bone, and starts to gnaw the meat right there in front of me. I turn away so I don't hurl. *Gross.*

"You might regret that later," he says. "Food isn't always plentiful here. When it is, you eat."

I don't respond, because if I open my mouth, I'm going to be sick.

We sit in awkward silence while he eats every last bit of meat, and I wonder what I'm going to do next. He answers my question when he stands, stretches, and yawns.

"Water is crucial. Every day, it's important you drink as much as you can. Fortunately, we have fresh water sources here on this island, and I'll show you where they are."

I stand and walk with him, wincing when my feet hit the rough terrain again. He frowns, looking down at my feet. "Those are a hazard," he says. "Take them off."

I look down at my feet, then back up to him. "Question," I ask, frowning right back at him and tipping my head to the side curiously. "Were you the self-appointed leader here or something?"

He narrows his eyes at me but doesn't respond.

"There are ways of suggesting someone do something without ordering them around. I'd like to remind you, Cy, that I'm not one of your lieutenants."

He crosses his arms on his chest but still doesn't respond. Stupidly, I go on.

"Do you know what *my* job is back in America?"

His face is impassive, his jaw granite. I go on. "I'm a journalist for the *The Times*." Still, no response. "I write about women's rights and feminist ideals?" I explain, waiting for some kind of recognition from him. "I've spent my entire career studying the plight of the modern woman and how we can maintain our autonomy and freedom without losing our identity or the gains we've made."

He still doesn't respond, and it's starting to make me angry.

"Honest to God, have you nothing at all to say?"

"Oh, I've got plenty to say," he says in a low, dangerous voice that makes the hair on the back of my neck stand up.

Damn it.

I swallow but stand my ground.

I go on. "I just think that if you and I are going to... inhabit... this island together..." I sound like a fool and I know it, but I can't seem to stop talking. "We could... maybe learn to communicate a bit better."

"How interesting," he says thoughtfully. "I was just thinking the same thing."

I blink in surprise, but I'm happy we seem to be making some headway here. "Oh?"

"Oh, yeah," he says. The still-narrowed state of his eyes should warn me. Maybe the sun got to me more than I realized. "I think I've been way too fucking polite."

My jaw falls open in surprise. "What?"

He takes a step toward me, and my heart leaps, but I don't step back. I won't let him physically intimidate me.

"Yeah," he says. "I've buried four men on this island." When he reaches me, he grabs for my hair and fists it. What is he doing? I come up on my toes and slap fruitlessly at his hands, both terrified and furious. I will *hurt* this son of a bitch.

His hold is tight, though not as painful as I anticipated. He's immobilizing me, not assaulting me. I feel like a puppy being held by the scruff of her neck.

What if he's going to hurt me?

Oh, God. Maybe he's no better than the man that tried to rape me. The only difference is this one bided his time.

"Let me go!" I protest, still trying to smack him off me. The beast. The fucking *beast*.

"Four fucking men," he says. "You got off that ship of your own accord. That was your choice. Now you're on my turf. And I'll be fucking damned if I bury another body on my watch. You want to skip eating a fucking meal because somehow meat I roasted with my own two hands is too good for you? Fuck that. You'll eat what I give you and do what I tell you until it gets through your thick skull how much fucking danger you're in. You get me?"

I slap at his hand again, angry that tears well in my eyes. He's too big for me to fend off, and I hate that the only companion I have here indefinitely is showing his true colors as the barbaric douchebag he is.

He yanks my head again and holds my gaze with his, then to my shock, cups my jaw almost tenderly with his other hand. "This could go many ways, Harper. You think on that." And on that note, he lets go of my hair, turns me around, and slams his palm against my ass so hard I stumble. "Now take off those fucking shoes before I have to do it for you, and if I do it, you'll be over my knee during the process."

Then he's stalking out of the cave, grabbing the empty coconut shells on his way, and I'm staring at him.

What the hell just happened?

He's at the mouth of the cave now. "You have thirty more seconds."

I take five seconds to wipe the angry tears from my eyes before I fumble with the clasps of my shoes and yank them off.

He really is no better than the man who lies dead.

I have to get off this island.

SEVEN

Cy

I'VE BEEN on this island for God-knows-how-long, I haven't seen a woman in fucking eons, and the first one I see has a death wish, a smart mouth, and a fucking agenda.

I'm used to being obeyed. I commanded an army of men before I landed on this island. I have no patience for people who make no effort toward self-preservation. If she were my subordinate, I'd punish her.

Hell, I still might.

Maybe it's because I've been on this island so long. Maybe it's because I've lost touch with civilization and polite society. Or maybe, somehow, this island is poisoned, affecting the mind in insidious ways. Because being around Harper inspires the filthiest, basest desires in me.

When I fisted her hair in my hand, and her mouth parted in pain, I could imagine that mouth wrapped around my cock. When her eyes flashed at me and dared to defy me, I imagined her strewn over my lap, bucking and kicking while I held her down and spanked her to tears. I want to dominate this woman. Punish her. And the harder she pushes against me, the more insistent the urge becomes.

I remember now. Parts, anyway. I've always been a dominant man. Not the most popular in school, you might say. But when I enlisted, I found my place. Deeply dedicated to discipline and structure, welcoming pain and rising to the challenges before me.

She poses a challenge, and I fucking like it.

After she takes off those stupid shoes, I stalk toward the watering hole and gesture for her to follow me. I rub a hand across my sweaty brow. I haven't thought much about my past recently. Starvation and the lack of real human companionship made survival prominent in my mind.

Now that my belly's full and there's another human with me, I start to remember things I haven't thought of in a very long time, as if my mental clouds part and my vision clears.

I remember who I am. And how I became the man I am today.

Maybe I shouldn't be so hard on her.

But when I look over my shoulder at her, I see a fragile creature who's too young, too beautiful to die. A woman who could grow to be a companion on this island. I don't want to see her injured, or worse, fucking killed. And my patience has all but fled.

"Keep up," I snap. She winces when she steps on a tree root, and I toy with the idea of swinging her up onto my back and carrying her to the water. But no. She wants her independence. I'll give her that.

When we're paces away from the water, I hear a sound that makes me freeze. I hold up my hand for her to stop, and she does, looking at me with wide, fearful eyes. And for one moment, I feel badly for her. She shouldn't be here. She should be vacationing, kicking back with one of those drinks with a tiny umbrella in it, listening to the sound of waves crashing on shore, her only concern how even her tan line is. She shouldn't be here.

Not on this unpredictable, godforsaken piece of earth.

Not here with me.

If Will is hiding, he knows where the cave is. He knows where this water hole is. I don't trust the motherfucker for a second.

I wish I had a goddamn gun.

But I know how to use my knife.

We stay immobile, waiting for another sound, but nothing comes. Finally, I shake my head. If the asshole attacks, I'm ready, but it'd be damn stupid of him.

I finally gesture for her to come nearer, wordlessly pointing to the water below. She nods, and steps toward it. I hand her one of the coconut shell halves and take the second, kneel beside the cool water, and scoop it into the shell.

"Don't you have to boil it or something?"

"No," I mutter. "This particular water source is clean, a freshwater spring."

"How do you know?"

I sigh. "We found out the hard way. This is the only one we can drink straight."

Frowning, she follows my lead and takes a cup of water to her lips. I realize as I hold her gaze with mine that this is an act of faith. An act of trust. She has to believe that I'm not lying to her, that she can bank on me telling her the truth.

"Drink up," I order. "It's important not to get dehydrated."

"Right," she says, before she takes big gulps of water. When she's sated her thirst, she tips some into her palm and runs it along the back of her neck. It's hot and humid today, with not a sign of rain in the sky. She hasn't acclimated to the weather like I have.

"I'd give anything for a shower," she says. Sitting on the bank by the stream, she lifts the hem of her dress and drizzles cool water on her bare thighs. With a sigh, she does the same to her shoulders. The wind blows, and I inhale her scent.

Wait. Her *scent*? I close my eyes and breathe deeply, her feminine fragrance stirring need in me. I inhale again.

Christ, I know that smell, though it takes me a minute to put it together. It's the sweet, musky scent of her arousal.

Her arousal? I look at her curiously, but she doesn't look my way.

Why can I smell her so intensely? Have I been a savage so long on this island that I've actually adopted the traits of an animal?

Without realizing what I'm doing, I take a step toward her. She looks up at me, her eyes panicky. If she runs from me, she's in danger. I take another step toward her. I have to keep her close. I gentle my voice so I don't scare her off.

"There's another watering hole we use to bathe," I say. "It's fine to splash yourself with this water, but we like to keep it for drinking." She hasn't let any of the water drip back into the fresh water, and she has no soap or anything that could harm our drinking supply, but it's a simple rule we all have kept consistently.

"Oh," she says, flushing. "I'm sorry."

"Don't be."

I take another step toward her, keeping my voice calm, because she's skittish. I swallow hard being near her, because when we're close, I'm vividly aware of everything about her.

The gentle swell of her breasts beneath the thin fabric of her dress. The way the dress dips into a low vee in the front, showing the valley between her breasts, gently freckled. I swallow. I want to lick each one of them, leaving marks with my teeth down the length of her body.

When she stands up, her skirt clings to her, the hem too high on her thighs, revealing her beautiful legs. I turn away when my mind goes to laying her down on a bed of leaves, parting those legs, and fucking her hard, right here, right now. I shake my head. The insistent, rampant need unsettles me. I'm not an animal. Then why does my body act on instinct as if I am?

What is going on with me? I've heard of men growing savage when put in certain conditions. In the military, it's not unheard of. Deprived of basic necessities, humans lose their civility, their hold on decorum.

But this... this is something else altogether.

I take another step closer to her, unabashedly letting my gaze roam over her body. When I come near her, I hear a low rumble, and it takes me a moment to realize I'm growling. I'm fucking growling. My heartbeat accelerates, and my breathing becomes ragged. My fingers curl, even my eyesight sharpens until I can see every hair on her body, her pulse beneath the thin skin at her neck, the rise and fall of her shoulders. My own lungs expand with every breath she takes. I can almost taste her, almost feel the way her soft, sweet body will yield to me.

She should run. She should gather her skirt about her and flee, because I'm the predator, she's the prey, and she doesn't stand a fucking chance. But she doesn't run.

It surprises me that she grows a little shy, her gaze roaming over me in turn. Her eyes linger on the muscles at my shoulders and arms, before traveling the length of my body. When she captures her lip between her teeth, I swallow hard. She's scoping me out from the top of my head to the tips of my toes. Christ, she's as turned on as I am.

"Come here," I murmur. She blinks and twists a piece of hair between her fingers but doesn't move.

"Harper," I say, louder, this time crooking a finger in her direction. "Come here."

Her eyes on mine, she walks toward me.

"Good girl."

She's so close to me now, I could let out a breath and rustle her hair. I draw my index finger along her hairline, gently moving a strand of hair off her brow, before tracing my finger down the side of her face to her lips. I outline her full bottom lip, then the top, gently parting her lips with my thumb. She doesn't stop me, but moves in even closer. Complying. She feels this, too. Her tongue peeks through and teases my thumb. When

I don't stop her, she grows bolder, circling my thumb with her tongue.

My dick throbs, my balls ache, and I want to own this woman fully. I swallow and pull my hand away with great reluctance, and it seems almost physically painful to turn away. She blinks as if waking and cocks her head to the side.

"It's strange here," she whispers. "Do you feel it, too?"

I'm glad she has the savvy to speak truth and not hide. I nod.

"I do." I shake my head. "I haven't decided if this island's enchanted or cursed. When food vanishes overnight, it's cursed, but when a woman like you ends up here..." I shake my head.

"There's no such thing as enchantment or curses," she says. "That's... that's fictional. I don't believe in that at all. It's got to be something psychological." She shakes her head and brushes imaginary dust off the skirt of her dress. "I should hate you after the way you treated me."

I give her a sidelong look that makes her blush. She has no fucking idea what I could do to her. What I *want* to do to her.

I turn back to the watering hole to refill my shell, though it takes everything in me not to lay her down and kiss her so thoroughly she begs for more. I want to tear her clothes off and make her mine, right here on the bank. The need is so pressing I'm shaking when I bring the shell to my lips.

I stand, and don't look at her. I don't trust myself.

We stand in silence for long minutes. I'm lost to my thoughts that quickly turn to fantasy. It doesn't matter if

I'm finally losing my mind, or if I'm just starved for human affection. I need to school my thoughts, control my impulses.

The memory of Will in the woods, Eugene's dead body, and the bodies of the others we've lost, does just that.

"Show me where you wash?" she asks.

I nod. "This way. Stay close," I order.

Her eyes narrow on me, and I realize she's hurt, maybe feeling scorned even. She'd better not do something foolish and reckless on the way.

"I want something clear. We're not fucking around here. Don't get any ideas in your head. You get me?"

Her pretty eyes narrow. "Ideas in my head?" she asks, her voice dripping with sarcasm. "What on earth are you talking about?" She snorts and turns away from me, rolling her eyes heavenward.

I shake my head. "I'm talking about staying safe. Nothing more, nothing less."

"Safe," she repeats.

"Safe. Now follow me and behave yourself."

I know I'm being a dick. I know I'm an asshole. But in the middle of an idyllic place like this, it might be easy to forget the danger that lurks in every corner.

Regardless of her objection, she follows me down through the woods and back to the beach. We walk in silence for the five minutes it takes to get there. I'm watching for any sign I can find of anything at all out of place, but I see nothing. I frown. This isn't right. Nothing here is.

A flutter of wings overhead catches her attention. "Oh, wow. What kind of birds are those?"

"Pretty sure it's a kind of duck, or somehow related.

They make for good eating," I respond. I have no idea what they're called. We didn't have them in the northwest.

"Oh, ew. God, I don't want to get used to that."

"To what?" I ask over my shoulder, as we take the final steps to the beach.

"Eating roadkill."

"Here we go again. There's a big difference between eating roadkill and surviving off the land," I protest.

I look over my shoulder at her, frowning.

"Here we go again is right. What the hell do you expect?" she retorts.

This girl will end up over my lap before the night's through. Ha. Fucking twist my arm.

She follows behind me, muttering to herself. "Not *this*," she says, and her voice is strained as if she's trying not to cry. I turn to see her wincing with every step she takes. Christ, I forgot she doesn't have her sandals on, and her feet aren't yet accustomed to this terrain.

"You need help?" I ask her, pausing with my hands on my hips. I could easily swing her up and on my back or in my arms and help her get to the beach, but I'm not sure she won't slap my face if I do it without asking her.

Not that I care.

"What do you mean?" she says, swiping angrily at tears I'm sure she doesn't want me to see.

"I could carry you."

Her jaw clenches, and I can tell this is killing her. I don't know much about this woman, but from what little she's told me, I know she's worked her ass off getting to where she is. I know that it takes great effort for her to admit defeat.

"I'm fine," she says, though her voice wobbles and she doesn't meet my eyes.

I turn away from her and don't respond. She can suit herself.

When we get to the beach, she whimpers with every step she takes on the hot sand. I look again at her, but she won't meet my eyes. The heat's made her hair sweaty, and her face is red, the rest of her skin a light pink. Fortunately, we avoided the brightest sunlight, but it's still hot as hell here. She looks gratefully to the water, and it seems we both realize the same thing at the same time.

We don't have a change of clothes. Her bag is back at the cave.

She looks down at her dress and up to me.

"Well, this was poorly executed," she mutters.

"Yeah. Well, I'll turn away. You take your clothes off and hang them on a branch."

"Cy," she says bracingly.

I raise a brow to her. Her eyes say what she doesn't want to out loud. The attraction between us is fucking dynamite.

"Yeah. That's why I said I'd turn away," I remind her. "You can air dry or something, then put the dress back on."

A corner of her lips quirks up, but she doesn't respond.

"Okay," she finally says. "But make sure you turn away."

I give her a look that turns her suddenly shy and a bit more humbled. "Please. Turn away, please."

I respectfully do what she asks, but it doesn't help like I thought it would. I can hear the rustle of her clothing as she removes it, and a second later I watch as she hangs them on a branch that extends to the watering hole.

I swallow hard. She's naked. Christ, I want to see her. A little voice whispers in my ear, tempting me to just take a peek, but I don't. If I do, I'll be joining her and then we're screwed. We're both barely hanging onto self-control already.

But God, I need to wash, too. So I step away from her and go to the other side of the hole. I'll be practical and logical and safe. I step out of my jeans and toss them on the bank, then wade into the water a few yards away from her. From the corner of my eye, I can just barely make out the gorgeous slope that leads from her side to her hips.

I start counting in Spanish.

Uno. Dos. Tres.

Doesn't help. Damn.

I count to twenty to try to stop myself from getting a hard-on.

Doesn't work.

I start reciting the prayers I learned in grade school. Maybe some kind of religious memory will trigger the need to stay celibate or something. Next thing I know, I'm imagining her in a Catholic school girl uniform.

Yeah, that didn't work.

I dive into the water and close my eyes, drowning everything out in the muted depths. We swim in the ocean but have sighted sharks offshore. If we stay in the shallows we're fine, because it's the depths that are more dangerous. Here, in the watering hole there are no sharks to worry about. Nearby, there are waterfalls. It's idyllic, and I stay beneath the surface, schooling myself for as long as I can.

I surface to the sound of her screaming.

Christ.

I whip my head around trying to find her. She's clutching her arms across her chest and screaming her fool head off.

"What the fuck?" I ask her, looking to where she points. In seconds, I'm on the bank grabbing for my machete when I see a boa constrictor just inches away from her. Huge and deadly, though it isn't poisonous, it's very capable of strangling her to death. And even if it wasn't dangerous, it's another food source.

We lost a man to a snake. I won't lose another. She screams again and again while I wield the knife and lunge. The boa strikes at the same second I bring my knife down, but it doesn't get far as the thick, sharpened metal lops its head off. Her screams become bloodcurdling, and she's crying freely now.

I hate this for her. Hate it.

With the end of my knife, I pick up the snake and toss it to shore, then turn back to her. She walks toward me, and without thinking, I open my arms to hug her. Thunder rolls overhead, and before she reaches me, huge drops of rain pelt down from above. She reaches me as the rain falls in sudden torrents. We both speak at the same time. The poor girl's trembling.

"I'm sorry, I froze—"

"Those things are deadly—"

"I tried to get away—"

"It killed one of the men here."

"You saved me, I couldn't—"

And then she's in my arms, soaking wet and utterly

naked, and I don't even try to stop this. She's shaking but framing my face with her hands as I bring my mouth to hers and kiss her. Oh, Christ, it's been so long since I kissed a woman, and never in circumstances like this. We're soaking wet and disheveled, but stripped from every possible modern convenience, there's nothing but raw sexual attraction.

She's holding onto me while I frame her waist with my hands, and my *God,* she feels so fucking good, even soaking wet and shivering. Her skin is like silk, her body easily melding to mine. My cock's a steel rod between us, but she's either as turned on as I am, or she doesn't care. She only presses herself closer to me and rocks. I slide my tongue in her mouth and skate my hands down her trim waist to the fullness of her ass.

I want to see how she responds to being dominated. Something tells me she might be an independent woman, but she won't fight this. So I grip her ass before taking one of my hands away and when she moans, I lace my fingers through her sodden hair with one hand, and with the other, slap the fullest part of her ass.

She sighs into my mouth and draws nearer. I spank her again, and again, as I continue to kiss her, yanking her hair between my fingers. I fucking love the way she molds to me like this, as if welcoming me to do more. I bring my hands to her underarms and hoist her into my arms. Her legs wrap around my torso, my cock pressed up against her ass. Christ, I want to fuck her right this minute. With her still holding onto me, our lips still joined together.

My need for her is so strong, I can't think, I can't speak. I need in this woman, and now.

I lay her on the ground and she yields to me,

moaning when I pull my mouth off hers and trail my tongue from her neck to her collarbone. On instinct, I wrap my fingers around her neck, feeling the way her pulse quickens on my palm while I cup her pussy with my other hand.

"I want to own this pussy," I say in a ragged whisper. Her eyes widen and her lips part when I flex my hand on her neck. I shove my hand between her legs and spread her thighs. She's dripping wet in more ways than one. I effortlessly glide my fingers through her folds until she's grinding against my hand.

"Fucking gorgeous," I say in a low rumble, working her pussy while I look her over. Jesus, how I want to fuck her. I drop my mouth to one breast and lap at her nipple while I finger her, reminding her who's in charge of this with gentle pressure to her neck. She moans and bucks her pussy against my hand. I suck in a nipple, suckling for a moment before giving it a harsh nip with my teeth.

She gasps, though it's muted with my hold on her. I release her nipple and lap the hardened bud with the flat of my tongue, circling to stimulate her. She moans and whimpers. I release her neck and move my hands to her wrists, cuffing them.

"Stay there," I whisper. "Do exactly as I say, or I'll punish you."

Her eyes look a little frightened, but her body vibrates with need. There are little pink fingerprints on her neck where I choked her, her hair wild and crazy from being pulled.

I'm drawn to her in a way I can't control, a way I don't understand but can't stop. I need her like I need to fucking breathe.

"I need to fuck you," I whisper. "I need to fuck you *now*."

"We shouldn't," she whispers, but then she's moaning and spreading her legs like she can't stop herself either.

I line my cock at her entrance and tease her clit with the head, and when she's moaning and on the cusp of climax, I plunge myself into her. She sighs deliciously and opens her legs wide.

"Fuck me," she says through gritted teeth. I place one hand on her neck again and gently squeeze, holding both wrists in my other hand, and shove my cock in her channel. Christ, it feels amazing. I don't even remember the last time I had a woman. I do know it was way before I even set foot on this island. She's so tight I groan, building a rhythm, oblivious to where we are or what we're doing, our only focus chasing our ecstasy.

I thrust and her head goes back with a moan and she pulls on her wrists, but I hold fast.

"Fuck me, you're gorgeous," I manage to rasp out. I thrust again, harder, and she screams, but it doesn't stop me. Again, I thrust and again she moans, her legs wrapped around my torso anchoring me to her. I pull my cock out so the very head is at her center, and slam into her again, loving the way she writhes on the edge of bliss, loving the way her pussy milks my cock, loving the momentary reprieve from all responsibility as I do what I've been created to do, what I have to do. This woman was mine from the moment she set foot on this island.

I close my eyes when her keening moans increase and her pussy clenches on me. She's on the cusp of climax and I'm on her heels. She throws her head back with reckless abandon and screams her climax when my seed lashes into her. I pump my hips and claim her body, marking her with my come. I don't stop until she's sighing and panting and fully relaxed beneath me.

"Gorgeous," I say, leaning down to plant a kiss on her cheek.

"My God, what was that?" she whispered. "I got turned on looking at you. This isn't me. I'm not—"

"Me neither," I tell her. We're still entangled together. I've just fucked her, but I'm not sated. I want *more*.

"Something's happening here," she whispers. She looks in my eyes searchingly. Hers are a delicate, bright green.

"I know." I don't know what else to say, so I lean down and kiss her again.

"Dear God," she says, when I pull away. "This place *is* bewitched or something."

"Or something," I mutter. "*Christ*. Get your dress on before I fuck you again. We've got to get up to the shelter and secure things before nightfall."

She pulls away reluctantly, jumping back in the water to clean off but I don't look this time. I can't. If I do, I don't trust myself not to fuck her again.

EIGHT

Harper

I HAVE no idea what just happened. I mean, I do. I just fucked a man I hardly know, in the middle of nowhere, like a wanton whore.

Who am I?

It's like we both lost total control at the same time. He went all animalistic on me and I caved like a house of cards. But God, I don't regret it. I don't regret it for a minute.

I've had polite sex, and lackluster sex, and pretty damn good sex, but never anything like *that*.

My throat still hurts a little from where he wrapped his hand around it. I touch the tender skin and smile to myself.

I liked it. God, I *loved* it.

My ass still stings from where he spanked me, and my scalp still burns from when he pulled my hair. I look down at my breasts, not surprised to see pink bite marks around my nipples. I turn away from him so he doesn't see me smile. I feel so... *badass.*

What the hell is that about?

The rain stops as suddenly as it started. I shake my head as I make my way up the bank, wiping as much of the water off me as I can.

He manhandled me and I begged for more. My pussy clenches at the memory of his thick, hard cock gliding in and out of me.

I start when I think about what we just did.

Birth control.

I took my birth control pills yesterday.

Are they still in my bag? How many more do I have?

And is birth control enough? I don't even know the man. I just had unprotected sex with a savage, wild man I met *today.*

Am I out of my mind? Honestly, I think I am. I really, truly, think that I've lost all semblance of reason. There's something in the air, or hell, the *water* on this place. I look back at the pool I just stepped out of as if I expect magical purple smoke to be rising from it, but of course there's nothing of the sort. I see the dead snake on the shore and cringe.

Something caws in the distance, shaking me out of my head. I grab my dress and pull it off the branch, whipping my head around to look to Cy.

"Just a bird," he says. "Still, we have to get back up to shelter."

He isn't looking in my eyes but hungrily at my body, and I swear he's hard again just looking at me. He swallows hard.

"We don't have time for another round, cowboy," I

mutter. He shakes his head as if to clear his mind and shoots me a lopsided grin but doesn't reply.

I can't believe I just fucked him, like a sorority girl at a frat party in need of a one-night stand. It's the island. It's got to be. Because when I see him standing there, still dripping wet and flushed from fucking, I can't help but smile back at him. If he stalked over to me right this very minute and manhandled me again, not gonna lie, I'd let him.

"Any ideas for dinner?" I ask him. My stomach growls, and he gives me a withering look.

"Hungry?" he asks.

I nod reluctantly. I will not admit I should've eaten the rodents. No way.

"A little," I say, tugging the dress over my still-damp body. "Not starving."

"Yet."

When I tug my head through the neckline, I see him swallowing hard again, his Adam's apple bobbing.

"Should've eaten the food I made you," he mutters, staring at my breasts.

I grimace and step over toward him. "I... think I'm fine. Please, tell me there are other sources of food on this island?" I have protein bars, still, but they won't last long.

"Sometimes there is, and sometimes there isn't," he says, tearing his gaze from mine and stepping past me to pick up the dead snake.

"Noooo," I groan, even as my stomach aches with hunger. The breakfast buffet this morning seems very, very long ago. He slings the snake around his neck, and I grimace.

"Really?"

"Really."

He walks toward me and takes me by the hand to help me up the steep bank.

I look longingly over my shoulder at the beach. "Can we explore the beach a bit? It would be better than walking through these woods."

I wince when my tender foot comes in contact with the rough branches. Without asking me, he bends, lifts me in his arms, and effortlessly walks while holding me. My arms instinctively wrap around his neck. I've never been carried by a man. I feel his muscles flex around me. He's warm and strong, and I feel weightless in his arms.

I like this.

"No," he says with determination. "It's too dangerous until we know where Will is. We're too exposed down there."

I don't fight him. I let him carry me. And maybe that's the catch. This is still my choice. Even when he dominated me on the bank, that was my choice, and I loved every second.

"Not so crazy about being the helpless female," I mutter.

"That's too bad," he counters, his voice deep and husky. I look up at him, but he doesn't make eye contact, he's so intent on making sure we're getting back to safety. If I believed in things like werewolves, I'd think I was being carried by one, and it's not just because of his long, ragged hair and beard, or the thick snake draped around his neck like a scarf. I shudder and look away from it. There's more to it than that. There's a certain ferocity in the way his eyes roam about the forest. Sometimes when he speaks his voice is rough and raspy like he's half-growling, and the way he killed that snake...

I swallow.

He's a man, not a beast.

Is he both?

His lips twitch. "I, on the other hand, quite like you being the helpless female."

And just like that I'm turned on again and more than a little irritated about it. I'm no *helpless female*.

"Is that right?" I can't keep the ire out of my voice. "I just arrived here. Give me some time—"

But then I stop speaking when I realize what I'm saying. I'm not taking it for granted that I'm going to be here a while. I don't want to be. I want to be home, back with my brother, back to my job and my home, the little piece of heaven I built for myself.

And yet, when he looks down at me, and his full lips quirk up at the edges, my heart does a little flutter in my chest. He leans down and brushes his lips to mine. I stop breathing.

"You've got no one here to prove anything to, Harper," he says and then, with a shrug, his lips tipped up and eyes twinkling, he brings his mouth to my ear. "No one to come save you. No one to hear you if you scream." I shiver, and my pulse ratchets harder. Even though he looks a bit playful, the rough sound of his voice in my ear affects me. "I own you now, Harper."

I feel my cheeks heat, and a full body tingle shivers down my body.

I should protest, but I don't trust myself to speak.

I own you now.

The way he says that makes my heartbeat thud.

No one owns me.

But there's something about being alone with him that makes me wish it were so.

I toss my head back, which doesn't have quite the dramatic effect I'm aiming for since he's holding me to his chest, and I tip my chin in the air.

"You don't own me, sir," I say with as much haughty dignity as I can muster. My voice sounds high and squeaky. I'm trying to play off being teasingly serious, but I only end up sounding like a child play-acting.

He sobers, his lips thinning and his grip on me tightening. "We'll see about that, now, won't we?"

Is he serious? Is this some wild man form of flirtation?

Though I like being held by him, I can't help but try to fight this.

"Put me down, Cy." I push against his wall of a chest.

His jaw clenches. "No." He isn't even winded.

"Yes," I counter lamely as he steps over a large, fallen log.

"Talk back again and you'll find yourself over my knee."

"Excuse me?"

A muscle ticks in his jaw. "You heard me."

Why does the threat of a spanking make my heart race even faster? I crave his domination and control so hard it scares me a little.

I decide to push it a little. What if he *does* spank me? I'll live. And I want to know what it's like. So with my heart racing, and my palms all sweaty, I put on a brave face and clear my throat.

"Put. Me. *Down*."

My timing brings us right to the foot of the cave.

Oops.

"Is that how we're going to play this, princess?" he says.

I clear my throat. "I'm not playing!" But I am, and I shouldn't be. I should mean what I say. I don't know what's come over me.

Still holding me to his chest, he falls to the ground of the cave and kneels on one knee. I cringe when he yanks the snake and tosses it behind him.

Gah.

I start to second guess my choices here.

"Okay, so maybe you should just let me go—ahh!"

I squeal when he flips me over and places me over his bent knee. My hands flail, my legs scissor, but he holds me in place with one arm. My heart races because I've never been spanked, and I'm not so sure why I'm doing this.

"Put me down!" I scream, because I feel like I should protest, that I shouldn't just lie over his knee and let him discipline me.

Without a word, he whacks his palm on my ass. It hurts a lot more than I expect, and my breath leaves me in one fell swoop. I'm gasping for air when he spanks me again, his huge palm as heavy as a paddle. I must've been crazy to want to see what this was like.

"Okay!" I protest. "Okay, alright!"

But he's unaffected by my words.

"This what you need, Harper?" he asks. He lands another slap, then another, building a fire on my ass unlike anything I've ever felt. I throw a futile hand back to try to stop him, but he effortlessly cuffs my wrist and pins it to my lower back, adjusts me over his knee, and continues the relentless assault on my ass like he's been waiting for this moment.

"You wanted to see I meant what I said, didn't you?" he asks with another smack.

I don't respond, because he's right.

"Has this cleared things up for you?"

"Hmmph!"

My dignity might be bruised, but my body vibrates with pleasure. It confuses me.

"Put me down."

He gives me another good spank.

"That demand is what got you here in the first place."

Oh, right. Dammit.

"Cy!" My belly hurts pressed up against his knee, and my cheeks flame. "I'm not a child!"

"Didn't say you were," he says before he gives me another hard smack that goes straight to my core. My pulse races and it hurts. It really, truly hurts, though every stroke of his palm makes me want more. There's something beyond this pain, though I don't know what that might be.

"You'll do what I say, Harper. You'll eat what I give you. You'll keep yourself safe while under my watch, or your ass will pay the price."

"Okay, alright, yes," I tell him. "Please?"

He gives me one more smack before lifting me off his knee. Spinning me around, he cradles me in the crook of his arm. His eyes are narrowed, his brows furrowed as he looks searchingly at me, as if trying to determine if I've learned my lesson. A delicious shiver runs through me.

"Much better," he rumbles approvingly, which makes me suddenly want to hide. I'm too raw, too exposed, and *so fucking turned on*. I can't bring myself to look at him, so I bury my face on his chest. The little dark, curly hair on his bare chest tickles my nose. I place my hand palm down on him as if to steady myself. I don't know what I want right now, but it isn't this. I don't want to cuddle. I'm sort of angry and wildly turned on and confused as fuck.

He holds me there tentatively at first, then squeezes me to him and kisses my forehead. The rough feel of his whiskers and gentle touch of his lips evoke unexpected emotion. I swallow hard, not knowing why I'm so raw and vulnerable right now.

Gently placing me on the ground of the cave, he leaves me rubbing my sore ass, gets to his feet, then walks toward the fire.

"It's gone," he says grimly.

"What is?"

"The rest of the meat I cooked. Gone." He turns to look at me with his hands clenched into fists, white-knuckled and betraying the fury he barely holds at bay. "It might feel like we're alone here, but we're not." I pity that lone man that crosses him now. I saw how he lopped off the head of the snake. I saw him end the life of the man who tried to rape me. Whether it's time spent on this island or something more, Cy is wild and untamed, and I don't know what he's capable of.

When he stalks to the foot of the cave, the setting sun illuminates the muscles in his body, taut and glistening with a fine sheen of perspiration. He throws his head back and *howls* into the night.

"Where are you? Come at me, motherfucker! You're not getting us. You're not getting *her*."

I stop breathing and blink in surprise. I practically expect him to pound his chest.

He continues to lament and howl, but I don't hear much beyond what he just said.

You're not getting her.

I own you.

Should I be afraid of his unabashed proclamation of ownership?

He waits, panting from the exertion of screaming to the other man who inhabits this island, before walking back to me.

"The ship might come back," I remind him stubbornly. If it does, I'm leaving. I have to. I have a job and a brother and would prefer the simplicity of a predictable meal in my belly, thank you. I clear my throat. I try another approach though. "If it does, come with me."

He holds my gaze for a minute before shaking his head and looking away. Finally, he sighs. "No one's coming, Harper. They brought you here for a reason."

Who?

I shake my head. I don't believe it. "You're lying."

His jaw firms. "I don't lie. Let's cook that snake."

"Cy, you can't just change the subject."

Walking toward the snake, he doesn't meet my eyes. When he speaks, his tone is mild but resigned. "You don't have to believe me," he says, his tone gentler at first than I've ever heard from him. Then his tone hardens. "But there's no ship coming, Harper."

NINE

Cy

AFTER I TELL her we're stranded here, she pulls into herself a little. She grows quiet and introspective. I don't really blame her. Today has been *intense.*

I honestly feel bad for the girl—woman. Whatever. I feel bad for her, because she's been through so much in such a short time.

I build a fire in silence, and we eat the snake. I'm honestly kinda proud of her. She makes a face but doesn't protest this time, taking the roasted meat from me without a word of complaint. When we finish the snake, we eat another coconut for dessert, polish off the coconut water, then walk silently down to fetch water to drink. When we come back up to the cave, the sun's already set, and the night's grown cooler. She shivers. Without a word, I drape my arm around her shoulders and pull her closer to me. She doesn't protest.

We sit by the fire in silence, and it feels almost nice, the crackle of the flames and her soft breathing beside me. Without the trappings of polite society, it feels as if there's no need to keep up conversation. We sit in silence for a while until her head begins to droop.

"Harper." She jerks her head up and blinks at me, her auburn hair hanging about her in messy but adorable waves. We stayed mostly out of the sun today, but she still has a light pink tinge on her cheeks. The flickering fire lights her green eyes so they look like little bits of glimmering jade. My chest swells with pride, and I want to gather her up to me and hold her.

I'm not used to this urge I have, to protect her, to keep her safely by my side. It's foreign to me but feels right.

I saved her life today. I fucked her. I spanked her ass.

Like I said. It's been an intense day. But it's left me with the need to cherish this woman, though I hardly even know who she is.

I need to get this sleepy girl to bed. "Let's get some rest, baby."

She looks from me to the fire, then back to me again. *Baby.*

Why did I say that? I don't regret it, though.

She yawns, like a sleepy little kitten, then gets to her feet. I take her hand, but before we go to the cave, I look beyond us to see if there's any indication at all that Will's out there. It was one thing when I was a loner on this island. Now that I have a woman to care for, it's altogether different. But I see nothing at all, though the pitch blackness doesn't help matters.

"Wait." She freezes at the foot of the cave, turns to me, and frowns. "Um. Where do you sleep?"

Isn't it obvious? I point to the cave. "In there." Did she not realize that?

"Um..." she worries her lip. "Are there bats?"

I nod. "Yes."

She shakes her head. "Oh God oh God oh God." It sounds like she's about to cry. "I can't sleep in there!"

"Course you can," I say, taking her by the hand and giving her a little tug. "The bats won't bother you, and it's safer in here than outdoors. Outside the cave you're susceptible to much more." Snakes. Rodents. Spiders.

The other man on this island.

Christ.

"How will I sleep with bats in that cave?" she asks in a high-pitched, terrified voice. She begins to whimper. "Cy, oh God, seriously there has to be another option."

I work my jaw before I reply. "There was, back when the men on this island were friendly. But it's too dark now to go to the shore." We had a few makeshift shelters we built, all six of us. One much sturdier than the rest. Back when we weren't enemies.

Frowning, she looks out to the darkness beyond the cave and yawns widely.

"Harper, you can do this," I tell her. "I promise."

Now that the fire is almost dying down, it's pitch black, the sliver of a moon offering little light. She shivers.

"Harper," I repeat. I take her hand and give her a tug, pulling her close. I run my fingers through her hair and bring my mouth to her ear. "You don't have to be afraid. I'll keep you safe."

"I'll keep you safe, too," she says. I grin. Christ, she's cute.

"Thank you."

"You're laughing at me. You don't think I can keep you safe? I keep my brother safe. I'm his guardian. I not as helpless a female as you think." I want to know about her brother, and how she keeps him safe. I want to know what matters to her.

"Never said you were a helpless female."

"You'll see," she says, ducking her head. "There will come a time when I need to keep you safe."

It's then that I realize she's really just stalling. She doesn't want to go into the cave.

"I believe you," I say, though I'm not so sure she's convinced. Hell, I'm not. "But now we need to get some sleep."

She takes a tentative step toward the cave. "What if the bats burrow in my hair?" Her voice is little and high-pitched. The poor thing is terrified.

"I will rip them out of your hair and kill them with my bare hands."

"Oh, ew, that sounds brutal."

I shrug. "Sometimes brutal works."

I tug her hand again and she takes another small step. "Is it cold in there?"

"Not that cold. Cooler than it was earlier but bearable."

"Do you have a blanket?" she asks.

I have a tiny scrap of a thing I fashioned out of a few t-shirts, but it's not much of a blanket.

"Sort of."

"I have some clothes in my bag we can—oh." She

looks around her. "Um, Cy? Have you seen my backpack?"

Mother*fucker*.

We walk into the cave and look to where we left it earlier. It's dark, our only light the moon and the fading flicker of fire, so it's hard to see, but she left it at the foot of the cave. It's gone. I should've thought of that, dammit.

"Son of a bitch," I curse. Had to have been Will.

"I need that," she says. "There's... things in it I need. Like *bad*."

"Like medicine?"

"Yeah. Like medicine."

Christ.

"We'll track him down tomorrow," I tell her. "Promise."

I lay down on the floor of the cave, the softest part covered in moss, and pat the ground beside me. I can hardly see her in the darkness, this far away from the fire.

"That looks terribly uncomfortable," she says, but then she looks to the back of the cave and falls to her knees. "Oh, God, I think I saw one."

She definitely did, but it's night, so they won't be sleeping in here. "Since they're nocturnal, they'll be flying outside hunting dinner."

She cringes.

Now that she's beside me, I pull her onto my chest, away from the mouth of the cave. "You'll be fine," I assure her. "You likely did see one, but they won't hurt you." I swallow hard before I make a promise. "Nothing will hurt you."

I can hardly see her, but I can hear her yawn. "Oh, God, I'm tired."

I nod, and take the threadbare, makeshift blanket and pull it up over her.

"You need it, too," she says.

"It isn't big enough for both of us, and I run hot at night anyway."

"You run hot any time of day," she says coyly, then she's giggling to herself. "Sorry. I'm exhausted and getting a little giddy."

"Don't apologize." I'm grinning, though she can't see it. It's the most entertained I've been since I landed here.

I hold her on my chest and quietly run my fingers through her hair, until her breathing slows and I'm sure she's asleep. My cock stirs beneath her belly, and I want to bury myself in her. I close my eyes and grit my teeth. *Here we go again.*

I hate that I have no control over this, that every time we're in close proximity I want to fuck her senseless. I've been here longer than she has. I know things she doesn't yet, and one thing is for absolute certain: our being on this island is no accident.

In the distance I hear the howling of what sounds like a wolf. She stirs and murmurs so softly I'm not sure she's awake.

"There are no wolves in the Cayman Islands." And then she's lightly snoring again.

What the hell is she talking about?

Does she think she's in the Cayman Islands? I have no idea where we are, but those are inhabited. Tourist locations. Not the middle of fucking nowhere.

When the howling dies down and there's no sound

but the soft rustling of trees outside, I close my eyes and finally fall into a deep sleep.

For the first time since I got here, my dreams are salacious and lewd, every one of them involving Harper. On her knees, sucking me off while I choke her, tied to one of the trees while I whip her perfect ass, spread face down on the beach while I take her from behind.

I wake up with a raging hard-on and groan. Was I that sex-deprived that having a pretty woman this close to me affects me this deeply? I try not to fidget because I don't want to wake her.

"Can't sleep?" she whispers. It's still the middle of the night. Her voice is soft and raspy in the quiet coolness of the cave.

"I'm fine," I lie. "Go back to sleep."

"Can't sleep either. You must've done something to my psyche or something, because I'm having one sex dream after another."

I can't help but smile.

"Is that right?"

Her hand travels down the length of my chest to my cock. I groan when she rubs me straight through my jeans.

"Fuck," I growl, reaching for her breasts and cupping them in my hands. "Stop that."

"Don't have to get up for work tomorrow," she murmurs. "Might as well—"

But I stay her wrist with one hand and smack her ass with the other. I'm not fucking around with her doing what I tell her.

"Get some sleep."

She rubs her ass and rolls, snuggling back up against my chest.

"If you say so."

"I say so."

Soon, she's gently snoring again, and I can't seem to get comfortable, not with this beautiful woman pressed up to my crotch. After a long time, I finally fall into a fitful sleep. When I wake with a start hours later, the pink rays of dawn filter through the entrance to the cave.

Harper is still on me, but her leg is hitched up on mine, her arm strewn possessively around my chest. Well *hello,* Sleeping Beauty.

Fuck, she's gorgeous. Her dress has risen up, revealing her perfect, shapely legs, and the very edge of the pretty pink panties she's still wearing. Her feet are bare, her useless sandals long forgotten. I stare at every inch of her, from her full breasts pulled up to my chest to her bright red toenails.

Fuck her.

The impulse is so insistent and powerful, I feel momentarily out of control. I blink in surprise. This is really fucking weird.

I swallow and gently shift so that I can stretch, but when I do, Harper wakes.

She blinks, looks around the cave, then sighs and buries her head on my chest again.

"Oh, this isn't awkward at all," she says.

"What?" I ask, running my hand down the back of her head, untangling the mass of waves. I continue until I reach her ass and give one of her cheeks a little squeeze.

"Morning breath. Waking up with your hard-on

pressed up to me. Lying on the chest of a man I hardly know, in a cave in the middle of nowhere."

"Could be worse," I muse.

"Yeah?"

Fuck her.

The insistent voice in my head speaks again, and before I know what I'm doing, I'm rolling until I've got her pinned beneath me on the cave floor. My growls echo in the cave, but I can't seem to stop myself. I have to have her, and now. Her eyes are round and wide with fear. I'm the hunter, and she knows she can't get away. I can feel her racing pulse with her wrists in my grip, hear her ragged breath, and smell the provocative scent of her arousal. My need to fuck her trumps all else.

I transfer her wrists to one hand while I rake her dress up with the other. When she tilts her head back, and I get a view of the delicate skin at her neck, I lean down and sink my teeth into her. She's sweet and salty and it makes her squirm deliciously beneath me. I rock my hips against her sweet body while I suckle the abused flesh between my lips.

I'm vividly aware of how fragile she is. How easily I could hurt her. I frame her body beneath mine as I lick and bite my way down to her belly.

"Cy," she moans, but I only growl in response. The need to fuck her permeates every pore of my body, every thought in my mind, my instincts fully trained on fucking this woman until she screams for mercy. I managed to tame my need to fuck her last night, but now I've lost all self-control.

I unzip my pants, grab my cock, spread her legs, and thrust so hard she screams, but as I sink into her hot, slick pussy, her screams grow hoarse. I silence her with my mouth on hers, gentle at first, then a rougher clash of teeth and lips. I bite her lip and her tongue touches mine, pulling away at the faint coppery taste of blood, my growl deepening. When I release her wrists, she throws her arms around my neck, pumping her own hips as I fuck her hard. Her nails scrape my back, and I slam my palm on her thigh, the impact stinging my hand. She whimpers and moans but submits.

She won't control this. I will.

I thrust again and again, her hot, tight cunt gripping my cock with every fevered movement, until she relinquishes everything, submitting her body to mine. When she screams my name at the top of her lungs, my own climax rips through me. My muscles contract and my pulse races, and fevered ecstasy washes through my limbs.

I own her.

She belongs to me.

I will mark her so even the skies above know she belongs to me.

My pulse begins to slow, and I stare at her wide-open eyes, and slightly parted, swollen lips. She brings a hand up to her mouth. "Turn around," she says.

"What?"

"I want to see your back."

I give her a view of my back.

"My God."

I pull out of her with great reluctance. "What?"

"I scratched your back. What the hell?"

"And I bit your lip."

She sticks her tongue out curiously as if to check and runs it along her lip. "No, I think I'm okay. But what the hell *was* that?"

"I woke up and needed to fuck you," I say, as if that explains anything.

"I woke up and needed to be fucked, so that was convenient. But now I need to go... clean up or something."

I nod, and take her by the hand, helping her to her feet. "We need to eat breakfast, clean up, get some water, and find your fucking backpack."

"We sure as hell do."

"What kind of medication do you have in there?" I ask her. I need to know. Is she sick?

She gives me a pointed look. "Birth control."

Jesus. Has the island affected me so badly that I'm operating under animalistic instincts? How the hell could I have not thought of that?

"We'll find it." Jesus, we'll have to.

She gets to her feet and stretches, yawning, then looks at the foot of the cave. "Can't say it was the most comfortable sleep I've ever had. Any chance we can make our way down to the shelter you built?"

"Yeah." Will can kiss my ass. I'll bring her to the shelter and get us outfitted properly. We'll make it our own.

"But wow, is that beautiful," she breathes. Standing at the foot of the cave, we get a full view of the valley below. The beach stretched out beyond the trees, the fingertips of sunrise painting the pale blue sky with ribbons of gold and cotton candy pink.

"It is," I tell her. "As much as I want off this island, there are some things I can't help but appreciate. And that's one of them."

We walk in silence down to the water; drink fully, and then clean up a bit.

"Coconut for breakfast?" I offer. "Today we'll catch some fish."

"Sounds good." I appreciate the fact that she isn't griping anymore about eating food in the wild. I crack open the coconuts and we eat, sitting by the embers of last night's fire.

"You know," she says, looking up above her to the trees. "If I didn't know any better, I'd think that was a bird's nest up there."

I look to where she's pointing.

"Hell yes, it is," I say, getting to my feet.

"What are you doing?"

"Need to see if there are any eggs in that nest."

She grimaces but doesn't protest.

I've had enough practice climbing these trees that it's an easy matter for me to shimmy up the trunk and haul myself up. There are three large, rounded eggs nestled in a nest in the branches.

Score.

"I need something to put them in," I say to her. "I can't hold them and get back down."

"Can you take the whole nest?" I look carefully at the interlaced twigs and shake my head. "No. If I take it off, it'll fall apart."

"Okay. I can catch them?"

I look down at her. She's already assuming a catcher position, her legs spread apart and knees bent, her hands cupped in front of her. It's honestly kinda cute.

"Babe, if you drop them, we lose a meal, and meals are fucking hard to come by here." Not sure she believes that, though, because oddly since she arrived, we haven't had an issue.

Her brows furrow together, and she nods with determination. "Got it. I won't drop them."

I give her a curious look, but she stomps her foot. "C'mon. We don't have all day here."

This girl is something else. "Alright," I agree. I take one of the eggs out. "Get ready."

I toss it as gently as I can. With a little squeal, she catches it in her cupped hands.

"Yes! One."

She gently places it on the ground, then assumes her position again. "Ready!"

I smile. Adorable.

I toss the second one down, and she catches that, too, and lays it beside the first.

"Do it!" She's ready for the third. I take the third, but when I toss it, something catches her eye and she looks away.

"My backpack!"

The egg smashes on the ground, the shell cracking and raw egg splattering near her feet. She doesn't even notice.

"Son of a bitch," I mutter under my breath. Did Will bring her backpack back?

I shimmy back down the trunk, frowning at the smashed egg on the ground, and with a sigh pick up the two that she caught. She's already over by her backpack, unzipping it and inspecting the contents.

"He must've come last night," she says. "Oh, God, do you think he was here when we—"

"I don't give a fuck if he was. Let him. I want it super fucking abundantly clear that you're mine."

She looks at me curiously for a moment, and nibbles her lower lip, before walking over to me. When she reaches me, she gets up on her tiptoes and puts her hands on my shoulders, lifts her face to mine, and kisses me. The kiss starts out tender and sweet, but soon she presses her body up to mine when I deepen the kiss.

She pulls away and whispers in my ear. "You're right, Cy. I want him to know that, too."

TEN

Harper

I PULL AWAY from him with reluctance. Knowing that there's another man on this island who's watching us creeps me out. I'm not afraid, though. I can defend myself I have to. I can defend *us*. And there's not a doubt in my mind that Cy will. Sometimes when I'm near him, I feel like he's part beast, and it isn't just that he's bearded and wild. It's who he is. How he holds himself. Hell, the way he walks and talks.

Something about waking up on this island, having slept in the same clothes I wore the day before, disheveled and starving, makes the reality of my situation a lot more real. I don't let myself think about it, because if I do, I'll cry.

I can't spend the rest of my life on this island. I *won't*.

The ship came here once. It will come back again.

I turn away from him and see the cracked egg on the ground.

"Oh, shit. *Man.* I totally flaked out, didn't I?"

He shrugs, and bends to pick up the two remaining eggs. "There are two of us, and we have two eggs. We're good." I'm glad he doesn't scold me for not paying attention. I wouldn't blame him if he did. That was my fault.

"I'm sorry."

"Don't be."

"I shouldn't have let myself be distracted."

"Harper, enough."

I hate when I drop the ball. I hate when I don't do what people are depending on me to do.

We don't say much else as he builds up the fire again. "How are you going to cook those eggs?" But he has a plan, involving some sort of flat rock and frying them, and it's messy, but in the end, we have cooked eggs. They're larger than chicken eggs, so it's almost like having two each.

"What kind of birds did these come from?"

"I'm not sure, but they're edible, like chicken or turkey."

"Not exactly the cruise buffet, but not bad," I tell him. "But I'd give damn near anything for a cup of coffee."

"Anything?" he asks teasingly, raising a brow at me.

"Anything," I repeat. Does he actually have coffee? "Yes, I will absolutely whore myself for a cup."

That makes him give me a low, rumble of a growl. "Wish I had some," he says. "I would take you up on that."

He smiles, and as he looks at me, his gaze grows dark. I bite my lip and shift a little beside the fire. I've never been around a man who looks like him, and it's doing something to me. I feel a little shy when I lick my lip, feeling where he bit me. My body has been marked by him, but it only excites me.

"So," I say casually, looking away so we don't tear each other's clothes off right here and go at it again. What *is* it with this place? "Can you tell me about yourself? Where did you live? What did you do?"

He stands and stretches, and I swallow hard looking at his tats and muscles. Fuck, he's beautiful, ruggedly handsome, and uncivilized. Raw alpha male, unencumbered by anything to hold him back. It's a damn good thing we've managed to establish some form of trust here. He's not the type I'd want to be on the wrong side of.

"I fought," he says simply. "Gotta be honest, I didn't remember much about who I was or how I got here until recently. It's coming back in bits and pieces."

I frown. "Like you hit your head and got confused or something?"

His jaw tightens and he's quiet and sober for a moment before he nods. "Or something. I know I grew up on the streets, inner city New York. I don't remember parents or siblings. When I was old enough, I made my money in the ring as a teen, then enlisted the day I was old enough to. Never looked back." He gathers a few twigs to clean up the area by the fire and tosses them on the pile. "You?"

I stand and smooth out my wrinkled skirt. "I grew up in the midwest," I say, and my mind is immediately transported to the tiny house I grew up in, surrounded by corn fields, the laundry hanging on clotheslines outside. It was a simpler place and time. "Both of my parents were teachers and valued education. I learned to read at a young age, and I was writing by the time I was five." I give him a small smile. "I've been a journalist since I graduated college. Got the job I have now after grad school."

Had? Will I make it back? Will my job still be there for me if I do?

He beckons for me to follow him back to the cave. When we reach it, I take out clean clothes and *thank you Jesus,* my toiletries.

"You mentioned a brother," he says.

"Yeah." I swallow hard, suddenly choked up. "Daniel is my younger brother and I'm his guardian."

Thankfully, he doesn't ask questions, and I don't supply any more details. I don't want to talk about the accident, my parents, or my brother's brain damage.

"You write about feminism?" he asks, folding the makeshift blanket and placing it under his arm. His question surprises me. I wasn't sure he was paying attention.

"I do." I say nothing more right now, because something tells me he'll have opinions on the subject matter, and I don't want to get into it right now. I reach into my bag and breathe out a sigh of relief. My pills. But then I frown. The food is gone. "He took the food I had in here." It wasn't much, but it was mine, the jerk.

"Of course, he did. Bastard."

I don't mention that he took some food himself yesterday, but yesterday seems like a very, very long time ago.

"I think we should go to the beach today," I tell him. "That way, if the ship comes, we're right there."

He doesn't respond, just gathers up his few belongings, but his lips are tight, and it makes me angry. Does he not care at all?

"They'll come," I tell him, arguing the point he doesn't voice. "It doesn't make any sense that they would just leave. Especially, when they realize I'm not there, and—"

"Harper. Listen to me."

He stands with his hands on his hips, and I try to pretend like I'm not feeling the pull again. I'm hyper aware of his strength and raw masculinity, and it's so damn disconcerting I don't know what to do with myself. I don't know much about psychology, but the logical part of my brain tells me that this isn't normal, that there's something going on here that neither of us fully comprehends. Our attraction to one another is abnormal.

I think?

How would I know? I've lived a carefully regulated life. The men I dated were educated and refined. We used condoms and discussed everything, and when I broke up with them it was after a series of logically thought out reasons.

Every time. Every damn time.

"They're not coming back, babe."

"Yeah, I know you think that," I say nonchalantly, and even as I speak, I know this will anger him. "But I don't believe you."

I'm pulling a brush through my hair and untangling it, and it feels nice to actually have a little sense of normalcy.

He takes a step toward me. "You don't have to believe me. I'm telling you, you being brought here wasn't an accident."

I feel my blood pressure rise. Does he know something? "Oh, yeah?" I ask, pointing my brush in his direction. "You don't know that, Cy. You're not God. You're not a magician."

He crosses his arms over his chest—his beautiful, muscled chest—and shakes his head.

"I'm not, but I'm also not stupid."

What the hell is that supposed to mean?

He takes a step toward me.

"And I am?"

"Oh, for God's sake, I didn't say that. I'm not the enemy here, Harper."

"Right," I say through gritted teeth, waving my brush at him. "I know that."

He isn't the enemy, but he's also not my friend.

"This conversation is going nowhere," he says. "Let's go to the beach. We'll see for ourselves which one of us is right soon anyway. And for the record? I sure as fuck hope it's you."

"Really?" I ask him. The hopelessness of it all, the near desolation I feel being alone with him on this island, wells in my chest and I feel I'm going to cry. But I won't show weakness. I fucking won't.

He takes another step toward me. "Really," he says. "I hope they do come to save us. But babe, they won't."

"You said that," I say, my hands shaking with anger. "Stop saying that. Shut up!"

With another step in my direction, he's standing toe to toe.

"No," he says. "I'll always speak the truth. I'm not a liar."

"Oh, how noble," I say. I'm not sure why I'm so angry at him, but when he reaches for me, I shove him away. He stumbles and nearly falls. "Don't touch me."

His eyes flash at me with a warning I should heed. He isn't safe. I shouldn't provoke him. But God, I'm angry.

"I'm going home. I'm going to find a way." Now that I've gotten started, I can't seem to stop. I go on irrationally. "And when I get back there I'm going back to my job and I'll write about this, about the caveman I found on the island who always knew everything."

"Nice," he says sarcastically. "Terrific. You do that."

"How even in the middle of nowhere he thought that somehow his patriarchal ways were needed."

This is the stupidest argument I've ever made, but I'm out of my element and reaching for anything to get my footing again. I've worked my entire life defending the plight of the repressed woman, only to be manhandled by this ogre with no help for it.

He's so close now I can see a smudge on his cheek where he must've rubbed soot from the fire. He smells like burning embers, and when he takes another step toward me, I remember. The way it felt to be pinned beneath him and fucked. The way I felt strewn over his lap while he spanked me. The way his touch *ignites* me.

"You know what you need?" he asks. His voice is all rumbly and dangerous. My belly clenches with need and arousal, *goddammit*.

I swallow hard and I feign bravado, because I'm quaking inside right now. "Something tells me you think you know *exactly* what I need."

He shakes his head at me. "You need a real man to take care of you."

I'm so taken aback, I laugh out loud. "Is that right? And let me guess. You're the perfect one for the job."

But apparently, he isn't finished yet. "You need to be put in your place," he continues, reaching for my hand. At first, I think he's actually trying to be all tender, when he plucks my hairbrush from my fingers.

"You asshole," I hiss. Is this still present day, or have I somehow been magically transported back in time? It's like he's some kinda goddamn Scottish highlander who thinks he's the boss of me, that just because I'm a woman I need keeping. Give me fucking heels and a broom.

Before I know what's happening, he's kneeling and hauling me over his lap.

"Stop!" I shout, because I know what this brought me last time, and *who the hell does he think he is?*

But he's bigger and stronger, and it's an easy matter for him to turn me over his knee and pin me there. Now I know why he took that brush. My solid, wooden hairbrush. *Jesus.* Without a word, he smacks my brush down so hard on my ass that I scream out loud.

"Ow! Hey!"

"You need someone to take you in hand," he says, with another hard *thwack* of the brush.

"Oh, and you're the one, are you? You jerk! Let me *go!*" I scream furiously, which just earns me another hard spank.

"Thankfully, yes," he says, unruffled, and for some inane reason, I'm turned on and it pisses me off.

"Put me *down!*" I scream, scissoring my legs and wriggling as hard as I can.

"Not until I know you're going to behave yourself," he says with another whack of the brush.

"Behave myself! As if I'm a child! I will do no such thing!"

"Alright, then," he says. "Suit yourself."

Warm air brushes my ass as he lifts my dress and pulls down my panties. My God!

"Cy! You stop that!" I scream, but it's not just because I don't want to be spanked, though there's that. I'm ridiculously turned on and mad as fuck about it.

"I don't think so," he says, before he smacks the back of the brush on my bare ass. I squeal and squirm. My hairbrush is solid wood with a flat back, and it hurts like hell. "I think that not only do you need someone to bring you to heel, but you *like* it, too."

"I do *not*, you big ogre!" I screech, bucking and wriggling, but not able to actually get away from him at all.

"Oh yeah?" he asks, rubbing the back of the brush over my scorched ass. "So, if I part your thighs, I won't find you wet as fuck?"

"No!"

"You're lying," he says. "And if you lie to me, you'll earn a harder spanking."

I don't respond, since I'm not sure what to say.

"Tell me," he says, spreading my thighs apart with the back of the brush, before he scrapes the bristles up and down my inner thighs. "Tell me, Harper," he repeats. "You're not at all turned on when I punish you?"

I swallow hard, because just hearing him say the words makes my heart thud in my chest and my pussy clench. I whimper when he glides the brush between my thighs. The need for pressure right there makes my mouth go dry and my pulse ratchet even higher.

"I think if you'd let me take care of you, you'd like it more than you know," he says.

I already have, I protest silently. But it's a silly argument. I'm putting modern expectations on a situation that's so outside the norm.

"I didn't say—I didn't mean—" my voice trails off, since I'm not sure what I want to say.

"We're in the middle of nowhere, babe," he says, smoothing the varnished wood over my ass as he talks. "And this argument is over." He calls me *babe* like we're dating, and for some reason it seems fitting.

I gasp when his hand is between my legs again, his palm cupping my pussy. My clit throbs and I want him to touch me so badly I'm whimpering.

"Okay, okay," I tell him, and in my head, I beg, *touch me.* I can hardly think beyond my need for relief. It's so insistent it's nearly painful.

I won't fight him, not now. Desperate times call for desperate measures, and if ever there were a desperate time, this is it.

I close my eyes when I feel his hands between my legs. I can't breathe or speak or move, my only focus the persistent, furious pulsing between my thighs.

"That's a girl," he encourages. "See, it isn't all bad now, is it?" If I wasn't so turned on it'd seem condescending, but I don't care now. He strokes and fondles, and I'm so aroused I'm already near climax. I'm so ready for this, a few more strokes of his fingers and I soar into bliss right there, climaxing right over his knee, panting and writhing while he wrenches pleasure from my body until I'm spent.

I'm in a haze when I feel him dressing me again. He turns me over and sits me on his knee. Taking my chin in his fingers, he keeps my gaze locked with his. I'm still breathing heavily, my pulse simmering down to normal. I feel shy and a little embarrassed at how hard and easily I climaxed.

"I'm in charge here, Harper," he says. "Whether you like it or not. Got it?"

I nod meekly, because I have no more power to deny him than I have to get myself off this island.

"We end up back home, then you can go back to whatever it is that makes you tick. You get that, too?"

"Yeah," I whisper. Because we will get back, damn it, and I want back to my normal life again.

When we do... will we ever see each other again? Or will we part ways, strangers once more?

Why do I care?

I'm not even sure what I'm consenting to, or if I'm even consenting. It's more that he's just telling me the way it is, and between being out of my element and my insatiable need for sex, I don't have a lot of resistance left in me right now.

"Good," he says, righting me. I'm still trembling so I stumble a little, but he holds me by the arm to steady me. "We're heading down to the beach." He hands me my hairbrush. "Put that in your bag for now."

Meekly, I obey, then go to sling my bag on my back, but without a word he takes it from my hands and takes the bag himself. Birds twitter overhead, and in the distance, I hear the soothing sound of waves crashing on shore. The sun is rising higher in the sky, and a gentle, warm breeze warns of the heat of the day ahead of us. Everything seems normal, but nothing is normal at all.

ELEVEN

Cy

IT DOESN'T MATTER to me where she came from.

It doesn't matter to me who she was before she landed on this island.

Now that she's here, she's mine. Fully. Entirely. Under my protection, under my watch, and in my bed, makeshift as it is.

She may have ideas in her head about how things should be, but I've buried four men and fuck if I let her be another casualty.

Today, we'll go to the beach. I'll take her back to the shelter the six of us built when we first got here, and we'll head to the shore. I'll show her the lay of the land on this island and introduce her to what it means to survive here. For now, food is plentiful, so we'll spend our time stocking up on what we can.

And I'll find the other motherfucker who threatens our safety. I watched as one by one the other men degenerated into being animals. If Will is hungry, or the poison of this island has affected him, he may have become like one of others. Barely human. Fucking dangerous.

And even if he hasn't, I want to know where he is.

When I was younger, I dated a few girls. I was the guy who always sat so he could see the door in a restaurant. I slept near the door in the bedroom. I walked on the outside of the street. It's part of who I am to know where danger lies and to be the first one to face it when necessary.

And now it's fucking necessary.

I spanked her good and hard this morning, and I don't regret it. Hell, I'm hard as a steel rod now, but we've got more important things to do right now than fuck... *again*. We both have admitted this island's some sort of aphrodisiac or something, and we have to fight against the constant irresistible attraction between us.

For now.

We'll have time.

I'm holding her hand as we walk to the beach, her bag slung over my shoulder. This time, we won't let anyone else touch it.

If Will wants to mess with us, then why did he bring the bag back?

Or does he want us to know that he's out there watching?

Either way, I will draw that motherfucker out, and if he tries to hurt my girl, I will end him. I will fucking *end* him.

I've done it before. I'd do it again.

The first human life you take guts you. It makes you

hyper aware of how fragile and temporary life on this earth is.

The second becomes easier. And the third. As a soldier, I learned to mask my fears and focus on my ultimate purpose. Back then, it was to serve my country and protect those who couldn't protect themselves.

Now it's Harper.

She's not a helpless female, though I'm sure a part of her thinks I think that. She's held her own on this island, and honestly better than half the men who died before she got here. Though she has her moments of grousing about our circumstances, she's ready to get shit done when necessary. Hell, I love that about her.

"Oh, wow." We've come to the entrance to the beach where we built the shelter long ago. It's a part of the beach she hasn't seen before, and from where we stand now, it looks like a fucking postcard. White sand as far as the eye can see, the beach dotted with picturesque shells and flat rocks on the shore.

"Yeah, it's beautiful," I agree.

"All that's missing is a cabana and someone to serve us drinks with little umbrellas in them."

It's missing a fuck of a lot more than that, but I don't argue with her.

"Looks idyllic," I agree. "But you can't swim in that water."

Frowning, she turns to me. "Sharks?"

"Yep."

Her gorgeous green eyes narrow on the water as we make our way to the sand. "Did you find that out the hard way, too?"

I close my eyes, instantly assaulted at the memory of the body torn to shreds. We did everything we could, but we didn't have the tools to save him. Watching him die didn't solidify our bonds as it could have, as it does sometimes in war. Instead, it served as a brutal reminder of how easily we could die here. We began to turn on one another.

"Yeah."

She doesn't reply, but I notice she's walking slower now.

"There's a place close to the beach where you can swim, though. You got sunblock in that bag?"

"I do." She looks over her shoulder at me. "Where?"

I point beyond the beach to a more distant alcove. "That inlet over there. Enough water gets in and out, but the opening isn't large enough for a shark to get through. It's almost like a little pool."

We reach the beach and she digs her toes into the white sand. "Wow, it's already heating up, huh?"

I nod. There are days when the temperature's nearly unbearable.

"Can we go for a swim?"

"We? Nah. I'm not interested. You can, though."

"Why don't you want to join me?" she asks, her head tipped to the side. She looks at me so coquettishly, I would almost give her anything right then.

"Need to keep watch."

She looks to the beach, then back to me again. "Fair enough."

"We have a few things to do today, though."

"Check out the shelter."

"Gather some water."

"Stock up on some food supplies?"

Neither of us says the other item on our agenda out loud: find Will.

I nod, glad that we're on the same page. "Absolutely. It will be better to wait to get your swim in later, once it isn't so hot out."

"Later this afternoon?"

"Yeah."

Without another word, she sits on the beach, drawing her knees up to her chest. "I'm game for whatever we need to do. I just want to look at the water for a minute. It's so beautiful."

I cover my eyes and look out at the vast expanse of endless blue-green water. Neither of us speak, but I sit on the beach next to her and we watch the waves coming in and out in silence. Wispy white clouds dot the sky.

"It's as if someone painted paradise," she says softly. "All the different shades of blue and blue-green. Turquoise. Cobalt. Ultramarine. Sapphire. Cerulean."

"Yeah, makes it sound a lot better than just 'blue.'"

The sky is lighter where it meets the ocean. Dotted with wisps of white clouds, it gradually becomes a darker blue, a breathtaking contrast to the greenery that surrounds the beach. Palm trees that surround the island bow their heads and branches as if in adoration of the ocean.

"You could almost imagine something hidden in those depths," she says.

"There's no doubt in my mind there are things hidden in those depths."

"I mean like... mermaid kingdoms, and kings that rule with tridents. Buried treasure and the like."

"I mean sunken ships and sea creatures."

She smiles softly but doesn't reply.

"We should get out of the sun," I tell her. "Only a

few minutes in direct sunlight like this, and your fair skin will scorch like a lobster."

"Mmm, lobster," she says, getting to her feet. "Sounds delicious. Is there lobster here?"

"Not sure," I reply. "But I've caught at least a dozen types of fish." Not during the famine, though. Not when there was no food to be found anywhere.

"Where *are* we?" she asks. "Do you think we're near the Cayman Islands? That's where we were supposed to be landing yesterday."

Was it only yesterday?

"I have no idea," I tell her. "What port did you sail out of?"

"Miami."

"Are you sure?"

She looks at me quizzically. "Do you think I forgot something as simple as that?"

"No." I don't supply the rest of my answer, and she doesn't push it either. I think that she was manipulated into being here. That she wasn't left by accident. Unless she saw evidence that she actually sailed out of Miami, she could've been literally anywhere. I'm not above a conspiracy theory. In fact, I'm pretty damn well convinced we have good reason to be concerned.

"Let's go over the food supplies we could stock up on," she suggests.

"First, let's get to the shelter and see what condition it's in. We have to be sure Will isn't there."

"Do you think he might've gone there?"

I shrug. "No idea." I don't think he would, to be honest. He had to know eventually I'd make my way back there, and hopefully the guy's scared of me.

Unless he really has become feral.

Like the rest of them.

What if *she* becomes like the rest of them, snarling and beyond recognition as a human? The look in their eyes when they go past human comprehension or reason...

It makes me glad the others are dead.

"How far's the shelter?"

"Not far."

We walk on the beach to the edge of the woods, because it's easier walking this way but still out of direct sunlight, with the wide branches of the palm trees above us giving us shelter.

"Can you tell me about the others?"

"I will. Not now."

She doesn't push it. I don't want to talk about it right now.

"I've never been in a place like this."

"Has anyone?" I laugh mirthlessly. Idyllic but dangerous, the island's like the mythological sirens, luring us in with their beauty only to have us crash to death on the rocky shores. Dangerously seductive.

"I mean like a vacation spot. My parents were very simple, and we had hardly any money. We would camp here and there, but we never went to a beach, and we never visited an island."

"What about when you were grown up? An adult? No trips to Cancun on spring break even?"

"Nah. I was already guardian to my brother and had no time or money for anything like that."

"I can relate to that." I want to know how she came to be guardian of her brother, but we have time to learn more about each other. Christ, all we have is time. Endless time.

I hold the branches on a low-hanging tree in front of me so they don't smack across her face. She ducks and follows my lead.

"How so?" she asks.

"I went straight to the Navy. But I did get to travel then. I saw some beautiful sights, much like this island."

The memories are still coming back in wisps and glimmers.

"Oh yeah? Like where?"

We're only a few paces off from the shelter. We both freeze at the loud, cawing sound of a bird nearby.

"What's that?"

I shrug. There are so many birds on this island I haven't even begun to catalog them.

"Oh! Cy! Is that passion fruit?"

I haven't seen it here before, so it takes me by surprise. "Maybe?"

"We totally can gather this," she says. "It'll keep better than the more perishable foods and it nourishes."

"Perfect." I know enough about hunting and building fires, and even constructing a shelter, but beyond that, I'm no botanist.

"Hell, I can even maybe find some greens to make a soup."

"Turtle soup is also an option."

"Oh, God!" She grimaces. "Did you cook before you got here?"

I shrug. "Yeah, a little. I mean, I've spent enough time in the Navy, I ate what they served me. I can flip a burger and cook a steak, but a turkey dinner's a bit beyond my field of expertise."

"Oh, God, don't talk about steak." Her hand comes to her stomach and she groans.

"Tell me about it. I'd give fucking anything for a good steak right now."

"With buttered potatoes."

"Stop," I groan. She laughs, then sighs. "Up ahead," I tell her, pointing to where the shelter still stands. It's more like a hut than anything, but we put our best efforts into it, and it's withstood tropical rain, storms, and kept creatures out, keeping us clean and dry inside.

"Wow," she muses. "So, tell me again why you were sleeping on the floor of a *cave* when this shelter was right here all along?"

She walks around the edge, taking in the details of the perimeter. It hasn't been tended to in a long while, and needs a good cleaning, but is otherwise in good working order.

"They were fighting over it. Eugene inhabited this place last, and he would attack anyone that came within a twenty-foot radius of it. He was the guy that attacked you," I remind her.

She turns to me and raises a brow but doesn't ask any more questions.

"Well, let's investigate," she says. Then she pauses and looks at me quizzically. "Deal?"

Is this her way of asking me permission?

I nod. "Let me open it up."

She steps to the side to let me in. I open the door, not surprised to see several large spiders skittering across the floor. Thankfully she stands behind me and doesn't see. Something tells me she wouldn't be a fan.

"Wow," she says. "It's like really kinda cool in here. Does it offer much protection against the elements?"

"Yeah. We get mostly rain here, but it stays dry."

"Cy, seriously," she says over her shoulder. "I can't

believe you had this place up your sleeve and you made me sleep in the cave with *bats*."

I smile while I check the door, make sure the foundation hasn't been weakened by any storms, and when she isn't looking, make sure that every damn spider is gone.

She sets about to tidying up the place, straightening the stack of wood by the fire pit, and taking up the roughly hewn broom we crafted out of twigs, she sweeps the dirty floor clean.

"It almost makes me look forward to sleeping tonight," she says, whistling to herself. I'm still turned on after our little session by the cave this morning, and the reminder that she'll be sleeping tucked up next to my side brings to mind the vision of her on her back.

Christ, I need to get a handle on this rampant need to fuck this woman seven ways to Sunday.

"Get your mind outta the gutter, Cy," she says, waving the broom at me, but her own eyes are bright, and there's a pink color to her cheeks. I swear I can smell her arousal from where I'm standing.

"What gutter? I was just thinking about sleep." I fake a yawn. "Cave sleeping's for the birds. I'm tired."

"Suuuure," she says, then she freezes, broom paused mid-air.

"Did you hear that?"

I stop and listen.

"What's that sound?" she whispers. "It's like a deep, low rumble, like giants snoring or something."

"Thunder, babe," I say, looking out the doorway as charcoal-gray clouds roll in. I frown at the sky. "There's a storm coming in, and soon."

"How soon?"

"No telling, but we should get some food quickly before it hits us."

She stands the broom up against the wall, and the two of us hike past the beach to where the palm trees sway, heavy with coconuts. We cart back half a dozen to the shelter and get her bag to get more food. I frown as we gather an ample supply of starfruit, guava, and a bunch of callaloo, a green similar to spinach that I recall from my travels. This shit *wasn't here* before.

"Oh, *yes!*" she hoots, pumping her fist in the air, then points to green, oval-shaped fruits. "Mangos. Perfect."

I don't rejoice with her, though. I'm grateful for the food supply, and I don't know how long I've been on this island, but it's long enough that all six of us have explored every inch of this place. And there were no mangoes. No coconuts. No bright green swaths of callaloo. I would know.

"Why do you look so down about this? This is awesome!" She looks at me curiously. "Do you not like mangoes?"

"Harper, I'll eat anything. It's just weird that you arrive here and suddenly there's all this food."

She shakes her head. "Well, I wouldn't say 'all this food,' she says. "Honestly, some mangoes and coconuts hardly make for an abundance of food."

"Compared to what we were eating before? It is."

"Maybe you guys just didn't know where to look."

"We spent days and weeks scouring every inch of this place," I protest. There were days we literally rummaged for grubs just to get something in our belly.

"Maybe they're just ripe now?" she offers helpfully,

gathering the fruit to her bosom. I help her pick some of the ripest ones.

"No," I tell her. "There has to be another reason."

She walks back to the shelter, laden with fruit, and yells over her shoulder. "Not sure what you're talking about, Cy. I think the island's getting to your head. You're like this conspiracy theorist, but I'm not seeing it."

Of course she isn't. She hasn't seen what I have.

Large drops of rain fall as if someone just opened up the heavens.

"Run!" I tell her. Once this rain starts, we could lose our way too easily. It was how we lost our second man.

She starts to run, then trips and falls in front of me, mangoes scattering on the ground around her. I leave the fruit and take her by the arm, helping her to her feet, but she's slipping in the mud. Without thinking, I give her the fruit I'm carrying to hold, lift her into my arms and carry her back to the shelter.

"The mangoes!" she shouts.

"We have plenty for now," I tell her, shouting to be heard above the sound of the wind. We make it in time, just as an enormous tree branch crashes on the ground behind us and lightning tears across the sky. I place her down in the shelter and shut and secure the door behind us.

"Wow, that came on so fast," she muses.

"Yeah, tell me about it."

"Is that always the way it is?"

I shake my head. "Sometimes we just get a little rain, then we go for days and days with nothing but heat. But when a storm comes in, it comes hard and fast. And they're dangerous as hell. Flooding, winds so hard they rip full trees out of the ground, and I worry we'll eventually see a tornado."

She nods, then sits on the floor cross-legged.

"Hopefully we'll be fine this time."

I nod, and we take the fruit and vegetables out of the bag.

"So, Cy. You keep saying this food wasn't here before. Where would it have come from? It's not like someone air-dropped a pile of mangoes from the sky."

"Yeah. I have no idea." I really don't.

"It's unsettling," she says, worrying her lip.

"It is." In silence, I peel some of the fruit and hand it to her. It feels like a feast, with the coconut and fresh, tropical fruit. I wish I could enjoy it, though. I like to be in control, and the unpredictable nature of this island makes me feel anything but.

"We can use the callaloo for turtle soup later, if we can catch a turtle."

She grimaces but nods. "Feels wrong, but okay. I've eaten stuff like that before."

I smile at her, drinking the remains of one coconut. I'm proud of her. She's getting over her aversions quicker than I expected. "Have you?"

"Yes, but it was in a restaurant, not for survival."

I wonder who she is, that she even ate in a high-end restaurant.

I snort. "Well that makes perfect sense. Just like how lobster used to be a mainstay for the poor and somehow became a delicacy."

"Not sure I'd want the lobster without butter," she muses, and that we definitely do not have. The wind howls outside. In silence, we clean up the shells and rinds, and place them neatly by the door.

"Are you sure that's just the wind?" she asks.

"What else would it be?"

She looks to the door. "A wolf or something?"

"Yeah." I don't reply at first. Then there's another noise I haven't heard before, not since before I was on this island, but one I'm very, very familiar with.

I'm at the door before she can stop me, my heart thudding so hard it feels like I might burst.

"Cy?"

I'd know that *chop chop chop* sound in my fucking sleep.

It's a helicopter.

TWELVE

Harper

HE HEARS SOMETHING OUT THERE, but I don't know what since I can't quite place the choppy sound, and the shrieking wind and rain don't help. But he told me it's dangerous out there, and in my gut, I know it to be true. When he opens the door, it's so dark outside it's as if it's night, and a huge branch bigger than I am goes flying past. I scream, covering my mouth when he dives headfirst into the storm. Is he crazy?

"Be careful!" I shout, but he's already gone. Where the hell is he going?

"Hey!" he's screaming, waving his arms overhead.

And that's when I realize what he's doing. It's a helicopter. My God, it's a helicopter.

"Cy!" I shout. "Be careful!" Though I'm as desperate as he is to be rescued, I can't help but realize they'll never hear us down here, they'll never see us. He looks back at me, standing in the doorway.

"First sign of anyone coming to save us," he says. "I can't not look. I can't help but try. I have to go, but don't follow me. You hear me, Harper? Stay *inside*."

And then he's gone. He just turns away and runs. I take a step toward him, but the wind is so vicious and fierce, it's a force of its own, pushing me back inside. I wrap my arms around myself and shake my head.

Why is there a helicopter flying overhead?

If it isn't a plane, does that mean we're closer to civilization than we think?

But how would we even find that out? I look helplessly at the woods and the machete. We could make a boat, maybe.

God.

And then what? Sail off in shark-infested waters… where? We could die before we got anywhere.

"Cy!" I scream, my voice dying seconds after leaving my mouth. I shield my eyes and try to peer out into the woods where he fled, but I can't see anything but wind and trees. I'm already soaked, rivulets of rain plastering my hair to my cheeks and forehead, my dress sodden. Reluctantly, I step back inside and shut the door. I can't do anything out there.

Where did he go? He was trying to attract the attention of the people flying the helicopter, but without fire or any way to get a signal to them, how would they even see us?

And as I pace around the cabin, I make myself think about what it would be like if he didn't come back. What if I'm all alone here?

What if… what if the other man really has turned into a savage, and he and I are the only ones on this island? I snort to myself, momentarily amused. As if Cy's any better.

He is, though. I know he is.

How has he built those fires? Do I even know how to do it if I had to?

How would I catch the fish he's talking about?

I'd have to... clean them and... I dunno, scale them or something. Whatever you do with fish before you can eat them.

I shudder. If he dies, I'm becoming a vegetarian.

Am I really thinking like this? He can't die. He won't die.

I walk back to the door. How did they even construct this thing? I couldn't build a house of cards, much less a real shelter with a real working door. How would I fix it if it somehow broke?

Oh, Jesus God, I cannot be the only person on this island. I can't, I can't, I *can't*. I will go crazy. I'll go literally insane.

And then a pang hits my chest so hard and fast, tears spring to my eyes.

I don't want him to die.

I like the barbaric guy. I really like him. And even though I'd give fucking *anything* to get off this island, if I have to spend it here with him, there are worse ways to be stranded. I miss him. I want him back. The loss is a physical pang in my chest. I blame whatever force has driven us together to tear each other's clothes off for what I'm feeling now.

I don't love him. I can't love him. But hell, if a part of me doesn't want these feelings I have inside to go there.

I pause my pacing when the torrential sound of rain

and wind stops as suddenly as it started. Is it over that quickly? I stand in the middle of the darkened room, listening. It's quiet.

Too quiet.

The quiet after a storm should be peaceful, not like this. Utter silence devoid of the sound of birds twittering or wildlife scurrying through underbrush. This silence is deadly.

I open the door and tentatively peer into the woods in front of me. The storm that came so suddenly ravaged the woods around us. Huge, massive limbs are strewn about everywhere, full tree trunks uprooted, like a giant just went through here having a temper tantrum.

At least we'll have firewood when it dries.

"Cy!" I yell, then clamp my hand on my mouth. Screaming for him when the other man is still out there is fucking stupid. I might as well put a spotlight on me.

If I'm alone... if I'm the only survivor...

A sob rises in my chest, and I have to swallow it down. I'm letting the island get to me. There's no reason to believe that either of them—Cy or Will—didn't make it.

I'm probably not alone. He'll probably come back.

To my right, a pile of coconuts litters the ground like overgrown hail, and a hundred or so more paces in front of me lies a bed of fallen fruit. I pick them up and haul them back to the shelter. I'll have food for days. I shiver, and then remember I'm soaking wet. If I'm going to be taking care of myself here, I need to use my head and some common sense already.

I strip out of my drenched clothing and pull on dry clothes, grateful I have at least these two items of clothing to wear for now. I find some low-hanging, wide branches, and hang my wet clothes up to dry, when I realize I'm super thirsty. I haven't had any plain water today, just the coconut water earlier, and Cy said one of the most important things for survival was staying hydrated.

Dammit, how do I get to the fresh water area from here? I shake my head. I can drink some coconut water until he gets back.

If he gets back.

I go back to the shelter and take a coconut in my hand and shake it, as if hearing the sloshing of water inside assures me this is a good one. I eye his machete, the huge, ominous knife, as if it's a snake about to bite. I stroke one finger along the handle, like I'm trying to make friends with it or something.

"You can't be that hard to use," I say to it, and when I realize I'm talking to an inanimate object, I get a little nervous.

Is this how insanity begins?

"Okay, alright," I say out loud. "We're going to work together, you and I."

Not much better, Harper.

Deep inside, in the darker recesses of my brain I'm currently denying, I know there might come a time I use this thing for more gruesome tasks than splitting open a coconut.

"Come back, Cy," I whisper, swallowing the lump in my throat as I raise the machete. I prep the coconut and swing the machete hard, hitting the coconut straight across the middle the way I've see him. It cracks just a little, a few dribbles of water leaking onto the shell beneath it. I lift the machete and slam it down again, this time cracking the thing in half.

I lift the coconut shell half and drink it greedily, feeling pretty damn badass about using the weapon to open the coconut all by myself. I swear it even tastes better, having been procured by my own two hands. Maybe I can even build a fire.

I look out to the woods. Yeah, that's not happening anytime soon. The woods are absolutely soaked.

How long has he been gone? Is he coming back? I stand in the doorway and frown, looking down to where the beach is. I'm sure I could find my way back here from the beach.

I don't like that I'm so in my head. It's weird, having no one to talk to and nothing to do with myself.

"Hello," I say quietly, just to hear the sound of my own voice. I clear my throat. "Hello," I repeat. My voice sounds scratchy from disuse.

What if I get to the beach and he goes back to the shelter? Will he wonder where I am?

A lump rises in my throat again. I haven't been here long, but it feels like an eternity, and I miss the guy. I miss the arrogant, bossy jerk. I don't like being alone. And if I'm honest? I'm afraid.

Could I take care of myself? Yes. Do I want to?

Hell no.

And maybe it's contrary to everything I've worked for, to everything I write about. But when I advocated for the modern woman, there was no chance of being stranded alone on an island. And it isn't that I need him just because he's a man. I mean, another woman here would be helpful, too.

I frown.

Why are there no other women?

I make it to the beach, grateful now that the sun has

come out as quickly as the rain came. It's hot as hell, the sand already scorching hot on my bare feet, but it feels good after the cold of the rain. It's a surprise to me how quickly the temperature changes, but it's indicative of us being in a tropical climate. I shake my head. *Duh.* I ate coconuts and mangoes. Of course, we're in a tropical climate.

I make my way to the inlet.

"Hey."

I nearly jump out of my skin when I see Cy sitting by the edge of the pool. He has an angry-looking gash on his arm, which he's bathing by the water.

"Cy! Oh my God what happened to you?" I run to him, my thankfulness that he's okay quickly overshadowed by concern.

"Yeah," he says, but he's dejected. "I missed the helicopter. No idea if it was even real or just a vision." He looks to me. "Was it a hallucination? Did you see it, too?"

A little pang of sadness hits me in the chest. He's been here so long; he's got to be feeling hopeless, questioning his own sanity like that.

"I did, Cy. It wasn't just in your head."

He sighs. "Yeah." He quirks a smile. "But God, it's good to see you." He lifts one arm for me to come over to him. I sit beside him and dip my feet into the water.

"It's good to see you, too." I don't tell him that I worried he didn't make it, or that I went through the mental gymnastics of having to fend for myself here. "What happened? Why are you cut?"

"Tree limb hit me. I should've known better than to run out in that. It's too fucking dangerous." There's a note of resignation in his voice that wasn't there before.

"Yeah. Why was there a helicopter anyway?"

"Who knows?"

"I was thinking if there was one, that we couldn't be as far from civilization as we might think. Right?"

He shakes his head. "Not sure if that's true. Military helicopters can fly a lot further than regular ones, and even regular ones can fly up to three hundred and fifty miles. Far enough that no matter where they originated, it's not possible for us to get there without knowing where we're going."

I don't protest. He was in the Navy. He ought to know.

I speak to him in what I hope is a cheerful tone. "In good news, the storm knocked down tons of fruit. I carried a bunch back to the shelter."

He nods. "Good girl," he says approvingly. My chest warms a little. I like it when he calls me that. I like the approval.

"Do you think after the storm is a good time to fish?"

"It's an excellent time to fish." He pushes himself to his feet. "Let's get some food while we can and get some water. Tonight, when the sun begins to set, we'll pull some fish in."

He uses the term "we" like I'll have anything to do with smelly fish. I'm all about making soup or getting the greens and fruit, but I would rather never eat another fish than actually have to catch the things.

He looks at me with concern. "I was just going to clean my arm then head straight back to you. But you found me first." He looks me up and down as if he's just seeing me, then levels me with his hard gaze. "Why did you change?"

"I got soaked."

He frowns, giving me a stern, reproving look. "I told you to stay inside. Did you go out in the storm after I told you not to?"

His tone holds a corrective edge that makes my pulse quicken. I shake my head. But a part of me wonders if I should tell him I did. Give him a reason to go all alpha on me. Maybe it would restore some of his energy, and wipe away that forlorn look in his eyes, and maybe— aw, hell. Maybe I like when he does. Maybe I feel special and protected when he shows concern. And hell, maybe I need this.

"No. I just stood in the doorway and yelled for you."

It sounds so silly now, like a little lost puppy pining away with her nose pressed to the windowpane.

"I'm sorry I took off so fast," he says.

"Don't be. It makes sense that you'd want to try to catch them."

He stands and takes my hand, and we walk hand in hand to the beach. I'm glad to see after he's washed the cut on his arm it isn't as bad as it first appeared. Mostly superficial.

"Do you think that other guy survived that?"

He shrugs. "No idea. Hope not."

We walk in silence back to the shelter. Earlier today, I wanted to swim. Now it's the furthest thing from my mind.

It seemed at first that this was a sort of paradise. But between the uncertainty of what lies ahead, and the dangers we face, it feels so much more like a prison.

We head to the watering hole, but before we get

there, I hear something. I pause and hold a finger up to my mouth.

His brow furrows and he looks ahead of us. But we see nothing.

"What was it?"

I shake my head. "I wondered if it was the other guy."

"This would be a good place to stake him out," he says. "Unless he's already transported enough water to wherever he is."

But he's out there somewhere. We both know it. We hear nothing after a few minutes of silence.

"No damage to the shelter?" he asks, after we get some water. I shake my head.

"One time, we had a storm and it leveled the shelter. It was a bitch reconstructing. I suspected we wouldn't have that issue this time, because the eye of the storm was further out to sea." His jaw tightens. "I shouldn't have left you."

"Look, I appreciate the sentiment and all, but I'm glad you tried. I mean, we would've wondered if we made a mistake if you hadn't, right?"

He looks at me silently, holding my gaze for long minutes. "And just when I think I'm in hell, you're sent to me," he says. He turns around and reaches for my hand, tugging me close to him before drawing his fingertip down my cheek to my chin. "I love that you have an attitude like that. You're a good girl, Harper."

"I'm a woman," I protest in a whisper, because I don't trust my voice. I swallow hard. I want to kiss him so badly I can taste it.

"You sure as hell are," he says with a lascivious grin. "But when you're with me, you're my girl."

And how could I not love that? Maybe I should protest, but I don't know if I want to.

Then he's bending down and brushing his lips to mine. So tender. So gently, it feels like the flutter of butterfly wings at first. With a sigh, he pulls me tighter to him, cups my jaw, and intensifies the kiss.

His rugged whiskers tickle my skin, his lips softer and gentler.

I'm so grateful to have him back, at first, I let him take this kiss. I surrender to this moment. I give it to him freely.

I fought a mental battle back at that cabin. And I came to a realization.

He wants me as much as I want him, and I'm not going to fight it. There's no damn point.

Cupping my jaw in his large, rough palm, he brings his mouth to my ear and whispers, "I want you, Harper."

I swallow hard. "I know."

"I want to fuck you day and night and leave the memory of my lips on yours, the taste of me on your mouth, the feel of my cock between your legs." His voice is just above a growl, low and seductive. I pull closer to him because I love this, his warmth, the possessive way he holds me, the dirty words he says that make me want for more than just a kiss. "I want to seduce you and shower you with attention, bring you to climax again and again, until every bit of resistance seeps out of you and you belong to me."

"Oh?" I ask in a breathy whisper. "Sounds manipulative. Also sounds pretty damn good, so I can deal with that."

His low, dark chuckle makes the little hairs on my arm stand up on end.

"You've made me forget my troubles, Harper, and I'll be forever grateful to you for that."

"Um. You're welcome?"

Still chuckling, he gives me a playful slap to the ass and I smile to myself.

I belong to him on this island, and until our circumstances change, there's no turning back.

THIRTEEN

Cy

DAYS GO BY, then weeks, and we fall into a familiar routine. We spend our days gathering food, until we have such a solid store, we're set for a while. Though we have no way of storing the roasted fish, we store everything else.

There's no sign of human life besides the two of us. Maybe Will died during the storm after all.

No helicopter returns, either.

We make the turtle soup with the greens, and Harper actually admits it could almost be chicken and spinach.

"Almost," she says. "Let's not talk about the turtle shell."

I still can't get her to eat the all the varieties of rodents I catch. She was pretty fit when she came, but after a few weeks of island fare, and the miles of walking we do each day, she's tanned and more lithe than before, whereas I've filled out more.

She's got razors in her bag, which she uses sparingly, but I ask her to help me shave the ridiculous beard I've grown while on this island. It's kinda of a bitch to shave, but together we do it. It feels so fucking good to get that hair off my face and neck. We use some of the knives we have back at the shelter to cut as much of it off as we can, and when I've cut it down as far to the skin as it can go, she shaves me. It's intimate and sexy, and it's no surprise that once she's shaved me clean, I thank her by pulling her onto my lap and kissing her sweet mouth.

It's almost comfortable like this together. No. It isn't the two of us that make this complicated, but our situation.

With Harper? It's fucking perfect.

One day she admires her muscles in the reflection of the water.

"My hair must be a sight," she muses. "But wow, look at those guns. And my *ass*."

She turns to look at herself, and I do, too. It's almost as good as an invitation to lie her down and fuck her right by the shore, so I do just that. She doesn't complain.

We've both stopped fighting it. We don't understand why or how this attraction between us flames to life at the merest whiff of the other's scent or the slightest touch of the other's skin, but it does. I'm no more capable of self-control when I'm around her than she is. So, after a while, we don't even try to stop it anymore. We make love when we wake up and take a nap during the day and wake to another go around.

Most evenings, we can't help ourselves and end up in bed all over again.

She can take me. She fucking loves it when I pin her down or restrain her with makeshift ties from what I find. When I place her belly-down and smack her ass while I fuck her from behind, she melts and takes every last stroke of my cock. We bathe by the watering hole and skinny dip, but there's so much more I want to do to her.

One night by the fire, I sit her on my lap, and when she's nestled good and secure, I cup one of her breasts.

"Cy," she warns.

"Mmm?"

"I'm sleepy," she says on a yawn.

"So? Be sleepy. I didn't say I wanna fuck you."

"As if you ever announce it," she protests on another yawn.

"This is true. But you know, there are a few things we haven't tried yet." There's a *ton* we haven't tried yet, but I'm easing her into the kinkier, deeper stuff. She responds well, but I don't want to scare her off.

"Oh," she asks breathily, wriggling her ass on my crotch when I roll her nipple between my fingers.

I bend my mouth to her neck and kiss her there, making her giggle.

"That's ticklish."

"You know what else is ticklish?"

"No, but something tells me I'm going to find out."

"Mhm. My stubble between your legs while I eat you out."

Her gasp says enough. "Cy," she whispers.

"You ever had that done to you?"

"Of course, I have," she whispers, but I think she's

lying, because she won't meet my eyes, she seems really fucking turned on and a little embarrassed.

"Really?" I ask her. "You never had *my* mouth between your legs."

"Mmmm," she moans when I suckle her neck while I roll her nipple between my fingers. "Maybe we... maybe we should go back to the shelter."

"We could," I say. I have no interest in laying her out in the middle of the forest when there's snakes and insects everywhere we turn. "But you said you were tired."

"Not like I have to get up for work tomorrow," she says, but her laugh fades to sighing.

I stand and lift her in my arms, carrying her to the shelter. If she starts talking about work, she'll get all melancholy again. She'll be reminded of Daniel, and her home, and the job that she left behind that she loves. When I carry her, she lays her head on my shoulder.

"Cy?"

"Mmm?"

"Do you think they think I'm dead?"

"I don't know, baby," I say truthfully.

"I hate the idea of Daniel thinking I'm gone," she says ruefully. "Who will take care of him?"

"There's nothing you can do about that right now," I tell her. I want to draw her to my chest and soothe her. Rock her until she falls asleep in my arms, no longer worried about what she can't control. The woman brings out a tenderness in me unlike anything I've ever felt before. There's more than just raw sexual attraction here. It's far deeper than that. Stripped away from anything superfluous, we're left exposed and vulnerable. Apart from civilization, we've only got each other.

"You're right," she says with a sigh. "I can't. But maybe we can send some signals or something."

I smile to myself. "Maybe, yeah."

"Maybe the helicopter will come back."

"I hope so. But for now, the only thing I want on your mind is my mouth on your pussy."

"Cy," she protests in a whisper.

"Harper," I whisper back.

"That's so dirty."

I go on. "I can't wait to taste you. To suck your sweet clit until you lose your mind."

"Oh God," she says on a moan. "You know, I could do the same thing."

The vision of her sucking me off makes me groan out loud.

"Fuck yes, you could."

I carry her back to the little shelter she's made into a home. She keeps it tidied and surprisingly pretty, gathering wildflowers and placing them in empty coconut shells, sweeping it, and straightening the blanket. She's resourceful, and has our food stores neatly organized and arranged, our weapons hidden, but sharpened and ready. It's almost cozy here, and there's something about it that disturbs me a little.

I don't want to grow complacent.

I don't want to accept this as our new norm.

I want to be sure that no matter what happens, we don't lose sight of the fact that we want off this island. That we still have our entire lives to live. That this isn't where we'll die.

I won't accept this. I have to be sure she doesn't, either.

So, though we make sure we've taken care of everything necessary and made our stay here as comfortable as we can, I don't lose sight of the fact that this is temporary. That we aren't meant to stay here forever, and someday we'll either find our way off this island or be rescued.

I hate being passive. I don't want to wait here for someone to come along, but hell if I can find a way off this fucking place.

She mentioned the idea of us being near another island, when the helicopter flew overhead. And there's a distinct possibility that we are indeed somewhat close to civilization. The thought kills me, to think we pushed ourselves to such extremes when civilization might be near. But there's no safe way for us to find out.

Or we could very well be truly isolated, far from anyone and anything remotely civilized. If only we knew. If only we fucking knew.

Harper gives me a coy look from where she stands, over by our bed. I don't know what she found or how she did it, but she's somehow made our bed thicker, more comfortable, and softer. With no artificial light, we go to bed when the sun sets and wake when it rises, and between having her next to me, the rigorous physical efforts every day of survival on this island requires, and the more comfortable bed situation, I sleep like a baby.

Tonight, focused on the lack of control I have over our survival, I'm craving control of another type.

I want to have her begging. I want to make her

come until she's hoarse from screaming, boneless, and high on endorphins.

I give her a series of short, rapid commands. She responds well to me instructing her, and when I'm ready to master her body, I like to get her ready. Mentally and physically.

I can hear the soft rustle of her clothing and wish we had more light in here. But there's a certain mystique to making love without seeing one another, as if the other senses are magnified.

The sweet, musky scent of her arousal makes my dick hard, and I growl as I make my way toward her.

"Hands on your breasts," I tell her. "Work your nipples."

"Cy—"

I'm close enough to fist her hair and give her a hard tug. "Work. Those. Nipples."

Her breathing is ragged when I drag my hand down her body to make sure she's obeying my instruction.

"Good girl." With my mouth at her ear, I finger her pussy. "Good and wet for me already. This cunt's mine, Harper. Say it."

"Yours." She's teasing me.

I pinch her clit between my fingers, and she lets out a little scream. "Say the whole thing"

"This cunt's yours. Mmm." She's rolling her hips and working her nipples, and her sweet, seductive scent permeates my senses. I close my eyes and work her clit harder, faster until she's writhing and panting.

I freeze.

"Cy," she whispers, pleading. I'll have her begging harder than that.

"Lie down on your back," I whisper in her ear.

"Spread your legs and work your nipples. You come hard, babe. Tonight, you don't come until I tell you."

She whines a little, and I punish her with a swift but moderate smack to her pussy. I want to shock her, not hurt her. Heighten her senses. Get her ready to come harder than she ever has before.

She gasps.

"Say *yes, sir*."

Slowly, gradually, I'm bringing her to where I want her. Introducing her to what I like.

Absolute fucking control.

"I—you want me—"

Another smack to her pussy and her words come out in a rush. "Yes, sir."

I can tell by the way her whisper ends on a sigh that she likes that.

"Now do what I said."

I remove my hand and feel her obey, down on her back with her thighs spread wide for me. I lower my head to her belly and kiss her there, before I lazily drag my tongue along the sweet, tender skin. My cock's hard as a fucking rock as she moans and trembles beneath me.

Kneeling over her, I cup her ass cheeks and lift her to me. I can almost taste her, almost feel her trembling before she shatters. Swallowing hard, I breathe hot air on her belly and work the sweet skin with my tongue. Circling. Grazing. Suckling. She's whimpering and doing exactly what I said, rolling her nipples between her fingers, like a good girl who knows what's coming.

"That's it, baby," I whisper, my breath hot on her pussy. "Work those nipples while I work your pussy." I squeeze her ass cheeks and kiss her mound. I'm dying to bury my tongue between her folds and taste her sweet essence, but I want her craving it before I do. I kiss her inner thighs and groan when I can already taste her, so wet, so ready. I pinch her ass and make her gasp, and when her hips rise, I kiss her pussy again.

"No coming without my permission," I remind her. "If you do, I'll make you regret it."

"Yes, sir," she whispers. I groan. I fucking love this. *Love* it.

I slide the very tip of my tongue between her folds, a gentle tease, and she lifts her hips for more, but I don't give it to her yet. It takes all my self-control to only tease. I blow my hot breath on her clit, then part her folds and drag my tongue slowly but fully along her center. Just once, but she's already bucking and moaning. I remove my tongue and breathe on her again. I love sensation play. Hell, I love all kinds of play, but we've had to get resourceful on this island without my kinky tools. I can do plenty with my hands, my tongue, my cock.

Without warning her, I bite the sweet, supple, slightly damp skin between her thighs, first her left leg, then the right.

"Cy," she whispers.

I bite her again. "Sir," I remind her.

"Sir," she purrs.

I slap her thigh when I realize she's waiting for me and not working her breasts like I told her.

I punctuate my words with measured smacks of my palm on her bare skin.

"Work. Those. Nipples."

She gasps and writhes but does as I tell her, fondling her breasts.

"Good girl."

She's earned this. It's time I gave her orgasm number one.

I bury my face between her legs and suckle her clit. She keens with pleasure, bucking beneath me. I lap and suck lazily, stroking and suckling, while she moans and does what I tell her. I know she's at the edge of climax when she tenses.

"Ask me," I instruct.

"Please, sir. *Please*."

I give her one lazy stroke of my tongue. "Beg."

"Please. Oh, God, Cy. I'm dying here. Please, sir. Let me come. Please let me come."

The strong woman who holds her own is reduced to begging and pleading, and it makes me so fucking hard I feel like a goddamn king.

"Good girl. That's my very good girl."

I return to her pussy but don't give her permission to come yet. Releasing one of her ass cheeks, I take my fingers and plunge them in her core, flexing and pumping while I suck her clit.

"Sir. Oh, God, sir, please sir. *Please...*" her voice pitches off into a whine.

I nod my head. "Good girl. Come, baby."

I pump and suck and work her pussy until she tenses, throws her head back and screams while she comes on my mouth.

Fucking.

Gorgeous.

I don't stop until she's panting and falls back to the bed. I want in her so bad my balls ache.

"On your knees," I order with a swift slap to her thigh. "*Now.*"

She scrambles beneath me and I can feel her fall to her chest and do what I say.

"I want your ass," I tell her. "Next time, I'm taking your ass."

"Oh, fuck," she whispers, still trembling when I line up my cock at her pussy, gliding the head through her slickness, and dragging it to her asshole. "Not tonight," I tell her. "But I will fuck every hole in this sweet body of yours until you're fully owned by me."

"Mmm," she says, letting me know she's as turned on as I am. Maybe I don't need to take it easy on her. She's fucking perfect.

I slide my cock in her center and groan with relief. She's so tight and wet, I effortlessly glide in and out, pumping hard into her while I hold her hips. She braces beneath me, able to withstand the savage thrusts. I reach for her hair and wrap it around my fingers, giving it such a hard tug, she gasps, but she doesn't quake or tell me to stop. She knows I need to own her, and she doesn't try to stop me.

I thrust in and out, a perfect rhythm ratcheting up my own need, until I can't hold back anymore. Yanking her head back by the hair, I bend down and kiss her neck as I thrust one final time into her and fly into euphoria. Fuck, this is good, so fucking good. My heart pounds as I spill into her, spasms of bliss wracking my body with a powerful, earth-shattering orgasm, the best I've ever had, and our lovemaking has been fucking epic.

"So fucking beautiful," I groan, pumping harder and harder, and she withstands every stroke of my cock, every tug of her hair. "Fucking perfect."

I lay my face on her bare back holding her to me. Feeling her pulse. Savoring every second of this.

I love you.

I'm not a sentimental man. I've never felt this way about a woman. But with Harper, I do.

But I don't say it. Not yet. I don't want to scare her.

But I will show her. I love this woman. No matter what happens, I won't let her forget that.

FOURTEEN

HARPER

I'M SNUGGLED up on his chest. Boneless. Still riding the high, I can't deny how I feel toward him.

We've been with each other removed from all civilization and the complications of polite society. There's a stark, beautiful honesty about our relationship I didn't know could exist between two people. It makes me wonder. Is this what people experienced on the frontier? Did pioneers have this desolate sort of longing for one another? Two people who otherwise might never have even given each other the time of day... falling in love?

You're just sex drunk, I admonish myself.

But I remember what it was like when I thought about losing him.

You just don't want to be alone.

Maybe I am affected by the sex. But honestly? Every time we come together like that, every time we unite our bodies and minds and pleasure into one, we grow a little closer.

It can't be helped.

But if I were transported back home right this very minute, miraculously rescued from this island, and back to where I was even a month ago... would I still remember him? Would I want to do normal things with him? Have a cup of coffee... get dinner... go to a play or movie.

Would I be able to bear an alpha male like him? I've been alone so long I've come to like it. I like being in control of everything in my life, from my income, to my surroundings, to when I go to the gym, and when I visit my brother.

My brother.

I close my eyes at the sudden rush of emotion. I miss Daniel so badly, it's physically painful. I have to accept the fact that he's in good hands now. Legally, once they think I'm dead...

Do they? Do they think I won't come back?

I swallow hard. *Will I?*

Still holding me to his chest, he reaches for my hand and entwines my fingers with his. "What's on your mind, babe? I can feel the shift."

"You can feel it?" I whisper. "How?"

He shrugs a shoulder. "I don't know. The same power that makes me want to fuck you day and night makes me understand you better, I guess. I don't know how to explain it. But I felt you happy and all blissed out, and then the temperature shifted a little. What's troubling you?"

I sigh. It's a little odd being so easy to read like that. "Daniel."

"Your brother."

"Yeah."

"Tell me about him?"

And so, I do. I tell him everything. How Daniel, my younger brother, looked up to me. How I would take him with me when I went shopping or to the movies, and how we had a standing Friday night tradition of going to see a movie together. Before the accident. When movies could hold his attention.

I tell him about the accident, but I don't go into details. I don't like reliving the particulars of the tragedy of losing my parents and losing the brother I knew.

"Brain damage," I whisper. "He lived, but now he'll mentally be a child forever. He can't live on his own, and with my job, the demands and travel, I couldn't watch him as often as needed. He has a seizure condition and needs constant supervision. So he lives in a state-funded group home. I visit as often as I can." I smile. "And every day's his birthday."

He smiles sadly. "Yeah?"

"Yeah." I tell him how Daniel thinks when he wakes up every day that today's his birthday. How the staff at his residence celebrates in small ways, with balloons or birthday cupcakes or ice cream.

"It must be nice to have a birthday every day," Cy says, and there's something about the way he says it that makes me smile. I like that he finds my brother's quirks cute. I want him to meet him. Daniel would love him, and for some reason this knowledge makes me pull even closer to Cy.

"Eh, I dunno," I tell him wryly. "A birthday a day and you'd age pretty damn quickly."

He chuckles. "You haven't aged a day. How old are you again?"

"Twenty-five."

"You look like a teen."

"Does that make you a creeper?"

Our conversation's cut short with a howling sound outside our walls so loud and insistent we both freeze. There's a second, then a third. I draw closer to Cy and he holds me tight.

"Wolves," he whispers.

"There are no wolves in the Caymans."

"Babe, we aren't in the Caymans."

I shiver.

"Then where are we?"

"No fucking idea."

The howls are so loud and insistent, it seems as if an entire pack is prowling the perimeter of the shelter.

"Don't be afraid," he whispers. "They can't get to us."

"But where did they come from? How did they get here?"

He shrugs and doesn't reply.

It goes on for hours, the howling and pacing outside our shelter. We try to sleep, but it's nearly impossible with the sounds outside. It isn't until the wee hours of the morning that the noise finally dies down, and I fall into a shallow, restless sleep.

We both wake to the sound of rain pelting down so hard, it sounds as if the ceiling itself will buckle under the weight of it, and the wind outside is coming through the slats in the walls.

Cy sits up and quickly dresses. I do the same.

Just as the sound of wolves fade, a more savage sound rents the air around us. Another howl.

Human? My blood runs cold.

"Wolves are gone, only to bring the storm," I muse out loud. "It's weird."

But Cy only stalks to the door, tight-lipped.

"Don't do this to me again, Cy. Please," I beg.

"Do what?" he says, turning to me with his hand on the latch.

"Leave me," I say in a voice that quavers and doesn't sound like my own. "Make me wonder if you'll come back. Make me think about what it would be like to be here, stranded, and all alone. Take me with you."

His eyes gentle and he comes to me, wrapping me into his arms and pulling me to his chest. "Baby," he says softly, bending down to kiss my forehead. "I'm not leaving you. Do you understand me? I'm not leaving you here alone." And right there in that moment, I wonder if I'm falling in love with this wild barbarian of a man. Because who wouldn't love a man like that?

"No one ever says, 'today is the day I'll die,'" I protest.

He sighs, as the wind howls outside the door. "And what are you going to do out there anyway? We should just stay inside where it's safe. I need to be sure the roof stays put. That no huge branches crash into this place and kill us. Gotta make sure we're safe. I want to make sure the motherfucking wolves are gone," he says. "Wish I had a goddamn gun."

I wonder inanely if he'd know how to use a gun and then I realize, of course he would. He's military, a street fighter, and something tells me if he had a weapon, he'd find his way around it easily.

"Take me with you, then," I insist. "I can handle myself."

"No," he says stoutly.

"Cy, I can—"

But a quick tug of my hair interrupts me.

"Hey!"

"Hey yourself," he says, and the tone of his voice brooks no argument. "You'll do what I say or I'll tie you up, and once things settle, punish you for giving me shit."

Goddamn it, even as the threat of a punishment raises my ire, I still feel the little tingle in my chest that turns me on. I love being dominated by him, even when I hate it.

Figure that one out.

"I don't have to do what you tell me," I protest, though I know the argument's weak. Of course I do. He's stronger than I am, and there's nowhere else for me to go.

"We playing that game again?" he asks, with his hand under my chin. "Really, Harper? Did you somehow forget in the middle of the night who I am? Who you are? And what happens if you get all headstrong and silly on me?"

"It's not headstrong and silly to want to go out there with you," I insist, mustering up my courage, because defying a man like Cy is no small task. I swear my butt tingles just thinking about him pulling me over his lap again, and even though a part of me likes it, it also fucking hurts.

"Cy, we can compromise," I try.

"No."

"*Yes.*"

He growls, tugging my hair again. I still his hand in mine, put my hand on his chin and give him my most pleading look. "Please?" I ask.

He looks into my eyes, and I can tell he's softening when he whispers, "Goddamn you, woman."

"What?" I say, giving him my most innocent expression.

"You know I can't tell you no when you look at me that way," he growls. "I should punish you for trying to manipulate me."

"Or better yet," I say brightly. "You can let me manipulate you and then punish me later."

His lips twitch as his eyes narrow. "Deal."

Welp.

"So you'll let me go?"

"I'll let you go," he says. "But I'll warn you, I have an excellent memory."

I nod. Something tells me I might regret this bargain with the devil, but I don't care right now. "Got it. Let's go!"

He sighs, takes me by the hand, and reaches for the latch.

"Fine," he says. "We're only checking out the perimeter for now, but I want it clear that you'll do exactly what I say, and if you don't, I *will* bring you back here, tie you up, and whip your pretty ass when we're done."

"Deal," I squeak, because he's a man of his word and hell if that doesn't scare me.

And I know right then, while the winds howl outside the shelter, and the memory of wolves pacing outside is still fresh in my memory, isolated on this island in the middle of nowhere, *I know.*

I like being with a man that scares me a little.

I can't think anymore, though, because the next thing I know, he's opening the door, and we're covering our heads as we survey around the cabin. There's no sign of any wolves, and rain beats down so hard and fast, it's hard to see anything.

"Harper!" he's yelling at the top of his lungs. I look to him just in time as a small palm tree comes toppling over. I duck as he pulls me to the forest floor. We're safe for now, but we need to get back to the shelter.

"I don't see anything," he says, and as we get to our feet, a flash goes by several yards in front of me so quickly I stifle a scream. I peer into the darkness and see masculine features and dark blond hair before he's gone.

It was a person. I saw a person. I know I did.

"Cy!" I shout, but my voice is drowned out in the wind. "Cy!" I scream so loudly it hurts. He's dragging me to the shelter, but what if the other person—Will, or whoever the hell it is—went inside? So I pull back on his hand. He gives me a quizzical look and shakes his head.

He mouths something to me, but I can't hear him. And what good does it do staying away from the shelter anyway? If someone's in there, we'll have to deal with it. We aren't safe out here with the winds and rain.

My heart pounds in my chest, and I wish I could warn him.

"Cy!" I scream, tugging his hand. He finally turns back to me, lifts me up in his arms and bends his face down to me.

"I saw someone!" I scream, my voice drowned out quickly with the gust of wind.

"What?"

"A person!" I shriek. "There was a person!"

"Where?" he screams back, and I point vaguely ahead. He nods, places me back on the ground, lifts a huge stick off the ground and hands it to me, then wrenches a branch as big as a small tree trunk from the earth. We walk hand in hand, slower now, but prepared to defend ourselves.

We fight the wind and rain as we go the few paces toward the shelter, and he opens the door ahead of me. He's got his stick in his hand, and he's posed like a baseball player up to bat. Ready to strike. He's prepared to attack if he has to, fight anyone who might've gone in before us, but there's no one there.

"Come out if you're hiding!" he screams, his voice sounding so much louder now that we're out of the storm and in the shelter. But no one responds, neither inside nor out. He looks to me and holds the stick—I guess it could be called a club, it's so big—in his hands like a baseball bat. I wouldn't want to cross him now. Seriously, anyone who did would have cast iron balls.

Or... be reduced to savage instincts.

Not merely a man anymore.

He's told me that's what happened to some of the others, how some of them became savage, like animals, not like him but beyond human comprehension or reason.

"What did you see?"

"Just a blur, but it was definitely a human," I tell him. "But I couldn't see in the rain. He was a man for sure."

He curses under his breath and paces the room.

"Must've been Will," he says. But when he describes him, it doesn't meet the description at all.

"No," I say, shaking my head. "I didn't get a good view at all, but that's nothing like what I saw. This man was smaller than you, but he had dark blond hair. He wasn't little. He was big, but not as big as you, and I couldn't see much else."

He frowns. "That's not possible."

What?

"I know what I saw."

"Maybe you're hallucinating," he says. "You're positive it was a human?"

His denial of what I'm telling him makes me angry. I take a step toward him.

I saw the savage look in the man's eyes. I glare at Cy.

"No less than the man who tried to rape me."

His eyes darken and his jaw clenches at the reminder of my assault.

"So someone's here, then," he says. "But it can't be..."

His voice trails off.

"What? What are you talking about?"

He shakes his head. "Harper, the blond guy... the only other blond guy on this island... he's dead."

The wind has begun to die down, the rain slowing as well, but I shiver as if a gust of wind just ripped through the shelter.

"How is that possible?" I whisper.

He shakes his head and changes the subject. "No fucking idea. But if what you're telling me is true..." his voice trails off, and his gaze comes back to me. "We're not alone."

I swallow hard.

"But we're together."

He drags me to his chest and holds me, then kisses the top of my head so fiercely it hurts. I close my eyes. Something tells me this is going to get harder before it gets easier. I swallow but don't speak. His next sentence takes me off guard.

"Once the storm is totally clear, I'm going hunting."

"Let me go with you," I say, more of a statement than a plea.

This time, he doesn't even disagree with me.

"There's no point in trying to keep you safe by keeping you away," he says. "So yeah, babe. You can come hunting. For now, let's get some sleep. We got hardly any last night." His eyes look heavy, and there's a weariness about him I didn't notice before.

But he doesn't sleep. He takes his club and barricades the door, leads me to the bed in the dark, and lays me down. I lay on his chest for long minutes. He's still rigid. Awake. Watchful. Listening.

Finally, I fall into a deep and dreamless sleep.

FIFTEEN

Cy

IT MAKES NO SENSE.

No sense.

How can someone else be alive? It has to be Derek. He was the only one who fits the description she gave.

But it can't be. How could it be?

Attacked by insects only six days into our landing here, he died. I saw his blank, lifeless eyes myself.

Is she going mad?

She got angry when I suggested she was mistaken, but I'm completely bewildered.

When Harper finally falls asleep, I get up, carefully, so I don't wake her, and pace in the darkness around our shelter. I listen for any sounds at all of someone approaching. If it *is* Derek... and somehow, he... fuck, I don't know, came back to life? No, what the hell am I saying? I'm a reasonable, rational human being.

Nonsense.

I shake my head.

But this island... this island isn't normal. Not since the day we arrived. The very fact that I can't remember how I got here is telling. The way Harper arrived here is too random. After God knows how long of me being stranded here, a cruise ship shows up? No. I don't buy it.

And now a man I thought dead—fuck, I threw the dirt on his body myself—now he's alive? No.

No.

I can't sleep. I pace the small shelter and listen for a sound, anything at all that will tell me to be aware of danger, but there's nothing but the gentle sound of wind outside the shelter.

I hear Harper's soft, whiffling snores, and I'm grateful she can sleep after tonight. She's been a fucking champ through this. The girl is made of sterner stuff than any woman I've ever met. And I will see to it that she gets what she deserves.

A home. A family.

Which means off this fucking island.

Finally, I lie back down beside her. She rolls over and nestles against me, her back pressed up to my chest as if she's meant to be here, just like this. I hold her to me and breathe her in and give thanks for this moment. I have no idea what will happen tomorrow, or the day after, or the *year* after. Or if we'll even make it to the next year. We have to take it day by day. And today, I'm grateful for this sweet woman I'm holding. I could be here alone, but instead I've got her.

She's all mine. Whoever's out there—Will, or Derek, or whatever or whoever the fuck else might threaten her—they'll have to come through me first.

I finally fall asleep.

When my eyes flutter open hours later, sunlight floods the shelter through the roughly hewn windows.

"Morning."

She's up and snuggled up to me like she usually is in the morning, her hand flat on my chest, one knee hitched up on me. Her auburn hair hangs about her in crazy, untamed waves. I reach out and tug a lock.

"Carrots," I whisper.

She smirks. "I wish I had a slate to smack over your head."

I smile and kiss her pretty freckled forehead.

"Took you a while to fall asleep," she says.

"Yeah." I don't say much else. I don't want her to be frightened.

Her stomach growls, and she yawns. "I am so starving," she says. "You?"

I sit up suddenly. I don't know if it came to me in my dreams or my subconscious was working overtime, but the realization hits me so hard it startles me, before I feel anger begin to take over.

Jesus.

Motherfucker.

"What?" she asks, sitting up and staring at me.

"This happened before," I tell her. "Same pattern."

"What pattern?"

I get to my feet. "Wolves. Storm." I frown. I don't want to tell her what else, but I have to. "If this is the same pattern, when we go out this morning, there will be no food left."

She stands beside me and blinks, before she pales. "Cy, you're not making sense."

I sigh. We'll know soon enough. "We have to see if the food is gone."

She shakes her head again, and the look she's giving me leads me to believe she thinks I'm out of my mind. "Cy," she says gently, like trying to talk to a patient in an insane asylum you don't want to upset, "you just need to get something to eat, and you need more rest. I think what I saw last night unsettled you."

Unsettled me? Goddamn right it did.

But she'll see for herself. Hell, I hope I'm wrong.

"There's so much food out there," she says. "Fish and coconut, fruits and vegetables. We've had nothing but an ample supply for weeks on end."

"We have," I say to her. "I'm not denying that, babe. What I'm telling you is that I've seen this before. And Christ, I *hope* I'm wrong."

It was just like this before. We woke up after the wolves and storm, and the food supplies had completely vanished overnight.

Three days into starvation was when they began to grow feral.

"Well, let's go look," she says. I nod.

Before we go, we eat a simple meal in silence. She freshens up a bit with some of the water we've stored, and I do the same. I hand her the stick I gave her the night before, and I tuck a knife into the loop on my pants. We are not going out there unarmed.

I open the door, half expecting someone rabid to attack, but the only sound is the gentle twittering of early morning birds. It's gorgeous out here, the sun rising over the ocean, casting golden light on the blue-green horizon, belying the danger we're in.

"No matter what happens," she says softly. "No matter what, I won't forget mornings like this."

A bird calls overhead, and I squeeze her hand. "Me neither."

The first sign that something's wrong is the missing callaloo. The closest source of food for us, it grows right outside our door. Beside it stands the tree where we get our coconuts, but it's bare. *Bare.*

"Well that's strange," she muses. Foreboding grows in my chest, because this was how it all started before.

"Come on," I say quietly. We need to check the fruit and other coconuts trees.

We walk in silence until we get to the cluster of trees we always go to. She's frowning.

"No coconuts? What? Where did they all go to overnight?" She shakes her head and looks all around the ground around us. "If they were knocked down by the storm, they'd be on the ground. But there's nothing."

I sigh. I won't repeat what I told her this morning. There's no need.

I know what we're going to find.

Goddamn it.

Our search for fruit yields the same. We walk to the water, and the usual signs of sea life are just as quiet as before. It's as if someone's set off an atomic bomb, and all signs of living creatures have vanished.

There's nothing.

Fucking *nothing*.

"It's a damn good thing we have some food put away," she mutters under her breath. "How could a storm have wiped everything out like that?"

I don't think it was the storm, but I have no idea

what else the reason could be, so I don't answer. And I'm not sure how long the stores we have will give us.

"We'll have to make our supplies last," I tell her. Until we have food again.

If we have food again. What if this time there's no resurgence?

We spend the day looking for something, anything at all that we could use as a food source but find almost nothing. Finally, when we're reaching midday, Harper looks thoughtful.

"Maybe we should go look on the other side of the island? Keep looking for anything at all?" It's a small island, and walking to the other side won't take long. It also means there's not much of a chance we'll find anything. The reason we built the shelter here to begin with was because of the close proximity to food.

I think about this before I agree. Nodding, I look up at the clear blue sky, dotted with only the faintest wisps of clouds. "We can at least go look by the waterfall," I tell her. I didn't look there before. It will at least give us something to do.

And maybe this *is* in my head. How would the island itself be conspiring against us? It isn't logical. But I've gone there mentally before.

I wish we could barricade the shelter so that no one else can get in, but any barricade we use short of a lock —something we definitely don't have—will keep us out as easily as it would someone else. We hide some of our food, though, and in various places, and then head to the waterfall.

We hear the waterfall before we see it. Vibrant orange and pink flowers line our way, reminding me of the fruit that I already miss. My stomach growls, and Harper gives me a sad, almost wistful smile.

"Hungry?" she asks.

I shrug. "Little. You?"

She shrugs. "I'm alright. I went for full days not eating when I was in college. I'd just get too wrapped up in what I was doing to care about it."

I chuckle. "So you're one of *those* girls."

"What?" she says, smiling yet defensive. "I don't know what you're talking about."

"Dedicated to her work and goals. Overachiever?"

She gives me a self-deprecating smile. "I suppose you could say that. Not you, huh?"

"Babe, when I was that age, I'd drink a keg for breakfast and a second for dinner. That was all I needed."

She snorts derisively. We're so close to the waterfall, it's almost hard to hear one another speak. "So you're one of *those* guys," she says.

"One of what guys?" I say warningly, drawing close enough to see the faint pink coloring in her cheeks at my warning look. Of course, she's just as welcome to tease me as I am her, but I like to play this game with her sometimes. It takes my mind off the dire straits we're in.

"*Those* guys," she says. "A frat boy who kills his brain cells with beer and gets laid more than he cracks a book open."

"Kinda. Not a frat boy, though. I enlisted before college."

It's the very short version of the story. There's more to it. I think, anyway. My mind still plays crazy tricks on me. Somehow, though, talking about this almost reminds me of something. *Almost.* I pause and frown, pinching the bridge of my nose to try to stoke my memory, but it doesn't work. There was something I was grasping for there for a minute, but it's gone.

"That's admirable," she says, swinging her arms as she walks easily through the trees, and hell if she isn't a sight to see, all tanned and freckled limbs, wavy, unruly hair, full lips and bright eyes that miss nothing. Her dresses have faded from sunlight and use and are a little baggy on her now.

"What is?" I ask. We reach the clearing that opens to the waterfall, and she smiles at me.

"Realizing your sorry ass needed discipline and doing what it takes to get there."

I shrug. "Part of growing up, isn't it?"

She nods. "I guess, yeah."

"So this waterfall is fresh water?"

I nod. "Most waterfalls are," I tell her.

"I thought most of the water on earth was saltwater?"

"It is. Only like three percent is fresh."

"Huh. So this doesn't flow from the ocean, then, clearly."

"Nope."

Turning to face the waterfall, she breathes in a deep, cleansing breath, then lets it out again slowly. "Wow, I forgot how pretty it is in here." A shadow crosses her eyes, but she doesn't say more than that.

I take her hand. This is the place where I found her. It's also the place where she was attacked. I doubt she's forgotten, and I bet she has mixed feelings about it.

If I have anything to do with this, we'll make a better memory here, just the two of us.

"What is it?" she asks.

"I want you to remember this waterfall," I tell her, tugging her over to me. "How pretty it was. How wild and untamed." I pull her hand to my mouth and kiss the back of her slender fingers. "Like you."

She gives me a shy smile and bites her lip. "Like me?" she asks teasingly. "Do you really think you haven't tamed me yet?"

I tug a strand of her wild hair and smile. "Not even close, babe."

"Good," she says with a twinkle in her eye I'm all too familiar with. She takes a step closer to me and encircles my neck with her arms, drawing me near.

"Kiss me," she whispers.

I cluck my tongue warningly. "Hmm. Seems a girl who's due a spanking should be watching her mouth a little more."

Her full lips turn downward into a pout. "I thought you forgot about that."

"I told you, I have an excellent memory."

"But you should conserve your energy," she says. "If we have no food..."

"Oh, I can conserve my energy just fine," I tell her. "I'll nap later."

"Cy—oh, look!" she points eagerly above, and I look to where she points. It's one lone bird, flapping its wings mightily. Only one, but it's one of the larger ones we've captured for food. She used to turn her nose up at it but has since learned to appreciate any and all sources of food.

But without a gun, I can't capture it. "It's a good sign, anyway," I tell her, when she gasps out loud.

"What?"

"It just... it just vanished," she says in a whisper. "It was... it was flying, and then, it was just... gone, like it was a... I don't know, like I was watching a movie and then someone hit the off switch or something."

I don't respond at first.

"You don't believe me," she says so quietly, it's almost to herself.

"Naw, babe. It isn't that at all. The problem is, I totally believe you."

She raises one brow, giving me a quizzical look. "What?"

I hold her to me, tip my finger under her chin, and raise her eyes to mine. "Something is off about this island. I don't believe in many supernatural things. Ghosts. Spirits. Whatever. If I did, I would say that I believe something weird is happening here. That the island is somehow responsible for what happens."

I close my eyes when my memory is assaulted by a flashback so vivid, I can't stop it.

Six of us. All of us taken. In a room, bound, while images are portrayed on screens. In front of us? I can't remember. All of us, aboard a plane. Drugged.

"What is it? Cy?"

I shake my head and open my eyes, looking around me. "We were taken here," I tell her. "But I don't remember how or why. A few things came back to me, but..." the memory is fading again. "And you know things don't add up on this island. You know there's something behind why we're here."

She frowns. I think she's finally starting to see that I have a point. "Things like what?"

"Like the way we feel about each other," I tell her.

"Our insane attraction. I can't control myself half the time, and neither can you." She doesn't deny it.

"The way the other men went slowly insane. The way you ended up here and there was no reason why or how."

Her eyes grow wide and frightened as I go on. "The fact that I knew there would be no food after the storm, and how it all just vanished. No fruit scattered on the ground or dead fish floating in the water. Nothing. Gone."

I hold her hand and gently squeeze. "What you just saw now. A bird that was here one minute and gone the next. Does that make *any fucking sense* to you?"

She swallows hard. "Not much of it does. But if there... *was*... something... supernatural or something, what could we do to stop it?"

"Babe, if I had any clue, I'd have already fucking done it."

She nods. "Yeah," she says quietly. "Honestly, so would I." She looks over my shoulder. "Hey, do you think those really vibrant flowers are edible?"

I shake my head. "No idea, but I doubt it. I've never seen any wildlife eat them, and we haven't tried." I sigh. "Let's go for a swim," I suggest, pointing to the beautiful, bright blue water by the falls. The temperature's been rising all day, and it's nearly unbearable. We're both already slick with perspiration.

"Sounds good to me. There are no, like... sea creatures, right?"

I shake my head. "Nope. Not here."

"If it's freshwater, no sharks then."

I smile. "Definitely not."

"Okay, then," she says. "Let's do it."

I stand there like an idiot when she begins to undress, because the sight of her naked never gets old.

"Fuck," I mutter.

"What?" she asks innocently, lifting her dress right up over her head and revealing her fucking perfect breasts. "Something wrong?"

I step out of my clothes and leave them on the bank by the water. My hardened cock springs to life. "Nothing's wrong," I groan. "You're just perfect."

She snorts, walking over to me. "I wouldn't say *that*."

"Good. If you got a big head, I'd have to take you down a peg or two."

"Oh, would you?" she says with mock displeasure. "And I bet you'd *like* it."

"I'd fucking *love* it," I say, taking her by the hand and leading her into the water.

I like that despite the fact that we're in danger, that we have very little food and no prospects of getting off this island, that we've somehow managed to grow this relationship. That somehow, despite all the odds against us, we've even... dare I think it... *fallen in love.*

"Hmmph, of course you would," she says.

I pull her into my arms when we step into the water. It's cold and clear and feels refreshing after the day we've had. She straddles my legs and wraps her arms around me, buoyed by the water, and I groan when she pushes herself against my hard cock. I can't keep my hands off her, even when it's inconvenient.

"Fuck, you're gorgeous," I tell her, before I bend my mouth to hers and taste her sweet, full lips. "So fucking gorgeous."

"Mmmm," she replies. I swallow her moan and

walk deeper into the cold water, submerging us up to our waists. I cup her ass in my hands, squeeze, and she opens her mouth, welcoming me to deepen the kiss. I'm teasing her with my tongue when I feel a quick, hard tug on my foot. I break the kiss and stumble, and she nearly topples into the water.

"What the fuck?" Another tug and I'm losing my grip on her. On instinct, I lift her and throw her as far as I can into the water, to the shallower part. To safety.

"Cy!" she screams, when my whole body gets sucked away from her. "Cy!" It's the last thing I hear as I'm pulled into the cool, dark depths.

SIXTEEN

Harper

"CY!" I'm barely holding onto the edge of hysteria as he's taken from me bodily, sucked right under the depths. He doesn't go willingly, though, but fights, his powerful, muscled arms rising above the surface as he tries to swim away from whatever's pulling him.

Whoever? My *God*. What enemy do we face now?

He surfaces and gasps for air. "Get to the bank!" he says, his words drowning in a terrifying gargling sound as he's sucked beneath the depths again.

"Oh God, oh *God*," I say, looking wildly about me for something, anything at all that I can use to save him. "Cy!"

On the bank I see the huge stick he gave me as a weapon. I swim as fast as I can to retrieve it, my limbs feeling as if they're made of lead, and hold it in my hands as if it's my lifeline. He must be getting pulled into some sort of undercurrent or something. I don't know how this works. We shouldn't have come here. Or maybe this island *is* demonic, and the current is meant to kill him. To take him from me.

I won't let it.

I can see him being bodily pulled to the waterfall itself, the powerful water that crashes into the pool below so hard the spray around it blurs my vision. It will kill him. It will crush his bones and destroy him.

I can't let that happen.

He's moving slowly, though, and I realize it's because he's fighting it. But Jesus, he's been underwater so long I wonder how he can breathe.

"Cy!" I scream, running on the bank so that I can reach him with the edge of the stick. He's such a big guy. Even if he can grab hold, how will I ever pull him out? But I love this man. And I refuse not to fucking try.

His head bobs up and I see him take a huge gulp of air.

"Take hold!" I scream, holding the edge of the stick so that the other end is within his grasp. This has to work. *It has to.*

"Cy, take hold!" I scream, my voice almost instantly drowned out in the deafening sound of the fall. "Take it!" My voice cracks and I swallow a sob. I need him to live. I need him to survive.

His head rises above the surface again, and he sees it, he sees me. With a massive thrust, he pushes himself forward and his fingertips touch the edge of the branch, only to sink below the surface again. I cry freely, begging for him to help himself, to take the branch and get out from under the current.

I run further down the bank.

"Oh, God, oh please, Cy, please," I beg, crying

freely as I hold the branch and watch him surface again. He reaches for it, and this time he grabs hold. I brace myself so I don't fall in, but it takes everything I've got. I see a thin, but sturdy tree hanging over the water, so I grab hold and anchor myself on it when his second hand wraps around the end of the stick.

"You've got it!" I scream. "Pull!"

He's fighting a losing battle, the current washing over his body with so much force it looks painful, but I'm not letting go. It takes every ounce of strength I have, but *I'm not letting go. I can't. I won't.*

He's holding on and I know I can pull him to shore, I know it. With a surge of adrenaline and a scream that echoes through the woods instantly drowned out by the terrifying crash of the waterfall, I pull with all my might.

They say that when mothers are in situations where their children are in mortal danger, they can move mountains, lift cars, or run at insane speed. It's the only possible explanation for what I do next. He's too big for me to lift and the current too strong, but with what feels to be inhuman strength, my heart pounding in my chest so hard and fast I feel it might split open, I haul him to the shore. When he reaches the edge, he grasps the bank, out of the current now. I sob with relief, as I reach down to him, pulling him onto the bank as he hoists himself up. He pants, coughing, on the shore, and I can only hold him, closing my eyes and weeping for the near loss of him. Long minutes pass with him coughing and wheezing and me crying like a baby, when I realize that his left arm hangs uselessly by his side.

"Cy," I say, wiping a hand across my eyes. "Your arm."

His eyes are closed and he's panting, but he nods. A moment later, he opens his eyes and breathes, "Dislocated, I think. Thank you."

"Of course," I say to him. "How could I not try to save you?" And in my head, I tell him the words that well in my soul, that I can't hold back.

I love you.

"Just like you would've done for me," I say, closing my eyes and holding onto him. He's belly down on a bed of leaves, and I lay my head on his back, my arms around him. "Just like you would've done." I stand with reluctance, not wanting to let him go. "Let's get you to the shelter. I need to see to your arm."

I say *see to your arm* like I will somehow know what to do to fix a dislocated shoulder. I'm no medic, and the very sight of blood makes me squeamish. I shiver at the thought of having to do something revolting like set his arm, but I'll do what I have to do to make it better for him.

But I've grown stronger on this island. I'm not the woman I was before I got here. I have eaten insects and even the disgusting rodents, and turtle soup. I've been fucked—*repeatedly*— by a barbarian of a man.

I will do what I have to.

He gets to his feet, still coughing and sputtering. I let him hold onto me for support as we grab our clothes from the bank and head back to the shelter.

"The knife. Don't forget the knife," he says. I grab it and he reaches for it.

He holds it with his good hand and tucks it into the loop at his waist. The walk back seems longer, and more arduous, both of us exhausted after the ordeal.

"It came out of nowhere," he says in surprise. "One

minute I was holding you and the water was still, the next, I was trapped in a current."

"God. I didn't know what was happening when you suddenly threw me like that."

"I wanted to get you away from the current."

I nod. "Thank you. It worked."

"If you hadn't saved me," he says, pausing just long enough to pull me to him and kiss my forehead fiercely. "Thank you."

I kiss him back, my lips brushing his cheek. "You're welcome."

It feels good to not be the one who always needs rescuing. To be the one that can actually do some saving, too, and I'm glad he's not too proud to admit it.

He slows when we near the shelter. "Something isn't right," he says.

I'm not sure what he's talking about, but I know by now to trust his intuition. That said, there are *lots* of things that aren't right here, so I'm not sure what this particular concern is.

"Yeah? What?"

"I don't know," he says. "It's a sixth sense or something."

The hair on the back of my neck prickles. "You don't have the stick," he says. "Get one to defend yourself if necessary."

In silence, I do what he says, grabbing a stout stick from the ground, and hold it like a baseball bat. He pushes open the door to our shelter, but there's no one in there. It doesn't surprise me. Even if there are others on this island, I don't expect anyone to be willing to take on a man like Cy.

We go in, and I know he's right. Something's off. I

can feel it in the pit of my stomach. It takes us a moment before we realize what the problem is, and it dawns on us both at once.

"The food," I say, at the very same time he says, "*Motherfucker*."

I want to cry all over again. All the food that we spent all that time gathering for us. Gone. I go through the places where we hid it, under leaves and clothing. Shitty hiding places if you know where to look. We were only trying to get it out of the immediate line of vision.

"My God," I breathe. "*My God.*"

"Son of a fucking bitch," he fumes. "It's fucking gone."

Even with his arm hanging by his side, useless, he's scarier than any other guy I've met. Intimidating. Ferocious.

We look everywhere, but it's clear that even our more clever hidden supplies have been ravaged.

Someone's watching us.

I hear a snapping of branches outside our door.

It takes a while for me to snap, but when I do, I *do*.

"I'll kill them," I say. "Kill them!"

I lift up his club, the mammoth one as big as my damn thigh, but with the furious outrage making my blood boil in my veins, I yank open the door. Cy's on the far end of the shelter near the bedding where we hid the coconuts, and he can't reach me.

"Stay here!" he shouts, but I'm already gone. The door swings crazily open, and I leap into the forest. I will kill them. *Kill* them.

"Come out!" I scream. "You goddamn thief. Show your face!"

Not surprisingly, no one responds to the welcome. I swing the club as hard as I can, striking a nearby tree so viciously tingles race up both my arms. I start when I hear a thud. I look around me, surprised to see coconuts on the ground.

What the fuck?

What the *fuck*?

As happy as I am to see some food, I drag my eyes away from the ground and shield my vision as I look far beyond where we are.

"Where are you?" I scream. "Where the fuck are you?"

Nothing. Not a sound. Not a bird twittering in the sky or a rustle of wind in the trees.

"Get your ass back here."

I turn to see a furious-looking Cy standing in the doorway.

"I will kill them," I fume. "I will beat his sorry ass until he—"

"Get *back* here." I know that look, and I'd be lying if I didn't admit it makes me squirm a little.

"He took our food," I say, as angry as a disgruntled child who lost her turn on the merry-go-round. "*Took our food.*"

"Clearly."

Then I remember. "But look!" I run to the tree, and he groans. I'm in trouble, and I know it, but I don't care right now.

"Coconuts, Cy."

I hold up several large, round coconuts in my hands. "I was so mad I whacked the tree with the stick, and these fell down."

He shakes his head. "They weren't there before."

"I know," I say, shaking my head.

"Hit it again," he says, pointing the hand of his good finger toward the tree trunk.

"Good idea." I lift the club off the ground, and before I do, I look to the top of the tree. "You see any coconuts?"

He shakes his head. "Nope."

I rear back and swing the club with all my might. Coconuts scatter to the ground at my feet.

"Oh my God," I whisper. "Are they... is it some sort of an optical illusion? Are we somehow not able to *see* them but they are actually there?"

"Looks like it," he says. "Harper?"

"Yeah?"

I turn to look at him. "I need you to help me with my shoulder. I'm useless like this. Gotta get the ball back into the socket."

Oh God, oh *ew*.

I look at his helplessly dangling limb and swallow hard. "Of course, I can," I say, even though the very thought makes me want to vomit. "Yeah, sure."

He chuckles. "Brave girl. You're white as a ghost. But I promise it isn't as hard as you might think."

"Hard? No. Gross? Yep."

He sets his jaw. "You can do this. I know you can. You're my girl, and you're not scared of fucking anything."

I feel a surge of pride at that. I swallow hard and nod.

"Let's do it."

"Take hold of my wrist."

I do, steadying myself with both feet planted on the ground, knees bent.

He gives me directions, and I do it on autopilot, lifting his wrist and rotating his arm. He hisses but doesn't make another sound, though the beads of sweat along his brow tell me it hurts like hell. Finally, he nods, swings his arm around, grimacing, then nods again.

"Good. You did it."

"Does it still hurt?"

He shakes his head, but his breathing is labored, so I'm not sure he's telling me the truth. We gather up the coconuts together and bring them inside the shelter.

"You know," I say thoughtfully. "Do you think that... that the other food items are somehow also an optical illusion?"

I frown at Cy, and he shrugs. "Worth looking, now, isn't it?" But it's hard to find places where the food used to be, without any colorful indication that the food was there. The forest is a camouflage of greens and browns, and though we think we remember the places where we've gathered fruit, everything seems weirdly muted.

"We're tired and thirsty," Cy says. "Let's get some food and water."

But when we go back, the coconuts are gone, too.

"Son of a *bitch*," Cy says. But that's all he says. He takes the club from the ground and whacks it against the tree so hard I wince myself. Even hungry and injured, he's so strong I wouldn't want to be his enemy. A handful of coconuts fall, but it's clear that whatever's up there is reaching its limit.

We crack open a few and drink greedily from the water, eating the coconut meat voraciously. I've always liked fresh coconut, but this seems like the most delicious thing I've ever put in my mouth.

"Mmmm," I say. "God, this is good."

He nods, and as we eat our food, he starts talking to me in a low voice.

"We need to find him. Them," he says. "They're hiding somewhere, and it's essential we find them."

"I agree."

In a whisper, he continues. "I think we should bait him."

I nod slowly. "Oh?"

"Yes," he says. "They will want you. Young woman. Beautiful. Strong." His eyes light up when he talks of me, and it makes me feel a little bashful and shy.

"Thank you."

He leans down and kisses first one cheek, then the next, before he brushes his lips across mine.

"I love you, Harper."

I swallow hard. "And I love you, Cy."

I know I do. I've known this for a while.

"I want you to know I will never, ever put you in danger. Do you know that?"

"Of course," I tell him. I know it down to my bones. "And I trust you."

He nods. "Good. Because what we're going to do next isn't easy. But it's as important as everything else we've done so far for survival."

I nod. He speaks in my ear.

"I'm going to pretend to go hunting, or to be looking for food. We have to pretend to get into a fight. I want you alone in here. I'm going to make it clear that all the weapons are gone, except I'll leave you with a knife. Okay?"

I nod.

"And once they're here, I'll be back."

I don't ask him what he'll do after that. I'm not sure

I want to know. I have no doubt that he'll kill them. And even though not too long ago I was a reasonable, rational human who abided by the law and thought things like *murder* weren't acceptable, I nod. Accepting. Agreeing. I'm already a goddamn accomplice.

He kneels in front of me and pulls me to his chest, giving me a hug so fierce I can't breathe.

"I love you," he whispers in my ear. "You saved my life today."

"And I love you," I whisper back. "You're welcome."

And then he's chuckling and kissing me, and I swear, that barbaric alpha male's eyes are actually glistening. He's moved. We both know that we've been leading up to this, skirting around the danger that others on this island pose, but we both know it's time to face it head on now. It has to happen.

He closes his eyes. "Forgive me for this," he says.

"Knock it off," I whisper.

He grins at me and whispers back, "I haven't forgotten that spanking you earned."

"No pardon granted for saving your life?"

He shakes his head. "Nope."

My body tingles and I want him to do more than kiss me right here, right now, but we've got a job to do. I know he feels the same when he groans and pulls away from me with obvious reluctance.

He puts his mouth up to my ear and whispers, "There's a knife under my pillow. Use it." Then he's on his feet, his face contorted in anger.

"That's it!" he says, so loudly I jump, I know this is part of the act, but I still don't like the way it feels when he's yelling at me like this. "I told you not to go out there. I told you not to leave the food. And you did it anyway. I'm out of here." He won't look me in the eyes, and I hate how that makes me feel. He turns from me and stalks toward the door, wrenches it open, and stands in the doorway looking at me.

"Go then! You only think of yourself anyway!" I scream, trying to come up with some kind of reason for our fake fight. I feel the lie in those words though. He isn't selfish at all. He's been so good to me. I swallow the lump in my throat that's threatening to choke me. He isn't selfish, and I love him.

"You can stay here. I'm *out* of here. You think you can fend for yourself? Fine then. Do it!"

And then he's gone. Even though he's acting, this feels more real than I imagined. It feels... God, awful.

I pace around the cabin, keeping up my end of the facade.

"Stupid jerk," I mutter. "I don't need him anyway." I pace around, saying all sorts of crazy ass stuff, when I hear someone coming toward me from the woods. It isn't Cy. I can tell just by the footfall that it isn't him. I shiver. Someone's coming toward me. Whoever it is, they're falling for the trap.

I pace near the bed and look where the makeshift "pillows" lie.

There's a knife under my pillow.

I quickly lift the pillow and remove the knife, sliding it under my dress and into my bra, when I hear footsteps drawing closer to the hut.

I turn around slowly, my stomach knotted with fear. I stifle a scream when I see a heavily bearded man who does *not* meet Will's profile in the doorway. He's lanky and lean, his once-blond hair matted and filthy.

Encrusted with dirt, his clothes are little more than rags. And his eyes. God, his *eyes* look ready to kill.

"Get out!" I scream, brandishing my knife. He doesn't even look at it but steps in the room anyway.

"I said get out!" I repeat, but he keeps coming at me. "If you come any closer, I'll kill you!"

He still doesn't stop.

I have no choice. Oh God, I have no *choice*.

With a growl, he reaches for my wrist, but I deflect him, and jab at him. This time, the blade catches his hand. Crimson blood spurts out from where I sliced at him, and he howls in agony. I ignore the scream and strike again.

And again.

And again.

I'm screaming, and I can't seem to stop. My hand is covered in red blood, but the man is still coming at me when Cy barrels though the doorway. With a ferocious roar, he lunges at the guy, tackling him to the floor. The man's head hits the ground with a sickening thud, and he passes out.

"Is he dead?" I ask, my voice shaking. "Is he?"

Scowling, he lifts his wrist and feels for a pulse. "No," he says. "Unfortunately, not. But I saw which direction he came from. We need to see if Will is with him. Let's go."

We tie him up with long, supple leaves that work almost as well as rope, and leave him outside our door. I follow Cy back to the cave where we stayed the first night I was here.

"He came from the hill, which can only mean he's been using the cave as a shelter," he says.

I nod. But as we draw near, I freeze.

"Cy," I whisper, pointing a shaking finger toward the cave, to where another man's mutilated body lies in a sickening heap. "Oh, God," I say on a sob. He reaches for me and draws me close. "Don't look, babe," he says. "Don't. There's shit you don't want to see." He sighs. "And *that* was Will. He must've been killed by Derek."

I nod. "Why?" I whisper. "Why would anyone do such a thing?"

He shakes his head. "It's not about fairness, Harper, but survival. And the better question is, how is Derek even alive still? I'm telling you, he was dead."

I shudder. "No idea. We should go back and make sure he hasn't done anything dangerous to himself or our shelter." But as we're about to turn away, something black catches my eye. Something that seems so out of place, I'm not sure what to make of it at first.

"Cy," I say. "Wait."

I hold up a hand to him. He turns back around to look at me.

"What is it?"

I point wordlessly to the pile of black metal and plastic on the ground.

Hand in hand, we walk together. I tell myself there isn't a dead man lying on the ground beside us. I pretend it isn't there.

It doesn't help.

"Oh my God," I whisper, shaking my head.

"Is that what I think it is?" Cy's frowning, when he falls to his knee in the cave and lifts the broken remains of something plastic and electronic in his hands.

"What does this mean?" I ask on a whisper.

His jaw tightens grimly. "It means Derek and Will aren't the only ones watching us."

I feel my eyes go wide, and I swear I feel panic right down to my soul.

"Watching us?" I whisper.

He points to the broken remains of security cameras on the ground all around us.

"Watching us," he repeats. "These are security cameras, babe. And they aren't old. We need to get back to Derek."

He stands and looks out beyond us. "It makes sense. It all makes fucking sense."

"What does?"

But he shakes his head. "We can't speak freely here."

Foreboding grows in my belly with every step we take back toward the shelter. I remember the dead, vacant eyes of the man killed in the cave. The savage, feral eyes of the man waiting for us in the shelter.

Will I become that way?

Will Cy?

And why the *fuck* were there—*are* there—cameras?

Cy knows something I don't, and I mean to find out.

We make it back down to the shelter as the sun is setting. What are we going to do with the man waiting for us?

"If he's fucking gone..." Cy begins, but when we get there, he isn't. He's waiting for us, still lying in the same position we left him. He watches us with cold, calculating eyes. I'm glad Cy is here. If I came across this man alone...

"We have questions for you," Cy says. "And I want you to answer." He swallows hard, and I can tell it costs him something to ask the next question. "Can you talk?"

The man nods.

"Take 'em off," he says. His voice makes my skin crawl. If a rabid, ferocious wolf could talk, it would sound just like this. I take another step toward Cy.

"Take what off?"

He nods to his restraints. "I'll talk if you take 'em off."

Cy narrows his eyes and crosses his arms on his chest.

"No."

"Then I ain't talkin.'"

Cy looks at me. "We need answers," I tell him. "The two of us can take him if we have to."

Cy stares at the guy. "Fine," he finally concedes. "You make one fucking move toward her, and I kill you without a backward glance. You get me?"

"Yeah." Frowning, he kneels and slices the rope at the man's wrists but holds the knife. The man sits up, rubbing his wrists, and looks me up and down before turning to Cy.

"Figures you got the girl."

I shudder at the thought of this guy putting his hands on me.

"I thought you were dead," Cy begins.

"Yeah," the guys says. "I was bitten by something venomous. It didn't kill me like you assholes thought, though."

Cy watches him through narrowed eyes. "Jesus," he says.

"You buried me in a fucking shallow grave. You remember the rain?"

Cy shakes his head. "We were already half starved by then," he says. "I don't remember much."

"Rain washed away the grave or I'd have been buried to death," he says.

"Jesus," Cy repeats. "I—"

"Shut up."

Clearly this guy has not forgiven him.

"I got out. Came to. Wasn't dead but in a partial coma. Starving. With every fucking day that passed, I felt more and more like an animal." He shakes his head. "A month in, I found the cameras."

The little hairs stand up on my arms. "What cameras?" I whisper.

"The cameras that are watching your every fucking move. *My* move. Made by the same people that brought us here. That brought *you* here."

"How do you know?" I whisper.

"Doesn't take a rocket scientist. How'd you get here?"

I tell him, and now that I'm saying this in light of what we know, it sounds implausible.

"Won a fucking cruise?" he says derisively. "You didn't win a fucking cruise."

"Christ," Cy mutters. "I knew that something was off. I knew that none of this was accidental."

"Like... like how?" I ask.

He shakes his head and rolls his eyes. "Not hard, sweetheart," he growls. "Brainwashing and drugs that honed your fuckin' animalistic instincts. The food that went missing? Manipulation. It's there. Fuckin' cameras and shit hide it. Sharks? Planted. Undercurrents? Planted. Poisonous fuckin' insects? Same. You ever hear of a wolf on an island? Me neither. Fuckin' *planted.*"

"Why?" I whisper. "Are they watching us now?"

"I got some of the cameras," he says. "There are three left. I did my job. Now you do yours."

"You have no idea who's behind this?" Cy asks.

The man turns to him, his eyes bulging, so wide now so I can see the whites.

"No, but I can guarantee you. It was no fucking accident."

"Tell me what you know."

He looks at Cy. "You don't remember anything, do you? You stayed the most sane of all of us, you bastard. But you don't remember fucking anything."

"I remember we were taken," Cy said. "We were... there were drugs..." his voice fades as he scowls.

"I don't remember everything either, but between me and Will, we pieced things together. *Someone* was behind our abduction. *Someone* kidnapped us, drugged us, affected our fuckin' memories. You can do a fuckin' lot to the human brain." He shudders. "I ought to know. Did it myself."

Cy stares at him, shaking his head. "What did they do to us?" he asks softly.

The man glowers, his eyes red and bloodshot. "Made us fuckin' savages. Manipulated our brains and bodies so we're more animal than human. We did shit, kept us together. At first. Will tried to kill me. I killed him first. And when I did..." his voice trailed off. He shakes his head. "It came as natural to me as a lion killin' its prey."

"Jesus," Cy mutters.

"They brought us here. They've been watchin' us. Made this happen. None of its real. None of its fuckin' real."

"God," I say, my voice shaking. "How do we get

off?"

"That's just it, sweetheart," he says. "We don't."

He shakes his head and lunges for the knife. Cy and I both reach for him but he gets it before we do and he retreats, holding it out. "Not gonna hurt you. But I want off this island, and I ain't ever goin' home. So I'm gettin' off this fuckin' island."

It's like it plays out in slow motion. His hand at his throat. The sickening sight of skin ripped open by sharp metal. Blood. Oh, God, so much fucking blood.

It splashes on the ground. I scream and scream, covering my mouth with my hands, screaming for the body in the throes of death at my feet and the life snuffed out so easily. Screaming for the knowledge that I was tricked, that I wasn't meant to be here. Screaming because I can't take this anymore.

I'm in Cy's arms and he's tucking me against his chest and carrying me away with his long strides.

"Your arm," I sob.

"Hush, baby," he says. "You're light as a feather. I'm only holding you with one arm."

I don't fight it. I don't say a word. He carries me back to the shelter, shuts, and barricades the door.

We lay down in silence and don't speak.

After a while, there comes a certain quiet after trauma. You can't cry anymore. You can't even really think. It's during that quiet that he holds me, rocking me gently against his chest. I'm hungry and thirsty, but I don't care anymore.

"You were right," I whisper.

"Wish that made it better," he whispers back, running his fingers through my hair from top to bottom. It feels nice. I sigh.

We lie in the silence for a little while longer. I can't help but feel the raw attraction to him that I always do, but I know now it isn't natural. It isn't part of who I am, but somehow...

"We have to find them, Harper," he says.

"We do."

I don't need to ask him who or what. We'll find the cameras, and the people behind this.

"We'll get off this island, baby."

We will. "But where will that leave us? And how?"

"I don't know, Harper. But I love you. And no matter what happens next, we're in this together."

I reach for his hand and entwine my fingers with his. "I love you, Cy. Together."

THIS CONCLUDES SAVAGE DOM: A Dark Romance, book one in the Savage Island Duet. The Savage Island Duet concludes with Savage Love, which you can find HERE.

I AM SO grateful for your support! Please read on for previews of my other books you may enjoy.

PREVIEWS

Beyond Measure: A Dark Bratva Romance (Ruthless Doms)

PREVIEWS

Preview: *Beyond Measure*

I scowl at the computer screen in front of me. As *pakhan,* the weight of everything falls onto my shoulders, and today is one day when I wish I could shrug it off.

A knock comes at my office door.

"Who is it?" I snap. I don't want to see or hear anything right now. I'm pissed off, and I haven't had time to compose myself. As the leader of the Boston Bratva, it's imperative that I maintain composure.

"Nicolai."

"Come in."

Nicolai can withstand my anger and rage. Over the past few months, he's become my most trusted advisor. My friend.

The door swings open and Nicolai enters, bowing his head politely to greet me.

"Brother."

I nod. "Welcome. Have a seat."

When I first met Nicolai, he wore the face of a

much older man. Troubled and anguished, he was in the throes of fighting for his woman. The woman who now bears his name and his baby. But I've watched the worry lines around his eyes diminish, his smile become more ready. While every bit as fierce and determined to dutifully fill his role as ever, he's grown softer because of Marissa, more devoted to her.

"You look thrilled," he says, quirking a brow at me. Unlike my other men, who often quake in my presence, having been taught by my father before me that men in authority are to be feared and obeyed, Nicolai is more relaxed. He's earned the title of *brother* more readily than even my most trusted allies.

"Fucking pissed," I tell him, pushing up from my desk and heading to the sideboard. I pour myself a shot of vodka. It's eleven o'clock in the fucking morning, but it doesn't matter. I've been up all night. "Drink?"

He nods silently and takes the proffered shot glass. We raise our drinks and toss them back together. I take in a deep breath and place the glass back on the sideboard before I go back to my desk.

"Want to tell Uncle Nicolai your troubles?" he asks, his eyes twinkling.

I roll my eyes at him.

I made an unconventional decision when I inducted Nicolai into our brotherhood. The son of another *pakhan,* Nicolai came here under an alias, but I knew he had the integrity of a brother I wanted in my order. I offered him dual enrollment in both groups, under both the authority of his father and me, and he readily agreed. We've come to be good friends, and I would trust the man with my life.

"Uncle Nicolai," I snort, shaking my head. None of

my other brothers take liberties like Nicolai does, but none are as trustworthy and loyal as him, so he gets away with giving me shit unlike anyone else. "It's fucking Aren Koslov."

Nicolai grimaces. "Fucking Aren Koslov," he mutters in commiseration. "What'd the bastard do now?" He shakes his head. "Give me one good reason to beat his ass and I'll take the next red-eye to San Diego."

He would, too. Nicolai inspires fear in our enemies and respect in our contemporaries. Aren falls into both categories.

"Owed me a fucking mint a month ago, and hasn't paid up," I tell him. I spin my monitor around to show him the number in red. "And you don't need me to tell you we need that money." As my most trusted advisor, Nicolai knows we're right on the cusp of securing the next alliance with the Spanish drug cartel. Our location in Boston, near the wharf and airport, puts us in the perfect position to manage imports, but the buy-in is fucking huge. We have the upfront money, but the payout from San Diego would put us in a moderately better financial position.

Nicolai leans back in his chair, rubbing his hand across his jawline.

"And you have meeting after meeting coming up with politicians, leaders, and the like."

I eye him warily. Where's he going with this?

"It's easy to say you need money. But that isn't what you need, brother."

I roll my eyes. "I suppose you're going to tell me what I need."

"Of course."

"Go on."

"You know what you need more than the money?" he asks. I'm growing impatient. He needs to come out with it already.

I give him a look that says *spill*.

"You need a wife," he says.

A wife?

I roll my eyes and shake my head. "Sometimes I think your father dropped you on your head as a child," I tell him. What bullshit. I look back at the computer screen, but Nicolai presses on.

"Tomas, listen to me," he says, insistent. "Money comes and goes, and you know that. Tomorrow you could seal a deal with the arms trade you've been working, and you know our investments have been paying off in spades. But a good wife is beyond measure, and Aren has a sister."

"You've been married, for what, two fucking days and you're giving me this shit?" I reply, but my mind is already spinning with what he's saying. I never dismiss Nicolai's suggestions without really weighing my options. Aren is one of the youngest brigadiers in America and has a reputation that precedes him everywhere he goes. He commands men under him, and I'm grateful he hasn't risen higher in power.

He grunts at me and narrows his eyes. "I've loved Marissa for a lot longer than we've had rings on our fingers."

"I know it, brother," I tell him. "Just giving you shit. Go on."

"Aren's sister is single, lives with him on their compound. Young. I don't know much about her, and haven't seen a recent picture, but I met her years ago when I first came to America. And she was a beauty then. I imagine she's only grown more beautiful."

Seconds ago, this idea seemed preposterous, but now that I'm beginning to think about it, I'm warming to the idea.

"You think he'd let her go to pay off his debt?"

"With enough persuasion? Hell yeah. And a good leader needs a wife. You've seen it yourself. There's something to be said for having a woman to come home to. The most powerful men in the brotherhood are all married."

He's right. Just last week, I met with Demyan from Moscow and his wife Larissa. He brings her everywhere with him. The two are inseparable. And he's risen to be one of the most powerful men the Bratva has ever known.

"And face it, Tomas. You're not exactly in the position to meet a pretty girl at church."

I huff out a laugh. The men of the Bratva rarely obtain women by traditional means.

I lift my phone and dial Lev.

"Boss?"

"Get me a picture of Aren Kosolov's sister," I tell him. Our resident hacker and computer genius, Lev works quickly and efficiently.

"Give me five minutes," he says.

"Done."

I hang up the phone and turn to Nicolai. "I want to see her first," I tell him.

"Of course."

"How's Marissa?"

He fills me in about home, his voice growing softer as he talks about Marissa, but I'm only half-listening to him. I'm thinking about the way a woman changes a man, and how he's changed because of her.

Do I need a wife?

The better question is, do I want Aren Kosolov's sister to be the one?

My phone buzzes, and Nicolai gestures for me to answer it. A text from Lev with a grainy picture pops up on the screen, followed by a text.

There are no recent pictures. This was from a few years ago, but it should give you a good idea.

Still, it's a full profile picture. I murmur appreciatively. Wavy, unruly chestnut hair pulled back at the nape of her neck, with fetching tendrils curling around her forehead. Haunting hazel colored eyes below dark brows. High cheekbones, her skin flushed pink, and full, pink lips. She's thin and graceful, though if I'm honest, a little too thin for me. The women I bed tend to be sturdier and curvy, able to withstand the way I like to fuck.

I don't want to have this conversation via text. I call him and he answers right away.

"Background?" I ask.

"Never went to college. Under her brother's watchful eye since her father died."

"Lovely," I mutter. He might not give her up easily.

"Temperament?" I ask, aware that I sound like I'm asking about adopting a puppy, but it fucking matters.

"Not sure, but she has no record on file at school or legally. Perfect record. Graduated top of her class in high school." He snorts. "Volunteers in a soup kitchen in San Diego and attends the Orthodox Church on the weekend."

Ah. A good girl. Points in her favor. Sometimes the

good girls fall hard, and sometimes they're tougher to break, but they intrigue me.

"Boyfriend?"

"None."

"Name?"

"Caroline."

"Caroline?" I repeat. "That isn't a Russian name."

"Her mother was American."

I nod thoughtfully. Caroline Koslov.

She would take my name.

Caroline Dobrynin.

I drum my fingers on my desk, contemplating. I nod to Nicolai when I instruct Lev. "Get Aren on the phone."

READ MORE

The Bratva's Baby (Wicked Doms)

Kazimir

The wrought iron park bench I sit on is ice cold, but I hardly feel it. I'm too intent on waiting for the girl to arrive. The Americans think this weather is freezing, but I grew up in the bitter cold of northern Russia. The cold doesn't touch me. The ill-prepared people around me pull their coats tighter around their bodies and tighten their scarves around their necks. For a minute, I wonder if they're shielding themselves from me, and not the icy wind.

If they knew what I've done... what I'm capable of... what I'm planning to do... they'd do more than cover their necks with scarves.

I scowl into the wind. I hate cowardice.

But this girl... this girl I've been commissioned to take as mine. Despite outward appearances, she's no coward. And that intrigues me.

Sadie Ann Warren. Twenty-one years old. Fine brown hair, plain and mousy but fetching in the way it hangs in haphazard waves around her round face. Light brown eyes, pink cheeks, and full lips.

I wonder what she looks like when she cries. When she smiles. I've never seen her smile.

She's five-foot-one and curvy, though you wouldn't know it from the way she dresses in thick, bulky, black and gray muted clothing. I know her dress size, her shoe size, her bra size, and I've already ordered the type of clothing she'll wear for me. I smile to myself, and a woman passing by catches the smile. It must look predatory, for her step quickens.

Sadie's nondescript appearance makes her easily meld into the masses as a nobody, which is perhaps exactly what she wants.

She has no friends. No relatives. And she has no idea that she's worth millions.

Her boss, the ancient and somewhat senile head librarian of the small-town library where she works won't even realize she hasn't shown up for work for several days. My men will make sure her boss is well distracted yet unharmed. Sadie's abduction, unlike the ones I've orchestrated in the past, will be an easy one. If trouble arises eventually, we'll fake her death.

It's almost as if it was meant to be. No one will know she's gone. No one will miss her. She's the perfect target.

I sip my bitter, steaming black coffee and watch as

she makes her way up to the entrance of the library. It's eight-thirty a.m. precisely, as it is every other day she goes to work. She arrives half an hour early, prepares for the day, then opens the doors at nine. Sadie is predictable and routinized, and I like that. The trademark of a woman who responds well to structure and expectations. She'll easily conform to my standards... eventually.

To my left, a small cluster of girls giggles but quiets when they draw closer to me. They're college-aged, or so. I normally like women much younger than I am. They're more easily influenced, less jaded to the ways of men. These women, though, are barely women. Compared to Sadie's maturity, they're barely more than girls. I look away, but can feel their eyes taking me in, as if they think I'm stupid enough to not know they're staring. I'm wearing a tan work jacket, worn jeans, and boots, the ones I let stay scuffed and marked as if I'm a construction worker taking a break. With my large stature, I attract attention of the female variety wherever I go. It's better I look like a worker, an easy role to assume. No one would ever suspect what my real work entails.

The girls pass me and it grates on my nerves how they resume their giggling. Brats. Their fathers shouldn't let them out of the house dressed the way they are, especially with the likes of me and my brothers prowling the streets. It's freezing cold and yet they're dressed in thin skirts, their legs bare, open jackets revealing cleavage and tight little nipples showing straight through the thin fabric of their slutty tops. My palm itches to spank some sense into their little asses. I flex my hand.

It's been way, way too long since I've had a woman to punish.

Control.

Master.

These girls are too young and silly for a man like me.

Sadie is perfect.

My cock hardens with anticipation, and I shift on my seat.

I know everything about her. She pays her meager bills on time, and despite her paltry wage, contributes to the local food pantry with items bought with coupons she clips and sale items she purchases. Money will never be a concern for her again, but I like that she's fastidious. She reads books during every free moment of time she has, some non-fiction, but most historical romance books. That amuses me about her. She dresses like an amateur nun, but her heroines dress in swaths of silk and jewels. She carries a hard-covered book with her in the bag she holds by her side, and guards it with her life. During her break time, before bed, and when she first wakes up in the morning, she writes in it. I don't know yet what she writes, but I will. She does something with needles and yarn, knitting or something. I enjoy watching her weave fabric with the vibrant threads.

She fidgets when she's near a man, especially attractive, powerful men. Men like me.

I've never seen her pick up a cell phone or talk to a friend. She's a loner in every sense of the word.

I went over the plan again this morning with Dimitri.

Capture the girl.

Marry her.
Take her inheritance.
Get rid of her.

I swallow another sip of coffee and watch Sadie through the sliding glass doors of the library. Today she's wearing an ankle-length navy skirt that hits the tops of her shoes, and she's wrapped in a bulky gray cardigan the color of dirty dishwater. I imagine stripping the clothes off of her and revealing her creamy, bare, unblemished skin. My dick gets hard when I imagine marking her pretty pale skin. Teeth marks. Rope marks. Reddened skin and puckered flesh, christened with hot wax and my palm. I'll punish her for the sin of hiding a body like hers. She won't be allowed to with me.

She's so little. So virginal. An unsullied canvas.

"Enjoy your last taste of freedom, little girl," I whisper to myself before I finish my coffee. I push myself to my feet and cross the street.

It's time she met her future master.

READ MORE

ABOUT THE AUTHOR

USA Today bestselling author Jane Henry pens stern but loving alpha heroes, feisty heroines, and emotion-driven happily-ever-afters. She writes what she loves to read: kink with a tender touch. Jane is a hopeless romantic who lives on the East Coast with a houseful of children and her very own Prince Charming.

What to read next? Here are some other titles by Jane you may enjoy. And don't forget to sign-up for my newsletter!

CONTEMPORARY ROMANCE

Dark romance
Island Captive: A Dark Romance

Ruthless Doms
King's Ransom
Priceless

Beyond Measure

Wicked Doms
 The Bratva's Baby
 The Bratva's Bride
 The Bratva's Captive

Undercover Doms standalones
 Criminal by Jane Henry and Loki Renard
 Hard Time by Jane Henry and Loki Renard

NYC Doms standalones

Deliverance
 Safeguard
 Conviction
 Salvation
 Schooled
 Opposition
 Hustler

The Billionaire Daddies

Beauty's Daddy: A Beauty and the Beast Adult Fairy Tale
 Mafia Daddy: A Cinderella Adult Fairy Tale
 Dungeon Daddy: A Rapunzel Adult Fairy Tale
 The Billionaire Daddies boxset

The Boston Doms
 My Dom (Boston Doms Book 1)
 His Submissive (Boston Doms Book 2)

Her Protector (Boston Doms Book 3)
His Babygirl (Boston Doms Book 4)
His Lady (Boston Doms Book 5)
Her Hero (Boston Doms Book 6)
My Redemption (Boston Doms Book 7)

And more! Check out my Amazon author page.

You can find Jane here!
The Club (Facebook reader group)
Website
Amazon author page
Goodreads
Author Facebook page
Instagram

Printed in Great Britain
by Amazon